THE GREAT REFORM ACT

History

Editor
PROFESSOR JOEL HURSTFIELD
D.LIT
*Astor Professor of English History
in the University of London*

THE GREAT REFORM ACT

Michael Brock

Vice-President and Bursar, Wolfson College, Oxford

HUTCHINSON UNIVERSITY LIBRARY
LONDON

HUTCHINSON & CO (*Publishers*) LTD
3 Fitzroy Square, London W1

London Melbourne Sydney Auckland
Wellington Johannesburg Cape Town
and agencies throughout the world

First published 1973

*This book has been set in Bembo type, printed in Great Britain
on smooth wove paper by Anchor Press, and
bound by Wm. Brendon, both of Tiptree, Essex*
ISBN 0 09 115910 5 (cased)
0 09 115911 3 (paper)

TO
MY WIFE
AND SONS

CONTENTS

TABLES

ACKNOWLEDGEMENTS

I wish to express my humble thanks for the gracious permission of Her Majesty The Queen to use material in the Royal Archives.

I am greatly indebted to the following who allowed material from their papers to be used in this book: the Most Honourable the Marquess of Anglesey (MSS at Plas Newydd and the Public Record Office, Belfast); His Grace the Duke of Bedford; the Right Honourable the Earl of Derby, M.C.; His Grace the Duke of Devonshire, P.C., M.C., and the Trustees of the Chatsworth Settlement; Russell Ellice Esq (MSS in the National Library of Scotland); the Right Honourable the Earl Fitzwilliam (MSS in Northamptonshire Record Office and in Sheffield City Library); the Trustees of the fifth Earl Fortescue's Will Trust (MSS in Devon Record Office); Sir William Gladstone, Bt. (John Gladstone MSS at St Deiniol's Library, Hawarden); Major General E. H. Goulburn, D.S.O. (MSS in the Surrey Record Office); Sir Fergus Graham, Bt., K.B.E.; the Right Honourable the Earl of Halifax (the Hickleton Papers); Viscount Hardinge, M.B.E. (MSS now in McGill University); the Right Honourable the Earl of Harrowby and the Trustees of the Harrowby Manuscripts Trust; Lord Hatherton (MSS in Staffordshire Record Office); Lord Kenyon, F.S.A.; A. C. F. Lambton Esq, M.P. (Durham MSS); the Most Honourable the Marquess of Lansdowne, P.C.; Brigadier A. W. A. Llewellyn-Palmer, D.S.O., M.C. (the Marquess of Lincolnshire's MSS); the Most Honourable the Marquess of Linlithgow, M.C., and the Trustees of the Hopetoun Papers Trust; the Right Honourable the Earl of Lonsdale (MSS now in the Record Office, Carlisle); L. N. H. Middleton Esq (Brougham-Granton MSS); the late Countess Mountbatten of Burma and the Trustees of the Broadlands Archives Trust (Palmerston MSS now with the Historical Manuscripts Commission); the Most Honourable the Marquess of Salisbury; the Right Honourable the Earl Spencer, F.S.A.; and His Grace the Duke of Wellington, M.V.O., O.B.E., M.C.

I record my thanks similarly to the following institutions: the Bank of England; Birmingham Public Libraries; the William L. Clements Library, University of Michigan (Croker MSS and certain MSS of Lord John Russell); the Very Reverend the Dean of Durham and the Warden of the Durham Colleges (Grey MSS); Gateshead Public Libraries (Brockett MSS); Harvard College Library (MS copy of Viscount Morpeth's diary); the University of Keele (Sneyd MSS); the University of Nottingham (Portland MSS); and the Library of University College, London (Brougham MSS, Parkes MSS). Transcripts of Crown copyright records in the British Museum (Additional MSS), and in the Public Record Offices of London and Belfast, appear by permission of the Controller of H.M. Stationery Office. For permission to quote from G. K. Chesterton's 'The Revolutionist: or Lines to a Statesman' I am grateful to Miss D. E. Collins and Methuen Ltd.

I acknowledge with gratitude grants made in connexion with my Reform Act studies by the Rockefeller Foundation, the Twenty-Seven Foundation, the University of Oxford, and the Worshipful Company of Goldsmiths. I record my thanks to Sir Douglas Veale, C.B.E., and to Lord and Lady Harrowby, who helped me at the start of my research, and to Professor Joel Hurstfield, editor of this series, and Miss Ann Douglas of the Hutchinson University Library. I have tried the patience of editor and publisher severely and never found it wanting. I am grateful to many fellow historians for their help and conscious that I have not been able in my notes to acknowledge more than a fraction of my debt to them. I have received much help with proofs and index from Miss J. Cunningham, Miss J. A. Gaines, and Mr A. H. Walker.

Finally, I record my most grateful thanks to those who read this book in typescript—Sir Isaiah Berlin, Sir Alan Bullock, Mrs C. R. Dick, Dr Brian Harrison, Sir Edgar Williams, and Mr P. M. Williams (the latter enduring this infliction twice). My debt to these readers is very great. If the book has any merit much of this comes from their suggestions. They bear no responsibility for its faults.

MICHAEL BROCK

Wolfson College, Oxford
March 1973

NOTE ON SOURCES AND STYLE

References to sources have been restricted to those which a student is most likely to need. Virtually all the manuscript collections, newspapers, and book titles which would have been listed in a bibliography appear in the notes at the end of the book (pp. 337–89). The full title of a book is normally given on the first mention in the chapter: thereafter a short version is used. If the place of publication is not mentioned the book concerned has a normal British imprint. No references are given to recently published and widely used works where the passages concerned are easily identifiable from the text. The index entry for a person includes dates of birth and death, and sometimes changes of title, so that he or she can be identified at once in such reference works as the *Dictionary of National Biography* or G.E.C.'s *Complete Peerage*. The sources cited most often are shown in List 1 below, and some useful reference books for the Reform crisis in List 2. Anyone using the volume and folio numbers in the manuscript references should remember that some collections, such as Lord Holland's papers and diary in Additional MSS, British Museum, are liable to be rearranged.

Spelling and punctuation have been modernized in the quotations. A capital letter for Reform denotes the parliamentary variety. In references to Parliamentary Debates (Hansard), when no series is mentioned, the passage is from the Third Series which started in October 1830.

LIST 1

The Journal of Mrs Arbuthnot, Ed. F. Bamford and the Duke of Wellington (2 vols., 1950). Vol. 2 contains the entries for 1826 to 1832. Cited as *Mrs Arbuthnot*.

Correspondence and Diaries of John Wilson Croker, Ed. L. J. Jennings (3 vols., 1884). Vol. 2 for 1829 to 1842. Cited as *Croker*.

The Memoirs of C. C. F. Greville, 1814–1860. As several editions of
this diary are available references to it are given solely by the date of
entry concerned. The best edition is by Lytton Strachey and Roger
Fulford (8 vols., 1938). Cited as Greville, *Diary.*

Correspondence of Earl Grey with William IV, Ed. third Earl Grey
(2 vols., 1867). Solely concerned with period from Nov. 1830 to
June 1832. Cited as *Wm. IV–Grey Corresp.*

John Cam Hobhouse (cr. Lord Broughton, 1851), *Recollections of a
Long Life*, Ed. Lady Dorchester (6 vols., 1909–11). Vol. 4 for Oct.
1829 to Aug. 1834. Cited as Broughton, *Recollections.*

D. Le Marchant, *Memoir of Viscount Althorp* (1876). Althorp succeeded
as the third Earl Spencer in Nov. 1834. Cited as Le Marchant,
Althorp.

Three Early Nineteenth Century Diaries, Ed. A. Aspinall (1952). Diarists
are Lord (later Earl of) Ellenborough, Le Marchant, and E. J. Littleton
(cr. Lord Hatherton, 1835). Extracts are all from period Nov. 1830
to 1834. Cited as *Three Diaries.*

Sir Robert Peel, from his Private Papers, Ed. C. S. Parker (3 vols., 1891-9).
Cited as Parker, *Peel.*

Wellington's *Despatches, Correspondence, and Memoranda*, Jan. 1819 to
Dec. 1832, Ed. second Duke of Wellington (8 vols., 1867–80).
Cited as *W.N.D.*

LIST 2

Pre-Reform

George Crosby, *Contested Elections* (York, 1841). H. S. Smith published
a similar collection (2nd ed., 1842).

G. P. Judd, *Members of Parliament, 1734–1832* (1955).

Parl. Papers, 1878, lxii, pt. 2, lists the constituencies and their MPs
during the last Parliaments before the Reform Act.

E. Porritt, *The Unreformed House of Commons* (2 vols., 1903, repr.,
1963).

Post-Reform

C. R. Dod, *Electoral Facts, 1832–53*, Ed. H. J. Hanham (1972). Dod
aimed to outline the principal interests in each constituency. The
new edition contains a most useful bibliography and a list of extant
pollbooks from 1832.

F. H. McCalmont, *Parliamentary Poll Book, 1832–1918*, Ed. J. Vincent and M. Stenton (1971).

General

S. Lewis, *Topographical Dictionary of England* (3rd ed., 1835, 5 vols. and atlas).

J. H. Philbin, *Parliamentary Representation, 1832, England and Wales* (New Haven, 1965). Brings together in convenient form material from *Parliamentary Papers* and elsewhere.

Text of the Reform Act

Collections of British constitutional documents covering the nineteenth century normally include the text of the Reform Act. *English Historical Documents, xi, 1783–1832*, Ed. A. Aspinall and E. A. Smith (1959), also gives the Scottish and Irish Acts. The less important clauses are summarized in these collections. Such summaries can mislead. The student who lacks access to the volume of statutes covering 1832 can find the full text of the main Act at the end of *Parl. Deb*, 3rd series, xiii.

Historiographical

Two collections of writings on the 1832 Act have been published in America. They are edited by W. H. Maehl, jr (New York, 1967) and by G. A. Cahill (Lexington, 1969).

I

THE OLD SYSTEM IN DECLINE

'I see no reason why there should be any great change . . . ,' said Mr Ferrars. '. . . We have changed everything that was required.' . . . 'The whole affair rests on too contracted a basis,' said his companion. (From the opening chapter of Disraeli's *Endymion*, set in 1827)

During the 1820s both sides in the Reform struggle gave up hope. The reformers became convinced that they were making no progress. In January 1820 Earl Grey, the whig leader, warned his son-in-law, J. G. Lambton, that there was little likelihood of Reform 'being carried during my life or even during yours'.[1] When the radical *Black Dwarf* ceased publication in 1824 its editor announced that England contained no public 'devotedly attached to the cause of parliamentary Reform'.[2] Lord John Russell found in 1826 that his Reform motions were met 'throughout the country' with 'growing lukewarmness', and announced that he would not bring the subject forward again.[3] In 1829 a whig reformer referred in the Commons to 'the now almost forgotten and ill-omened cause of Reform'.[4] Reforming circles had reason to be gloomy. It was stated in one of the Reform Bill debates, and not denied, that from the beginning of 1824 until the end of 1829 no petitions for Reform had been presented to Parliament.[5]

The shrewdest men on the opposite benches were not deceived by the reformers' failure to make headway. In March 1820 Peel surveyed the recent election and asked Croker: 'Can we resist for seven years Reform in Parliament?'[6] When Canning thought he was going to India in 1822 he said privately that 'Reform was inevitable; and he was not sorry to be away while the measure was accomplished'.[7] In 1824 or thereabouts one of Peel's closest friends reported:

Peel considers a revolution at no great distance—not a bloody one and perhaps not one leading to a republic, but one utterly subversive of the aristocracy and of the present system of carrying on the government. He thinks we may get on quite as well after this change as before; but he considers it inevitable.[8]

Peel and Canning were good judges of the Reform agitation. The lull in it was a product of their political skill. They could not be deceived into supposing that they had lulled it for good. They knew that, whatever advantage they might take of wind or tide, a deep current was eroding the unreformed system and would soon wash it away. A few sentences from Peel's letter to Croker in March 1820 indicate the erosion process. 'Public opinion,' he wrote,

never had such influence on public measures, and yet never was so dissatisfied with the share which it possessed. It is growing too large for the channels that it has been accustomed to run through; . . . the engineers that made them never dreamt of various streams that are now struggling for a vent.

This chapter is concerned with Peel's 'channels' and with the 'streams' running through them.

The volumes of the *History of Parliament*[9] covering the period from 1754 to 1790 give an authoritative account of the British electorate as it was when George III came to the throne. Britain did not then possess the prerequisites for popular or democratic government. Representative institutions are 'inapplicable', in the words of John Stuart Mill, 'when . . . only some small fraction feels the degree of interest in the general affairs of the State necessary to the formation of a public opinion'.[10] A system for expressing the people's views on political questions cannot function if there are too few views to express. In 1760 few people outside aristocratic and parliamentary circles understood politics, or took a continuous interest in them. The shams of the system symbolized and facilitated the ascendancy of these few.

Aristocratic magnates spent large sums in gaining and retaining control of constituencies, and so acquiring parliamentary weight. To have a clientele of several MPs was to be a person of consequence. Many boroughs with small electorates resembled valuable pieces of property in that the power of naming their MPs could be bought or inherited. But they were properties of a most uncertain kind; and the high prices at which some of them changed hands reflected the desire of various magnates to acquire a great political 'interest' rather than the likely cash return on the outlay. A borough owner could usually obtain places and promotions for himself and his family and friends; but seen solely in terms of these material rewards most boroughs were poor investments.

There was no secret ballot. Votes were cast openly, so that electors were subject to pressure from those on whom they depended for their living. Sometimes the patron or 'owner' was in a position to dictate to the voters, who were a mere handful of his dependants. More often he was obliged to dispense money and favours to keep his hold on the borough and exclude his rivals. Some owners could give orders: others had to give bribes. Some voters showed a stubborn independence. Some boroughs were fickle or unruly: others resisted all attempts at control. The electors at these 'open' places had an expressive nickname for their favourite candidate—'Mr Most'. Political considerations in the modern sense did not normally enter a great deal into all this. At this stage the system resembled, not so much the fortress of privilege, as a field on which the few played an expensive and chaotic game under rules which were complicated and sometimes uncertain.

This hey-day of proprietary politics was short-lived. In the latter part of the eighteenth century the phrase 'public opinion' came into use to denote a new factor which had begun to disturb the balance.[11] The enlargement of the political nation did not originate with the industrial revolution nor with the population increase. But much of its impetus came from these trends. The demand for information about public affairs increased. So did the capacity to meet it; for among the industrial processes revolutionized were those of paper making and newspaper printing.[12]

The growth of the press reflected and stimulated the diffusion of political views and knowledge. The newspaper heralded change in the politics of Britain in 1820 much as the transistor radio did in those of Africa in the 1950s. In 1813 *The Times* was printed at the rate of 250 sheets per hour, in 1827 at 4000 per hour. Newspapers also benefited from better roads and faster coaches. The circulation of stamped papers nearly doubled between 1788 and 1811 although the stamp duties helped to keep their price too high for the working man to buy his own copy. It was calculated in 1829 that each copy of a newspaper reached, on an average, twenty-five people. Professional men read them in the subscription reading room, middle-class[13] people and artisans in the coffee house; and Robert Southey, worried about working-class radicalism, told the Prime Minister in 1817 that such sheets as Cobbett's *Political Register* were 'read aloud in every ale-house'.[14]

In formal structure the electoral system of the 1820s was little

different from that of 1760.[15] By then the combined population of
Manchester, Birmingham and Leeds was approaching half a million,
having doubled since 1800.[16] Yet these three cities did not have one
MP between them. The eleven seaboard counties between the Wash
and the Severn, with Wiltshire added, still contained more than half
the English borough seats.[17] The unreformed House was not doomed,
however, merely because it had survived from a different Britain. Any
long-lived political system necessarily consists largely of survivals.
Institutions in use today, such as the House of Lords in Britain or the
Electoral College in the United States, have long outlasted the societies
for which they were created.

Any estimate of the stability of an institution surviving from another
age starts with certain questions. How powerful are those who have
a vested interest in its continued functioning? Do many influential
people think that they would gain by its disappearance? How risky is
the process of replacing it thought to be? Has it become obviously
inefficient in any way? Have the practices by which it is run given rise
to grievances or come to be regarded as morally objectionable? Are
the groups controlling it able and willing to adapt it to new needs?
Is the picture which its critics have painted of an entirely reformed
institution attractive to the moderates and the uncommitted? The notes
which follow on the pre-Reform system in its final phase are intended
to throw light on these questions. Its formal structure in the mid
1820s is summarized in Tables 1 and 2. Table 1 gives a general outline.
In Table 2 the English boroughs are classified according to the nature
of voting rights and the number of voters. These boroughs made up
more than half the House, and were the Reformers' main target. They
are therefore described first.

A nomination or pocket borough was one in which elections were
controlled by a single individual who had ensured that most, if not
all, of the voters there were his friends or dependants. The methods
of achieving control varied according to the number of voters and
the nature of the voting rights. In Group A (the scot-and-lot boroughs)
any man who paid poor rates could vote. Paying these rates was
deemed the equivalent of being obliged in the middle ages to 'pay
scot and bear lot'. The potwalloper qualification (Group B) was even
wider. It included every man resident for the last six months in the
borough, and not a charge on the poor rate, 'who had a family and
boiled a pot there'.

A number of the boroughs in Group A and B were 'open', in the

sense of containing sizeable electorates which exercised a certain freedom of choice. Others possessed very few voters despite the apparently wide suffrage and had fallen into the nomination category. Some
of these places had decayed into rotten boroughs, the number of inhabitants shrinking until hardly anyone was left to vote. In other cases,

continued on page 22...

TABLE 1

THE UNREFORMED* HOUSE OF COMMONS IN 1830

	County seats	Borough seats	University seats	TOTAL
ENGLAND				
York	4			
39 two-Member counties	78			
City of London		4		
Weymouth†		4		
195 two-Member boroughs		390		
5 single-Member boroughs‡		5		
2 Universities, Oxford and Cambridge			4	
Totals, England	82	403	4	489
WALES				
12 single-Member counties	12			
2 single-Member boroughs (Beaumaris, Montgomery)		2		
10 single-Member borough constituencies formed by grouping boroughs		10		
Totals, Wales	12	12		24
SCOTLAND				
27 single-Member counties	27			
6 single-Member counties, returning Members for alternate Parliaments only	3			
Edinburgh		1		
14 districts of burghs (constituencies formed by grouping burghs)		14		
Totals, Scotland	30	15		45

TABLE 1   *(Cont.)*

	County seats	Borough seats	University seats	TOTAL
IRELAND				
32 two-Member counties	64			
2 two-Member boroughs (Cork, Dublin)		4		
31 single-Member boroughs		31		
Trinity College, Dublin			1	
Totals, Ireland	64	35	1	100
TOTAL	188	465	5	658

★The reformed House is shown in Table 5, pp. 310-13

†Strictly the two boroughs of Weymouth and Melcombe Regis. They had been organized as a single constituency since the 1590s.

‡Abingdon, Banbury, Bewdley, Higham Ferrers and Monmouth.

TABLE 2

ENGLISH BOROUGHS, 1830

	A Scot and lot	B Pot-walloper	C Burgage	D Corpo-ration	E Freeman	F Free-holder	TOTAL
ELECTORS							
1. Over 5000	1	1	—	—	5	—	7
2. 1001 to 5000	6	2	—	—	24	4	36
3. 601 to 1000	7	5	—	—	9	1	22
4. 302 to 600	10	1	—	—	13	—	24
5. 101 to 300	8	5	10	1	11	1	36
6. 51 to 100	4	—	10	2	5	—	21
7. 50 or fewer	2	—	15	26	13	—	56
TOTAL	38	14	35	29	80	6	202

A1. Westminster; A2. Lichfield, Newark, Reading, Southampton, Southwark, Warwick; A3. Chichester, Leominster, Malton, Peterborough, St Albans, Stamford, Windsor; A4. Bridgwater, Bridport, Dorchester, Fowey, Marlow,

Penryn, St Ives, Tamworth, Wareham, Wootton Bassett; A5. Abingdon, Callington, Corfe Castle, Milborne Port, Shaftesbury, Steyning, Stockbridge, Wallingford; A6. Aldborough, Amersham, St Mawes, Seaford; A7. Gatton, St Michael.

B1. Preston; B2. Bedford, Northampton; B3. Cirencester, Hertford, Lewes, Pontefract, Taunton; B4. Honiton; B5. Hindon, Ilchester, Minehead, Tregony, Wendover.

C5. Appleby, Ashburton, Chippenham, Cockermouth, Haslemere, Horsham, Ludgershall, Northallerton, Richmond, Saltash; C6. Great Bedwin, Bletching-ley, Boroughbridge, Downton, Knaresborough, Newport (Cornwall), Newton (Lancs.), Reigate, Weobley, Westbury; C7. Beeralston, Bramber, Castle Rising, Clitheroe, Droitwich, East Grinstead, Heytesbury, Midhurst, Newtown (Isle of Wight), Petersfield, Ripon, Old Sarum, Tavistock, Thirsk, Whitchurch.

D5. Winchester; D6. Salisbury, Wigan; D7. Andover, Banbury, Bath, Bewdley, Bodmin, Brackley, Buckingham, Bury St Edmunds, Calne, Christchurch, De-vizes, Harwich, East Looe, West Looe, Lostwithiel, Lymington, Malmesbury, Marlborough, Newport (Isle of Wight), Portsmouth, Scarborough, Thetford, Tiverton, Truro, Wilton, Yarmouth (Isle of Wight).

E1. Bristol, Leicester, Liverpool, London, Nottingham; E2. Berwick-upon-Tweed, Beverley, Bridgnorth, Canterbury, Chester, Colchester, Coventry, Dover, Durham, Exeter, Gloucester, Hull, Ipswich, Lancaster, Lincoln, Maldon, Newcastle-upon-Tyne, Norwich, Oxford, Rochester, Shrewsbury, Worcester, Great Yarmouth, York; E3. Barnstaple, Carlisle, Grantham, Hereford, Maid-stone, Newcastle-under-Lyme, Sandwich, Stafford, Sudbury; E4. Arundel, Boston, Derby, Evesham, Great Grimsby, Hedon, Hythe, King's Lynn, Ludlow, Queenborough, Tewkesbury, Wells, Wenlock; E5. Bishop's Castle, Cambridge, Eye, Huntingdon, Monmouth, Morpeth, Okehampton, Plymouth, Poole, Woodstock, Wycombe; E6. Aldeburgh, Helston, Lyme Regis, Plympton, Totnes; E7. Bossiney, Camelford, Dartmouth, Dunwich, Hastings, Higham Ferrers, Launceston, Liskeard, Orford, New Romney, Rye, St Germans, Win-chelsea.

F2. Cricklade, East Retford, Shoreham, Weymouth; F3. Aylesbury; F5. Guild-ford.

Notes

(1) Boroughs with a mixed franchise are classified according to the qualification held by a majority of the voters. Thus the six boroughs in F were not the only ones in which forty-shilling freeholders voted, but those in which freeholders constituted the majority. Four of the six had been convicted of corruption and 'sluiced' by Act of Parliament, the neighbouring freeholders being added to the constituency to enlarge and improve it (see Chapter 1, n. 15, p. 338).

(2) In some boroughs electors needed a double qualification. It is usually more or less self-evident which qualification did more to determine the nature of the constituency. Thus boroughs in which the freemen were ineligible to vote unless they paid poor rates (scot and lot) are classed with the freeman group.

(3) Classifying the boroughs presents many difficulties. The absence of a registration system, coupled with the rarity of some boroughs being closely contested and 'polled out', means that the number of voters must often be uncertain. The partition between the corporation boroughs and the smallest in the freeman group (D6 and 7; E6 and 7) is the thinnest of all. Thus Lymington is classed in D, and Plympton in E. The justification for this is that in Lymington the mayor and burgesses were limited to a fixed number, while in Plympton there was no such limitation and the exclusive right of the corporation to elect the freemen had been challenged. But this challenge had never been pressed home (*Parl. Papers*, 1834, xxiii. 735–6); the two boroughs were essentially similar in type.

Sources

Among sources which apply to all English boroughs the following are especially useful:

Parl. Papers, 1830–1 (338), x.53–112; 1831–2 (112), xxxvi.489–604; Boundary Commissioners' Reports 1831–2 (141), xxxviii–xli. In some cases this material needs to be supplemented from Municipal Corporations Reports, 1835 (116), xxiii–xxvi.

The Extraordinary Black Book (1831 ed.), pp. 235–44.

Spectator, 1 Jan. 1831.

T. H. B. Oldfield, *Representative History of Great Britain and Ireland* (6 vols., 1816). Oldfield had been an active reformer.

...*continued from page 19*

there being no procedure for boundary revision, the movement of population had taken most of the townsmen outside the limits of the parliamentary borough. Either development might allow a single rich man to acquire and control the property within those limits. In Gatton (Surrey) the population had both diminished and shifted; and ownership was complete. The parish contained 135 inhabitants; but there were only six houses in the borough. Gatton was sold several times towards the end of its parliamentary life. At the last of these sales in the summer of 1830 the price was said to be £180,000.[18]

Groups C and D (the burgage and corporation boroughs) were more uniform in type than A and B and contained no open seats. Burgages were ancient pieces of property of various kinds, from which in burgage boroughs (Group C) the right to vote was solely derived. If one man had managed to acquire a majority of them he could nominate the Members for the borough. At this period Group C consisted almost entirely of nomination boroughs. A municipal corporation was a feature of most, but not all, parliamentary boroughs. The majority of these corporations had great electoral influence. On one side of this large category were the boroughs with no corporation, on the other the corporation boroughs proper (Group D) where the corporators constituted the entire electorate. Group D thus included the most striking examples of the 'close' borough, that is, of the borough in which the adult male population greatly outnumbered the voters. Most of this group were also under some degree of nomination. Corporators often welcomed a rich patron who could help their town or themselves. The magnate who had become a borough patron in this way had a good chance of maintaining his ascendancy. Corporations were normally self-electing, and for some there was no residence qualification. This meant that once a patron had his majority he might be able to consolidate until he obtained a complete dominance, in which the corporators consisted mainly of his family, his tenants, or even his servants. Marlborough (Wilts), where the patron was the Marquess of Ailesbury, provides an example of outright control. Its corporation was said to have consisted usually of the marquess' steward, butler, footmen, and dependants. At the time of the Reform Bill the mayor was one of his agents.

In Group E (the freeman boroughs) the voters were those who had taken their 'freedom' according to the local rights and customs. The methods of obtaining this privilege were usually inheritance; marriage with a freeman's daughter, or in some places with his widow; 'servitude', that is serving a local apprenticeship; and purchase. Like A and B the freeman group included both nomination and open boroughs. In a few of the largest freeman constituencies, such as Coventry and Liverpool, the corporation had no control over the register of voters. The smallest on the other hand were almost indistinguishable in practice from corporation boroughs. A patron controlled the corporation, and through them kept the freemen down to a handful. A united corporation, in a small town, could go far to prevent its opponents from taking out their freedoms.

In many freeman boroughs there was no residence requirement; and in these the freemen who had moved elsewhere, known as 'outvoters' or 'outsitters', formed an important part of the constituency. Moreover some corporations could make honorary freemen of people who did not reside in the borough and who might not have any connexion with it. After an interval of twelve months prescribed by statute such honorary freemen acquired parliamentary votes.

A carefully chosen band of outvoters could be a great help to a patron. Dunwich (Suffolk), which two patrons shared, was as snug a

nomination borough as any. After centuries of coastal erosion most
of it had fallen into the North Sea. There were about thirty freemen,
most of them non-resident. The borough of Cambridge, though
numerically less select than Dunwich, was almost as secure. Around
the turn of the century it had been managed for the Duke of Rutland
by a local banker.[19] The freemen had been kept down to about 200,
the patron's influence being exercised mainly through some eighty
outvoters.

The open boroughs in Groups A, B and E were not democratic
constituencies in the modern sense. In nearly all these places propertied
people could exercise a marked influence provided that they were
willing to spend. Many potwallopers were ready to vote as directed
in return for douceurs or a reduced rent. The large freeman boroughs
were even more accessible to money. Outvoters might account for
more than half of the electorate. In Lancaster only some 740 of the
4000 freemen were resident.[20] Paying the fares to bring a host of
outvoters to the poll, with liberal refreshment *en route*, and 'compensation for loss of time', could be extremely costly. In some places
freedoms were confined to the members of the trade guilds. Seventy
per cent of the freemen of Newcastle upon Tyne, for instance, belonged
to craft trades, and only eleven per cent to the upper and professional
classes.[21] In such boroughs most freemen were poor enough to see
nothing wrong in being paid for their votes. The Rochester freemen,
for instance, who numbered about a thousand, were notoriously
corrupt. In a petition of February 1831 they were said to include no
more than 350 residents, only 150 of these being rated to the poor at
ten pounds a year or above. This was not the most respectable constituency which Rochester could have supplied. The city and liberties
included about a thousand more householders rated at ten pounds or
above who had no votes.[22]

This summary does not reveal why Canning and Peel believed the
system to be impermanent. They certainly did not think it unadaptable
in any obvious sense. It had admitted the 'nabobs' to Parliament. It
now admitted the banker, the merchant, and even the manufacturer.[23]
It possessed that power of assimilation which has been a leading
characteristic of the institutions of the British aristocracy. 'People
think this new Parliament will be a curious one,' Lady Cowper wrote
in June 1826, 'such strange things have turned out. There are three
stock-brokers in it, which was never the case ... before.'[24]

If a successful merchant or millowner wanted a place among the *élite* he bought a landed estate; and if he was ambitious for his sons he cultivated any borough interest that went with it. Peel's father was a textile manufacturer who bought an estate, and at the age of forty became one of the Members for the neighbouring borough. Alternatively the self-made man could simply hire a close or rotten borough seat or buy his way into an open one. Most of the new men who became MPs entered the House by the latter route. There were always seats of one kind or the other available to someone with money.

Canning and Peel wanted to retain open voting so that the landlord could know how his tenants voted. They did not want the vote given to everyone who clamoured for it. They required of an electoral system that it should give great influence to the propertied few. But they did not believe that the system which had been acceptable in 1760 would be accepted much longer. They defended the unreformed system because it gave power to men of property. They despaired of it because it did so in ways that were coming to be thought provocative and corrupt. The system had proved adaptable to many changes. But little could be done to adapt it to an era in which its defects were being scrutinized as never before. In so far as it was based on nomination by individuals and on the influence of corporations there was no weight of public approval behind it.

The ideal constituency according to the doctrines current in the 1820s was a community which trusted the judgement of its leading members, and therefore deferred to them in electoral questions, not from fear, but by inclination.[25] Few even among the radicals objected to political deference when it was untainted by bribery or coercion. What happened in the nomination boroughs was far from this ideal. For the local magnates as a group to have great influence would have been, outside radical circles, entirely acceptable: for a single magnate, who might not even rank as an important local landowner, to be able to dictate was very different. It was thought legitimate that the buyer of a landed estate should acquire with it the political influence which every owner had over his tenants. It was not thought legitimate that, by buying certain burgages, a magnate could return the Members for the borough, when he did not care a scrap for the place except that it served his political ambitions. A standing order of the House of Commons forbade members of the Upper House to interfere in elections for the Lower. Everyone recognized that, with so many peers among the great proprietors, it must often be overlooked. But this did not mean that peers should be allowed to nominate MPs and flout it openly.

This was not a system based on property, but the caricature of one.[26] The borough proprietor might not own much in the place apart from his voters: they frequently owned nothing at all. He was often an absentee: so were many of them. The predominant interest in Banbury belonged to the Earl of Guilford. He did not live there; nor was he a property owner in the borough. It was a corporation borough; and he maintained his influence with the corporation through a number of non-resident corporators chosen from his family and friends. Similarly, the citizens of Knaresborough did not see a great deal either of the Duke of Devonshire or of the candidates whom he nominated to represent them in Parliament. The duke's agent dealt with the burgage holders, some of whom possessed their burgage deeds only while they were at the hustings going through the motions of voting.

The substantial citizens of Banbury thought themselves entitled to vote for their borough Member and would have found a parliamentary spokesman very useful on occasions.[27] They did not enjoy watching the corporation obey Lord Guilford's orders. But that was not the worst of it. Most corporations in parliamentary boroughs were damaged and corrupted by their electoral role. Corporators were branded as partisans. There could be no confidence that they would discharge their duties as magistrates impartially when the case in question bordered on politics.[28] The Banbury petitioners of February 1831 attributed a frightening 'spirit of turbulence and disrespect' among the lower classes of their town to their magistrates' reputation for partisanship and consequent lack of authority.[29] The venality of some corporations in the smaller boroughs was notorious. 'Everyone has heard,' the *Morning Chronicle* remarked in July 1830, 'of what Camelford cost the Marquess of Cleveland till the arrangement with the Marquess of Hertford. The Members who were returned for the marquess paid the voters in £1 notes enclosed in a deal box marked "China".'[30]

The corporations of certain large cities became equally notorious. In 1817 the whig corporation of Nottingham set out to make sure of both the town's seats through a wholesale creation of honorary freemen. The electoral misdeeds of three prominent corporations in the 1826 election provided an even larger scandal. The corporation candidate at Northampton was shown to have been paid £1000 out of corporate funds. The tories of the Leicester corporation, holding one seat, and determined to capture the second, outdid Nottingham by enrolling 800 of their supporters as honorary freemen more than a year before the dissolution. The city paid all the expenses of the operation except the stamp duty of £3 a head. One of the corporation candidates was promised £7000, and the other an unspecified amount, towards election expenses. The money for all this was found partly by raising the price of an ordinary freedom from £35 to £50, partly by the sale and mortgaging of corporate lands. One of the candidates returned by these means quarrelled with the corporation over his election expenses and the story came out in Parliament and the press.[31] At Coventry the corporation were supported by the weavers. They therefore allowed the latter to riot with impunity during the election. The Commons found the case against Coventry's mayor and magistrates so strong that they turned to the standard remedy and passed a Bill giving concurrent jurisdiction in the city to the magistrates for Warwickshire.

The aftermath of the 1826 contests highlighted both the sins of the corporations concerned and the near impossibility, while the electoral system remained as it was, of preventing their recurrence. On Northampton Peel said in February 1827 that 'if such an application of corporation funds shall be decided not to be illegal ... in my opinion a legislative remedy should be resorted to, to prevent ... recurrence'.[32] But Bills to prevent the use of corporate funds for electoral purposes were rejected by the Lords in 1827 and 1828. The Lord Chancellor told the peers in July 1828 that 'corporations ... held property not in trust; and over such property the corporation exercised the same right as individuals did over their property'.[33] The Coventry Bill too was killed in the Lords.

The abuses in local government which the system engendered were not confined to corporations. If a scot-and-lot-borough patron appointed the overseers of the poor he could disfranchise hostile voters by keeping them off the rate books. This was said to happen at Stockbridge, where the Grosvenors were also accused of making the road surveyor serve electoral purposes. He apparently employed unemployables who thus became ratepayers and grateful voters in the Grosvenor interest.[34]

None of these abuses was new in the 1820s though some of them had not been practised hitherto on so large a scale. The system was increasingly in ill repute, not so much because it was growing more corrupt, but because more was known about its corruption. Incidents which might once have passed unnoticed were now familiar to every newspaper reader. Visitors flocked to Old Sarum to see the field and ancient earthwork which returned two members to Parliament. Moreover standards of public conduct were rising. It was no longer entirely acceptable that Leicester's charitable funds should be reserved almost exclusively for voters of sound views, or that one Liverpool merchant should be exempt as a freeman from harbour dues while his rival was not.[35]

The system may well have had a blacker reputation than it deserved, since it was the worst corporations, and the most corrupt bodies of freemen, which attracted nearly all the publicity. The exclusiveness of most corporations made them a natural target for unfair criticism.[36] Their electoral functions were only one factor contributing to the defects of English local government. Many municipal problems were far harder to solve than was generally realized. A corporation's blunder might be ascribed to partisanship when it resulted in fact from an incompetence to tackle the town's problems which had nothing to do with the electoral system. Largesse from parliamentary patrons and candidates was not always directed towards corrupting the corporators or freemen. Some of it might even be of general benefit to the town.

The venality of freemen boroughs was easily exaggerated. A freeman who insisted on being paid for his parliamentary vote was not necessarily putting it up for sale. The candidate whom he favoured could not have it for nothing; but in many cases the other side could not have it at all. To say that all electors should be independent and respectable made a good slogan. Carried into action it would have meant disfranchising the working class in the absurd belief that no one else took bribes.

When all this has been allowed Canning and Peel were right. A system so disreputable was not likely to last.

Those who were dissatisfied with the borough system found some compensation in the 82 seats for *English counties*. Here property was given its legitimate influence in open constituencies. Apart from Westmorland, where the Lowthers ruled, no English county was dominated by a single nobleman. The most influential of the county families consulted together informally and chose the Members from among themselves. This group often managed to prevent a contest, with all its attendant rancour and expense. They contrived, in the phrase of the time, to 'keep the peace of the county'.

The county voting qualification had been fixed by an Act of 1430 at the ownership of freehold land or property worth at least forty shillings a year. A wide variety of properties, life interests and even church offices conferred the vote. The bell-ringer of Westminster Abbey was an *ex officio* voter for Middlesex. There was no residence qualification; but using 'outvoters' on a very large scale would have been prohibitively expensive and unpopular.

The majority of county voters were not as independent as the title freeholder might suggest. Centuries of rising prices had made the freehold qualification very small. It was no guarantee that the voter had the financial resources to stand up to his landlord. Many of those who voted as freehold owners owned nothing much except the patch which qualified them; in reality they were tenant farmers, dependent in some way or other on their landlord's good will. Thus the voters of an English county were not far from the ideal electorate of the propertied classes. A property qualification guaranteed, in theory at least, some respectability and independence. The number of voters made nomination by one person very difficult. At the same time the nature of the qualification ensured that most of the voters would be open to influence from above, and some to direction. The influence was not usually oppressive. Few county magnates wanted to quarrel over politics with a tenant who farmed well. Sometimes he was told how to cast one of his votes, but allowed to do as he liked with the other.

The governing class were less satisfied with the county system than this idyllic picture indicates. Contested county elections, while not very common, could be ruinously expensive.[37] Direct bribery was rare in counties. But in all other ways the poorer freeholders were almost as demanding as borough outvoters; and most counties contained several thousand of them. The poll was taken only in the county town, so that the bills for transport, lodging, refreshment, and compensation for loss of time, could reach enormous totals. There was no system of registering the voters in either counties or boroughs. Thus the process of voting included that of proving a title to vote and was extremely slow. The law allowed a maximum of fifteen days for taking the poll. The Yorkshire election of 1807, which held the record for expense, seems (when all allowances for exaggeration have been made) to have cost the candidates and their supporters over £250,000.[38]

While the expenses in other counties did not approach the Yorkshire level they could be very formidable. One candidate in a Warwickshire contest was supposed to have spent £27,000.[39] The risk of incurring expenses of this order virtually excluded a squire of moderate means from Parliament, however acceptable he might be to his fellow magnates and to the freeholders. In the eyes of many squires the county seats were too costly and too few.

The dominance which the larger landed magnates enjoyed in the counties was not secure. There were plenty of freeholders living in towns and cities. One of the Middlesex seats went to industry in 1820, and one of Yorkshire's in 1826. A good many urban freeholders had never bothered to qualify for a vote. To do so they would have needed to be assessed to the land tax for their freeholds, unless exempted.[40] In the late 1820s many Manchester freeholders were apparently not assessed.[41] The town was assessed for land tax at a comparatively small fixed sum. The assessors had no great inducement to keep individual assessments up to date. Lancashire had not been contested for a long time. No one had yet stirred the potential voters of Manchester to challenge the county grandees.

Some magnates in counties that had become partly industrial were uneasily aware that their rule rested in tradition and not on firm foundations of electoral law. A system in which registration provisions did not exist, and the polling arrangements were quite inadequate, would provide an expensive framework for a clash between land and trade. The dissatisfaction of a number of magnates did not mean that the county system won great approval from business and professional men. The industrialist's ambition was not to contest his county against the landlords. If he wanted any change, it was that the town which he had helped to create should be given the MPs to which its importance entitled it. He hoped that he could trust his fellow townsmen and employees to elect the man who had brought them prosperity.

The electoral laws of the rest of the British Isles differed a good deal from those of England. The *Welsh* system, which was the closest to the English, gave rise to comparatively few serious grievances. The Welsh counties were in general smaller and less populous than the English, and thus rather more liable to fall under a single dominating influence; but most of the borough constituencies were comparatively open. All but two of them were formed from groups of boroughs under a sixteenth-century Act which applied only to Wales. The

Carnarvon Borough constituency, for instance, included five boroughs and had an electorate of around 800.

  Scotland, by contrast, was a notable breeding ground of reformers. From the Act of Union in 1707 until the Reform Act it resembled in its electoral arrangements an unbroken series of close boroughs.[42] The burghs, except for Edinburgh, were grouped into districts for electing the fifteen burgh Members. This Scottish grouping system was far more oligarchic than the one which applied in Wales. The 'districts of burghs' employed a uniform system of indirect election devised at the Union, the voters at the first stage being the members of self-electing burgh corporations. The corporation of Edinburgh, who had an MP to themselves, formed a constituency of thirty-three in a city of 162,000. Scottish counties were hardly more open than the burghs. The characteristics of an English county were sufficient voters to give some appearance of an open and popular constituency, coupled with the ascendancy of the local landlord proprietors. All Scottish counties lacked the first and some the second.

  This arose from two differences between the Scottish and English voting qualifications. In the first place the Scottish qualification had not been devalued. It was based on 'the old extent,' that is, on land currently worth between £70 and £130 a year. As a result Scottish county electorates were small, ranging in the 1820s from a little under 240 (Fife or Perthshire) to 21 (Bute). Secondly, in Scotland the qualification was not related directly to land ownership. Under the 'superiority' system of Scottish law the vote lay with those who held directly from the Crown, but this right could be separated from ownership of the land itself. When this was done the superiority became simply a piece of parchment worth the price of a vote, and could be held by a 'parchment voter' who owned no land in the county concerned at all. In 1831 more than half of the 2500 odd voters for Scottish counties, including twenty out of the twenty-one for Bute, were said to be of the 'parchment' type. Superiorities without the corresponding land were held largely by three classes of people—attorneys, younger sons in middle-class families, and the nominees of great aristocrats. The attorneys traded and speculated in them: the younger sons hoped that, if they always used them in support of government candidates, they would be rewarded with official appointments; and the magnates acquired them to extend their 'interests'. By this means the Duke of Montrose, for instance, more or less controlled Dumbartonshire, though he had little property there.

Scotland was thus a country of close rather than of rotten or nomination seats. Its salient feature was not places which still returned MPs though wholly decayed, nor even seats under a magnate's unassailable control. There were a few Scottish nomination counties. Apparently at one Bute election the candidate had proposed and seconded his own nomination, and then voted for himself, he being the only person present apart from the returning officers. The twenty-four electors of Sutherland were said all to be tenants either of the Marquess of Stafford or of his younger son. But oligarchic exclusiveness rather than dictation was the norm in Scotland. In most Scottish counties and burghs the electors were just numerous and independent enough to require inducements and rewards.

As a general rule, where the voters were many and poor what a candidate needed most was cash: where, as in Scotland, they were comparatively few and drawn largely from the middle class, he needed patronage. Scotland was plentifully supplied with well educated but needy younger sons. These were the great beneficiaries of the Scottish system. The majority of the country's 45 MPs would support any government that was not obviously falling, in return for a steady supply of spoil for the oligarchies that elected them.

This electoral machine was not simply an alien imposition. It served the interests of the government in London more directly than those of Scotland. But its staff were Scotsmen and it provided Scotsmen with good things. Very few Englishmen sat for Scottish seats; and a large slice of the total patronage available went north of the border. As Sir Walter Scott, a stout anti-reformer, wrote, India was Scotland's 'corn chest'.[43] By the 1820s, however, the 'economical reform' movement had reduced the volume of patronage even in Scotland. The machine was past its best, and had powerful enemies. It sustained, and was sustained by, a powerful group of Scotsmen; but they were losing ground. Like most patronage systems it disappointed two voters for every one satisfied, and was loathed among those who would not earn advantage by servility. Moreover, some of the great proprietors felt that they were under-represented by it. As a means of representing the Scottish people it was utterly inefficient.

In any survey of the unreformed system *Ireland* must stand apart. Irish electoral arrangements were part of a governmental system designed to keep Catholic Irishmen in subordination; and they were attacked and defended as such. To give a coherent account of the transactions leading to the Irish Reform Act of 1832 would thus require another book. Nevertheless something must be said about the Irish system if only because the Reform crisis, like a number of others in British history, was sparked off in Ireland.

The Irish part of the system like the Scottish had been completed by an Act of Union. Since 1793 the Irish Catholics had been eligible for votes in both boroughs and counties; but until the Catholic Emancipation Act of 1829 they could not sit in the House of Commons. Under the Union of 1800, which ended Ireland's separate parliament and transferred the representation to Westminster, 84 Irish boroughs had been abolished, compensation being paid to the owners. As a result, in 1832, while ten of the thirty-three Irish boroughs were reckoned as close, and a further eight as nomination seats, none were so decayed that they could strictly be called rotten. More than half belonged to the corporation group. A law of 1792 allowed Catholics to become corporators; but this had little effect. The corporations were self-electing. Once Protestant, therefore, they continued to be so; and in many places would-be Catholic corporators could be subjected to unacceptable oaths of office.

Most of the borough patrons and Members were drawn from the Anglo-Irish aristocracy: some were not Irish at all. Part of an English nobleman's estates and 'interest' might lie in Ireland; or an Englishman might hire an Irish borough seat. Peel was given the seat at Cashel (Tipperary) by his father as a twenty-first birthday present. The first group, the men of the 'English pale' in Ireland, were not complete aliens like the second. But as all the Members and nearly all the patrons were Protestants, and many were absentees as well, they were anything but a representative group of Irishmen. The social barrier between the Member and most of those living in the area which he nominally represented was greater in Ireland than elsewhere; and outside Ulster there was always a religious barrier as well.

The Irish counties formed in 1825 the only sizeable section of the system where the opponents of the governing class had an obvious chance of seizing control. In the 1826 election the forty-shilling free-holders of Waterford shook off the dominance of the Beresfords who opposed Catholic Emancipation, and elected a pro-Catholic. Two years later, in a far more spectacular revolt, Daniel O'Connell was elected for Clare though a Roman Catholic and therefore ineligible to sit. After the Clare election the forty shillingers were not left with the vote. In 1829 the Irish county franchise was altered. The old

B

system, so long thought both impregnable and sacred in every part, was
shown to be neither.

For the purposes of a survey it is convenient to divide the unreformed
House of Commons into compartments. But the divisions are artificial.
The system was judged then, and must be judged now, as a whole.
Where nomination and influence are concerned the unreformed House
should not be regarded as a military unit neatly subdivided, with one
squad containing all the open borough Members, another all those for
close boroughs, and yet another those from the English counties. It is
seen better as a crowd straggling along a road. At one end are the
Members for the most populous and independent counties and the
two Members for Westminster. At the other come the MPs for Gatton
and Old Sarum. The rest of the House is strung out over the whole
intervening space, with every little group merging into the next.

The total number of nomination seats cannot be stated accurately.
At any time some boroughs would be crossing the borderline
between influence and nomination. There can be no agreed rule on
how to classify all of these. None of the contemporary estimates are
entirely dispassionate and trustworthy. J. W. Croker's calculation in
1827, which is one of the more reliable, gives 276 seats as being held
'not by influence or connexion, but by direct nomination'.[44] Croker
was trying to impress his chief, Canning, with the borough owners'
power, and may thus have included a few too many seats in his total:
on the other hand, he naturally did not include the handful of seats
under the direct control of the government. His figure may perhaps be
accepted as a rough practical guide.

A few of Croker's 276 nomination Members owned their own seats;
but most of them were dependent on patrons. These relationships also
were of a variety to defy classification. Some patrons seem to have put
certain restrictions on how 'their' Members voted although they had
been paid for the seats concerned at the full market rate. Others who
had been paid nothing left their MPs completely free. In many cases
the Member had a good deal of latitude, but felt an obligation to
surrender his seat, even before it should be demanded of him, if he
found himself disagreeing with the owner on a major issue.

These remarks on the unreformed system are an attempt to show
where it was vulnerable. Contemporary views and judgments have
therefore been emphasized. The effect of the rotten boroughs was
naturally exaggerated by both reformers and anti-reformers. Anti-

reformers stressed that it was the rotten seats which enabled either party to bring its brilliant young men into the House. Reformers recounted instances in which such seats were occupied by the owner's undistinguished, but obedient, dependants. In fact, most of the relatives, connexions, and friends, nominated by patrons, were well-to-do members of the governing class; and people of this kind would have been elected under any system then in contemplation.[45] Even the relationship by which a Member was at least as dependent on his patron as on his constituents was not confined to nomination seats. There was nothing to prevent a magnate from paying a candidate's expenses for an open seat.

The paradox of a system which few people thought defensible, and still fewer attacked, was apparent to contemporaries. 'The systematic corruption of Parliament, and its effects, are better understood now,' the radical *Examiner* pronounced in 1828, 'than at any former period; and yet . . . the demand for the remedy has been abating as the sense of the evil has been prevailing.'[46]

However low the reputation of the system, the obstacles in the way of an effective Reform movement were immense. Those who had a material interest in the survival of the old House formed a strong force in both Parliament and country. Despite occasional revolts, the people at the base of the system willingly sustained their masters' great power, since this was the source of their own small privileges. The poorer corporators and non-resident freemen feared household suffrage much as the poor whites of the American south hated negro suffrage in the reconstruction period after the Civil War. In both cases these fears prolonged the rule of the few. Moreover, the most ambitious of the new men naturally hesitated to attack a privileged system which they hoped to join.

This constituted a formidable vested interest; but its strength can be exaggerated. A large majority of the peers, and more than half of the House of Commons, had little to do with the rotten boroughs. Only the richest merchants or manufacturers could think of buying a borough or even of hiring a seat. By 1830 a seat cost perhaps £1200 to £1800 a year, or £5000–8000 for the life of a parliament. Most business men could afford neither the outlay nor the time involved.

The unreformed system would not have lasted for so long had it been sustained only by those who had a personal interest in its continuance. Like any well-established constitution it had given rise, not merely to vested interests, but to political habits which ensured its survival in the absence of a general and strong demand for change. It was regarded as part of Britain's free and Protestant constitution. No one had dared to tamper with municipal charters since James II's efforts in that direction had ended in his dethronement and exile. The system was supported, moreover, by one of the strongest political convictions of the time—the doctrine of the sanctity of property. Governmental interference with property rights was thought tyrannous. The rotten boroughs were bolstered by illegal practices; but they represented property of a kind. Abolishing them would be a bad precedent. Start down that road and no property would be safe. Parliament had no more right, Eldon told the Lords in 1832, 'to take away the elective franchise from the present holders of it, than . . . to take away from them the property in houses or land which conferred it'.

The stability of the system depended most of all on the views and interests of the political parties. In an era of tory governments most of the nomination seats were held by tories. Apart from the strength of toryism among the great proprietors, opposition politics were an expensive luxury for a nobleman who wanted to increase his interest or to gain a step in the peerage. By Croker's estimate members of the 'tory aristocracy' controlled 203 of his nomination seats, and the whigs only 73. These figures suggest that the tories, as a parliamentary party, would uphold the system, while the whigs would want to abolish it. The first part of the inference is truer than the second. The whigs held off from attacking the system for many years; and when they challenged it at last, between 1819 and 1823, they had no success. A glance at the course of politics during Lord Liverpool's premiership may help to explain this ineffectiveness.

The last tory to propose a sweeping Reform had been the younger Pitt in 1785. In Lord Liverpool's time nearly all tories, even those with no personal stake in the rotten boroughs, felt an interest in preserving the system which, among its other merits, provided one of the foundations of their party's ascendancy. The position of the whigs and independents[47] is not so quickly explained. Most whigs favoured some kind of Reform in theory. But up to the autumn of 1819 they proposed to wait indefinitely until there was a greater popular demand for it. There was no chance of a Reform Bill passing while the war with France lasted. To encourage an agitation, and unsettle men's minds when no good could come of it, was not thought proper work for a whig aristocrat. During the 1790s Grey had been involved in the radical

Reform schemes of the Friends of the People. But he told the Lords in 1810:

I doubt much whether there exists a very general disposition in favour of [Reform] . . . . Until this country shall have expressed its opinion upon this subject, the examples of the other nations of Europe should deter us from any precipitate attempt to hurry on to premature or violent operation a measure on which the best interests of the nation so essentially depend.[48]

In February 1817 he said that he did not regard Reform as a *sine qua non*. In September of that year he announced that there had been 'some modification' of the opinions of his youth.[49]

The independents generally started from a standpoint less friendly to Reform, but arrived at much the same practical conclusion. William Lamb, the future Viscount Melbourne, was a Canningite of whig origins and something of an independent. He sat for Peterborough from 1816 to 1819. His views at this period were recorded many years later by a whig country gentleman, Sir Robert Heron.

It is a proof [Heron wrote] of the high reputation of Lord Melbourne that he has never been charged with apostasy; yet he was brought in for Peterborough by the late Lord Fitzwilliam to oppose Reform, and did oppose it manfully. At that very time, however, in conversation with me he justified his future change: he told me that he thought Reform . . . was unnecessary and that the people did not wish it. 'If,' he added, 'the people should ever become seriously and perseveringly desirous of it, I should think it my duty to support it.'[50]

If enough people outside the governing class became reformers they would sweep the whigs and independents along with them. The system would then become almost impossible to maintain. Something must now be said about middle- and working-class attitudes to Reform.

The use of class terms to denote divisions of society was still new during this period. It is appropriate to concentrate on the industrial and commercial areas of England and to begin with the middle class, since William Lamb and his friends referred chiefly to this class when they spoke of 'the people'. The men who were given the middle-class label were extremely various in outlook and circumstances. It is possible to distinguish two main groups, however.[51] The first consisted of the successful merchants, manufacturers, and professional men. The second was a *petit bourgeois* group of small masters, shopkeepers, and lesser professional men. Much as the two groups differed from each other, they possessed certain traits in common. Most of them were affected by governmental decisions on such subjects as the corn laws and the currency. By the end of the Napoleonic wars most were well enough informed to grasp something of the issues involved. Their class was gaining in numbers, in importance, and above all in self-confidence. It was, and is, easy to exaggerate these gains: the contemporary image of the middle class current among the whigs owed something to romantic exaggeration.[52] It was true, however, that middle-class people were learning to voice their political demands with effect. Pückler-Muscau, who toured England in 1827 and greatly admired the English middle class, took particular note of their public spirit. 'They love their country passionately,' he wrote, 'but without any view of personal interest—without hope of sinecures, or intrigue for place.'[53]

Apart from the few who aspired to seats in Parliament these new men had little natural inclination to admire an old-fashioned electoral system. Those who had profited by the first explosion of industrial change were apt to see in it great possibilities of social progress. In the upper middle class the predominant outlook was characterized by a confident liberalism. The periodicals which catered for them, such as the whiggish *Edinburgh Review* founded in 1802, had little respect for ancient ways. Mechanical inventions to the young writers of the *Edinburgh* were merely one expression of 'the march of mind', and of 'the spirit of the age'. The more enlightened and progressive a country was, the more it outgrew its old institutions; and the safer it was to replace them with something better, as an out-of-date machine would be replaced.

The lower middle class had still less natural attachment to the existing order. They resented the nepotism and restrictions which, as they thought, robbed them of their rewards. Lacking capital and connexions, they were inclined to assert the rights of man as against those of property. The intellectuals among them had both the motive and the talent for questioning traditional authority. Edward Gibbon Wakefield called this group 'the uneasy class'.[54]

The industrial proletariat in the new mills and factories were less temperate than their masters in blaming the system. Political awareness had long been widespread among such groups as the London artisans. It was now spreading throughout the lower part of society. Whether conditions were in general harsher than they had been a generation earlier remains a matter of controversy. About the discontent which the new conditions generated there is no doubt at all. Trade had been dislocated by the Revolutionary and Napoleonic wars and their aftermath; and commercial conditions fluctuated greatly.[55] The workers even in the most flourishing industries suffered from recurrent slumps. Crowded into the insanitary parts of each town, and subjected to the new and inhuman discipline of the factory, working people naturally blamed their troubles on the government. Habits of deference and subordination to those higher in society were shaken. The existing order was no longer accepted without question. The have-nots acquired a new solidarity. In 1817 and 1819, during the post-war slump, industrial Britain seethed with discontent. The 'labouring poor' were turning into a new phenomenon—the working class.[56]

The rising middle class faced both ways. They could be moved, on the one side, by resentment against the squires, on the other, by fear of the workers. Both attitudes will appear as this story is told. During the first decades of the century the attitude of fear was dominant. This resulted largely from the effects of the French Revolution. The Terror of 1793-4 reinforced the fears about the working class which middle-class people entertained, and affected British politics for a generation. After the Terror, for each convert to the radicalism of Paine's *Rights of Man*, several were repelled. In the lower half of society the impressions left by the Terror faded fairly quickly; but among propertied people the lesson was learned for life. Henry Cockburn wrote of the Edinburgh of his youth: 'The revolution in France . . . , for above twenty years, was the all in all. Everything, literally everything, was soaked in this one event.'[57]

People of property became convinced that any constitutional change involved an appalling risk. It might disrupt the habits of obedience which constituted the only barrier against anarchy. Changes once set in motion would be hard to stop. Those who summoned the States General, or initiated a Reform of the House of Commons, were apt to be swept irresistibly towards revolution or democracy. The upper and- middle-class British people who had been young in 1793 held the view expressed by J. M. Keynes in middle life, that civilization was 'a thin and precarious crust erected by the personality and the will of a very few, and only maintained by rules and conventions skilfully put across and guilefully preserved'.[58] Around 1810 the crust looked too thin for any tampering with it to be allowed. This may seem a curious reaction to what had happened in France. It might have been more reasonable to attribute the Terror less to the summoning of the

States General than to the fact that they had been summoned far too late. Events of this kind produce, however, not calm reflection, but a revulsion from past attitudes and illusions. The Englishman of 1789 thought it admirable that the French should at last adopt the principles of 1688. Twenty years later, remembering the Terror, he shrank from the very idea of political change. The Englishman of 1914 cheered for the ultimatum to Germany. Twenty years later, remembering the Somme, he shrank from the very idea of war.

It is possible to exaggerate the degree to which the Terror and the war turned the middle class towards reactionary politics. Greatly as dissenters disliked revolutionary atheism, there was a wide gulf—for a Unitarian a very wide gulf—between the members of the older dissenting denominations and the establishment. The fact that most corporations were exclusively Anglican served as a continual reminder of the dissenters' depressed status.[59] The history of Methodism in these years is instructive, however. Its newer offshoots, the Primitive Methodists (nicknamed the Ranters) and the Bible Christians, appealed largely to various sections of the working class and were far from conformist. The main Methodist connexion, on the other hand, strained every nerve to achieve respectability. In 1819 its leading figure, Jabez Bunting, pronounced Methodism to be 'as opposed to democracy as it is to sin'. The Brunswick chapels still to be seen are a reminder of the Methodists' ostentatious loyalty in this period to the Royal House.[60]

No doubt some ultra tories and borough owners with a strong personal interest in the maintenance of the *status quo* did all they could to feed this alarm, and expressed more fear of Jacobinism than they felt. Some of those who enjoyed political power and rewards may have been well content that the middle class should be too scared to demand a redistribution of these benefits. But in Lord Eldon's time, as always, politicians could exploit only those fears which were already deep and widespread. In the shadow of the guillotine some mill-owners became as frightened and as diehard as any marquess. While the mill-owner continued to react like the marquess he was represented in the Commons—after a fashion—by the marquess's nominees. If views on the matter in hand hardly differ between two groups it makes little difference which group supplies the jurymen. Even the most daring of the rising professional men recoiled from the Jacobins and Napoleon. In 1807 the *Edinburgh* pronounced that an extension of the suffrage would bring no more than 'subordinate advantages'.[61] Yet this wary approach to Reform was too bold for many; and the tory counter-stroke, the *Quarterly Review* founded in 1809, quickly established itself. Despite the spread of political views and information the existing order was still safe. In this atmosphere, as far as the propertied classes were concerned, multiplying the politically minded meant multiplying reactionaries.

A few years after Waterloo the political weather began to change. The new generation did not share their elders' alarms. The ideas which had inspired the American and French Revolutions became more familiar and less horrifying to people of property. The memory of the Terror and of the War with France began to subside. 1793 was no more effective as a revolutionary bogey to the young men of this decade than 1917 was to those of the 1930s. To use the terms which were coming into use around this time, liberal influences began to gain on the forces of conservatism.[62] In the Commons itself liberals penetrated farther into both parties; and coming men willing to oppose Catholic Emancipation became hard to find.[63]

Politicians warned each other that 'the schoolmaster was abroad' throughout the land. An electoral system based on corruption and servility seemed unworthy of an age of rising educational standards. The foundation of the *Manchester Guardian* in 1821, and of the *Westminster Review* in 1824, showed that radicalism of various kinds was spreading among people of talent and education. The Benthamites[64] of the *Westminster* were eager to abolish the electoral system, which like many other institutions had failed to pass their test of utility. On this issue they regarded the *Edinburgh* as time-serving and half-hearted. The *avant-garde* of yesterday were being outpaced.

When the weather began to change in the period following the Peterloo massacre the whigs changed their tune. Their function was defined by a whig leader more than fifty years later as being 'to direct and guide and moderate popular movements'.[65] They saw a popular movement starting towards Reform, and decided that they would be better placed to guide and moderate it if they moved a step forward. Between the autumn of 1819 and 1823 most of the leaders and party magnates committed themselves to Reform. Grey told Holland at the end of 1819 that Reform was 'daily becoming more and more a subject of popular interest': it would 'be impossible for any party looking to the support of public opinion to succeed' without proposing a general Reform.[66]

Towards the end of the following year Grey was canvassing among his colleagues a scheme for taking a hundred seats from 'the most obnoxious' boroughs and dividing them 'between the large towns and the most extensive and populous counties'.[67] In January 1821 he told a Northumberland county meeting that his terms for accepting office would be a 'total change in the system of government'.[68] In April 1822 Russell obtained 164 votes for the plan of transferring a hundred seats, this being the highest Commons vote for a general Reform since 1785.[69] In the following August, after Castlereagh's suicide, it seemed possible that the whigs would be invited to form a government. Even Holland who described himself as 'a sorry and small Reformer' agreed that a whig administration must be based on a pledge to introduce a Reform, and that something as sweeping as the hundred seat plan might be required.[70]

Coke and Tavistock who were old Reformers had already said publicly that they would not support a whig government which avoided this pledge. Meanwhile those party magnates who had hitherto opposed Reform, or remained silent about it, were announcing their conversions. The announcements by leading borough owners such as the Duke of Devonshire naturally aroused particular interest. A minority of whigs were still not reformers; and the majority differed greatly on what kind of Reform they wanted. But in 1822 the greatest doubt was not whether a whig government would embrace Reform. It was whether anyone would live to see a wholly whig government.

The Reform movement in the whig party fizzled out. It had some popular support but not enough. The older generation are slow to lose their fears, or to make way for their juniors. The people inside a well-established and exclusive system can resist a good deal of pressure from outside. The demand from the non-voters has to appear over-whelming and threatening to become effective. The whigs gained very little independent parliamentary support for Reform because the independents were not convinced about the popular pressure for it. Most independents still thought of conceding Reform as dangerous and almost revolutionary. They did not yet believe that refusing it might entail an even greater danger of revolution. The electoral system might be clumsy and corrupt. But under it British institutions were preserved and the king's government functioned after a fashion. It was doubtful whether any other machinery could be devised through which these aims could be achieved.[71]

Cobbett saw 'the rotten part of the constitution' as the basis of the governmental system—of The Thing, as he called it. The parliamentary independents were inclined to think the same. Cobbett had become a reformer to destroy The Thing. They stayed aloof from Reform to keep The Thing in being. Liverpool's government was constantly in trouble between 1819 and 1822. But he stayed in power because, when it came to a vote of confidence, the independents showed that they preferred him to the reforming whigs.

The pace of change in the industrial revolution, and the alteration in the class balance by 1820, can be exaggerated. The older tradition was still very powerful. As late as 1830 agriculture still employed far more British people than any group of industries; and in England only one person in eighty worked in the cotton industry. The new industrial fortunes scarcely rivalled as yet the wealth of the greatest landowners. Moreover, each demand for Reform stimulated a strong reaction from the older England. There were plenty of old-fashioned people whose politics were to damn liberals, radicals and political economists, and to sustain existing institutions in church and state. Boroughs like Old Sarum were a safeguard against the heresies of the innovators, and a symbol that those heresies had little influence.

A great many poor men still had no politics and no notion that a vote was useful except to sell. Even among the politically insurgent part of the working class, support for a whig Reform was unreliable. The Reform cry rose with the discontent which bad times brought and fell as prosperity began to return. This does not mean that working-class reformers were solely the product of slumps and of personal privation. There were life-long reformers among the London artisans whose convictions did not weaken when trade was good. The leaders of the working-class Reform movement, in particular, were not the creation of bad times alone. They knew plenty about hardship and distress. But it was a measure of prosperity which gave some of them the confidence to take an insurgent line. A man with the initiative to become a leader was likely to have found his way into a flourishing trade. John Doherty, who emerged as an outstanding trades union leader in 1830, was a Lancashire spinner, and thus a member of one of the best paid working-class groups. These people were comparatively few, however. Most of the working-class backing for Reform came from men who were feeling the pinch. In the good years these supporters fell away, in proof of Cobbett's dictum that it was impossible to agitate a man who had a full stomach. The anti-reformers knew that they had only to ride out the storm. In due course with the boom of 1824 and 1825 the Reform agitation withered.

Secondly, radical reformers were naturally suspicious of schemes such as Russell's. The term radical covered a great variety of political attitudes; and some radicals were close to the whigs. Yet between whig and radical Reform schemes there was a great gap. For working-class radicals Reform was based not only on the belief that a different system of government could somehow cure unemployment and distress, but on a theory of rights. Every man capable of using a vote intelligently had a right to one. Whig reformers did not found their schemes on any such theory. They planned to make aristocratic government acceptable by purging away its most corrupt and expensive features. In 1822 Russell appealed to the aristocracy to unite for Reform on that basis.[72] This programme was hardly calculated to arouse overwhelming working-class support. It barely fulfilled even the minimum demands of the radical intellectuals who remained more or less at odds with the whigs throughout the 1820s.[73] Those who wanted to raze the fortress of privilege to the ground were not content with a redesigning scheme aimed at making it less conspicuous and cheaper to man.

Many middle-class people were still deeply impressed with the risks of Reform. Despite the most prudent planning it might give votes to the wrong men. Any prolonged Reform agitation would also harm trade. Even the most limited Reform of all, the transfer of MPs from boroughs convicted of corruption to great cities, did not win universal approval. In March 1828, when a project was under discussion for giving Members to Manchester and Birmingham in this way, Mrs Arbuthnot noted in her diary:

> In practice nothing can exceed the folly of giving Members to these populous towns. It causes riots and loss of lives and property at every election and is not needed; for the great merchants get returned for the rotten boroughs and can attend to the interests of their town much better than if they were obliged to pander to the passions of a . . . mob.[74]

This was the view of a staunch anti-reformer. But some of the leading men in the cities concerned seem to have agreed with it. As late as October 1829 the *Birmingham Journal* remarked that the city did not need MPs: 'The advantage of sending representatives,' it commented, 'is merely theoretical and is surely attended with disorder.'[75] The difference between the generations where the middle class were con-

cerned may be summarized in this way. The men who remembered
1793 were anti-reformers whatever happened. Many of the younger
generation lacked this firm commitment. They would support the
system only for so long as it looked like doing what they wanted.
If they acquired enough grievances they would take the risk and turn
to Reform.

Finally, fashions of thought among the younger tories and independents in the Commons were not favourable to Reform. Was
there any practical benefit in abolishing the rotten boroughs and
creating a host of new voters? Or would it merely make governments
at once weaker and less liberal? It is a mistake to identify the
reformers entirely with a progressive political outlook. In the
eighteenth century the Reform movement had been to some degree
backward looking. The House of Commons was to be turned into a
barrier against the executive.[76] This old-style hankering for weakening
the executive was not fashionable among the capable young politicians who surveyed the problems of the post-war era. They had
come into politics when the economical reform movement had
done its work;[77] and they thought the executive quite weak enough
already.

In June 1822 Brougham revived Dunning's motion of 1780 'that
the influence of the Crown has increased, is increasing, and ought to
be diminished'. The revival fell flat and Brougham was defeated by
216 to 101. The boroughs which the government controlled by
patronage were now a mere handful. In February 1831 an 'old whig'
referred to crown influence as having been 'completely destroyed' in
his lifetime.[78] A prime minister had now to rely on the boroughs
controlled by magnates who supported him. Many a tory magnate
still thought of his boroughs simply as his private property. He might
have little conception of the governmental system of which they
formed part. But the intellectual tory now put a high value on the
contribution to this system provided by the rotten boroughs. They
began to be seen as a necessary facility for the executive; and some of
the liberal tories were as keen to preserve them as anyone.

The liberals did not relish putting governments under the control
of an enlarged and illiberal electorate. The great issue for them was
Catholic emancipation; and it was generally believed that an emancipation bill would have a harder passage in a reformed House than in the
existing one. The Catholic Irish were easily made the scapegoats for
every ill. No-popery sentiment was so strong in all parts of the United

Kingdom except Ireland that increasing the number of popular seats would almost certainly entail increasing anti-Catholic strength in the Commons. The liberals were thus in one of the characteristic difficulties of the progressive. In principle they were well disposed to reforms and even to popular government. In practice they feared that the new voter created by a Reform act would show his ignorance of his own best interests by voting against every liberal measure.[79]

The liberal tories looked to Canning. His prediction about the imminent ruin of the unreformed system was made when he was waiting to leave for India. He never left. In September 1822 he accepted instead the Foreign Secretaryship and Leadership of the Commons which Castlereagh's suicide had suddenly made vacant. To fulfil his ambition he had now to falsify his own prophecy. He was not only a convinced anti-reformer: his political future was bound up with that of the rotten boroughs. A formidable Reform agitation would entail a whig government, or a tory split, or perhaps both. If he were to enjoy a prosperous premiership as Liverpool's successor the tory party must remain great and united; and to that end the system must remain unreformed and indeed unchallenged.

Canning had some reason to see himself as the only possible saviour of the old constitution. His experience and the rapidity of his mind qualified him pre-eminently to exploit the middle-class and liberal hesitations about Reform which have just been described. From 1812 to 1822 he had sat for Liverpool. He understood how to appeal to the business community. His analysis and recipe were simple. The government must at all costs retain the confidence of the younger commercial men. Every grievance acquired by the latter would make a few more of them doubt whether they would ever have fair play until a Reform act had given MPs to the new industrial towns. Once these people started a formidable Reform agitation they would soon win round the liberals in the House. Prevent the grievances and you had prevented Reform. 'We are on the brink of a great struggle,' Canning told his secretary two months before he died, 'between property and population. Such a struggle is only to be averted by the mildest and most liberal legislation.'[80]

Canning also managed to convince many whigs that with their help he and the liberal tories could stand up to the anti-Catholic ultra tories and pass emancipation. Sir Francis Burdett, who had been one of the foremost parliamentary advocates of a radical Reform, was one of those convinced. He told Lambton in 1825 that 'the main object ought to be to form an administration on the express basis of conceding the Catholic claims'. 'I said,' Lambton reported to Grey, ' "What, without any stipulation on Reform?" He answered: "Certainly, that is a secondary consideration".'[81]

The extent of the tory government's achievement during Canning's ascendancy from 1822 to 1827 is controversial; and any appraisal of it lies outside the scope of this study. But his political success is undoubted. He 'flashed such a light around the constitution,' said Coleridge, 'that it was difficult to see the ruins of the fabric through it'.[82] Russell's decision to discontinue his Reform motions has been mentioned already. He told the Commons in 1827 that he believed the 'growing lukewarmness' on Reform to be

attributable to the improvement which had taken place in the manner of conducting the government. Whether the people of the Kingdom were wrong or right in allowing themselves to become indifferent upon such a cause, it was not now for him to examine; but he did believe that, as long as they saw the general affairs of the country well conducted, and actuated by a spirit of improvement, they would not look too narrowly into the constitution of that House of Parliament.[83]

Everything which Peel had written to Croker in 1820 remained true, however. A *tour de force* does not alter the political facts; and it cannot be kept up indefinitely. The price of beguiling the reformers was too high. Every liberal concession which Canning made increased the tories' suspicion of him. The bulk of the party distrusted him, and could not perceive, as he did, how precarious the system had become. His attempt to hold the allegiance of the middle class seemed to them a hunt for 'low popularity' dictated by his unprincipled ambition. The more he put Reform in the shade the safer they felt to indulge in a party split and refuse allegiance to him. Liverpool had a stroke in February 1827; and Canning became Prime Minister in April. Six members of the late cabinet refused to serve under him;[84] and Wellington even resigned from the Commandership in Chief as well as from his cabinet office. The tory party, the main bulwark against Reform, was shattered. Canning, who had been ailing before the crisis began, died in the following August. The unreformed system was free from attack; but its defenders had been utterly disorganized.

Like Joseph Chamberlain after the Boer War, Canning was too dynamic and ambitious to stand by while the tories drifted into a decline. Both statesmen adopted a new policy, calculated to win new support. Both split the party and broke their health by doing so. The task of warning the tories that the system could be pushed over, without encouraging the reformers to push, may have been beyond any man's powers: it was certainly beyond Canning's. His origin outside the circle of wealth and power exposed him (as it did Chamberlain) to the distrust of many aristocratic tories; and this was increased by several episodes in his career for which he was open to censure. For success he would have needed not only his 'outsider's' vision, but an 'insider's' prestige and an unblemished record. 'There has been but one man for many years past,' Greville wrote in his diary at the height of the Reform crisis, 'able to arrest this torrent, and that was Canning: and him the tories—idiots that they were, and never discovering that he was their best friend—hunted to death with their besotted and ignorant hostility.'[85]

It is doubtful whether Canning's formula for preventing Reform would have worked for long even if he and Liverpool had both survived and retained the party's allegiance. Despite his claims the unreformed system afforded plenty of practical grievances in the mid 1820s; but it also afforded the prospect of their removal. He had not settled any of the test cases in the ways desired by the middle class; but he had convinced them that such settlements were on the way. There still seemed a chance of gaining their ends by safer means than Reform. They tolerated the old system in the hope that their champion, Canning, would soon be in charge of it. Liverpool's health in his last year of power, like Palmerston's a generation later, was obviously failing. Those who wanted changes knew that they had not long to wait.

It is likely that several difficult decisions could not have been deferred for much longer. It is certain that, when at last made, they could not have been manipulated to please everyone. Even Canning could not settle 'the three C's'—the corn, currency and Catholic questions—without giving middle-class people grievances. Apart from the divergence between the land and industry, merchants and manufacturers were divided among themselves on banking and the tariff; and the collapse of a boom late in 1825 sharpened these divisions. The opponents of the Catholic claims were unlikely to accept any compromise on emancipation: they were determined to oppose it in any form, since the Protestant constitution symbolized for them as nothing else did the traditional England which the liberals threatened. When decisions have to be made, a system which must please everyone to survive cannot survive for long.

By 1827 even Canning's flashing light could not conceal the ruined state of the constitution. The tale of corporation misdeeds in the 1826 election showed no signs of ending. The election had sharpened governing class worries about the problem of election expenses. Grey's reforming views were not weakened by paying some £15,000 for his son's unsuccessful attempt at a Northumberland seat.[86] Yorkshire, having acquired two extra seats from the disfranchised borough of Grampound, seemed more expensive than ever. It was not contested in 1826. But the fifth candidate for this four seat county did not retire until the eve of the poll. By then the election had cost around £150,000.[87] Althorp chaired a select committee on the election expenses problem and introduced a Freeholders Registration Bill, and an Expense of Elections Bill while Canning was premier. Neither was passed and the worries remained.[88]

Canning's tragedy was followed by a ridiculous four month epilogue. Goderich, his successor as premier, succumbed to the incessant bullying of his sovereign, his colleagues, and his wife, and resigned tearfully in January 1828 without even waiting to meet Parliament. This failure advanced Reform too, though in a lesser degree than Canning's. Canning had broken the tory party; but he had also split the whigs. He could not complete his ministry and obtain a majority without calling on the whigs. Grey was opposed to entering a coalition. But most of the other leaders disagreed with him and a number of whigs, Lansdowne among them, took office. The collapse of Goderich, and of the coalition which he had inherited, discredited Lansdowne's leadership and paved the way for a whig reunion under Grey.

Wellington followed Goderich as Prime Minister. Canning, foreseeing that the duke would outlive him and would soon succeed to the premiership, is said to have made a final prophecy: 'Two years will undo all that I have done.'[89] But after his own premiership there was not a great deal left to undo.

CATHOLICS, CORN AND CURRENCY

*Died full of good works, deeply lamented by every HONEST BRITON,
MR. CONSTITUTION... on the 13th of April... 1829, at the
House of the Incurables. (Birmingham Argus,* 1 May 1829)

The government which Wellington formed in January 1828 was
directed towards tory reunion and headed by a staunch anti-reformer.
Yet it completed the disintegration of the tory party and converted
multitudes to Reform. Some of its misfortunes may be attributed to
the duke's defects as a Prime Minister. He was very competent in
politics within a limited range. He could deal with almost any problem
which he could envisage. But judging public opinion was beyond him,
chiefly because by prime ministerial standards he lacked political
experience. Unlike Liverpool, Grey and Melbourne he knew little
about the Commons. He had sat there for a few years only, and then
not for an open constituency such as an English county. If he had
been aware of the lack of insight which resulted from this inexperience,
the defect might have done him less harm; but he did not know about
his political myopia. 'He is exceedingly quick of apprehension,'
Greville noted in August 1830, 'but deceived by his own quickness
into thinking he knows more than he does.' The duke was so isolated
by eminence and deafness that those of his lieutenants who could see
the danger hidden from him failed to give him any effective warning
of it. Only after the Reform storm had begun to blow did he recognize
the change in the political weather.

It was the duke's qualities, however, as much as his political defects
that destroyed his ministry and the system on which it rested. He did
not believe in government by postponement; and by January 1828
there was a great need to settle the Catholic, corn and currency questions. He decided sensibly in all three cases: but in all three he added
to the enemies of his government and of the system, and so greatly
increased the strength of the Reform movement. The 1828 corn law

was a fair compromise having regard to the balance of parliamentary forces at that time. That did not make the measure satisfactory to the Manchester manufacturers. Their aim was free trade in corn and they did not recede from it. They merely knew after 1828 that before it could be attained Parliament must be reformed. It was, however, Wellington's settlement of the Catholic question which damaged the system the most. To understand this episode it is necessary to glance at the problems which faced the duke in his premiership.

Wellington's attempt to restore Lord Liverpool's regime never looked like succeeding. In the first place, his effort to reunite the two sections of the party failed. He appointed Canning's leading political heirs to his cabinet, William Huskisson becoming Colonial Secretary. But he found the Huskissonites[1] impossible and soon forced them out of the government. His opportunity to do this came on a Reform question, namely, the disposal of the two East Retford seats which that borough was to forfeit because of its corruption in the 1826 election.[2] East Retford was a mere pretext for him, however: if another issue had provided a similar opening he would have used that just as readily.[3] Secondly, he was soon in trouble on the Catholic question. There was now nothing to hold back the pro-Catholics. They were freed from their long fear of embarrassing Canning. They had protected themselves against the dissenters' displeasure by carrying the repeal of the Test and Corporation Acts, and so removing the political slurs on dissent. In 1827 an emancipation proposal had been lost in the Commons by four votes. On 12 May 1828 Burdett tried again and secured a majority of six.[4]

In the last week of May 1828 Wellington therefore faced two problems. He needed a new President of the Board of Trade, preferably a pro-Catholic, to succeed one of the Huskissonites. Secondly, he needed to reassure Peel who had been shaken by Burdett's success. Peel believed, in his own words, that he could not stay in office indefinitely 'being in a minority on the most important of domestic questions'.[5] He could not resign while the government was being reorganized without bringing it down. But he asked the duke not to shut the door on emancipation during the forthcoming debate in the Lords. Both men were on record as opponents of emancipation. But Wellington was not such a prominent champion of Protestantism as Peel.[6]

The duke appointed Vesey Fitzgerald to the Board of Trade; and a few days later, on 10 June, he made the kind of statement in the Lords for which Peel asked. 'If the agitators of Ireland would only be quiet,' he told the peers, it might 'become more possible to discover the means of doing something' for the Catholics. Both appointment and statement were sensible; but the conjunction of them was unfortunate. Until the present century acceptance of office or promotion entailed being re-elected to Parliament:[7] in Fitzgerald's case there would be a by-election for County Clare. Wellington knew that by promoting Fitzgerald he was running some risk of a by-election defeat. Indeed Fitzgerald secured a handsome promotion partly because he would not have undergone the expense of re-election, with some danger of being beaten, for a smaller one.[8] The risk did not seem great; and Wellington had compelling reasons for accepting it. Fitzgerald's position in Clare, from his support for emancipation and his family property and personal connexions, was very strong;[9] and in the absence of the Huskissonites there were no other pro-Catholics of requisite calibre available. What the duke had not foreseen was how his speech of 10 June would strike Daniel O'Connell.

O'Connell had naturally been disturbed when the cabinet's pro-Catholic wing was weakened by the ejection of the Huskissonites. Coming on top of this the speech of 10 June horrified him. It seemed to him and his colleagues in the Catholic Association a deliberate attempt to undermine their position and split their movement. As O'Connell read it, the message of the speech was this: if the Association would not relapse into total inactivity it was to be branded as the obstacle to emancipation.

The Association included an influential moderate wing, largely inspired by the Catholic bishops, who would be inclined to take Wellington's hint. They had been strong enough in February 1828 to prevent Reform from being written into the Association's programme. If O'Connell and his colleagues now defied the duke and continued the agitation the bishops might secede taking many of the priests with them. The moderates, who had always disliked the method of mass agitation, would say convincingly that it was actually harming the cause. It is doubtful whether O'Connell wanted emancipation at the price of his own eclipse; and even if he had been self-denying enough for this, his hold over his wild men, though remarkable, was not so strong that he could keep them quiet for months on end. Engineering an immediate crisis represented the only means by which he could escape from his predicament and prevent a split in the movement. He had to prove to the government that his word, not theirs, ruled Ireland, and that emancipation must be conceded at once, and to agitation, not at leisure when all agitation had been abandoned. By promoting Vesey Fitzgerald to the cabinet Wellington had given O'Connell the chance to prove just this.

At an Association meeting on 14 June O'Connell denounced Wellington's speech and called on the Clare electors to reject Fitzgerald. On 16 June he launched the campaign against Fitzgerald and appealed for money for it. He also made a plea for unity in face of the 'efforts now making to create divisions' among the Association.[10] On 18 June the Association decided after a debate to oppose Fitzgerald, despite a warning that an unsuccessful contest would be disastrous. On the following day J. W. Doyle, the most active and influential of the Irish Catholic bishops, addressed an open letter to Wellington. It was amicable in tone and suggested securities for the Protestants which might be written into an Emancipation Bill. After that O'Connell stood with his back to the wall: he had to win the Clare election somehow.

The Association had still not found a candidate. They applied to two who were judged to have a chance of success under their colours. By 23 June both had refused to stand against Fitzgerald. Just over a week from nomination day O'Connell thus faced a humiliating fiasco. At this point the suggestion was made to him that he might stand himself. Although as a Catholic he was debarred by the oath from taking his seat, there was no law to prevent his being elected. O'Connell stood. On 27 June Dr Doyle sent him a letter of support. In what Peel called a 'fearful exhibition of sobered and desperate enthusiasm'[11] the peasants of Clare defied their landlords and overwhelmed Fitzgerald. On the fifth day of the poll, 5 July, he conceded defeat.

By winning the election in Clare O'Connell produced the crisis which he needed. The Association's victory there might be reproduced at the next general election in almost every county in Ireland. In the meanwhile the government feared to give any Irish county Member either an office or a peerage. 'I see clearly,' Wellington wrote to Peel in September 1828, 'that we have to suffer here all the consequences of a practical democratic Reform in Parliament if we do not do something to remedy the evils.'[12] The Association's achievement and the government's reaction to it foreshadowed the Reform crisis. The Irish landlords' machine had been snatched away and used against them. Wellington decided to replace it by a system which would be less vulnerable to agitators.[13] The electoral qualification in the Irish counties must be raised to £10.

Without emancipation, however, it was impossible either to persuade the House of Commons to raise the franchise, or even to govern Ireland. After their triumph in Clare the Association had it in their power to reduce the country to anarchy and financial chaos. They could refuse to pay rent to alien landlords and tithes to an alien church. There were also signs that they meant to try organizing a run on the banks by demanding payment in gold. The Orangemen of the north had already started a counter-agitation, so that civil war was in prospect as well as rebellion. If emancipation were to be delayed the Irish government would need great coercive powers, although the regiments there were so unreliable that it was doubtful whether such powers would be effective. In any case, coercion required an act of Parliament; and once again the Commons would not pass a coercion act without emancipation.

There was no question for Wellington of obtaining a House with a 'protestant' majority by dissolving. In Ireland an election would entail bloodshed and the tightening of O'Connell's grip on the country; and his successes there would reduce, and might even cancel, the 'protestant' gains elsewhere in the United Kingdom. The duke had therefore to deal with the existing House, and to accept emancipation as the preliminary to any legislative remedies against the Association's power. He decided that he was the man to sponsor the Emancipation Bill. He thought with good reason that a cabinet led by himself and Peel was the only one which could impose the Bill quickly on both Parliament and king. He was unwilling to see it delayed until a rebellion or a civil war had broken out. Peel agreed, and was thus easily persuaded of his duty to stay in office and see the measure through the Commons. 'It is a bad business,' the duke remarked to Lord Sidmouth when these plans were announced; 'but we are aground.'[14]

Wellington and Peel were subjected to much abuse for 'ratting' from their outraged 'protestant' followers. The Dowager Duchess of Richmond decorated her drawing room with stuffed rats named after them and their fellow apostates.[15] When Peel resigned his seat for Oxford University and stood for re-election he was defeated amid uproar. A little later Wellington answered a statement from the Earl of Winchilsea by challenging that nobleman to a duel. But the duke's surprise tactics, though they entailed the maximum anger and shock, were successful. Government influence created large pro-Catholic majorities in both Houses. The emancipation resolution in the Commons, for instance, had one of 188. Some MPs who had voted against Burdett the previous year now abstained. Some who had abstained now voted for the resolution. Fifty-eight government supporters actually reversed their votes.[16] The Emancipation Bill was introduced on 10 March and received the Royal Assent on 13 April.

The accompanying Bill raising the Irish county qualification to £10, and so disfranchising about 80,000 former voters,[17] went through without much difficulty. O'Connell and his colleagues made no attempt to save the votes of their supporters; and most of the pro-Catholics in the Commons had shown as early as 1825 that they were willing to accept this restriction of the franchise to gain emancipation. The Bill making the Catholic Association illegal had the quickest passage of all and became law before the end of February.

The Emancipation Act had an immense effect in advancing the cause of Reform. It carried the disruption of the tory party a stage further and thus weakened and divided the anti-reformers' forces. It drove a wedge between the country gentlemen and the 'ministerial interest' and so shattered the precious link on which the tories' supremacy depended. It naturally started a rumour that Wellington and Peel might 'rat' on the unreformed system as they had ratted on Protestantism. This widely held suspicion unbalanced Peel's judgment in face of the Reform agitation, and was the source of the duke's greatest difficulties and of his worst tactical mistakes.

Even more important was the unpopularity of the Act. Once it had been passed the unreformed House was presented in the harshest possible light as a machine for thwarting the popular will. The ultra tories' explanation of their defeat was simple. The Act had been passed against the will of a protestant country because of a pack of unprincipled borough owners. These renegades had gone counter to their convictions in order to keep their slices of government patronage. The Earl of Winchilsea, announcing his conversion to Reform in March 1829, told the Lords that

'when he saw . . . those who were possessed of close boroughs . . . sacrificing their principles, in order that they might be able to patch up fortunes which had been broken and ruined by their vices, he had no hesitation in saying "let honest people have the representation which these have so grossly abused".'[18]

The spectacle of the renegades, Greville noted in February 1829, 'has given a blow to the aristocracy which men only laugh at now, but of which the effects will be felt some day or other'.[19]

A good deal of the ultra-tory account was myth. Many of the converts on emancipation had nothing to do with the rotten boroughs. Apart from this the suggestion that the renegade borough owners were thinking solely of patronage was an absurd oversimplification of their motives. They had all kinds of reasons for following the duke besides their liking for honours and jobs. He led their party. They respected him. What he said on emancipation made sense to them. But on the main point the ultras were right. There was no popular majority for Wellington's policy. Despite Peel's huge majority in the Commons on the resolutions he was in a minority among the English and Welsh county Members. The events of 1829 showed 'no-popery' to be quite as strong as liberals had feared. In a reformed Parliament emancipation would have been passed more slowly if at all.[20] In an entirely representative House of Commons it would have been defeated. Wellington was a champion of the old system. But he used it in a new way; and by so doing he persuaded a great many people that it ought to be abolished.

The incident which made the greatest sensation was Peel's election for Westbury, where some unsavoury and far-from-private arrangements were made to serve the government and thwart the people.[21] By the time the day's polling closed on Friday 27 February it was certain that the Oxford University by-election would end in Peel's defeat. He was due to move the Commons resolution preceding the Emancipation Bill on the following Thursday, 5 March. The Secretaries of the Treasury had prepared against this emergency by arranging for a seat to be vacant just then. On 23 February a writ had been moved for a by-election at Westbury (Wilts). This was a pocket borough belonging to Sir Manasseh Lopes; and he made the vacancy by resigning his seat there. He regarded this service as worth a peerage. But the only reward he seems to have received for it was the appointment of one of his protégés to the Consulship at Pernambuco.[22]

Peel was elected for Westbury by Lopes's favour on 2 March, despite a shower of missiles, while the 'protestant' candidate was still on the road from London. Lopes, who had been twice fined and imprisoned for electoral bribery, and whose misdeeds had cost Grampound its two MPs, was the most notorious borough owner of his

time. The procedure of Peel's nomination and election was conducted
entirely by Lopes himself, his nephew, who was the Mayor, and the
Mayor's brother-in-law. Every other member of the corporation and
voter refused to have anything to do with it. Nothing could have
given more publicity both to the system's seamy side, and to the
government's determination to use the facilities it gave them for
defying majority opinion. No one, Richmond remarked two years
later when defending the Reform Bill in the Lords, was likely to
'forget Westbury'.[23]

The package deal on emancipation destroyed the mystique of an
unalterable, Protestant constitution. Only a few ultra tories could
break their habits to the extent of joining the reformers there and
then. But nearly all of them began to talk like reformers. To support
their demand for an immediate election they maintained that the
ministry had no right to enact the Emancipation Bill in the existing
unrepresentative House of Commons: it should be referred to the
people first. One opponent of the Disfranchisement Bill told the
Commons that the Irish forty shillingers 'had as good a right to their
franchise as the owners or voters of . . . Gatton'.[24] Another warned
the Lords that if the Bill were passed 'a year would not elapse without
some general measure of Reform being called for'.[25] The first remark
was made by Lord John Russell, the second by the ultra-tory Duke of
Richmond.

Anger at the betrayal led some tory magnates into imprudence.
The Duke of Newcastle was an out and out supporter of the unreformed system in which he had a considerable stake.[26] But in 1829
he behaved like a radical agitator. He was involved, for instance, in a
plan to frighten the king by bringing some thousands of men to
Windsor to present an anti-Catholic petition. Such methods of
opposition, which an indignant Canningite described as 'radical all
over',[27] were not adopted wholeheartedly enough to halt Wellington.
They merely helped to spread reforming and democratic ideas.

Many years later G. K. Chesterton warned a tory leader of the
dangers of such conduct:

> If I could water sell like molten gold,
> And make grown people do as they are told,
> If over private fields and wastes as wide
> As a Greek city for which heroes died,
> I owned the houses and the men inside—
> If all this hung on one thin thread of habit

I would not revolutionize a rabbit.
                    . . .
Walter, be wise! Avoid the wild and new,
The constitution is the game for you.
                    (*Lines to Walter Long*, 1912)

Others besides tory noblemen learned from O'Connell and Wellington that the constitution could be altered. 'It is desirable,' the radical
Examiner remarked in August 1828, 'that agitation and organization
which have been working such wonders in Ireland' should be made
assistant to the Reform cause. The borough owners, said the *Manchester Times* in May 1829, 'may yield to importunity what they deny
to justice'.[28] O'Connell's success in enforcing his demands led to the
founding in July 1829 of the London Radical Reform Association.
It was to imitate his 'catholic rent' by charging each member of the
public who attended a meeting a 'radical rent' of a penny.[29] At the
Leicester Reform dinner in August 1829 one of the city's Members,
Robert Otway Cave, recommended 'the establishment of a club or
committee, resembling the Catholic Association, to take advantage of
every favourable opportunity for working Reform'.[30]

The most important of those who acted on O'Connell's lesson was
Thomas Attwood of Birmingham. He was a country banker of tory
connexions and an old enemy of the Act of 1819 re-establishing specie
payment. This measure, with which Peel had been particularly
associated, was brought into complete effect over a period of ten years.
An Act of 1826 had forbidden the English country banks to enlarge
their note issues. But notes for amounts under five pounds which had
already been stamped could be put in circulation until 5 April 1829.[31]
The critics of the 1819 Act argued that the withdrawal of these notes
would intensify its deflationary effects to the point of disaster.

These critics, the exponents of some measure of currency inflation,
were drawn largely from two groups—farmers, and the manufacturers
in Birmingham and the Midlands. With the farmers must be classed
a number of landlords and county MPs bound to them by interest and
sympathy: with the manufacturers, those bankers, merchants, tradesmen and workmen who depended on Birmingham's industrial
prosperity. A policy of inflation naturally attracts debtors. To creditors
and the holders of fixed-interest securities it is apt to look less attractive.
Many farmers had contracted debts during the war or just after it;
and as the value of money rose with the return to cash payments the

burden of these seemed to be unjustly increased. Birmingham was a city of small scale businesses many of which were short of capital, and few of which dealt directly with export markets. In consequence most Birmingham manufacturers saw great advantages and no draw-backs in a degree of inflation involving easy credit and rising prices.

In other cities, especially those of the West Riding, labour-saving machinery embittered the relations between capital and labour. But it was not much used in the small workshops characteristic of Midland industry. In Birmingham marked social mobility blurred class distinctions. Journey-men rose to be masters, and then if they failed fell back again. These factors combined to produce a higher degree of understanding and cooperation between masters and men than was known elsewhere. During the years following the financial crash of 1825 the city's metal industries were depressed. Employers and employed suffered together, and demanded the same remedy. They believed in currency reform as the cure for a slump and unemployment.

When the small notes had been withdrawn Attwood made a last effort to convert the government to his views. He convened a Birmingham meeting and organized a petition which carried 8000 signatures and was presented in both Houses. The government rejected it with some appearance of contempt.

At this meeting Attwood had made an admiring reference to O'Connell's success and had called for 'an array not less formidable than that legally exhibited in Ireland, before which ministers were compelled to bend'.[32]

His speech showed that he regarded a Reform agitation as a last resource, not to be employed unless the government and the unreformed House remained obdurate.[33] The failure of the petition decided him. Reform now seemed to provide the only means by which his theories might be adopted. The unreformed House would never alter the currency: therefore it must go. When unrepresented cities like Birmingham had been given MPs, and the county representation had been increased, it might be possible to secure the repeal of Peel's Act of 1819. 'Men do not generally act from abstract principles,' Attwood wrote years later in explanation of how the final Reform agitation arose, 'but from deep and unregarded wrongs, injuries and sufferings.'[34]

On 14 December 1829 Attwood and fifteen others founded the Birmingham 'Political Union for the Protection of Public Rights'.

'The general distress which now afflicts the country', the 'requisition' for the first meeting ran,

and which has been so severely felt at several periods during the last fifteen years, is entirely to be ascribed to the gross mismanagement of public affairs. Such a mismanagement can only be . . . permanently remedied by an effectual Reform in the Commons House of Parliament. For the legal accomplishment of this great object, and for the further redress of public wrongs and grievances, it is expedient to form a GENERAL POLITICAL UNION between the Lower and the Middle Classes of the People.[35]

The chances for such a Union did not seem very good even in Birmingham.[36] Many middle-class people thought political associations factious. In their eyes meetings of bodies where concurrent political opinions formed the only tie were socially divisive and almost unconstitutional. When the High Bailiff of Birmingham was asked to convene a Town Meeting from which the Union might be launched he refused.[37] The Union's opening meeting on 25 January 1830 was not attended, to quote Joseph Parkes, 'by the more opulent and influential public characters of the town'. Parkes, who was a local attorney and active as a whig-liberal in Midland politics, attended this meeting, but did not join the Union.

In Birmingham the leading whigs had particularly strong reasons for keeping clear of any such Reform agitation. The whig cabal, as the local tories called it, represented the ruling group of the town. They were engaged in establishing the electoral guilt of East Retford and the necessity of transferring its two seats to Birmingham. The inherent delicacy of this operation was enhanced by the fact that the most powerful interest in East Retford was held by a whig magnate, Earl Fitzwilliam. The Birmingham whigs disapproved of a tory demagogue blundering into their preserves. They disliked having their clothes stolen while they took their statesmanlike bathe in muddy waters.

On Reform the Union's organizers looked diffident if not lukewarm. In his opening speech to the 25 January meeting Attwood produced, in the words of an indignant reformer, 'a small text of Reform, but . . . a ponderous volume of currency'. The petition recommended to the meeting was one already used at Cambridge which did not even mention Reform.

By the end of the inaugural proceedings, however, the future of the Union was assured; and its supporters had shown their attachment to Reform unmistakably. Twelve to fifteen thousand people attended on 25 January. The Cambridge petition was forgotten and a far more specific one, demanding Reform, substituted for it. This attracted some 30,000 signatures. Attwood's reasons for the substitution are a matter of surmise. It doubtless reflected a new-found confidence. Having launched their scheme successfully the Council of the Union wanted their own petition. Moreover the meeting had made it imperative to speak out on Reform. The only opposition to Attwood had come from whig reformers. He needed to disprove the whig taunt that he was no true friend to Reform. Finally, the meeting probably brought home to Attwood and his colleagues how many people saw Reform as a panacea. When Parkes warned those present that all their 'distresses' were not the result of misgovernment, and implied that some could not be removed even by a reformed Parliament, he found only a single supporter.

Parkes's lonely protest contained much truth. A reformed House of Commons, faced with hopes which were conflicting as well as extravagant, was sure to disappoint a good many of those who had agitated for it. Attwood's Reform politics like those of many other people were based on an illusion. He was not experienced enough to measure the support which could be expected for a change in the currency. If he had been, he would have seen that a reformed House was little more likely to adopt his currency schemes than the unreformed. Manchester industrialists wanted no tampering with the currency.[38] 'While the small Birmingham manufacturers', Professor Asa Briggs writes,

looked to high wages, high profits and high prices as indices of economic prosperity, the Manchester manufacturers put their trust in low wages, competitive profits and cheap prices. While the iron interests in the Midlands were insular in outlook, preoccupied with an expansionist credit policy at home, the Manchester cotton lords were internationalist in outlook, surveying with eager interest movements in international prices and on the exchanges.[39]

Political calculations were, however, at least as difficult then as they are now. Attwood was extremely capable despite the naïveté of his politics. Statesmanship was required as well as the talents of the showman and the revivalist to build up the Birmingham Political Union. It was strictly law-abiding. By making sure that it kept this reputation Attwood not only attracted middle-class recruits but deprived the government of any chance to suppress it. At an early stage he put his currency schemes into the background until Reform should have been won. He gained the support of politicians of many shades, enlisting, for instance, both O'Connell and the ultra-tory Marquess of Blandford.[40] During these crucial first months he also had the favour of Cobbett, who gave the Union's proceedings important publicity in his *Political Register*.[41] A motley but powerful Midland army was thus enrolled for Reform. On 11 February 1830 Huskisson told the Commons that it would be wise to give East Retford's seats to Birmingham, since Attwood was likely to be less dangerous inside the House than outside.[42] In the following November Francis Place, the London radical, called Attwood 'the most influential man in England'.[43] These two statements can give an exaggerated idea of Attwood's standing. He was not leading a national movement. Until the railways were built no popular leader could do that. Indeed it was still illegal for one political society to correspond with another.[44] In each locality the magnates were expected to give the lead; and they operated through the traditional means of the county or town meeting. Even in Birmingham the political union's position was not assured.[45] None the less Huskisson's prediction was sound. The union was likely to survive and grow until Birmingham had MPs.

The process whereby the 1829 Acts undermined the unreformed system was all the more dangerous because partly hidden. Emancipation did not put the Wellington government in any immediate danger. The whigs and Huskissonites on one side and the ultra tories on the other did not dare to turn it out. They could not defeat it decisively except in combination; and they were unwilling to combine. An agreement to overthrow the duke between two parties which had so little in common with each other would look factious; and, as the party complexion of the succeeding government could not be predicted, each side feared that making such a compact might mean handing power to the other. Although Sir Richard Vyvyan, acting on the ultras' behalf, approached Palmerston in October 1829 with a coalition proposal nothing came of this.[46] Until the 1830 session opened the whig leaders would have nothing to do with any Reform agitation. Grey and Russell both refused during the emancipation crisis to suit the newly converted ultra-tory reformers and embarrass the duke by taking up Reform again.[47] The attitude of the Birmingham whigs in shunning the proposed political union was close to that of the party as a whole. Few whigs or liberals cared to admit that the

House of Commons which had just passed the Emancipation Bill was dangerously unrepresentative.

Despite this lull, some observers quickly concluded that the survival of Wellington's government, and probably that of the unreformed system as well, depended on his success in winning back the ultra tories. 'Croker talked very boldly,' Lockhart wrote to Sir Walter Scott on 30 March 1829, 'of the duke's confidence that the tories would all reunite ere next session under his banner. I doubt it. But if they don't, adieu to the aristocracy of England, church and all.'[48]

Some months later Wellington urged George IV, if he could not or would not turn the government out, to give it proper backing and quell the activities of the ultra Duke of Cumberland. 'By suffering the present state of things to continue,' he said, 'I must entreat Your Majesty to consider that you may hazard the existence of all the institutions of the country, and even of the monarchy itself.'[49]

The anger of many ultra-tory magnates was untinged by these fears. Some of them had no idea how precarious the system had become. Newcastle continued to treat the voters under his influence almost as if they were his property. In October 1829, when reproached for evicting tenants who had voted against his candidate, he wrote publicly: 'Is it presumed then that I am not to do what I will with my own?'[50] Even those who were less indiscreet than Newcastle gave little credit to warnings which came mainly from the turncoat government. The refusal of most ultras to rally to Wellington must rank as a notable example of political short sight. But it can no more be ascribed entirely to that than the renegades' actions can be ascribed entirely to lust for patronage. Emancipation was not the type of measure which the ultras could be expected to overlook from considerations of prudence the moment it was on the statute book. 'Protestantism' was a matter of passionate conviction for them at the heart of their political creed.[51] Moreover, they were in a baffling predicament. The accusation of ratting had a wide and continuing application. It could damage not merely those tories who had helped Wellington to pass emancipation, but any who forgave him for it; not merely those who accepted offices, but any who seemed to seek them. An ultra county Member returning to the duke's following would not be regarded as disinterested by most of his constituents. At the next election the charge lately levelled against the renegades, of abandoning principles in the hope of place, would be levelled at him. He would be contributing to the unity of the tory party, but also to his own unpopularity and possible defeat, and to the impression outside Parliament that the only upright and consistent politicians were the liberals and whigs. The Marquess of Chandos, a leading ultra county Member, refused the Mastership of the Mint early in 1830. He would apparently have liked to accept, but feared that if he did so his constituents would turn him out at the next election.

The experiences of the Duke of Rutland show that Chandos's fears were not groundless. Rutland commanded a powerful and broadly based political interest backed by great wealth. Although he had always taken the 'protestant' line his connexions with the government were close; and he found Wellington's appeal to support the Emancipation Bill hard to resist. But 'this county is very hot', he wrote from Belvoir to Mrs Arbuthnot in February 1829, 'they want to petition the King and to do God knows what besides.'[52] He wobbled when the Bill was in the Lords, voting for the second reading and against the third. Thereafter he and his Members supported the government. As a result his two brothers holding his county seats were opposed in the 1830 election. One was defeated in Cambridgeshire; and warding off the challenge to the other in Leicestershire cost nearly £6000.[53] Thus the ultra-tory leaders might not have been able to end disunion even if they had all realized how dangerous it was.

Ultra-tory disgust with the system did not rally the liberals to its defence. The diehards turned to Reform because emancipation had been conceded. The liberals turned because, once the concession had been made, there was little reason to fear the Protestantism of a reformed House. The reformers gained friends on all sides. The sophisticated had long found the system an anachronism. The unsophisticated now began to see it as the cause of all their difficulties. As in other eras, people too ignorant to know how their troubles had originated needed a scapegoat. They had long cast the Catholics for this role. They now started to blame their ills on the 'rotten' system under which the Catholics had been favoured, and to look to a Reform Act for a cure.

The sense of the country was against the system, and the nonsense too. Silently an enormous coalition was forming. This included intellectuals and anti-intellectuals, those who welcomed technical change and those who feared it, currency reformers and their bitterest critics, and corn law repealers along with sworn enemies of repeal.

It represented one of the oldest of all political phenomena—a Cave of Adullam, wherein, as in King David's time, all the discontented gathered. Each group supposed that Reform would bring with it their particular remedy. Many of these hopes were foredoomed. A Reform was unlikely to accelerate the repeal of the corn laws or the alteration of the currency, and still more unlikely to deprive the Catholics of their new rights. The discontented had the power to make great and much needed changes, but not the changes on which their hearts were set.

After emancipation Reform was unavoidable. Wellington's claim that the rotten boroughs were used in 1829 to serve the country's interests was just. So was the ultras' charge that the boroughs were used to thwart the country's will. The influence of these boroughs had been seen, and judged intolerable. The tory party, which had exploited and defended them, was damaged and disunited. The unreformed system had been exposed to view, and therefore to attack.

Tory disunity takes a prominent place in any account of the coming of Reform. Feuds and mutual suspicion in the anti-Reform party gave the reformers their chance.[54] The converts to Reform were largely disaffected tories. The attacking army was reinforced by deserters from inside the fortress, where the remainder of the garrison kept themselves busy fighting each other. The connexion between tory weakness and Reform strength went deeper than this. Lord Liverpool's tory party, like Lord Salisbury's at the end of the century, lived on fears which both held the party together and left the champions of change without influence. Under the shadow of the French Revolution and war, or during the 1880s with their threat of the radical programme and then of Home Rule, almost any sacrifice seemed worth while to a tory to keep his party in power and the radicals out. And the alarms which united the tories weakened their opponents. Moderate and uncommitted people were afraid of the radicals.

Gradually these fears faded; and as a result the tory party deteriorated and fell apart. The efforts of the most perceptive and dynamic of the leaders to check the decline were mentioned earlier. The new remedy for the party's weakness, in Canning's case liberalism, in Joseph Chamberlain's tariff reform, merely hastened disintegration. Neither statesman managed to convert the party as a whole. The fainter his fears grew, the less a disgruntled tory, who distrusted these programmes and their purveyors, cared about the party's decline. The prospect of

C

a whig or liberal government no longer looked menacing. In 1829 the whigs seemed to have deserted Reform, just as in 1905 the liberals seemed to have shelved Home Rule. Tory unity and predominance had thus lost their over-riding importance for many members of the party. Moreover, these long spells of power included such admirable but politically dangerous measures as Catholic Emancipation and the Balfour Education Act. By 1830, as by 1905, the tories had plenty of inducements to quarrel with each other or become deserters, and few fears to stop them from doing so.

This disgruntled complacency was misplaced. The lessening of fear which made the tories rebellious also made the uncommitted voters and moderates ripe for radical experiments. It was a short step in 1829 to the Reform Act, and an equally short one in 1905 to the People's Budget. The party of the right were in the greatest danger when they felt safe; partly because they would then quarrel among themselves, partly because if they felt safe others would soon feel radical.

There were no obvious signs that the session of Parliament which opened in February 1830 was ushering in a reforming whig government. When it ended the whig party's internal difficulties were as great as ever. They were still at sixes and sevens with the ultra tories, and therefore still unwilling to enter the only combination by which they could supplant the duke. Their showing in important divisions had not improved much. On 4 February they would have defeated Wellington on the Address had not a group of them voted against the ultra-tory amendment in order to keep the government in being. On 6 July, in the last important division of the session, they were in no danger of winning: their motion on the Regency was beaten by 247 to 93. On 1 July *The Times,* certainly the most influential and probably the most independent of the London papers, remarked that 'if disunion be weakness' the opposition were 'a quicksand'.

In reality, however, the whigs underwent a great revival between February and July 1830. When the session began they suffered from two weaknesses which looked hard to overcome. First, they lacked leadership and organization. Secondly, the king might leave them in the cold, and choose the ultras for the new ministry, if Wellington fell. By July both these weaknesses had disappeared. The whigs, though still beset by problems, were tolerably well organized and well led; and they were certain to predominate in any new government.

The first moves towards cohesion were made in the Commons. Now that the borough owners were joining the papists as leading public scapegoats the opposition had a fine chance to revive the traditional whig demand for governmental economy. The revelation of what crimes against Protestantism a borough magnate would commit, to make sure of his slice of the Treasury loaf, naturally brought this demand back into fashion; and despite all the reductions of the last fifty years the list of offices and salaries still presented some tempting targets.[55] The economy campaign was started by Sir James Graham. A few weeks of Graham's free-lance operations threw the whig benches into such confusion that they were obliged to end their anarchy. They realized that they would soon become ridiculous unless they could secure some control over their skirmishers. A group of whig MPs met twice early in March 1830 and chose Althorp as their leader in the Commons. This organization, though an important first step in building up the party, was originally confined to questions of economy. The group was not very large. Twenty-seven Members attended the first meeting, forty the second.

A whig government would need heavier metal than Graham or even than Althorp. Grey was the only whig leader of premiership calibre. At this time his party did not greatly admire him. Many whigs criticized the pride and bitterness which he had shown when opposing a whig junction with Canning in 1827; and his romantic attachments were sometimes ascribed to a damaging weakness for flattery. 'His vanity,' Greville wrote in December 1830, 'has all his life made him the fool of women.'[56] But Grey possessed two attributes of commanding importance. Whatever the reservations of his middle age, he had been a parliamentary reformer all his career. In 1794 he had nearly been tried for treason as a Friend of the People. Secondly, he was a parliamentary speaker of immense distinction. After hearing Grey on Queen Caroline's case in 1820, Creevey wrote: 'There is nothing approaching this damned fellow in the kingdom when he mounts his best horse.'

Grey was hard to move. Late in 1829 his attitude towards Wellington's ministry was one of friendly neutrality. He thought that any attempt to weld whigs, Huskissonites, and ultra tories into an active opposition would fail; and he did not mean to take part in one. He decided to spend the first part of the 1830 session at home in Northumberland away from all intrigue, and to come to London only at Easter. He wrote to his brother-in-law, Edward Ellice, in October:

I feel myself very comfortable in my situation as spectator, which I shall not easily be tempted to relinquish ... [The ministers'] great security is in the impossibility, almost, of forming any efficient and united party against them. As to the internal distress, those who might be the most willing to attack them have been themselves too much implicated in the measures which have led to it to make it a convenient ground of opposition.[57]

Two developments moved Grey from this position, the first and less important being a blow to his pride. He learned in December 1829 that Wellington did not mean to offer him office. Grey was the whig leader for whom the government were expected to make a bid now that emancipation was out of the way. At the beginning of December he was told by Lord Ponsonby that, while the king's hostility to him was an obstacle, Wellington should soon be able to overcome it and offer him the Lord Lieutenancy of Ireland. Later in the same month, however, Rosslyn, one of the whigs whom the duke had recruited, visited Grey and made clear that the government were not thinking of any such offer. Rosslyn said that the king's known objections were regarded as decisive.[58] In the later part of his career Grey never had much appetite for office. He would probably have refused an offer. But he would have liked one to be made. Rosslyn's news inclined him against the duke.

The state of the country provided the second and greater propellant towards opposition. By the beginning of 1830 the conjunction of a long continued slump and a weak government had begun to alarm Grey. The recovery from the financial crisis of 1825–6 had been slow and irregular. The 1829 harvest was poor; and most areas suffered from a good deal of unemployment and a slight decline in wages. 'The distress is so general and so intense,' Grey told Princess Lieven on 29 January,

the remedies so difficult, and this administration so weak in its general com-position, that notwithstanding the personal power and influence of the duke, I begin to doubt their being able to encounter the storm that is collecting about them. I think I never saw symptoms so alarming ... I think it impossible that, with the feeling now rising in the country, there should not arise out of the various parties existing in Parliament some new combination, which the duke may find more formidable than any that he has hitherto had to encounter. When I say this I am speaking very much against my wishes, for what I desire most is that the present men should take such measures as should enable me to give them my support.[59]

The government viewed the outcry about 'distress' differently.

Paradoxical though it may sound, Grey was probably better informed on the views of squires and bankers than they were. He was a North-umberland magnate. Opinion in the West Riding was known to him through his son-in-law, Charles Wood, and Lord Morpeth. His brother-in-law, Edward Ellice, and the Whitbreads kept him informed about the city of London and the commercial world. Wellington had no such facilities for putting his ear to the ground. His ministers in the Commons had all been brought up in the governing party and occupied seats which were convenient for someone in office.[60] None of them had saddled himself with exacting constituents and with the prospect of expense at each re-election. No cabinet minister sat for an English county. The duke and his colleagues suspected, as Mrs Arbuth-not wrote in March 1830, that 'nine tenths of the cry [about distress] has been made by the Brunswickers[61] [i.e. the ultra tories] out of spite upon the Catholic question'. The cabinet referred in the Speech from the Throne to the prevalence of 'distress in some parts of the United Kingdom'. Their reluctance to admit how bad things were caused great indignation; and they were lucky, as was related, not to be defeated in the Commons on the Address. Grey was incensed by their blunder. Two further extracts from his letters to Ellice show how his mind was moving:

6 *February*: But what in the name of God can be meant by talking of increased ... distress in *some parts* of the country. I should like to know what part is exempt.

2 *March*: I am afraid that the ministers are deceiving themselves very fatally as to the real situation in the country and the spirit that is rising in it. This is, in consequence of the king's speech and the subsequent conduct of the ministers, assuming a character of great bitterness against them; but I much fear that it is likely to go further unless some relief can be found. The news-papers in their attacks upon the landowners have succeeded in destroying all respect for rank and station, and for the institutions of the government. Another year like the last and who can answer for the consequences?[62]

On 5 April he wrote to Princess Lieven, referring to a scandalous press attack on a cabinet minister: 'All this is too like what took place in France before the Revolution.'

Grey began to oppose the government, not so much because he wanted to supplant it and be Prime Minister, as because he thought it a danger to society. He would not have wanted to join the duke. He was not ambitious to be the duke's successor. He told his son, in a letter about the whig union under Althorp and the cabinet-making speculations to which it gave rise, that his name must be excluded from these. At sixty-six he was physically and mentally 'altogether unequal to the discharge of any laborious office'.[63] But he remembered the French Revolution and saw explosive materials being accumulated. He gradually reached the conclusion that the duke's cabinet had neither the standing nor the insight needed for dispersing these explosives, and that they might if left in office end by putting a match to them.

It is thus a mistake to explain Grey's actions in 1830 solely in terms of personal ambition. He was concerned with the public weal as he understood it; and he had a large personal stake in it. As a landowner he was dependent on prosperity and social peace. He did not want his rents unpaid and his ricks burned. When he looked to his own interests he did not see gaining office as the greatest of them.

Grey's alarm was well founded. Professor W. W. Rostow has compiled a 'social tension chart' for these years.[64] It is based on the supposition that unrest in the industrial working class originated largely in the combination of high cyclical unemployment and high food prices. The index number rises for the years when work was plentiful and food cheap, and falls for the bad years. During the two four-year periods from 1822 to 1825 and from 1833 to 1836 it falls below five only in 1833, when it is four. The intervening years provide a stark contrast:

1826	$\frac{1}{2}$	1830	$1\frac{1}{2}$
1827	$2\frac{1}{2}$	1831	2
1828	$2\frac{1}{2}$	1832	1
1829	0		

The causal relationship between distress and unrest may have been more complex than such a chart would suggest. Indeed its author readily concedes this. Nonetheless the force of Cobbett's remark connecting agitation with empty stomachs cannot be denied. For the cotton handloom weavers the misery after 1825 was even worse than Professor Rostow's figures show. The 'permanent dividing line,' Dr Bythell writes, 'between relative (although not unbroken) comfort and a standard of living normally below that of other workers came with the slump of 1826, when the piece-rate really tumbled and never subsequently recovered to any appreciable degree'.[65] At the very least the Rostow chart shows that Grey was not exaggerating when he called the distress 'general and intense'. Grey foresaw that in desperation men might try to smash the established order, blaming their troubles on it, and believing:

> Hungry guts and empty purse
> May be better, can't be worse.

Early in April Wellington suffered a misfortune which tipped the political balance against him. It became known that the king was fatally ill. The prospect of his death both strengthened the whigs, and made it more likely that they would become the duke's out and out opponents. The heir to the throne, the Duke of Clarence, although not exactly a liberal, had none of the liking for the ultra tories and dislike for Grey which had influenced George IV.[66] Grey and the whig leaders thus knew at last that, if Wellington resigned, they and not the ultras would form the core of the succeeding government. With the king dying and the emancipation crisis receding, the influence of the ultra tories was declining sharply. They had owed much of their weight to George IV's support, and to the belief that he might be willing to overlook their lack of talent and put them in office. They had owed something to the excitement over emancipation, in which they had acted as the sole representatives of 'a Protestant people'. By June 1830 this excitement had cooled a little. Although those who had 'ratted' to the Catholics were hated as much as ever, the whigs, being judged honest on the question, had been largely forgiven.

Now that the whigs were clearly the senior members in any alliance, they had far less objection to cooperating with the ultra tories. But this was not the only reason why the prospective change made such cooperation more attractive. The Duke of Cumberland was the ultra whom the whigs most distrusted and whose prominence had previously scared them off. He would have little or no influence with the new king. The cabinet hoped that increasing whig hostility might make the tories more friendly. But Wellington was sufficiently impressed with the difficulties which the king's death would produce to draft a letter asking Peel to take over the premiership.[67] The new reign would add a few to his supporters, but many more to his opponents.

The law as it then stood required that Parliament should be dissolved within six months of the sovereign's death. The fact that a dissolution

was thus imposed on the duke did not in itself involve a great alteration to his plans. He had probably intended to dissolve some time
during 1830 in any case. The succession of William IV meant that he
would fight an election in different and probably less favourable
conditions. But the indications are that, even if the law had not
compelled him to hold one, he would still have chosen to do so.[68]

The prelude to the election was, however, unfortunate for Wellington. The king's final illness was fairly prolonged. The election was
thus virtually certain more than three months before it could take
place. During the intervening period the duke was deprived of the
sanctions normally at the command of a British Prime Minister. He
could not resign, and so desert a sovereign who was mortally ill; and
he could not yet dissolve. The opposition and the independents could
therefore indulge in electioneering while the old Parliament lasted,
knowing that the cabinet must accept any defeat however damaging.
In these circumstances the duke's lieutenants lost control of the Commons, while the whigs enjoyed themselves.[69]

Grey's arrival in London in April gave his entourage a chance, by
working on his foibles as well as his fears, to involve him in the
opposition plans. His son-in-law Durham, who had some influence
with him and supplied the ambition which he lacked, was especially
active in this direction. Towards the end of May the whigs began to
confer at Lansdowne House. Although Grey's ambition and belief
in his own vigour had shrunk, his pride had not. He must have known
that if he did not join the opposition now forming he would be
disregarded and forgotten. He probably did not welcome this end to
his career. A letter of 23 June speaks of him as 'thick' with Brougham
at a great whig dinner at Brooks's.[70] On 25 June he was in collision
with the duke in the Lords over a minor Reform question. The king
died on the following day. The whole political world knew that
Wellington was now free to offer Grey a post. Grey decided to define
his position. On 30 June he declared in the Lords that the government
had shown themselves 'incompetent to manage the business of the
country'.

This indictment did not originate in the heat of debate. It was part
of the strategy which Grey and Althorp had worked out. The king's
death forced Grey, if he wanted to voice his loss of confidence in the
government, to do so at once. A delayed attack would be attributed
to the rage of a disappointed place hunter. Grey said then and later
that his words were not meant as a declaration of war.[71] He wanted,

he explained to Princess Lieven on 2 July, to show the ministry that he would join them only if they offered him a prospect of real influence and undertook to change some of their policies. He was anxious, he wrote, to put himself in a good position for rejecting a poor offer. In other words he needed to preclude the sneer that he was refusing solely because he greatly overvalued his own services. If he emphasized where he disagreed with the cabinet no one could say with any show of reason that it was his vanity which made him reject a post of no influence. Grey was too proud to be ready to look vain.

A letter from Arbuthnot to Peel on 3 July suggests that the ministry interpreted the speech much as Grey himself did to Princess Lieven.[72] But Wellington and Peel were not prepared to pay the high price which Grey demanded for his services. The attack may have been neither intended nor interpreted as a declaration of war. But when no offer came it acted as one. Looking back in 1834 Tavistock called it 'the speech . . . which closed the door upon all chance of a coalition'.[73] The opposition had at last acquired a leader of premiership calibre.

The whigs were still faced with two problems which they had to solve if they were to form a government. They could secure help from either the ultras or the Huskissonites; but they needed it from both. The first could supply the necessary margin of numerical strength in both Houses, the second front-bench talent. Since the ultras distrusted Huskisson this triple alliance was not easy to forge. Grey decided not to commit himself to either group for the moment. Some days before George IV died he declined Huskisson's offer of a formal alliance, though declaring himself ready to act with the Huskissonites 'when the occasion should offer'.[74]

The whigs' second problem was their leading lawyer, Henry Brougham. Most of his colleagues judged him to be without rival both for attacking power in debate and for unreliability. Excited by the possibilities which the king's death opened up, he added rapidly to his reputation for disruption. In many ways his situation resembled Grey's. But unlike Grey Brougham thirsted for office. The new reign subjected him to conflicting pressures. It gave him a powerful inducement to overthrow the ministry, since their successors would now be whigs. It also inclined him to make up to them, since they were now free to enrol him. It was his part on Queen Caroline's behalf in 1820 that had debarred them from doing so while George IV lived.

In this dilemma Brougham behaved erratically. At one moment he showed his anxiety to join the cabinet, at the next his anxiety to destroy it. The whig aristocrats began to think that he was either mad or a villain. Many of the party refused to cooperate in any scheme originated by 'Wickedshifts', as Creevey called Brougham. The humiliating whig reverse of 6 July, mentioned earlier, was largely attributable to Brougham's part in the motion; 'for,' as Althorp told his father, 'at the present moment all our people hate him so cordially that it is only necessary for him to say or do anything for them to dislike it.'[75]

By July 1830 the whigs had turned against Wellington, although they were still some way from defeating him. They had not yet turned decisively against the unreformed system.[76] During the 1830 session Reform was a serious topic of debate in the Commons for the first time for some years. Whigs were no longer obliged to shun the subject as they had done during the emancipation crisis. The long-drawn-out proceedings to disfranchise East Retford helped to push them into taking a reforming line. The bribery in this freeman borough was of an unusual kind. The freemen had established a tariff of twenty guineas per vote.[77] The essential qualification for an East Retford candidate was that his ability and willingness to pay should have been well established. Contests were deprecated. The East Retford voters preferred a safe forty guineas at each election to high risk politics. Thus the candidates in 1818 and 1820 had paid for promised votes which had never been cast. From 1812 to 1825 the largest local interest, that of the Duke of Newcastle, was dormant in East Retford. The seats were divided between 'the independent interest', in which the corporation had a large say, and that of Earl Fitzwilliam, who had possessed a leading interest since 1812.

In October 1824 both the sitting Members announced that they would not stand again. The usual machinery was set in motion. Each interest produced a candidate of guaranteed financial soundness. In September 1825, however, the independents' man developed doubts about his health, and perhaps about his finances, and retired. The Fitzwilliam interest now hurriedly brought forward a second candidate.[78] This provocative move shattered the system. The corporation replied by running a no-popery candidate with the Duke of New-castle's support. He was defeated after a violent contest and petitioned against the return. The corruption of the borough was brought to light.

By 1830 the resulting disfranchisement proceedings had become most embarrassing to whig reformers.[79] They disliked opposing a

process which would give Birmingham two seats. They found it
equally awkward to support disfranchisement, and so admit that a
leading whig magnate had been involved in buying votes. To escape
from this difficulty a number of them claimed that East Retford was
no more guilty than many other boroughs: it was absurd and unfair
to single out one place for punishment when the only effective remedy
was to reform the whole system.

These reforming views would not have been advanced so force-
fully had they originated solely in embarrassment. There was conviction too in the whig protests about East Retford. As usual, the
petitioners looked just as corrupt as the party which had topped the
poll. Moreover the men being singled out for punishment could at
least claim the merit of having resisted bigotry and intimidation. The
methods of the no-popery squad had not been attractive. They withdrew custom from tradesmen who opposed them, and made the streets
unsafe for Fitzwilliam supporters for several months before the
election. During the poll they started a riot. If the evidence given to
the House of Lords can be believed, they chased a man with a broken
arm into a river and did not spare women. Their candidate spread
a rumour that one of his opponents kept a Catholic priest in the
house.

Whig politicians were finally outraged by the passing of an Indemnity Act which protected the East Retford freeman from subsequent prosecution, and so obliged him to give evidence incriminating
himself and his friends. Grey's reply to this was to indict the system.
If he were given an Indemnity Act covering the Members of both
Houses, he told the Lords in July 1830, he would guarantee to 'disfranchise half the boroughs in the kingdom'.[80]

During most of the session the whig approach to Reform was
tentative, however. To some extent this reflected a desire not to
offend potential ultra-tory allies by being too reformist. But it reflected still more hesitations and differences within the whig party
itself. Grey's advice to his son in February 1830 illustrates these
hesitations. Howick told his father that he meant to divide the House
against the East Retford Bill on the ground that a general Reform was
the only fair and effective way of dealing with offences such as East
Retford's. Grey was alarmed to see his son becoming a committed
reformer. He knew by long experience that an aspiring politician was
unwise to tie himself to such a millstone as Reform. 'The only objection I see to (your plan),' he replied to Howick,

is its pledging you perhaps to parliamentary Reform more than, under the present circumstances, might be expedient. There is certainly at this moment the appearance of a stronger feeling in favour of that measure than has for some time, or perhaps ever, existed. But it is a feeling which will subside if any means can be devised for diminishing the present prevalence of distress. And I do not see what advantage you would derive by hampering yourself with a question which will always be opposed by the Crown, and on which you cannot rely on the support of the people. Assist in carrying the measure if a fair opportunity should offer; but do not pledge yourself in such a manner as may give ground hereafter, if you should be connected with the government, as I hope to see you, for reproach in not pushing it. *Experto crede.*[81]

In other words Grey was not yet convinced that support for a general Reform was either politically profitable or socially necessary. While the depression lasted people would blame the unreformed system for their troubles and feel that they had nothing to lose by a change. But good times might return; and then the demand for Reform would evaporate. Grey's increasing uneasiness at Wellington's doings did not entail much modification of this view. He remained a reformer by personal conviction; but his objective at this stage was to scrap or remodel the government rather than the system. Wellington and his colleagues if not removed would jeopardize the social order. There is no indication that Grey yet believed the continued existence of the rotten boroughs for another twelve months to be equally dangerous.

The majority of whigs and Huskissonites and many ultra tories wanted some kind of Reform. But there was no agreement between the three groups on which kind to advocate. When the session began Russell decided that a very moderate scheme was the most likely to secure widespread support. He accordingly moved on 23 February to give two Members each to Manchester, Birmingham, and Leeds. The Huskissonites split on this motion. A number of ultra tories abstained on it. They had little use for a proposal which gave the new seats to manufacturing towns, instead of to the counties to strengthen the agricultural interest. Russell's motion was defeated by 188 to 140.

On 28 May O'Connell proposed triennial Parliaments, complete manhood suffrage, and vote by secret ballot. Brougham and Russell spoke against ballot and Althorp in favour of it.[82] As hardly any whigs agreed with all three of O'Connell's proposals, they brought forward their own Reform scheme as an amendment to his. At this time the prospect of a new reign overshadowed the whigs' plans on Reform as on everything else. Now that they might be invited to form a government they had to be careful not to pledge themselves to too much. Nor did they wish by appearing intransigent to make it impossible for Wellington to admit Grey and their other leaders into his cabinet. It was a moment of great uncertainty and therefore one for caution. Their scheme, which Russell propounded with some embarrassment, was of the hundred seat type. Like Russell's earlier proposals it included monetary compensation for borough owners.[83] The amendment attracted neither ultra-tory nor Huskissonite votes, and was defeated by 213 to 117. It fell as flat outside the House as inside. Though much less restricted than the motion of 23 February it was not bold enough to arouse popular support.

Neither the whigs nor anyone else yet knew whether the Reform movement in the country would become really strong. The indications were that it was spreading and gathering strength. Attwood's political union was being copied. On 25 March a meeting was held, for instance, at Stow-on-the-Wold (Glos) to promote a union on the Birmingham model.[84] The Leeds radicals held a mass meeting on Hunslet Moor at which the banners of 1819 were seen again. In London a mass meeting on 8 March inaugurated the Metropolitan Political Union for Radical Reform.[85] O'Connell claimed that it was attended by 30,000 people. In April the more 'respectable' of the London reformers founded a society, the Parliamentary Reform Association, which was linked with the radicals in the House of Commons.[86] The reformers were backed by most of the London press. *The Times* despite its general support for the government championed Russell on this issue.

Most politicians were impressed by such Reform activities: few or none were convinced by them. Taken together they did not supply adequate evidence that Reform was a winner. It was fairly easy to collect, and still easier to claim to have collected, a large crowd for a London mass meeting. But many of those attending it would not have understood what was going on and certainly could not be classed as active reformers. O'Connell admitted that the petition emanating from the meeting of 30,000 in March bore only ten signatures.[87] Speaking in the debate on 28 May he and Russell agreed that 'the country was in a state of perfect tranquillity'.[88] Only fourteen Reform petitions were said to have been presented to the House of Commons during the whole session.[89] Absence of demand still provided the anti-reformers with what Russell later recalled as 'an argument not to be resisted'.[90]

The Birmingham union was as yet the only one to look formidable.[91] In August 1830 its membership was said to have reached 6000.[92] Attwood was effective because he had the support of both middle and working classes. From the first he secured money and leaders, from the second numbers. It was not certain whether his methods could be used successfully anywhere except in his own town with its exceptional facilities for cooperation between classes. A good many of the attempts to form political unions elsewhere came to little or nothing. According to a Reform source there were 27 unions in existence in November 1830.[93] Few of them included many leading local figures. Some exerted no influence. Nottingham had one, for instance;[94] but in October 1831 Attwood seems not to have known of its existence.[95] The unions formed in London during this period had no lasting effect. The Radical Reform Association of 1829 collapsed within a few months. The Metropolitan Political Union made a more successful start, but was disrupted by resignations in August 1830.[96] The more moderate Parliamentary Reform Association proved no more influential.[97] The most enduring of the London organizations was the one based on the rotunda in Blackfriars Bridge Road.[98] This hall was hired in 1830 by Richard Carlile and quickly became a centre of working-class radicalism. Between 5 November 1830 and 4 March 1831 645 Reform petitions reached the Commons. The radicals of the Blackfriars Rotunda supplied five of these. Of the remainder, only four are recorded as coming from political unions.[99]

At this time there was nothing approaching a single Reform movement. The Reform proposals discussed were of three kinds. At one extreme came the schemes of the new ultra-tory converts. In April 1830 a writer in *Blackwood's* explained that the county candidate's expenses must be reduced by the provision of polling places in each locality. In boroughs middle-class householders should be added to the electorate. A general aboliton of close boroughs would be a mistake. 'The great manufacturing towns,' the article continued,

ought to have Members to attend to their local interests; and if twelve or twenty were added to the House . . . on account of this we cannot see that it would make any difference to the general interests of the country. But we dissent wholly from the doctrine that the manufacturing interests have not sufficient influence in Parliament.

These adjustments would ensure that the landed interest achieved their proper supremacy. It was time for the smaller squires to unite and 'act independently of the peers'.[100]

In the middle of the spectrum were the proposals with which the whigs and liberals hoped to attract the middle class. Something has been said about these in the first chapter. They represented an attempt to base the legislature on property in ways which were both up-to-date and morally unobjectionable. They went farther than the ultra-tory scheme described in *Blackwood's;* and they showed a much less pronounced bias in favour of the landed interest.

At the other end of the spectrum from *Blackwood's* came the radical demands. Early in July 1829 Cobbett and Henry Hunt, the radical leaders with the largest followings, issued a joint manifesto. They warned the working class:

listen not to those who may tell you that . . . , in the old adage, . . . half a loaf is better than no bread. In this case half a loaf *is* no bread. . . . Never . . . present a petition which shall not distinctly pray for annual parliaments, universal suffrage, and vote by ballot.[101]

Cobbett's approval for the Birmingham Union's moderate pro-gramme could not last for very long. At the end of July 1830 he aecused Attwood of being in collusion with the whigs against the radicals.[102]

It is easy to see why politically minded working-class people were chary of moderating their demands. They knew that the member of the ruling class who turned to Reform did so, not to destroy the system, but to keep it in being. They looked on manhood suffrage, annual Parliaments, and secret ballot as the only guarantee for the kind of Parliament which they wanted. By manhood suffrage they would gain the vote for the whole working class. By annual Parliaments they could make sure that their MPs obeyed them. By ballot they would protect themselves against intimidation by employers or landlords. Workers of all kinds had a natural reluctance to agitating in order to obtain votes for their employers. They did not want to make their masters still more powerful. Indeed, they wanted Reform as a protection against those masters.[103] Their demands were bound to scare off middle-class moderates. This was the great difficulty in establishing and maintaining an effective Reform agitation.

In 1830, as in 1820, the House of Commons would not reform itself unless confronted with an agitation too strong to be disregarded.

Complaints from some middle-class people about sinecurists and borough owners would not be enough. Any Reform programme towards which the workers remained apathetic would fail. Yet a demand from the working class for their own remedy of manhood suffrage might be even more dangerous than working-class apathy. The more that this demand was voiced the more plausible would become the anti-reform argument that no concession within reason could satisfy the Reform movement outside Parliament. The reformers had somehow to achieve the difficult combination of a feasible programme and working-class support.

On the other hand the Reform movement showed certain novel signs of strength. In the aftermath of emancipation it was attracting support from propertied people hitherto friendly to the existing order. The discussion at a Kent County Meeting[104] on 12 March suggested that it was now very difficult for an ultra tory to swim against the Reform tide. The meeting resolved to include Reform in both their Address to the Crown and their Petition to Parliament. Sir Edward Knatchbull, the ultra leader who was one of the County Members, dare not do more than object to its inclusion in the Address on procedural grounds; and Earl Stanhope, another ultra, answering an interrupter, declared himself a reformer.

The Wesleyan Methodists were beginning to shift their political stance. While the Catholic question remained open their quietism often shaded into toryism. Many of them preferred a tory candidate to one who favoured the papists. As a body they still took no part in general politics. But individual Wesleyans became politically more active and insurgent after emancipation. Moreover the one cause to which the Wesleyans gave official support was growing in strength. By 1830 it was clear that the British government had failed in its repeated efforts to secure an amelioration in conditions for the West Indian slaves.[105] With an obstinacy which appeared even to the sympathetic *Quarterly Review* 'little short of insanity' the slave-owners of the colonial legislatures had refused to remove even the worst abuses of the system.[106] On 15 May 1830 a crowded and excited meeting of the Anti-Slavery Society rejected the deliberate approach of the Society's chiefs and petitioned Parliament 'to proceed forthwith' to abolish slavery. One speaker remarked that the anti-slavery cause needed a 'black O'Connell'.[107]

There was a close connexion between the anti-slavery movement and Reform. The abolitionists believed that destroying the rotten boroughs represented the only way of defeating the West Indian interest.[108] There was some reason in this. The West Indians stood for the kind of old-established but declining interest which was over-represented in the old system, and could expect to be cut down to size in a new one. Like the borough owners they were concerned to preserve the less legitimate types of property. A writer in *Black-wood's* commented a few months later that Anti-Slavery proposals, and the like, were 'so many nurseries of jacobinical agitation . . . , all useful . . . to unsettle men's principles, and to disturb the sacred foundations of property'.[109]

'Pull down an abuse where you can,' a *Westminster* reviewer commanded in January 1830, 'especially where it is one, like that of slavery in the West Indies, whose supporters support all the rest.'[110] Brougham thought it necessary to remind the 15 May meeting that Wilberforce, like himself, had an immaculate record as a parliamentary reformer. Some 2600 petitions against negro slavery reached Parliament in the autumn of 1830, all but 400 of them being initiated by Nonconformists. Challenging the unreformed system looked almost as difficult as ever. But some much needed friends had been lost to it and its enemies were gathering.

All this spread the impression in Parliament that, while Reform was not imminent, in some form or another it was on the way. People had become used to the idea; and the younger generation at least were clearly not afraid of it. A rising whig, supporting the proposal of Members for Manchester, Birmingham, and Leeds in February, warned the House against refusing Reform when the people were becoming both more enlightened and more distressed.[111] When Huskisson saw Russell's Reform proposals for the debate of 28 May he commented: 'I cannot support those; but before long something of that kind will be carried in Parliament.'[112] J. C. Hobhouse noticed in this May debate that the House 'would not listen to' some of the speeches against all Reform.[113]

Several members of the cabinet took care to trim their sails to this breeze. Peel, making the closing speech for the government on 11 February against the renewed proposal to give East Retford's seats to Birmingham, explained that:

if on a future occasion a majority of the inhabitants of any borough should be proved guilty of bribery and corruption, he should not object to the transfer of the franchise to a large town, with this understanding—that there should be a division of franchise at the disposal of Parliament, alternately between the landed and commercial and manufacturing interests.[114]

On 23 February Sir George Murray, speaking against Russell's motion, told the House:

he was quite ready to admit ... that it was expedient to give representatives to the great towns ...; but he could not agree to carry that object into execution in the way which the noble Lord proposed.

When the Lords in their turn had decided on 20 July not to transfer East Retford's Members to Birmingham, Ellenborough noted in his diary:

I spoke shortly. I guarded myself against being considered as pledged to any other measure, intending to decide all measures according to the special circumstances of the case. The duke was not so cautious as I was, and spoke strongly against giving the franchise to great towns. Lord Holland said to the Chancellor, 'He will live to see it done.' I think I may, and therefore was cautious.[115]

The escape route to Reform to which these speeches referred was not of much use. The conditions which Peel laid down for giving a city MPs were extremely hard to satisfy. Two small boroughs had first to be proved indisputably corrupt, so that there would be seats for disposal to both the landed and the manufacturing interests. In each case the corruption would have to be pervasive enough to require extinguishing the constituency, as opposed to 'sluicing' it by adding the freeholders of the surrounding area.[116]

Proving bribery on this scale was enormously difficult, since voters did not expect a Member to pay until the seat was safely his, and knew that they could whistle for their money once disfranchisement proceedings had been started. In consequence virtually no payments would have been made for the last election in the series, this being the one under particular scrutiny. Moreover the borough to be disfranchised would have to lie in an area so well provided with borough MPs that reducing them by two through its extinction could arouse no complaints. The list of corrupt boroughs was admittedly long. But the chances were against any of them passing tests as stringent as these.

It was intrinsically absurd to make the question of MPs for Birmingham depend on a quasi-judicial process for punishing delinquent boroughs. East Retford was revealed during the proceedings in the Lords as harbouring an active committee for promoting its own disfranchisement. Guided by a sharp attorney or two, this body met in the Turk's Head Inn to tackle the hard task of making the borough appear even more corrupt than it actually was. By 1830 one committee member wore 'a very handsome gold watch' presented, in gratitude for his exertions, by Birmingham well wishers. The prospect of borough candidates, whose sole real interest would be in starting a petition leading to the disfranchisement of the borough concerned, was not inviting. During 1830 more and more people came to accept that disfranchisement proceedings were no substitute for a Reform measure.

Despite their disclaimers and escape clauses the government were slipping into an anti-Reform position which left little room for manoeuvre. This stumbling march towards the last ditch is not difficult to explain. In the first place, most of the cabinet were less inclined for concession than the three ministers whose remarks have just been quoted. Peel and Murray being commoners were sensitive to the changed atmosphere on Reform. Ellenborough as an ex-whig disliked committing himself to the system as it stood. But seven of the eleven members of the cabinet were peers; and few of the seven, from the premier downwards, had begun to realize that the reformers might soon be formidable.

Secondly, the cabinet were dogged both by their past and by immediate political necessities. They were bound to oppose the whig motion to transfer East Retford's seats to Birmingham. Wellington had driven the Huskissonites out of the cabinet in May 1828 for becoming involved in this proposal. He could not now adopt it himself. Besides, after the Address debate in the Commons the first objective of cabinet policy was to win back the ultra tories. If the cabinet had adopted the Birmingham scheme, or even allowed a free vote on it, they would have annoyed the ultras. They could not have given two seats to the manufacturing interest without suggesting that they preferred whig to ultra support; for the alternative to the transfer to Birmingham was to throw East Retford into the Hundred of Bassetlaw where the ultra Duke of Newcastle possessed an 'interest'.[117] The ultras duly voted with the government for Bassetlaw; and Birmingham was defeated by 126 to 99.

Much the same considerations applied when Russell's motion was debated on 23 February. It would have seemed absurd, after refusing to transfer Members to Birmingham, to vote to create them for Manchester, Birmingham and Leeds. There was a precedent for transferring seats but not for creating them. Once again the cabinet probably hoped to conciliate the ultra tories by opposing this whig motion.

All this does not quite explain, however, how a statesman of Peel's intelligence can have allowed himself to be pushed into an anti-Reform position just as the reformers were gathering strength. It is hard to believe that he entertained any conscientious objection to the most moderate kind of Reform; and his record on the question if he had wanted to turn moderate reformer was not particularly embarrassing. When the session opened, although he had often voted against Reform, he had never spoken against it in any great debate.[118] In February he received a moderate Reform scheme from Croker which did not involve increasing the total number of seats. It is equally unlikely that he had any illusions about the possibilities of creating new seats when boroughs were disfranchised for corruption. He can hardly have supposed such switching to be an effective and acceptable method of Reform. A peer could fall for that kind of notion, but not an exceptionally clear-headed leader of the Commons. Peel became a diehard on Reform with his eyes open.

For two or three years after 1829, that is throughout the Reform crisis, all Peel's decisions were affected by the repercussions of emancipation. He had to face constant insinuations in the debates of the 1830 session that he would surrender on Reform as he had on the Catholic question; and, as a cotton manufacturer's son moving uneasily among the patricians, he was peculiarly sensitive to these sneers. Political misfortunes can often be traced to reactions of this sort. In 1962 Mr Macmillan allowed a junior minister to resign over the Vassall case and was heavily criticized for doing so. This put him in a poor position for dealing firmly in the following year with the Profumo affair. It was only a year since Peel had ratted. While that was in all minds he was determined not to rat again. The tories would have repudiated a leader who, having committed the sin of giving in to agitators, repeated it in a different context only a year later. The Emancipation Act had brought on the agitation for Reform. It had also aligned Peel against every Reform proposal. He had been pledged against emancipation, and had then felt obliged to sponsor it. There was to be no immediate repetition of this performance. He would not pledge himself as being opposed to a Reform of the most moderate kind. But his determination not to sponsor even that, let alone something larger, was immovable.

So Peel made no move towards Reform and settled for Bassetlaw in the East Retford case. Even if he had wanted to make a Reform move he might not have been able to impose this policy on his colleagues. It is worth noting that, while to the House of Commons Bassetlaw represented the diehard solution, the peers in the cabinet thought of it as a compromise. For them the diehard line would have been to forgive East Retford and leave it as it was. Peel had difficulty in persuading them even to persevere with the Bassetlaw scheme in the Lords. Left to themselves they would have abandoned the Bill. But he insisted that he could not oppose a general Reform effectively unless delinquent boroughs were punished and their constituencies improved. Even if Peel had been prepared to rat to Reform he would have had a struggle to take the cabinet with him. It would not have been easy in May 1830 to drag the duke and his friends into the nineteenth century.

3

THE 1830 ELECTION

I know that this is not the light in which the Treasury views the returns; but I see in them the seeds of the most troublesome and unmanageable Parliament since that of 1640 which overturned the monarchy. (J. W. Croker to Viscount Lowther, 13 August 1830)

There is nothing . . . so convulsive to society as the strain to keep things fixed when all the world is . . . in eternal progress. (Thomas Arnold to J. T. Coleridge, 1 November 1830)

The election which took place in July and August 1830 weakened the Wellington government and brought a great access of strength to the reformers.[1] Wellington needed and expected to emerge with a substantial gain. His whips calculated that a vigorous use of the influence commanded by the government and its friends would win a number of seats. The Canningites and Huskissonites were the opposition groups most vulnerable to these methods. As they had been members or supporters of the government in 1826 some of them still occupied seats which the government whips could influence or control. They were to be replaced in these by reliable government supporters.

The expected increase in numbers did not materialize. The government's gains were offset by heavy and in some cases unexpected losses. They ended with no more followers in the new Parliament than in the old and with their prestige badly damaged. There were various interpretations of the results. But no calculation showed a decisive numerical change for either government or opposition.[2] To some extent this outcome reflected no more than over-optimism in the government's forecasts. It had been forgotten that a gain in one place often entailed a corresponding loss in another.

The migration of Sir George Warrender illustrates this process. He was a Canningite and had sat since the 1826 election for one of Lopes's seats at Westbury. By 1830 he was opposing the government which his patron still supported. He therefore abandoned Westbury, where he was replaced by a ministerialist, for Honiton. His new seat was under the influence of his ultra-tory brother-in-law, the Earl of Falmouth. The situation at Honiton had been the reverse of that at Westbury. The patron had joined the opposition, while his MP, whom Warrender replaced, had remained a government supporter. Thus Warrender's migration cost the ministry a seat at Honiton to offset its gain at Westbury.

The government's most dangerous losses were, however, of a very different kind. They resulted from well-publicized contests for county seats. The damage to prestige caused by these defeats was even more serious than the failure to gain in numbers.[3] Some politicians were prepared to support any ministry which looked strong enough to deal with the troubles that threatened. After the election Wellington did not look strong enough; and this kind of supporter began to desert him.

The campaign against the Huskissonites and Canningites was a disastrous failure. The gains were tiny; and the leaders were not kept out of Parliament. Charles Grant held Inverness-shire against a government candidate; and when Robert Grant was driven from the Inverness district of burghs, he went to Norwich where he defeated Peel's brother, Jonathan. The campaign probably helped to convert the Huskissonite leaders to Reform. It certainly provided them with an excellent excuse for announcing their conversion. The 1830 election was the first for some years in which the facilities available to the administration had been vigorously used. No group had been placed in 1826 as the Huskissonites were placed in 1830. The duke's assault thus came as a shock. The election repeated the lesson of the emancipation crisis: the facilities which the system gave a government were tolerated only if they were left unused. The Huskissonite leaders now began to favour electoral arrangements which could not be manipulated by the ministry of the day and its borough-owning friends. They became enemies not merely of the government but of the system as well.

Warrender took the opportunity of a speech in the Haddington-shire (East Lothian) election to foreshadow his conversion to Reform. The government had refused his request for their neutrality in Haddingtonshire, and had insisted on supporting the sitting ministerialist. This refusal accorded with the standard practice of the time. But Warrender was able to refer to the instances of illegitimate ministerial interference in support of his complaint. After a recital of them all, in which the county of Inverness formed the climax, he said:

He would tell the ministers this; such was the view taken by the public of their interference that they would lose all the counties and great towns in England though they might gain by it in the rotten boroughs and in Scotland . . . . He had always considered that the elective franchise was wisely distributed and fairly exercised; but from what he had recently seen he doubted very much whether at the end of this general election he might continue of the same opinion.[4]

The Canningites and Huskissonites were not the only members of the parliamentary class to be brought nearer to Reform by the election; nor were the government's mistakes the only means by which such people were converted. The election was the occasion for widespread protests against the electoral system. Electors in many places expressed their discontent with Parliament and its doings by revolting from their usual allegiances. The dominant magnates were challenged from the hustings in both counties and boroughs. Many county freeholders refused to take the magnate's journey money and vote for his candidate. They preferred to pay for themselves and vote for the popular man. In some boroughs the hustings were merely the prelude to argument before an election committee against the particular restriction of voting rights on which the magnate's dominance rested. These revolts revealed, not only how unpopular those with electoral influence had become, but the extent to which the whole aristocracy was by now involved in this unpopularity. Powers which were so intensely resented had ceased in some places to be entirely effective. There were signs where the revolts were most formidable that facilities long exploited by the magnates might soon cease to work to their advantage.

People outside the political system could only call for a Reform act. Those who were to some degree inside it could do more. Apart from demanding a change in the system they could begin to effect one. By tearing holes in the network of nomination and influence they could produce a kind of Reform without the passage of any Reform act. The more open-minded members of the governing class ceased to have any use for a system which was unpopular and productive of revolts. The Irish counties had been brought under control through legislation.[5] By the end of the election some politicians were wondering whether a similar technique might not be used more promptly, more liberally, and on a far larger scale.

Electoral control by the great magnates had become noticeably more difficult and uncertain during the 1820s. An impression had prevailed for several years that it was harder than ever before to maintain a borough interest. Edward Lytton Bulwer's novel, *Pelham*, published in 1828, described how the Borough of Buyemall, after being 'long in undisputed possession of the Lords of Glenmorris', had lately become 'open to all the world'.[6] In January 1830 the *Morning Chronicle* explained the conversion to Reform of tories such as Thomas Attwood with the comment:

in counties where whig and tory families coalesced to spare the expense of a contest . . . there will be found men ready to come forward for the express purpose of putting the aristocratical candidates to an enormous expense, it not being necessary for themselves to be at much expense . . . . In almost every county there are now a number of freeholders about the towns who would willingly second any third candidate in an object of this kind.

Such observers predicted that an election in the aftermath of emancipa-tion would subject the magnates' control to severe strain. In many boroughs, the *Morning Chronicle* remarked on 26 July 1830, there had been a

progressive increase in the number of voters. Thirty years ago, for instance, Warwick had from five to six hundred. . . . The voters are now upwards of 1200. The purchase of 1200 votes is a very different thing from the purchase of 400. . . . Stafford, which had not above 400 voters in the time of Mr Sheridan, has now upwards of 860. Everywhere the number of voters has been doubled and trebled. In Coventry . . . , Leicester . . . , Liverpool . . . , Preston, they have been trebled.[7]

'From the number of moneyed men in this country,' the *Chronicle* added on 28 July, 'and the improvement of late years in the science of breaching boroughs, we should not be surprised if many places reputed close were opened ere long.'

Now that the ultra tories were as ready as the whigs to criticize the system, the press rang with complaints that willingness to spend a huge sum was the sole qualification for a county candidate. In the last week of July the *Standard* imagined someone asking who were the new candidates for a particular county. When told, he replies: ' "Who are they? I never heard of their names. . . ." "Nor I," rejoins the res-pondent, "but they have money." '[8] With the political prospects highly uncertain there was a shortage of county candidates willing to spend fortunes. Sir Francis Burdett told the Birmingham Political Union that the largest English counties were 'going a-begging'.[9]

The electors were urged by every shade of reformer to take advantage of this situation, and to 'reform' the system by using their votes honestly, instead of selling them. The ultra-tory writer in *Blackwood's* told the voters in April 1830: 'reform yourselves; and this will have no small effect in reforming the House of Commons . . . give your votes at the next election uprightly and wisely.'[10] Joseph Hume, the radical, said in a Commons speech on 7 July that it was 'really in the power of the people of England . . . to send a majority to this House independent of the boroughmongers and the administration'.[11] 'The state of parties,' said the whiggish *Globe* on 22 July, 'the disgust of rich men at the expense of contested elections, . . . *tempt* electors in large counties and populous towns to exercise their rights with something like honesty.' 'Englishmen,' the *Morning Chronicle* added four days later, 'will at last be forced to be pure because Members are too poor to buy them.' It is doubtful whether the speakers and writers who gave this advice foresaw all the effects of honest voting.

Lord John Russell was defeated at Bedford, where his family had returned one Member unopposed for more than forty years. His father listed among the causes of this defeat 'anti-aristocratical . . . feelings'.[12] One of the Marquess of Anglesey's brothers was beaten in Carnarvon borough. This family also had held their seat for forty years. In Chester, where the Grosvenors had held both seats, they prevented a contest by announcing before the election began that they were giving up one for good. At Lichfield Viscount Anson secured the return of both his nominees, but was obliged to make and publish an agreement that 'at the next dissolution . . . and for ever afterwards . . . the independent interests of the city' should return one of the Members.[13]

Each of these boroughs contained some hundreds of voters and provided an unusually good opportunity for revolt. The member of the Russell family who had sat for Bedford in the previous House had often been an absentee from his parliamentary duties.[14] In Carnarvon borough the Anglesey interest felt the full weight of no-popery, as the retiring Member had been a fervent supporter of emancipation.[15] Earl Grosvenor could afford to give some ground at Chester. As his eldest son was becoming one of the Members for the county he no longer needed both city seats. In Lichfield the independent interest's success would have been impossible had not the Marquess of Stafford sold his property within the borough some years earlier.

These were the only places in which the borough rebels won an outright victory, but by no means the only ones in which they produced an effect. A revolt aimed at purging a corporation, or at showing that the favoured few had no legal title to the exclusive enjoyment of their privileges, represented only the first shot in a campaign. At Truro the Earl of Falmouth's candidates received 14 votes each from the capital burgesses, and the Reform candidates 179 votes each from the inhabitants, every one of the latter being disallowed by the mayor. It required the chairman's casting vote in the House of Commons committee to reject the resulting petition.[16] The proceedings established that Falmouth's methods of maintaining control had barely squared with the law. About half of the capital burgesses were non-resident although the borough charter required them to reside. Similar tactics were used at Calne, Dartmouth, Marlborough and Wigan.[17] None of these petitions succeeded. At Dartmouth, however, although the Houldsworth family retained their seats, their position was much weakened. As a result of Quo Warranto proceedings in the King's Bench, five of the eleven resident Houldsworth voters resigned the freedoms which had enabled them to vote.[18]

Some corporations and patrons were subjected to a war of nerves. At Marlborough, where two 'popular' candidates were challenging the exclusive voting rights of the Marquess of Ailesbury's corporation, the mayor refused amid uproar to make a double return. He was told that this might cost him £4000 in the courts. When he and the corporators retreated after electing Lord Ailesbury's nominees their gowns were torn off their backs.[19] At Shaftesbury the Grosvenors bore down the independent candidate by the weight of their property, despite his promise to compensate any of his supporters who might be evicted for their votes. The election ended with a riot in which Lord Grosvenor's managers were in some danger and with a threat from the independent party of a larger revolt next time.[20] At nomination day in Truro one of the independent candidates, William Tooke, was threateningly explicit: 'the question', he was reported as saying,

would certainly come before the House of Commons. . . . The mayor would be placed in a very serious predicament, should he decide against the clear rights of the burgesses at large in favour of a select body that, as he [Tooke] believed, had no longer a legal existence, there not being a majority of them resident within the borough, and a majority of the whole of the capital burgesses being necessary to perform any corporate act. The mayor might avoid this dilemma by making a double return, leaving it to the House of Commons to decide where the right was.

When the mayor had reluctantly allowed the matter to go to a poll

the capital burgesses, after tendering their votes, were asked by Mr Tooke whether they were elected by two aldermen and thirteen resident capital burgesses, and whether thirteen capital burgesses reside in the borough, to which the reply given was that they did not know.[21]

Unseating a proprietor's nominees was extremely difficult. Mounting an effective campaign of propaganda against him was not. The actual success achieved by the borough revolts was afterwards exaggerated for partisan purposes. A speaker at an anti-Reform meeting remarked in November 1831 that 'the number of boroughs ... daily opening ... never had been so great as at the elections of 1830'.[22] In fact, some revolts started, and most ended, as propaganda exercises. One or two of the tales of revolt seem to have been near to inventions. More than one paper carried a story about the Earl of Beverley's borough of Beeralston. It was said to contain only two voters. 'These two,' according to *The Times,*

determined at the last election to throw off the Beverley yoke; and, accordingly, through friends, they negotiated to return two gentlemen for their own profit, instead of that of his lordship. The Portreeve is Dr Butler, of Plymouth; but he is merely returning officer, and has no vote. Dr Butler, accompanied by an attorney's clerk, ... met the voters under a great tree, the place usually chosen for the purpose of election. During the time the Portreeve was reading the acts of Parliament usually read on such occasions, one of the voters handed in to him a card containing the names of two candidates, proposed by himself, and seconded by his friend. He was told by the attorney's clerk that this was too early. Before the reading was completed, the voter on the other side handed in a card corresponding with the former, and he was told he was too late. The meeting broke up. The Portreeve and assistants adjourned to a public house in the neighbourhood, and then and there made a return of Lord Lovaine and Mr Blackett, which was not signed by a single person having a vote.[23]

The truth of this tale may be doubted. There was no petition against the return and the constituency of Beeralston numbered nearer thirty voters than two. But the basic facts could not be denied. Lord Beverley owned the borough and controlled it through the merest handful of his dependants.[24]

A recital of these incidents does not in itself explain why the borough elections of 1830 caused such dismay. The technique of posing as a borough's popular champion had been discovered long before 1830. Many borough owners were well used to the trouble and expense of defeating revolts and the petitions which followed them. In several places the rebels were merely trying to improve on their 1826 performance. This was true both of Marlborough and of Lord Lansdowne's whig borough of Calne. Yet the contrast between 1826 and 1830 was striking. In 1826 established interests were little threatened unless they were pro-Catholic. In Leicester, for example, the Protestant corporation were the attackers. In 1830 all the established interests were on the defensive, the Protestant capital burgesses of Truro being just as unpopular as Lansdowne's whig corporators in Calne. The target was no longer the liberals and pro-Catholics. It was not even the turncoat ministers who had surrendered to liberalism. It was the whole parliamentary and electoral apparatus. Everywhere the men of the establishment found themselves naked to the wind.

The other established powers were almost as unpopular as the ministers. The protest was directed more at the system than at the government. In Bedford and Carnarvon borough, where the revolts fell on a whig and a liberal tory, they produced government gains of a sort. Now that the whole parliamentary system was hated, the aristocratic parts of the opposition were beginning to share the unpopularity of the ministry. The Catholic question had accustomed whig magnates to unpopularity. But it was one thing to suffer for religious liberty, and quite another to do so in defence of privileges which whig doctrine proclaimed to be obnoxious. For a tory magnate who had hitherto used no-popery as a shield, to be vilified to this degree might be a new and hateful experience.

The disturbance to the usual order of things in the counties was unprecedented; and these proceedings were still more ominous for the stability of the system. 'Almost invariably,' Lady Georgiana Stuart-Wortley reported to her mother who was abroad, 'where a great county struggle has taken place the old established county interest has been defeated.'[25] Suffolk was contested for the first time for forty years, one of the sitting Members who had represented it for nearly twenty-five years being defeated. He was accused on the hustings of not supporting Graham on economy and of asking for a crown living for his son.[26] The initiative in turning him out came from the freeholders and not from a rival magnate: they had some difficulty in persuading their chosen candidate to stand. 'One great feature of the county elections,' a young whig wrote, 'is that the small gentlemen and the independent farmers separate themselves from the aristocracy.'[27] In Surrey the pro-government candidate, Colonel Jolliffe, was beaten by a thorough going reformer. Jolliffe's 'ownership' of the borough of Petersfield made him unpopular with the county voters. But he was a large local landowner and had the weight of property on his side. The reformer (if an opponent can be believed) 'only inhabited a cottage in the county'.[28] His more substantial supporters paid to carry his voters to the poll, and this enabled him to counteract Jolliffe's long purse. Joseph Hume, driven by the government's influence from his Scottish burgh seat, was elected unopposed for Middlesex. It was apparently the Middlesex tories who invited this famous radical to stand for their county.[29]

In one or two counties the insurgents produced no more than a scare. On 27 July the *Manchester Mercury* carried a notice asking 'the freeholders of the county resident in Manchester, in Preston, in Warrington, and other great towns in Lancashire . . . to withold the promise of their votes for a few days' as a commercial candidate would shortly be announced.[30] No such candidate materialized. At Warwick, where both the county Members were standing for re-election unopposed, three or four hundred men from the Birmingham Union, accompanied by a band, invaded the hustings. Attwood spoke at length and cross-examined the candidates. Peel regarded the Union's 'daring attempt to overawe the nomination of representatives at Warwick' as one of the worst incidents in the election.[31] The candidates, on the other hand, seem to have treated the affair with amusement and some contempt. One of them was already on record as a reformer. The other declined to give the pledge of supporting Reform which the Union demanded.[32]

In Devon the revolt was not merely a scare. A reforming whig, Viscount Ebrington, beat E. P. Bastard, whose family had represented the county since 1784. Bastard was one of the few candidates in the county contests who made no pretence of being any kind of reformer. The opposition to him was spontaneous. Ebrington did not appear in Exeter until the contest was over. His supporters bore all the expenses of his candidature; and the lawyers advising his committee charged nothing for their services. The new Irish county electorate did not prove notably deferential. Captain John Hely-Hutchinson was a member of a Tipperary family who had supported emancipation for many years, his own pro-Catholic record being immaculate. He was beaten in the county election by a stranger to the county.

The dominant interests sometimes faced a difficult future even where the revolt failed. In Huntingdonshire these interests put forward a placeman and a placeman's son, both heirs to peerages. This pair luckily escaped a contest by securing enough promises for success before 'the committee for preserving the independence of the county' could find a candidate.[33] But the committee might be better prepared next time.

The return of Brougham for Yorkshire was the most sensational county result, and the one which had by far the greatest effect on whig opinion.[34] Its impact was all the greater in that the whigs had scarcely suffered at all in the other counties. T. W. Coke, the whig veteran, wrote on 25 August that in Norfolk the independent movement had broken tory strength, and 'the like spirit has manifested itself in most counties, which leads me to hope we shall live to see the Parliament independent'.[35] Independence was not always won from the tories or the government, however. When the West Riding manufacturers backed Brougham their target consisted of whig aristocrats and squires.

Three of the four Members for Yorkshire refused to repeat their experience of 1826 and announced their retirement by the beginning of July 1830. One uncontested election costing £150,000 was enough for them and too much for the other Yorkshire squires. The party magnates on both sides therefore embarked on a search for candidates who were popular enough to be elected without spending money. The idea was to obtain undertakings from squires and substantial farmers that they would pay for conveying themselves and the neighbouring voters to and from the poll, and so guarantee the candidates against expense. On 7 July Lord Wharncliffe wrote to his whig counterpart, Viscount Milton, suggesting an understanding between the two parties in the county that the election should be conducted on this basis. If it were to be as expensive as the last Yorkshire election, Wharncliffe wrote, '[we should be prevented] from having those to represent us whom we should all wish'.[36]

Limiting expenditure became more important than ever in mid-July when a Yorkshire squire of disruptive views named Martin Stapylton announced his candidature on the sole issue of purity of election. To the embarrassment of both parties he said that he was standing in order to promote Reform, and added privately that he would keep the poll

open as long as any freeholders remained unpolled who were ready
to pay their own expenses and vote for him. However much Stapylton's promises were discounted, he had ended any hope of an uncontested election.[37]

The surviving Member was a tory; and by mid-July the tories were
on the track of a well-known squire who would have a good chance
of being elected to their second seat without spending his money.
The whig magnates had a far harder problem. They soon settled on
Viscount Morpeth for one of their vacancies. But they were determined
not to concede the third seat to the tories: once conceded it might be
hard to regain. They therefore needed a second runner. Moreover, a
great many of their voters were in the West Riding. The two candidates had to be acceptable, not merely to the squires, but to the liberal
leaders in Leeds. At a meeting in Leeds on 14 July the latter accepted
Morpeth grudgingly, and then rejected every other name from the
squirearchy which was mentioned. These were not candidates, it was
explained, for whom the West Riding freeholders would travel to
the poll at York without being paid. It was eventually agreed that a
general meeting should be called at York on 23 July and that the
West Riding liberals should be entitled if they wished to make a
nomination.

Edward Baines, the editor and proprietor of the *Leeds Mercury,* was
not content to nominate a West Riding industrialist by leave of the
squirearchy. He meant to show the world that he and his fellow
liberals were independent of the county magnates and held the whip
hand. He would force the squires to accept a candidate who was as
far as possible from their traditional mould and who would dominate
the election. On 15 July it was known in London that Brougham was
to stand for Yorkshire. Two days later his name was put forward in a
Leeds Mercury editorial.

Brougham was a shrewd choice. Baines and his friends, for all their
defiance of the aristocracy, were not radicals. 'The factory question'
tended to keep masters and men apart in Leeds.[38] The mill-owners were
suspicious of their operatives' distinctive type of 'tory radicalism', and
willing to accept a whig as their champion. Brougham's anti-slavery
work, which he had capped with a fine speech on 13 July, made him
popular with West Riding dissenters, and especially with the Methodists. He bore no resemblance to a traditional whig candidate for
Yorkshire. He owned no land in the county. When triumphantly
elected on 6 August he was the first non-Yorkshireman to represent

the county since the Reformation, and the first lawyer since the Commonwealth.

At the York meeting on 23 July the West Riding leaders told the whig magnates that Brougham would be run as a candidate whether he had official whig endorsement or not. After many recriminations the magnates surrendered. The meeting was reported at length in the press; and Brougham's efforts to conciliate the defeated squires were not thorough enough to heal the wounds. His address on election included what a whig politician called an 'ill conditioned fling at the whigs'.[39]

No well-informed politician regarded this as a triumph which could be repeated, either in Yorkshire or elsewhere. Brougham's candidature could scarcely have prospered if the Fitzwilliam interest had been deployed against it from the start. But Viscount Milton who controlled the interest preserved a careful near-neutrality for some time between Brougham and the squires. His position and that of his fellow magnates sustained no lasting damage from the elevation of what a local tory called 'the Bainesocracy of Leeds'.[40] Brougham was unlikely to hold the seat for long, as he told Milton. His chances of gaining office within the next few years were good. He could not afford to fight a by-election in Yorkshire on appointment. When the whigs came in he would be obliged to retire to a borough or to the Lords. Men like Baines could take the initiative in county politics only where the proportion of town-dwelling freeholders was high. The combination of a four-seat constituency, immense election expenses, and an exceptionally high proportion of town freeholders, made Yorkshire quite unlike any other county.[41]

All that the whig magnates lost at York was prestige—and their illusions. Grey was as closely affected as anyone, since his son-in-law, Charles Wood, had been among the opponents of Brougham's candidature at the adoption meeting. Wood and the rest of the whig nobility and squires of the greatest county in England had been toppled in public by a Leeds newspaper owner. The whig patricians suddenly looked almost as weak and unpopular as the government or the borough owners. They realized how much popular support their hesitations and reticence on Reform had cost them. They had assumed that it would never be too late to step in and control the Reform movement, because people like Baines would wait indefinitely for a lead from above. They now abandoned this assumption. They had long thought it desirable to give Members to industrial towns, such

D

as those of the West Riding, and to make county elections less expensive and more controllable. They now concluded that this was imperative and urgent.

An anonymous opposition pamphleteer, widely believed to be Brougham, gave as his verdict on the whole election: 'The aristocracy has been taught a lesson ... The secret has been imparted, ... the secret of their weakness.'[42] 'The aristocrats' power,' the ultra-tory *Durham Advertiser* announced on 20 August, 'is fast crumbling beneath their feet.' The elections have shown 'in some places', said a writer in *Blackwood's*,

how the ancient fashion of the country is losing strength. We have seen political power and importance dissevered from property, and thousands of people fill, with their approving breath, the political sails of those who have no ballast to keep them steady, no cargo of their own on board to make them anxious, above all things, for the vessel's security.[43]

As long as middle-class people accepted the unreformed system its defects were overlooked by most of the governing few. Now that its enemies could no longer be dismissed as ignorant mobs, this tolerant attitude disappeared. A system so widely hated among people of some property and education had not merely ceased to serve the aristocracy, but had begun to menace it. The longer that the aristocrats insisted on maintaining the whole ramshackle affair the more the hatred which it inspired would be directed at them. The best course would be to scrap it and so recover popularity.

In the short run most borough patrons could defeat attempts to open their boroughs. Some had only to call up their outvoters to out-number the radicals. Others relied on legal rights so firmly based that an election committee was sure to decide in their favour. But these would be Pyrrhic victories. Repeated recourse to outvoters and election committees would involve any but the richest magnate in ruinous expense. The position was the same in the counties. The great county families could not spend a fortune on a contest every few years. Even if they did, they would not have any assurance of winning. A candidate popular enough to pay nothing for bringing his voters to the poll or for legal services was now better placed to contest a county to the finish than a magnate or even a group of magnates. A reformer, looking back on this change from May 1832, wrote that the county contests of 1830 had taught the small freeholders their real importance, and . . . shown how titled wealth may be driven from the field. When swarms of independent yeomen repair to the county town at their own expense, . . . the unpopular candidate, who is sweated by attorneys and agents and feasting committees, retires wan and discomfited.[44]

By October the reformers of the *Morning Chronicle* had decided that they wanted the county arrangements to remain as expensive as they were. 'As to Mr Brougham's plan for diminishing the expenses of county elections,' a leader pronounced,

we question whether, if carried, it would not be injurious. It would merely give rich landholders a greater facility in carrying county elections. At present the popular Members have the disinterested voters; and the aristocrats must pay for the conveyance of theirs to the poll. Whatever assists in breaking up overgrown aristocrats is a benefit to the country. Allow [the voters] to poll in districts and, if the tenants of the aristocracy are not protected by the ballot, . . . [you] give the candidate of the aristocracy a positive advantage over the popular candidate. At present a popular man can, at very little expense, put the aristocratical Member to a very heavy one.[45]

The *Chronicle* was right. The system did not serve the interests of the county and borough magnates running it unless the number of seats contested against them by the independent interest remained small. But it was now involving them in such unpopularity that the risk of this kind of contest was increasing in almost every type of seat. The only way by which the aristocracy could obtain a less expensive, and more controllable, system was to give up the rotten boroughs. Once that concession was made, the necessary changes would follow. A Reform Bill could reduce costs for borough candidates by abolishing the outvoters. By giving votes instead to respectable inhabitants it might prevent election contests from degenerating into orgies of bribery and drink. Making the counties safe for aristocratic magnates would not be objectionable as part of a general Reform. Enough polling places must be provided to take the freeholders' votes with a reasonable economy of time and travel; and the urban freeholders must be prevented from swamping the agricultural interest of the county. While the system commanded consent many politicians put up with its defects rather than give ammunition to radical agitators. Now that consent had been withdrawn the argument for putting up with them was less strong.

Observers of all political shades predicted that the new House would be unmanageable. The events of the election brought urgency

to the whigs' championship of Reform. 'Two years ago,' wrote Sir
Robert Heron, 'I thought Reform of Parliament almost hopeless. I
now believe it to be certain and approaching. The longer delayed, the
more it will be radical.'[46] 'I was not till within a few months a strong
reformer,' J. N. Fazakerley wrote to Viscount Milton in December
1830,

but the last election and the manner in which several counties broke loose
from the old influence of aristocracy and property convinced me of the
necessity of dealing largely with this question. Otherwise it was, I thought,
clear that if the excitement went on to the next election the forty shilling
freeholders throughout England would take the game into their own hands,
return Members of extreme popular opinions for every county, and throw
such a body into Parliament as would deprive any government of the power
of controlling or shaping any measure of Reform.[47]

'Wellington . . . has lost an opportunity,' Abercromby told Lansdowne
on 17 August, 'of at least attempting to carry us on for a time; . . .
the people have shown that they know their power.'[48] Robert Grant
told the Commons in March 1831, when explaining his conversion
and that of his political allies, that 'the events of the last general
election and particularly at the county elections . . . had made a deep
impression upon him . . . . Upon these events, and upon the most
mature deliberation, he had felt himself called upon to support' the
Reform Bill.[49] 'We are in a very ticklish state,' Anglesey wrote to
E. J. Littleton on 1 September, 'those who reform first will have the
best of it; and those who delay will have nothing left to reform.'[50]
   The last four of these statements were by reformers of very recent
standing. Fazakerley and Abercromby belonged to the group centred
on Lansdowne and Holland which had hitherto been lukewarm about
Reform when compared with most of the whigs.[51] Grant and Anglesey
were Huskissonites who had lately served under Wellington.

   By revealing and stimulating these movements in the constituencies,
the election increased willingness among the governing class to concede
a Reform measure. Moreover, the 'do-it-yourself' Reform policy
which a revolt embodied was normally coupled with a demand for a
Reform bill. The ways by which the demand for a legislative Reform
grew during the election now need to be outlined.
   Daniel Whittle Harvey, who was re-elected for Colchester, adopted
all the reforming attitudes which were becoming fashionable. As a
radical of some effrontery he interspersed exhortations to the electors

to vote honestly and assert their freedom with a request to his Colchester outvoters to take less of his money. Early in July he was reported as telling those who petitioned for Reform that in the election they should support 'none but . . . friends of the measure', and should vote in a 'disinterested' way.[52] He then opened his Colchester campaign by warning his London outvoters that they were too expensive. The borough had brought two of his predecessors to financial ruin, he said, and, in eighteen years, had cost him over £25,000. 'The spirit of searching economy is abroad,' he added, 'and you must come down in the market.'[53] Like Harvey's calls for Reform, this glimpse into the system's seamier parts received excellent publicity. The end of the election found Harvey on his county hustings declaring, as the *Colchester Gazette* reported, that

the heads of all the great families met just before election time, and settled who should be . . . Member, driving the yeomen voters like swine before them. He had saved Maldon from being a close borough; and he was determined to do the same in Essex. This was the origin of all the aristocratical hate that was displayed against him.[54]

The East Retford case had focused attention on election expenses and malpractices; and Whittle Harvey's remarks shared the spotlight with many other reports. There were probably no more sordid electioneering incidents than usual: it was the publicity attracted by them which was exceptional. Lord Rancliffe was widely reported when he gave, as one of his reasons for retiring from the representation of Nottingham, 'the disgraceful acts which he had been told took place at contested elections' there.[55] The dissenters' anti-slavery candidate for Bristol was defeated after his committee rooms had been sacked by his opponent's supporters. This riot, in which fourteen people were killed, emphasized the ragamuffin nature of a large constituency of freemen. Many dissenters felt that they would fare better with a reformed and respectable electorate. In March 1831 Francis Jeffrey listed the factors which had 'excited the impatience and zeal of the people' for Reform. One of these, he told the Commons, was 'the disgusting spectacle of corruption and venality . . . displayed at the general election' of the preceding year.

A number of candidates whose attitude to Reform was doubtful, when the election began, ended by pledging themselves to support some variety of it. No one knew how many parliamentary votes the reformers had gained by this. Not all of the pledges looked entirely reliable. A few were given by ministerialists under the impression that they were compatible with support for the duke. In County Wexford Viscount Valentia 'expressed himself very independently and avowed himself a friend to moderate Reform'.[56] With the help of this pledge he was returned unopposed. The government whips marked him as a 'friend'.[57] He may have expected Wellington to turn moderate reformer in the new Parliament. Perhaps the Treasury whips expected this too: otherwise they would not have regarded Valentia and some other moderate reformers as 'friends'. It was not clear which way these moderates would go if faced with a choice between the duke and Reform. In the event Valentia voted against the Reform Bill. So did J. T. Hope, a new Member for Gatton in 1830 from a well-known tory family. According to his later statement Hope had a 'confident expectation' when elected that Wellington would 'propose some measure of Reform'.[58] The expectation was widespread. *The Times* pronounced just before the election began that there was no inconsistency in supporting both Wellington and Reform.

It is extremely difficult to estimate the strength of the Reform demand which evoked these responses. Once the Reform Bill had been introduced this became a matter of political controversy; and it is necessary to begin by disposing of a myth which the opponents of the Bill then spread. They did not deny that the Reform cry had been strong in many constituencies. They were not in a position to do so, since everyone remembered that in November 1830 this cry had practically destroyed Wellington's government.[59] But, by arguing that the cry had been ephemeral, they were able to maintain that the government was being far too sweeping. The Bill, in this account, represented drastic and unnecessary surgery on a patient who had been suffering from a mere passing fever.

The fever was attributed by the anti-reformers to the news from France. The July revolution in Paris coincided with the election. Until news of the revolution came, Lyndhurst told the Lords in October 1831, 'the cry was all over the country for negro emancipation. But after the news arrived . . . the cry was changed, and the universal demand was for Reform'.[60] The essence of the Lyndhurst version thus was that there would have been very little demand at the hustings for Reform, but for the extraordinary chance that the election coincided with a revolution across the Channel. The facts do not support this account. The formation of the provisional government in Paris was announced by the English newspapers on 3 August; and with the reports published on that day it became clear that the revolutionaries had achieved a rapid and comparatively bloodless success. All the elections in Scotland and Ireland were then outstanding; but the effect of the revolution even on the few close contests in these countries was probably small.[61] On 3 August just over one hundred constituencies were outstanding in England and Wales of which less than forty were contested. The oustanding elections included all the contested counties, since the poll was taken later in them than in most of the boroughs.

Further study is unlikely to reverse the views which Professor Gash expressed after surveying some of the later contests. 'In the elections themselves,' he wrote, '. . . it is difficult to discern that the news of the French revolution was more than an accidental and superficial feature.'[62] The July revolution greatly affected British politics, but far less in the election than in the months that followed. It does not seem to have brought any material number of votes to Reform candidates, nor even to have accelerated the process whereby certain candidates accepted Reform pledges.[63] It helped to determine, not who was elected, but how those elected behaved when the new House met. It affected, not so much what pledges were given, as how far those given were honoured.[64]

Many of the governing class were too well informed to be deceived by this myth about a transient Reform fever. Indeed the lesson which open-minded politicians learned from the election was precisely that the Reform demand did not resemble a passing fever in the least. 'The demonstration in favour of Reform at the general election of 1830,' the Canningite Lord Wharncliffe told Wellington in November 1831, 'satisfied me that the feeling upon it was not . . . temporary and likely to die away.'[65]

The Reform cry was not overwhelming anywhere. It did not sweep the hustings and so provoke an almost equally intense reaction. The most significant fact was less that so many people demanded Reform than that practically no one opposed it. In Parliament the ultra tories were shy of an alliance with whig reformers. But on the hustings, and lower down in the social scale, these hesitations scarcely applied. The whigs had always stuck to their principles and attacked patronage-hungry borough owners. Why should not all honest men combine? Eldon, it was said, would have allowed his Northumberland tenants to vote for Lord Howick had the latter stood for that county. The ultra-tory *Brighton Gazette* rejoiced that 'the fawning parasite' was rejected, while 'honesty, consistency, and integrity, come they from whig or . . .

from tory, march in honour . . . at the head of the poll'.[66] Viscount
Acheson was returned for County Armagh on a liberal programme of
economy, retrenchment, and liberty of the press. His proposer
produced the other component for the mixture by making an
Orange tory speech, in which the electors were reminded that,
however 'a suicidal Parliament' might propitiate 'the Moloch of
Popery, the Boyne still flows; the walls of Derry are still strong'.[67]
Brougham's election speech at Leeds, in which Reform figured
prominently, appeared to the ultra *Standard* 'an unequivocal indication
of that union of the independent and undisgraced members of our
lately conflicting divisions into one country party'.[68]

In Cornwall Sir Richard Vyvyan, the ultra-tory leader, advocated
an alliance between whigs and ultras and said that a purely whig
administration would be tolerable. Some of Wellington's worst
measures could still be undone. The new Beer Act, for instance, gave
powers properly belonging to local magistrates to excise officers. That
must be repealed.[69] If Parliament reversed the duke's policies in this
way it might escape Reform. But if the new House

crushes the debtor by increasing his obligations; if it allows an organized
police, under the immediate control of the crown, to be increased and to extend
itself into all parts of the country . . . then may we be sure that the mass of
the nation will call aloud for a change in its formation.[70]

In Derbyshire the old tories lectured the government Member on
Reform and retrenchment and left the whig alone. 'It's like a whig
county now,'[71] the Duke of Devonshire noted in his diary.

These reforming signs were not lost on Brougham. He had been
campaigning among West Riding towns each of which wanted its own
MPs; and Reform had naturally been one of his principal themes. The
election left him ideally placed to become the popular Reform champion. He no longer depended for his own seat on a borough owner.
He was a Member for the greatest county in England, the birthplace
of the Reform movement; and Russell for the moment was not even
in Parliament. It would have been unlike Brougham to neglect such
an opening. At dinners in Sheffield and Leeds at the end of September
he announced that 'he would leave in no other man's hands the great
cause of Parliamentary Reform'. 'I have assisted others hitherto,' he
said, 'but I shall now stand forward as the champion of that cause.'[72]
There had not been much doubt that the other whig leaders would
take up Reform before this statement. After it there was none. They

were bound to prefer joining the movement to letting Brougham monopolize it. But there was hope for the anti-reformers in the speech too. A venture in which Brougham was taking a leading part was unlikely to go smoothly.

The 1830 election made the Fazakerleys, the Grants, and the Wharn-cliffes think it more dangerous to refuse Reform than to concede it. The disturbances of the months that followed tipped the balance of fear still farther in the same direction. The July Revolution in Paris was followed at the end of August by an uprising in Brussels. It was soon clear that these upheavals would disrupt British trade and the governing class became seriously alarmed. At the end of September Ellice told Grey of the 'general discontent among the middle classes from the dullness of trade and the little, or rather no, profit that attends all the industrious occupations'.[73] This alarm was increased by the realization that the trades union movement based on the Lancashire spinners had grown into a militant and formidable force. The Bishop of Carlisle told Graham that the operatives of his district had been enrolled as union members by a representative from Preston. Threats were used against the few recalcitrants. The organization was to be armed: 'Smiths were of the number and were manufacturing pikes'.[74] A minister who accompanied Wellington at the opening of the Liverpool–Manchester Railway wrote: 'Tricolour flags were displayed at some parts of the line. The spirit of the district was detestable.'[75]

An examination of the union movement led by John Doherty lies far outside the scope of this book. Although it had received a stimulus from the July revolution its origins lay in industrial, rather than political, conditions. The defeat of the spinners' strike in 1829 convinced Doherty and his followers that to succeed they must combine with other trades. They also regarded two moves by the masters as provocative. Manchester wages were brought down to the general level; and the principle was introduced whereby the spinner working more spindles in the wheel was paid a lower price.[76] It was estimated that by the end of September the membership of Doherty's union had reached 80,000, and the weekly receipts £330:[77] it had grown throughout October. A serious coal strike broke out in that month in the Oldham district which might well spread throughout the north-western coalfield; and the colliers were rapidly incorporating themselves in Doherty's union.

The weaknesses of the Lancashire strike movement which are so plain to the historian were not easily discerned from London at the time. Trades unions had been legal only since the Acts of 1824 and 1825.[78] The governing class had little confidence in the capacity of the Lancashire manufacturers to deal with the strikes. They doubted whether effective and timely combination against Doherty's union would be possible among men whose attitude to each other was one of rivalry and competition. Even if the masters did combine they seemed as liable to provoke trouble as to allay it.[79] The agricultural south east was no more peaceful than the north. Rick-burning and the destruction of threshing machines had been reported from Kent since June.

The city of London began to tremble. The great financial houses and the Bank of England were not proof against shocks to confidence on this scale. In the last fortnight of October even Rothschilds were rumoured to be in danger.[80] The first effect of the continental disorders had been that gold flowed into London for security. But this movement was soon reversed. On 28 October the Governor of the Bank of England felt obliged to enquire about the gold reserves in Dublin. 'Gold and silver have been taken pretty freely from this bank,' he wrote, 'since the unfortunate events which are still passing upon the continent, and, though we are very fully supplied, yet there is no saying how long or to what extent the foreign demand may continue.'[81]

Lady Georgiana Stuart-Wortley, whose election reports to her mother have been mentioned earlier in the chapter, wrote on 11 September: 'You have no idea how the wise and unwise of all parties croak, and no wonder; for the spirit of the lower classes at this moment is of a most alarming description.'[82] In July the notion of a revolution in Britain would have been scouted among the governing class as absurd; by mid-September the prospect that London might follow Paris was being mentioned everywhere. Lord Alvanley wondered how a dandy like himself would gain a living when all noblemen's estates had been confiscated. His proposal for supporting himself in the republican era was apparently that he should open a disorderly house with the Earl of Glengall as his headwaiter.[83] When Lord Hertford invited Huskisson for the shooting, he promised 'a good battue every day—unless the revolution comes here meanwhile'.[84]

Huskisson never received that invitation. On 15 September he was killed by an engine at the opening of the Liverpool–Manchester railway.[85] This made the absorption of the Huskissonites into one party or the other almost certain. They were hardly capable of standing alone now that they had lost their leader. It also increased their attractiveness to both parties. The problem for both had been to gain Huskissonite support without alienating the ultra tories. Huskisson's death removed this problem. While the ultras had distrusted him they did not greatly object to his colleagues. His disappearance thus freed both the duke and the whigs to bid for his group.

On 19 September Grey gave Holland a hint to sound Melbourne and Palmerston. Holland reported on 25 September that the accident had inclined these two away from the duke and towards the whigs, and that they would be more inclined to serve under Grey than under any other whig leader. This assurance was all that Grey needed for the next few weeks. He replied on 8 October that matters should be left there until the government's measures were known. A premature junction, he wrote, would not 'succeed with the public'.[86] Grey remembered the disaster of the Fox–North coalition. In 1830, as in 1827, he was very sensitive to any taint of an unprincipled alliance.

The government were less cautious. Before Huskisson had been dead a fortnight Peel persuaded the duke to offer Palmerston a Secretaryship of State. Viscount Clive was chosen as go-between. The move turned out disastrously; but it is not surprising that Peel and the duke were tempted to make it. Despite their sorties against the Huskissonites in the election the cabinet had never given up hope of seducing some at least of the group's leaders into office. Plans for assassination and for courtship had gone on side by side. A tentative and indirect offer of a place had been made to Melbourne in July, for instance.[87] It had not been possible, however, to offer anything to Huskisson himself, partly for fear of offending the ultras, but more especially because such an overture would have meant a loss of face for the duke. This had foredoomed any approach. Huskisson's followers were too loyal to him for any of them to accept a proposal from which he was excluded. By freeing them from this restraint the accident 'removed great difficulties', as Arbuthnot put it.[88]

Peel was in urgent need of a colleague on the front bench who could help him to cope with the new House in debate.[89] Yet if he had not become overstrained he would have seen that the overture was not merely foredoomed but might do considerable harm. Now that the Huskissonites were obliged to choose their side they had very strong reasons for choosing the whigs. Their late leader had been a declared opponent of any but the most moderate Reform. But they

were not pledged against it in the same way. His death thus enabled
them to come out as reformers. Moreover, they suspected that bolster-
ing up the Wellington cabinet was beyond them. No politician of
Palmerston's ambition and comparative youth was likely to join a
rickety government if he saw an alternative. Palmerston likened being
sounded about taking office with the duke to being invited 'to jump
off Westminster Bridge'.[90]

The government's negotiation with Palmerston dragged on for
about five weeks. Lord Clive does not seem to have been the ideal
emissary. According to Mrs Arbuthnot he was 'a very honest man'
but 'as deaf as a post and not very bright'. Palmerston was in no hurry.
He did not intend to engage himself with either side until Parliament
met and the strength of the opposing forces became better known. The
first phase ended on 12 October when he retired to Paris for a fortnight
to be out of reach of all emissaries. The second phase was shorter.
Palmerston and the duke met on 30 October at the latter's request.
In an interview lasting five minutes Palmerston demanded a total
reconstruction of the cabinet and the admission of the leading whigs
as the price of Huskissonite adherence.[91] Wellington and Peel agreed
at once 'that such notions put the matter quite out of the question'.[92]

The overture had not remained a secret and the news of it was
damaging the government. By making their foredoomed move
Wellington and Peel unwittingly convinced a good part of the
political world that they meant to make a concession on Reform.
This rumour was not new: it has been mentioned already in connexion
with the election. But until the last week of September it could be
dismissed as a malicious fabrication spread by those bent on destroying
the duke's good name as a statesman of principle. The Palmerston
affair suddenly gave it a compelling plausibility. One prominent
Huskissonite, Robert Grant, had declared for Reform during the
election.[93] At a Cumberland election dinner Sir James Graham, the
whig leader closest to the Huskissonites, had urged the government
to learn from the example of France, and to produce a 'moderate but
effective Reform in the representation'.[94] The Huskissonites were
most unlikely to accept office without stipulating for some concessions—of measures or men—to the moderate reformers. By
approaching them Wellington therefore seemed to confirm that he
was ready to sponsor a limited bill.

The duke and Peel had no intention of doing any such thing.
Wellington opposed Reform on principle with all the force of his

personality. Peel was equally determined not to be part of a reforming ministry. He would not repeat in a Reform context his reversal over emancipation. Both men intended to meet the Reform movement, and the alarm which it was arousing, with a firm front. Some observers, both in the government and outside it, believed a firm policy to have a good chance of success. This belief rested in what may be called 'the theory of the good fright'. By this theory Wellington's government would be strong enough to defend itself, and the unreformed system, provided that its natural supporters rallied to it. Holding the Government's majority together and resisting Reform was simply a matter of bringing these people into action; and nothing stirred them to action as effectively as a good fright. This doctrine embodied the experience of those who had watched Lord Liverpool's followers being brought into line between 1819 and 1822. 'The tories [i.e. the ultra tories] are alarmed at the general aspect of affairs,' Greville noted on 9 September; 'and I doubt whether they will not forget their ancient grievances and antipathies, and, if they do not support the government, abstain at least from any violent opposition.'[95] Ellenborough recorded five days later: 'Rosslyn thinks some of the whigs as well as of the tories will be alarmed by events on the continent and support government.' 'I can't help hoping,' Mrs Arbuthnot noted on 23 October, 'that the confusion in which France and Belgium are will a little alarm our people here, and they will feel it desirable to uphold the government and the existing order of things to avoid the confusion and ruin that is befalling those unfortunate countries.'

Wellington was less constant than some of his followers in attachment to the theory of the good fright. He inclined to it in August. Thus he thought the July revolution in Paris had strengthened him;[96] and when the first news came of the insurrection in Brussels he noted with satisfaction that it had been accompanied by 'plenty of plunder . . . [so that] those who have anything to lose will rally round the government'.[97] By mid-October he was less optimistic about the effect of alarm on people of property. 'Everybody is frightened,' he wrote to Mrs Arbuthnot on 15 October,

'Sir James Graham made a nice little attempt to terrify the government with Parliamentary Reform. But please God this will not answer. The gentlemen in Kent, so bold in Parliament, are terrified out of their wits with the burning of a few corn stacks, and the breaking of a few threshing machines. Lord Camden writes as if all was lost . . . I am more afraid of terror than I am of anything else.'[98]

But Wellington was too sanguine in temperament to despair. If the government stood firm people would recover from their terror. 'We must have patience,' he told Mrs Arbuthnot on 21 October, 'and all will get right.'[99]

The predominant reaction to the continental upheavals among the British governing class did not correspond either to the good fright theory, or to Wellington's views on terror. Charles X of France was universally condemned. No one, whether in the governing class or out of it, could say a good word for an ultra-Catholic monarch who had torn up his parliamentary constitution and muzzled the press. Revolutionary violence stemmed, not from radicalism, but from the provocations of rulers who refused to move with the times: this seemed the lesson of the July days. It was possible to make a stand against such rulers and establish a moderate and liberal regime: Louis Philippe's success proved that resistance did not always end in anarchy and blood. As the months passed, and reports came through of unemployment in Paris and of further upheavals, this image became tarnished. In the autumn of 1830 it was bright; that exaltation eclipsed for a time the memory of 1793. 'Confound these French ministers,' said Sir Walter Scott, contemplating the follies of Charles X's advisers; 'I cannot forgive them for making a Jacobin of an old tory like me.'[100]

It was resistance, not concession, which now aroused protests. Those who struck back against popular claims were widely condemned. In September Lord Exeter and the Duke of Newcastle were reported as ejecting tenants who had cast disobedient votes at the election. 'Those are the men,' Lady Georgiana Stuart-Wortley commented, 'that are answerable for a revolution if one does take place.'[101] 'Like the old French emigrants,' wrote Grey, 'they have learned nothing and forgot nothing, and, like them, would involve this country in ruin if they had their own way.'[102] To Tavistock the two noblemen were 'playing the game of levellers with a vengeance'.[103] Did Newcastle and Exeter see, *The Times* asked,

what it was that brought about this mighty French revolution of July 1830? ... When they expel honest men from their habitations for exercising a constitutional right ... they ... have perpetrated a *coup d'état* against the people of England which they, the people, ... may be apt to repay ... A better case for parliamentary Reform could never be imagined.[104]

A still more revealing comment was made by one of Lord Hertford's rotten borough Members. 'As to this country,' he wrote, 'a mere trifle will usher us in forty eight hours into bloodshed. Lord Exeter or the Duke of Newcastle, who on just and legitimate grounds quarrels with his tenantry, ... may touch the right spring; and then *sauve qui peut*.'[105]

The conviction grew among the governing class that it was no longer enough merely to abstain from provocation. At a dinner to Wellington in Manchester on 13 September the Earl of Wilton deplored that the people's 'hereditary attachment to the aristocracy' was 'lessened'. Lord Wilton did not know 'to what cause to attribute that diminution'.[106] Charles Tennyson, a reforming MP, speaking ten days later, explained it. He 'thought the solution was this. There had arisen in the minds of the wealthy and enlightened middle classes of this country a conviction that there did not exist between them and the legislature a sufficient link'.[107]

In the meetings held to celebrate the July revolution the non-existence of the link was startlingly apparent. A speaker at Leicester said of the aristocracy:

If they obstinately shut their eyes to those signs of the times ... and persist in exercising an arbitrary power ... , instead of receiving it at the hands of the people, ... ere many years shall pass not a vestige of nobility will be left in England. (Cries of 'the sooner it is done away with the better'.)[108]

The speaker was a well established manufacturer, brother-in-law to a candidate for one of the county seats.

By the end of October the 'agricultural revolt' had spread from Kent over much of south-eastern and southern England. Press reports and comment on the revolt revealed in its full extent the alienation of the middle class from the aristocracy and gentry. The *grande bourgeoisie* did not rally to the landlords when the latter fell into trouble: they jeered and cursed from the side lines. In August, a leading citizen of Manchester, speaking at a celebration of the July revolution, remarked, 'the march of intellect ... has lately been making an extensive tour through the agricultural districts'.[109] When in October Sir Edward Knatchbull passed light sentences on the first machine-breakers to be brought to trial, *The Times* asked: 'Must the public peace and safety be compromised because ... these Knatchbulls and others are conscious of the vile condition to which their system has degraded the poor?'[110] On 30 October the *Morning Chronicle*, surveying the outbreaks, inveighed against 'the busy, meddling parsons and small fry of magistracy' in the country districts. The *Chronicle* blamed the troubles on 'the system ... so long patronised by the English aristocracy', and, after an allusion to rotten boroughs, concluded: 'the middle classes of this country must bestir themselves ... let them go to the root of the evil. If they do not, there will soon be no security for property.'

Those who held the good fright theory had not over-estimated the degree to which the governing class would become frightened: they had mistaken the direction which the fearful would take. That it was right to stand out against demands which originated in the mob was not disputed. But with middle-class people demanding Reform the risks of resistance loomed larger than those of concession. The sort of people who had once feared the effects of Reform now feared those of refusing it. 'At home,' Howick noted in his diary on 22 October,

things do not look well. The most violent democratical principles are daily spreading and are avowed and proclaimed by bodies of respectable people in a manner not a little alarming ... I cannot believe that [Wellington] contemplates anything sufficiently comprehensive to satisfy any considerable number of persons, which would in my opinion give the best chance of escaping those violent changes which ... must ultimately be the consequence of an attempt to maintain existing abuses.

'If a rigid economy were resorted to,' Morpeth told the Commons in the Address debate, 'and if ministers no longer continued to refuse a Reform ... of Parliament, little danger could be apprehended to the institutions of the country.' Morpeth was a Canningite whig who had just been elected for Yorkshire. Another reformer said in the same debate:

You who are against granting those rights and privileges which not the lower orders only but all the middle classes ... demand, you may cry out against the reformers as revolutionary; but it is you that are bringing in a revolution by refusing to reform the Parliament.[111]

Even more interesting than these pleas from reformers was the acceptance by many anti-reformers that some sort of Reform was on the way. They neither feared it nor denied the necessity for it. 'I presume,' wrote Lord Hertford's Member, looking forward to the meeting of Parliament, that the duke 'has some declaration in store ... that will satisfy the nation.'[112]

People who thought like this were not yielding to terror; theirs was a calculated, not an irrational, fear. They were reconciled to

Reform much as the more reluctant southern moderates in the United States have been reconciled to civil rights legislation. They ceased to resist the reformers because they saw that the price of resistance had become too high. They had reached the conclusion which, more perhaps than any other, sets the scene for political change. They thought that, while concession might have ill effects in the long run, a diehard line could bring immediate disaster.

The benefit to be derived from a firm stand against change was thus smaller, and harder to win, than members of the government were apt to think. None the less they would have gained something from taking this stand had they taken it convincingly. But a convincing last-ditch stand was not compatible with a long and well-publicized search for front-bench speakers among the Huskissonites. Wellington had some inkling of this. 'Try what we please,' he wrote to Mrs Arbuthnot on 11 October, 'we shall make no coalition. These foolish liberals are looking for what they call moderate Reform, which is in fact radical Reform. They will not coalesce with us to resist that.'[113] 'None of these gentlemen,' the duke added on 18 October, 'will join the government unless we shall concede upon parliamentary Reform, upon slavery, and other follies. Peel is stout upon all these points.'[114] No one who accepted Wellington's analysis of Huskissonite attitudes was likely to regard a cabinet which coquetted with a prominent Huskissonite as being stout on any of these points. The duke had begun to learn this.

On 29 September Coke said at the Mayor's feast at King's Lynn that Wellington 'would bring forward next session parliamentary Reform' and other whig measures, 'not because he liked them, but because he was obliged to bring them forward or go out of office; and office he liked too well ever to leave it as long as he could keep it'. Had it not been for the rumours about the Palmerston overture these remarks would have made little stir. As it was they were reported, and given editorial mention, in the *Morning Chronicle*[115] and the evening *Globe* of 16 October; and the same evening the *Courier* commented: 'that the Duke of Wellington has something important in view we do not deny'. Wellington, the *Courier* added, 'expects from the House of Commons, and from the whigs collectively, a more generous and patriotic course than that of the Norfolk sage'.

Wellington and Peel were enraged and the editor of the *Courier* was obliged to explain that his remarks of 16 October had been written without authority or inside knowledge.[116] The *Courier* was regarded as the government's mouthpiece, however; and its disclaimer probably had little effect. A number of tory magnates, one of whom was Lonsdale, believed the rumour of a Wellingtonian Reform measure.[117] They let it be known that they could not continue to support the duke unless he stood firm against all Reform. 'There have been several meetings,' the *Court Journal* announced on 30 October,

> of . . . the independent members of the House of Commons, at which the supposed intentions of the Duke of Wellington were the chief topic of conversation. Several of the members stated at the last meeting that they had received positive information of the duke's having shaken off all negotiations with the friends of the late Mr Huskisson, and of his having formed an alliance with some of the ultra tories, who had made various conditions with him, one of which was that he should not propose or sanction any plan of parliamentary reform however modified.

The earlier rumour had been baseless: the new one was not. The duke, who had certainly not become a parliamentary reformer, was being persuaded by Lonsdale's threat to announce that fact in public. He did not appreciate, as he prepared to reassure Lonsdale, how unrepresentative the latter had become even among the tory borough owners.

If further persuasion to make an anti-Reform announcement was needed, E. J. Littleton unwittingly supplied it. Littleton called on Arbuthnot on 31 October to explain the attitude of the Huskissonite leaders, although he held no authority from them and had not consulted them about the call. He outlined the measures which they would require of the government as a condition of their adhesion. These included a bill to give 'Members now to the three great towns, and hereafter to other great towns, whenever there should be such proof of corruption as would cause the disfranchisement of some borough'.[118]

It seems likely that Wellington was disquieted by this conversation. Littleton would be telling his acquaintances that the Huskissonites had insisted on moderate Reform. Palmerston would let the same people know that the negotiation had not been broken off on the Reform question. The two stories in conjunction must give the impression that the duke had been ready to concede moderate Reform to strengthen his grip on office. And it would be insinuated that he was still ready to do so whenever it should be worth his while. Unchecked, these insinuations would have injured him. His method of checking them proved calamitous.

The whigs spent the last days of October struggling to coordinate their attack in time for the Address Debate on 2 November. Brougham favoured a formal coalition with the Huskissonites. Although Grey still thought this premature, a coalition offer appears to have been made to Palmerston on 31 October. He refused it on his own and his colleagues' behalf, just as he had refused the duke the day before, but he promised the whig deputation to support their party as far as he could without sacrificing his principles.

There were doubts about taking a bold initiative on Reform. 'The greatest danger which we run,' Althorp wrote to Brougham on 5 October, 'is the giving people an opportunity of saying that we were very moderate and mealy-mouthed as long as there was a chance of the Duke of Wellington taking us in, but that now we despair of this we are become violent.'[119] With the Reform cry growing stronger, however, Brougham's determination to start by challenging the government on Reform swept such doubts aside. Indeed their only effect was to help him to displace Russell as the party's Reform champion. 'I anxiously hope,' Grey wrote to Holland on 17 October, 'that Lord John Russell may be the mover'[120] of any opposition Reform motion. But if this motion were to be made right at the start of the session Russell could not move it, since he was not yet in the new House. On 18 October he told Holland that he had decided against an early publication of his Reform views. 'I believe,' he wrote, 'it is better to wait and let Brougham run riot as he pleases.'[121] Two days later he asked Ebrington to consider moving an Address to the king for strengthening Wellington's administration.[122] Russell thought that this would be acceptable to all parties: it would allow the duke to remain Prime Minister and to include Grey and Althorp in his cabinet. Russell's ideas on Reform tactics showed the same unseasonable caution. He wanted merely to revive his motion for giving Members to Manchester, Birmingham and Leeds.

On 31 October about twenty whig MPs met at Althorp's. 'Althorp announced,' Howick recorded in his diary,

that J. Russell meant . . . to give notice of the renewal of his motion for giving representatives to the three great towns. But the feeling of all present was so strongly expressed that such a motion, as not going far enough, ought not to be made, that he engaged to write to J.R. to induce him to give it up. Brougham complained that his plan of Reform had been much misrepresented and said he was determined to move certain resolutions preparatory to bringing in ... four or five distinct bills, for the purpose of enabling different persons to support those parts of his plan of which they might separately approve; and he repeated what he had said at Sheffield of being resolved not to give up this subject to anybody, that he had followed others long enough and he now expected them to follow him.

Brougham's success in the meeting presaged failure in the House. His efforts to produce a scheme which pleased every reformer looked too much like sleight of hand. When he was asked at the meeting 'whether he intended to disfranchise any boroughs, ... his answer,' as someone told Russell, 'was so confused that it could not be made out whether he did or not'.[123] Neither Brougham's 'plan nor the mover will satisfy the Benthamites or the radicals,' Holland told his son on 5 November, 'and the moderates, who would rather see the question in Johnny's hands, and who perhaps think it has been rather un-handsomely taken out of them, will not, I suspect, be very active or cordial in support of it'.[124] From the suspicions which Brougham aroused, the small attendance at the meeting, and doubts about the Huskissonites' attitude, there seemed little prospect of defeating the government and carrying the plan.

Althorp, Stanley and Denman dined with Brougham after the meeting and settled the outline of the Reform to be proposed. Brougham sent this outline to Graham on the following day and asked him to discover whether the Huskissonites would support it. Brougham was clearly prepared to modify it to suit them; and Graham expected them to demand modifications. On the same day Grey's assent to the plan was secured with some difficulty by Durham.[125] The prospect of the premiership had naturally increased Grey's anxiety not to offend the ultra tories. He wanted the prospective whig government pledged to Reform, but not to Brougham's particular proposals. It was agreed that Althorp and Grey should open the campaign by disclosing the party's insistence on Reform during the first day's debates. By the evening of 1 November all the arrangements were in train. But they were not Brougham-proof.

Brougham had aroused the resentment of many whigs by supplanting Russell. On 2 November he made himself still more unpopular by cheating Althorp of the limelight. He used the routine motion on the standing orders to announce, before the Address debate had even begun, that he would introduce his Reform on 16 November.

The plan could not have been launched less auspiciously. Brougham's statement, in Le Marchant's words, 'took the party by surprise and was coldly received'. Althorp's, deprived of any element of surprise, had 'comparatively little effect'. 'The independent Members,' Le Marchant continues,

who were believed to represent the opinions of large constituencies . . . sat provokingly silent. It was said, I recollect, that Mr Brougham's interposition with his notice had disgusted them. . . . Altogether the impression made on Lord Althorp by the night's proceedings was one of deep disappointment.[126]

The whig's blunder in the Commons was entirely eclipsed, however, by the duke's in the Lords. Grey declared for Reform 'very temperately', as Ellenborough noted. He adjured the peers to use the session 'by securing the affections of your fellow subjects, and by redressing their grievances, and—my Lords, I will pronounce the word—by reforming Parliament'.

Perhaps in the early part of my life [Grey continued] I have argued this question with the rashness of youth; but I have never thought that Reform should be insisted on as a matter of popular right, nor have I ever advocated the principle of universal suffrage . . . these are principles which I must deny, and claims which I must oppose. The right of the people is to good government.

Wellington replied that the government were 'totally unprepared with any plan' of Reform. 'On his own part,' he added,

he would go further, and say that he had never . . . heard of any measure . . . which could in any degree satisfy his mind that the state of the representation could be improved, or be rendered more satisfactory to the country at large. . . . He was fully convinced that the country possessed at the present moment a legislature which answered all the good purposes of legislation, and this to a greater degree than any legislature ever had answered in any country whatever. He would go further and say that the legislature and the system of representation possessed the full and entire confidence of the country. . . . He would go still further and say that if at the present moment he had imposed upon him the duty of forming a legislature for any country . . . he did not mean to assert that he could form such a legislature as they possessed now, for the nature of man was incapable of reaching such excellence at once; but his great endeavour would be to form some description of legislature which would produce the same results. . . . He was not only not prepared to bring forward any measure [of Reform]; but . . . as long as he held any station in the government of the country he should always feel it his duty to resist such measures when proposed by others.[127]

There are several stories of how the duke's colleagues reacted to these remarks. According to one version the duke whispered to Aberdeen as he sat down 'What can I have said which seems to make so great a disturbance?' 'You have announced the fall of your government: that is all,' Aberdeen replied.[128] This was an understatement. Wellington had announced the fall of the system.

4

THE WHIGS IN OFFICE

Now that this Reform has served their purpose so well, and turned out the duke, the opposition would be well satisfied to put it aside again, and take time to consider what they should do. . . . It is a hundred to one that whatever they do will not go far enough to satisfy the country. (Greville, *Diary*, 17 November 1830)

The cause of Reform had been advanced farther by Wellington in three minutes than by the whigs in a year. To make a most provocative declaration for the *status quo* just when the Reform movement was threatening to be formidable seems perverse. Yet, as the last chapter suggests, by the end of October 1830 the duke had a great inducement to make some such declaration. He explained some years later to Lady Salisbury that he had been trying to reassure Lonsdale and the other tory borough owners. 'When they all came up for the meeting of Parliament,' he told Lady Salisbury in 1836,

. . . I saw that it was a question of noses—that as many as I gained on one side I should lose on the other. The ultra-tories were beginning to take great alarm at the idea of Reform; and I heard at that time that Ld Lonsdale, upon being asked whether he was going up to town, said it would depend upon whether ministers intended to resist Reform.[1]

As the last chapter suggests, this was more than an excuse invented afterwards to give a heedless aberration some colour of rationality. Such observers as Arbuthnot and Tavistock explained the speech in the same way in 1830.[2]

If the statement had been confined to an unadorned declaration against any Reform it might have been defensible on grounds of principle or even of expediency. 'As he [the duke] believes it would be dangerous to begin Reform, he is right to say so,' John Gladstone wrote to his son William.[3] There was much to be said for an attempt to dispel the rumours which the Palmerston negotiation had aroused. Moreover, the duke's scepticism on the feasibility of moderate Reform

schemes was justified. Any scheme involving the minimum of disfranchisement was subject to a basic difficulty. The close boroughs
were the most unpopular and the freemen boroughs the most corrupt.
But these were not the rottenest and most decayed. It would not be
fair to select them for abolition while leaving Old Sarum untouched.[4]

Apart from this difficulty it is not certain that a moderate Reform
concession would have secured a majority for the duke, and so safeguarded the main outlines of the unreformed system. He could not
have placed much reliance on the whig and independent votes to be
gained from concession. As for the tories, more and more of them
were coming to want a Reform; and a good number expected the
duke to propose one. But this does not prove that they would all
have accepted it from him if he had. Whatever their private thoughts,
they would not have found it easy to follow him publicly in a second
reversal of policy. Some of the ultras who complained when he made
his stand would have called him a 'rat' if he had yielded. 'It would
have been impossible,' Le Marchant wrote many years later, 'for . . .
Wellington or . . . Peel, after their recent conduct on the Catholic
question, to ask the confidence of the country to carry a Reform
bill.'[5] Had Wellington and his cabinet realized all the risks of resistance
and concession they might still have decided to die hard. Although
the duke's colleagues strongly objected to the manner and timing of
his declaration the majority of them seem to have agreed with the
diehard line which it imposed. This was Peel's attitude; and most of
the cabinet disliked the prospect of ratting a second time almost as
much as he did.[6]

It may be argued that the ministers were doomed in any case: once
Brougham began to operate they were bound to unite the reformers
by declaring against Reform. Their best course was to prevent further
demoralization among the anti-reformers by making the declaration
at once. They could at least show that their refusal of a moderate
Reform sprang from principle, and not merely from the impossibility
of ratting twice in two years.

A well-prepared anti-Reform statement might thus have been
justified. But there can be little defence for the statement which the
duke actually made on 2 November. His every phrase showed that
he had not weighed the risks involved in resisting all Reform. A
leader who understood those risks might have made a declaration
almost as unyielding; but it would have been very differently worded.
He neither consulted his colleagues nor warned his party beforehand.

Almost as Wellington spoke, the mover of the Address in the Commons entered on a warm, though ambiguous, commendation of Reform. 'The awakening spirit of the age,' the mover said, 'called loudly for reform and improvement'; he was justified in presuming that 'in the work of reform', the government 'would not be found wanting'.

Wellington's declaration did far more than unite reformers of all shades and give the political unions the battle cry they needed. It convinced the moderates, first, that he must be removed from the premiership, and, secondly, that Reform was likely to pass. A Prime Minister who could talk like that in troubled times seemed to them both menacing and inept. He might provoke a revolution: he certainly could not stop a Reform bill. The prudent and the uncommitted had at last to face the question: how shall I stand politically if a Reform bill passes and I have opposed it to the last? The Reform movement was 'over the hump'.

The duke was indiscreet by conviction. He did not believe in using tentative phrases in debate. He thought with some justification that his political standing was based on his 'character for plain, manly dealing'. 'The people of England,' he remarked in 1828, 'must be governed by persons who are not afraid. You must state fearlessly and crudely your principle.'[7] He had been angered no doubt by Grey's taunt that the government might refuse Reform now, but would be compelled to yield it in the end, just as they had been compelled to yield emancipation.[8] He had endured a long period of frustration in cabinet and had watched misrepresentations spreading almost unchecked. At last the wretched Palmerston affair was ended and he was free to speak his mind. He was speaking it in the Lords where the atmosphere was not Reform-laden. He was thinking not of his unseen audience of newspaper readers as he should have done, but of the peers around him. Though his declaration was such as to cause disturbance even in the House of Lords there is evidence that some peers approved of it at the time.[9] It was only when they realized what popular indignation had been aroused that they began to wonder whether he had been a shade too forthright.

Wellington was concerned, not to appease or outmanoeuvre the enemies of the political system, but to stop disaffection from spreading among his friends. The roarings of Attwood and Brougham against the system left him unworried. But Lonsdale had only to drop a hint

to produce a startling effect. Wellington's declaration had the sudden-
ness and violence of a reflex action. Where tory suspicions that he
might truckle to Reform and radicalism were concerned he suffered
from an exposed nerve, left raw by 1829. Lonsdale had touched it.
In talking to Lady Salisbury the duke naturally presented his remarks
of 2 November as a calculated disclosure. They had arisen, he said,
from a count of noses. In this respect his explanation of 1836 contained,
like nearly all such explanations, an element of unconscious self-
deception. Whatever he might say afterwards the statement of 2
November was not calculated and deliberate.

To the duke conceding Catholic emancipation was one thing,
weakening on Reform quite another. He looked on the Protestantism
of the governmental system with calculating rationality: for the
constitution itself he had a romantic reverence. His view was entirely
altruistic: he possessed next to no borough interest of his own. It
was not related to what he knew of the borough system: he was well
aware of the failings of the tory borough owners.[10] It represented his
reaction against the evils of revolutionary anarchy and military
despotism which, to his mind, it had been his life's work to combat.
He was liable to obsessions in politics—'to being governed,' in
Greville's words, 'by one leading idea'.[11] His hatred of radicalism was
obsessional: it went beyond discussion or calculation, indeed almost
beyond reason. To him reforming, radical and revolutionary principles were all one. He had seen such principles at work among
Napoleon's armies and the Cato Street conspirators. He thought them
nothing more than a propensity to plunder.[12] It was intolerable that
his natural allies should suspect him of conniving at these iniquities.

Most Prime Ministers suffer from an exposed nerve somewhere.
Whether they make a serious misjudgement when it is touched de-
pends on their health, on the extent of their experience, on their
intelligence and awareness of their defect, on their accessiblity to good
advice, or merely on their luck. Wellington had exactly the wrong
equipment for dealing with the Reform crisis. By 1830 he was no
longer an Iron Duke in health. Some years earlier he had walked too
far forward, while watching the trials of a new howitzer. The per-
cussion had damaged one of his ears, and unskilful treatment seems
to have aggravated the trouble. He became partially deaf; and his
general health deteriorated. His isolation and unawareness of the
defects in his political equipment completed the damage. He had
become an advanced case of the malady which a later occupant of the

office thought common to all Prime Ministers. They 'suffer,' Bonar Law said in 1922, 'by suppression. Their friends do not tell them the truth; they tell them what they want to hear.'[13]

All this made Wellington hopelessly vulnerable to the effects of his basic misconception. No one would warn him that the events which were hurrying him into declaring himself an out-and-out anti-reformer coincided, not with a passing wave of panic in the governing class, but with a massive movement of opinion towards Reform. It is a mitigation of his blunder that this movement had not reached its climax when he made his speech. The most alarming news about the agricultural risings had barely begun to appear in the London papers by 2 November.

At the end of October the labourers were reported to have become bolder. They were now making their attacks 'in open day' and in one or two cases they had hoisted the tricolour.[14] It now appeared that many of the rural middle class sympathized with the risings and were unwilling to join any force which might be ordered to act against the rioters. On 2 November *The Times* carried a report of a meeting in the Canterbury Corn Exchange three days earlier. This had been convened under the chairmanship of Lord Winchilsea to prepare the ground for the enrolment of yeomanry. It had been adjourned without achieving anything, after a speech from a farmer asking 'Why are not the salaries of public officers reduced? Why are not useless places set aside?'

The Times reported on 6 November that there was great difficulty in persuading respectable people to serve as special constables in Kent.[15] On 13 November the London press described Lord Clifton's failure to win approval from a Rochester meeting for the enrolment of a yeomanry unit. One farmer present had attributed 'most of the evils that afflict this country' to 'corrupt representation'. The meeting resolved that it was 'the duty of landowners and clergy, by a liberal abatement of rent and tithes, to assist the farmers'.

Some of these news items aroused more alarm among the governing class than the facts warranted. The analysis of the agricultural revolts by Professors Hobsbawm and Rudé in *Captain Swing* (1969) shows that, while they might look like a revolutionary movement, they were anything but that. They were confined to the corn-growing areas of south-eastern and southern England. The labourers had little or no effective contact with urban radicalism. The origin of their protest lay in the agricultural changes of the last eighty years, which had turned them into a pauperized proletariat. Their objectives were limited and were expressed in economic and local terms. They demanded a living wage and the destruction of the threshing machines which deprived them of winter employment.

Most of their proceedings were not violent where persons were concerned. The uprisings were sparked off by the news which the local radicals brought of the revolutions on the continent. But there might have been explosions in 1830 without this spark. In an effort to lessen the rate burden which the Speenhamland system imposed, some parishes were reducing poor relief allowances. There had not been a good harvest since 1827. The labourers had few revolutionary ideas and no revolutionary plan. They moved because they could not stand the prospect of another winter like the last.

Moreover, it was soon discernible that collusion between farmers and labourers owed less to grievances against the governmental system than the press reports of early November had suggested. Most farmers disliked threshing machines as much as their labourers did. They used them only because they feared to give their rivals an advantage by not doing so: they were glad to see them go. Some smaller farmers joined in the labourers' demands because they were hard put to it to pay rent and tithe. For the rest, as *The Times* reported on 17 November, it was easy to see why farmers agreed to raise wages and dismantle the machines: they were not fools enough 'to refuse requests not unreasonable in themselves and put to them by 300–400 men after a barn or two had been fired and each farmer had an incendiary letter addressed to him in his pocket'. Faced with demands to enrol as special constables or yeomanry the farmers could not well admit to fear. Complaints against the system of government provided a more respectable ground for refusal.

Nonetheless, the farmers' discontent with the system was real and it increased the difficulty of re-establishing order in the areas affected. The revolts thus completed the train of events through which support for Reform became formidable. Hodges, one of the Members for Kent, spoke on the fateful first day of the Address debate. He quoted from an account by a Kent magistrate of the farmers' refusal to serve as special constables. 'The majority of them,' it read, 'refused to be sworn in, observing that their petitions for relief had never received the smallest attention, and that the cause in which the labourers were engaged was theirs.' He 'was convinced,' Hodges told the House, 'nothing would remedy the evil but that remission of taxation which could be effected only by a reformed House of Commons.' The unrepresentative character of the House entailed, as a reformer said in 1831, 'that the manufacturing artisan enrols his name in affiliated societies, instead of subscribing it to petitions, that the agriculturist winks at, if he does not encourage, the outrages of his labourers'.[16]

The special importance of the agricultural risings in forwarding Reform lay in their impact on the ultra tories. The people converted by events during and after the election had mostly been liberals and moderates. Fazakerley, Wharncliffe and the Grants all fall into this category. Among the Kent and Sussex landlords hit by the revolts were a number of leading ultra tories—Winchilsea, Knatchbull, and Richmond. Speaking in the Lords on 4 November Winchilsea demanded Reform. Richmond did the same a few days later. The Canterbury meeting had evidently left its mark on Winchilsea. 'If Reform, moderate Reform did not take place,' he told the Lords,

the noble duke (Wellington) . . . would himself speedily witness the destruction of the best institutions of the country . . . . Their Lordships . . . would neglect the duties they owed to their country, the confidence of which in the wisdom of Parliament had been much shaken, if they did not take some measures to win back the respect and confidence of the people. . . . They must do justice to the people, and then they would have the people ready to support and maintain those laws which were necessary to the security and prosperity of all.

The duke's declaration against Reform forced the whigs and Huskissonites into partnership at last. The Huskissonites met on 6 November and agreed to support Brougham's motion provided that it was worded vaguely and did not commit them to his scheme in all its details. Graham reported this to a dinner of whig leaders on the following day. The attendance at Althorp's meeting in the Albany on 13 November was the largest yet known. The Huskissonite condition proved readily acceptable. In the light of Wellington's speech there was everything to be said for a general motion, couched in terms to which no reformer could object. The motion on which the meeting agreed ran:

that this House do . . . take into consideration the state of the representation of the people in Parliament, with a view to remedy such defects as may appear therein.[17]

The cabinet discussed how to deal with Brougham's plan on 9 and

14 November. Ellenborough argued for agreeing to the motion, and then fighting the Reform proposals in detail. But the cabinet decided to meet Brougham with a direct negative. According to Ellenborough, Peel said that 'he thought the terms of the motion did not signify. It was "Reform, or no Reform". He never would undertake the question of Reform.' Peel maintained this position at the second meeting, though he admitted by then that a really successful resistance to the motion was unlikely. Even if the government secured a majority, Brougham would have most of the county Members: there would thus be no sound basis from which to resist Reform. 'I cannot understand his reasoning,' Ellenborough noted; 'if he thinks Reform carried why not vote the resolution and fight the details. It seems to me that obstinacy, and the fear of being again accused of ratting, lead to his determination to resist when resistance is, in his own opinion, fruitless.'

It is not clear whether any of Ellenborough's colleagues had the hardihood to join him in arguing for concession after 2 November. Lyndhurst had pressed Wellington to take in Grey and other whigs.[18] He was thought to be more devoted to the woolsack than to his leader or to the anti-Reform cause. On 7 November he gave a dinner, to the amusement of the political world, to the leading whigs. Murray 'confessed himself friendly to a Reform' in the Address debate on 3 November—words which even Peel could not explain away. But most of the cabinet were still for standing firm even apart from the Prime Minister's pledge. They might recognize some Reform to be necessary. The king said that, except for the duke, they all admitted this when they took leave of him on 21 November.[19] Even so, they were not prepared to propose one. Whatever might be the result of Brougham's motion, Peel wrote to his brother William on 12 November, 'it is better for the country and better for ourselves that *we* should not undertake the question of Reform'.[20]

Hardly a day passed now without some prominent magnate deserting the government. The duke must have foreseen some of these losses when he made his speech. Losing Stafford and Cleveland was serious because both commanded great political 'interests'. But as Cleveland was an acknowledged reformer, and Stafford's connexions were with the Canningites and whigs, it caused no surprise. The defection of noblemen with impeccable tory pasts such as Talbot and Bath was more sinister, and revealed how faulty was the duke's method of counting noses. 'Lord Bath came to town,' Greville noted on 12 November, 'intending to leave his proxy with the duke, and went away with it in his pocket after hearing his [the duke's] famous speech; though he has a close borough, which he by no means wishes to lose, still he is for Reform.' 'The potentates,' Hobhouse wrote, 'begin to tremble for their acres.'

The king and his ministers were due to dine at the Guildhall on Lord Mayor's Day, 9 November. Various reports, including one from the Lord Mayor Elect, suggested that Wellington was likely to be attacked during this journey. Even if he were not his appearance could cause a riot. On 7 November, after sitting for more than seven hours, the cabinet were persuaded by Wellington and Peel to cancel the visit. Their decision was entirely reasonable; but it tore away their last shred of prestige. In the city a government so incapable of governing that it could not reach the Guildhall was judged unfit for the times. Government stocks, which had fallen four points after the duke's speech on 2 November, now fell a further three. The shock, far from rallying effective support to the duke, warned the governing class that the established order was in greater jeopardy with every day that he remained Prime Minister.

On 11 November W. E. Gladstone, then an undergraduate of tory views, proposed a motion condemning the government in the Oxford Union. It was carried by one vote.[21] Ellenborough noted that the newspapers were turning against Wellington, 'like cats leaving the falling house'. The ultra-tory *Brighton Gazette* suggested that the alarm over Wellington's anti-Reform speech was unnecessary: the reformers had only to push vigorously and 'the pledge will be utterly disregarded'. The liberal *Manchester Guardian* hinted that the duke's reason for cancelling the Guildhall visit might have been a hope that the resulting alarm would strengthen his government. Both insinuations were baseless: both were current in parliamentary circles as well as in the press.

A good fright was no more help to the government in November than it had been six weeks earlier. Possibly a more skilful politician than Wellington could still have exploited people's fears with some success. More probably the good fright theory was no longer applicable by 1830. It was by now very well known to the progressives. They had suffered much from its application over the years. Tory governments had cried wolf too often. Their opponents could easily represent these cries as false alarms, designed to whip the doubtful into line. No one had much fear of what would happen if the government fell. Greville no longer gave weight to apprehensions about the whigs:

he now thought suggestions that it might be difficult to form another administration 'mere balderdash. . . . I have heard these sort of things said fifty times of ministers and kings'. Very few magnates, even among the great tory borough owners, seem to have been afraid of a whig Reform. They relied on Grey's well-known moderation, or perhaps on the whigs' equally well-known ineffectiveness in office. In view of the whigs' performance in 1827, and of their aversion from any Reform proposal which could offend the ultra tories, this complacency is not surprising. The Knight of Kerry, who held one of the Irish offices, tried to persuade Wellington to reconstruct the cabinet on a whig basis. The whigs, he wrote on 5 November, 'have no dangerous projects: even their Reform cannot mean anything injurious to the landed interest'.[22]

Brougham's Reform motion was never debated. On 12 November Sir Henry Parnell, a whig financial expert, gave notice that he would move to refer the Civil List to a select committee. The cabinet resisted this though it was bound to attract some doubtful votes. As Parnell was sounding the note of economy Members who had to defer to their constituents would not like to vote against him. But the considerations which made concession difficult on Reform operated on the Civil List also. To accept a committee on it would be a notable surrender for a cabinet which already had too much of a reputation for surrendering.

The most important of the ultra-tory groups, which was led by Knatchbull and Vyvyan, met on the day of the debate and decided to vote for Parnell's proposal. They hoped and expected that their support would give him a majority and so bring down the government. They were 'country gentlemen' with a tradition of independence in a whip's sense of the word: that is, no government could depend on them. They had strong reasons for turning against Wellington, and for choosing Parnell's amendment on which to do so. They wanted their revenge for Emancipation as much as ever, and had no use for a government which was unpopular in the country towns and among the farmers. They were united in favour of economy, but somewhat divided on Reform. They found Parnell's proceedings less embarrassing than Brougham's.

Both leaders of the group were county Members who had to please economy-minded constituents. Knatchbull sat for Kent. He was scarcely a reformer; but if a small Reform concession would help to

stop the rick-burning, he was willing to make it. The ultras were not
for the most part politicians of great subtlety and foresight. They
found it far easier to envisage their grievances against the existing
system than the possible disadvantages of a different one. They shared
the general belief that the whig and Huskissonite leaders would not
take Reform too far.[23] Like most rebellious politicians they neglected
Jezebel's pertinent question: 'Had Zimri peace who slew his master?'

When Parnell's resolution was debated on 15 November the
government were defeated by 233 to 204. Despite their shortsightedness
the Knatchbull–Vyvyan group at least had some sort of policy based
on reasonably accurate calculations. This was not true of all the other
seceders. A number claimed that they would not have voted against
the government had they known that the question was being treated
as one of confidence. These claims are hard to accept. But some of the
penitents had doubtless hoped, even as they voted with Parnell, that
he would lose. Two conclusions can be drawn from the division list.
First, there was little loyalty to the ministry remaining anywhere. The
new Member who had been the whips' original choice for moving
the Address voted with Parnell. All of the four cabinet ministers' sons
in the Commons were in town: none of them bothered to vote.[24]
Secondly, now that the government was losing its grip, a Member
with a considerable number of constituents was apt to court popular
favour by voting for economy. Only fifteen English county Members
voted against Parnell.

Peel had expected the defeat and was delighted at it. The strain had
told on him; and an honourable release from office was just what he
wanted. The duke told Lady Salisbury later of 'the extreme irrita-
bility . . . almost amounting to insanity' which Peel 'constantly displayed' in the weeks before the government fell. 'When the ministers
were beat on the Civil List,' Lady Salisbury noted, 'Peel arrived in one
of these states at Apsley House "suant à grosses gouttes," and calling
for tea, soda water, and messes of all sorts to calm his agitation:
walking up and down the room and insisting that they should resign
immediately.'[25] Mrs Arbuthnot who was present during part of this
scene wrote in her journal: 'I never saw a man so delighted as Peel.
He said when the opposition cheered at the division . . . he did not
join in but . . . it was with difficulty he refrained.'

The duke was not so well informed as Peel when the debate began.
Optimistic to the last he had exclaimed, on being hurriedly told the
division figures, that there must be a mistake: the government's

E

majority could not be as small as 29.[26] But he did not differ from Peel when he learned that the majority was not his. He too preferred to resign at once rather than risk giving Brougham a triumph which would embarrass the new cabinet.[27] He knew that Brougham's motion was vaguely worded, and expected the ultra tories to support it.[28]

We do not know whether this expectation would have proved correct, still less whether Brougham would have won. The ultras agreed at their meeting on 15 November to meet again on the following day.[29] It seems likely that they were deferring their decision on whether to support Brougham until they knew the outcome of the Parnell division. Brougham himself was not as confident as he made out. When the opposition were in the lobby on 15 November he begged them, should they be beaten, to stay in the House and try dividing again that evening.[30]

Wellington resigned on 16 November and the king immediately summoned Grey to form a government. The whig leaders' problem of what to do about Brougham now reached a crisis. The ministry would need support, or at least forbearance, from reformers of every shade. There would be a popular revolt if Brougham were not in the cabinet, and a revolt of the parliamentary moderates if he were given any post of real influence. Meanwhile he would not consent to postpone his Reform motion beyond 25 November.

Grey made a bad start. He allowed a rumour to spread that he wanted to keep Lyndhurst as Lord Chancellor;[31] and he offered Brougham the Attorney Generalship. Brougham answered the note conveying this offer by tearing it up and treading on the pieces. Grey was quickly brought to a more realistic view. The incoming cabinet met on the evening of 18 November and decided that Brougham should have the Lord Chancellorship. He had been regarded for some months as the right Lord Chancellor for a Reform government; and that very day he had called the Chancellorship the only appointment that 'is any temptation to me'.[32] Yet when he was offered the Great Seal on the following morning he refused. He wanted to be Master of the Rolls.

The Mastership was a permanent appointment worth £7000 a year, and compatible with a seat in the Commons. It thus represented a great catch to a man of Brougham's temperament and talents. Appointment to it would give him a high position while allowing him to remain the chief tribune of the people. Free from financial worries he would be well placed to influence, and perhaps terrorize, every government. The post was as good as vacant since there was little doubt of the present Master's willingness to become Lord Chancellor.[33]

Any politician less excitable and self-deceiving than Brougham would have realized, however, that his motives for wanting the Mastership provided the whig leaders with conclusive reasons why he could not have it. Left to himself Grey might have given way; but the king advised resistance.[34] Althorp was adamant. 'If Brougham is left in Parliament with an irremovable office,' he said, 'the ministry will not last three months; and I certainly will not belong to it.'[35]

Brougham's two brothers warned him on 17 November that if he stood out for the Mastership he might prevent the formation of a Reform government. By 19 November he must have had some inkling that his popularity as a reformer might not survive further obstruction. The whigs were seething with impatience. An hour or two after he had refused Grey he was visited by Althorp.[36]

Althorp told Brougham that he had until 2 p.m. to accept. If the Chancellorship were still vacant then Grey would return to the king and declare himself unable to form a government. In that case, Althorp said, Brougham would be responsible for a further twenty-five years of tory rule and for the whigs' failure to enact their reforms. Brougham surrendered.

The parliamentary moderates were delighted to see Brougham in the Lords. 'Thank heaven his tusks are drawn now,' the Canningite Lord George Bentinck wrote on 22 November; 'If it should become necessary to drive him from the Woolsack I do not apprehend much danger from any vapourings of his as a private peer.'[37] Moreover, once Brougham was out of the way, the moderates had plenty of ministers of their own complexion to counterbalance ardent Reformers such as Durham and Graham. Both the groups which had helped the whigs to defeat Wellington were represented in the cabinet. Knatchbull refused office; but the ultra-tory Richmond became Postmaster-General, while the Huskissonites obtained three Secretaryships of State and the Presidency of the Board of Control. This variety of political views was obtained without grave loss of cohesion. The new ministry were a tightly-knit group even by the standards of those patrician times. The whigs, as Melbourne put it, seemed to be 'all cousins'. Their cousinhood, extending beyond the strict confines of the party, embraced the Huskissonites and even one or two ultra tories. Melbourne had belonged to the inner circle from birth; and Palmerston also commanded the entry to it through his mistress, Lady Cowper, who was Melbourne's sister. Goderich had been in Althorp's form at Harrow. Richmond was Holland's second cousin.

Grey himself had the confidence of all but the most extreme reformers. In a long political career he had never intrigued for office and seldom held it. His record was thus both more consistent and more non-committal than those of the official tories could be. The moderates were reassured by his promise to stand and fall with the peerage,[38] and the radicals by the fact that he was Durham's father-in-law. The ultras remembered that he had been Canning's bitterest enemy, the liberals that he had never wavered in his advocacy of Catholic Emancipation. Though no currency reformer he had announced lately that he had an open mind on the currency question. The amount of patronage which he bestowed on his family was not popular; but the newspaper reader who learned that they were now receiving more than £18,000 per year of public money was reminded that Wellington's relatives and connexions cost far more than this. During the new government's honeymoon period most people were willing to overlook such blemishes.

A politician who has to persuade the few to give up their privileges should not look like a leveller. Grey retained what Byron had called 'the patrician, thoroughbred look ... which I dote upon'.[39] As the head of a Reform government he thus possessed what we are apt to regard as a prime requisite of political leadership—the ability to look one way and go the other. Mr Macmillan is reported as explaining that a Conservative leader can persuade his party to accept changes so long as he is wearing the Brigade of Guards tie. But this aptitude in its highest degree belongs only to statesmen such as Grey, in whom it is entirely spontaneous. Grey's patrician bearing was anything but a pose deliberately assumed for political purposes. His earldom had been created for his father little more than twenty years earlier. Fortunately for the cause of Reform he had that exaggerated respect for the charmed circle which sometimes characterizes those whose families joined it recently.

The extremely aristocratic character of Grey's government did not result from deliberate policy or even, to any great degree, from his patrician leanings.[40] It was an accident; and once again, despite the criticism aroused, it must be judged on balance a fortunate one. In their composition as a parliamentary party the whigs were much like their opponents. But long spells in opposition had given them a highly aristocratic leadership. In the early years of the century ambitious young men who needed official salaries and were prepared to work for them seldom became whigs. As a result the people available to lead the party were largely magnates; and the members of Grey's cabinet owned, or were heirs to, an enormous acreage. It was hard to believe that men with such a stake in the existing order would sanction a revolutionary change, or one likely to injure the landed interest. Moreover their wealth was regarded as a guarantee of integrity. They were too rich to have much need of ministerial salaries. Their dominant motive for Reform could hardly be a sordid desire to improve their own chances of staying in well-paid offices. Political life may have been harder for a new man in 1830 than it had been a generation or two earlier. The more the governing class feared radicalism, the more they felt 'lacklands' and upstart 'lawyers of fortune' to be untrustworthy guardians of an aristocratic system.[41]

A cabinet of high rank and broad acres stood well, not merely with the governing class, but with the country. Some aristocrats were becoming unpopular from their connexion with the unreformed system; but most Englishmen still 'dearly loved a lord' provided he were a reformer. 'The whole people of England,' Thomas Attwood told J. C. Hobhouse in June 1830, '[are] essentially aristocratic and imbued with respect for their superiors, and hatred of those neighbours raised by accident above themselves.' Wellington, who did not often agree with Attwood, said the same: 'This country has nothing to fear while the troops are officered by gentlemen,' he told Lady Salisbury on 18 September 1830. 'The spirit of the people is aristocratic.'[42] Althorp was not as famous as Brougham; but he had been Master of the Pytchley Hunt and kept a fine herd of shorthorns. To the forty-shilling freeholders who had the last word in the unreformed electorate he was a great man. Grey's cabinet of patrician amateurs had plenty of prestige. It was their capacity and experience in administration, and above all in finance, which were in short supply.

Althorp's sole qualifications for the Exchequer were two first classes in his mathematical exams at Cambridge, a short spell as chairman of the finance committee of the Commons, and some well-kept estate accounts. Auckland was President of the Board of Trade, though he had 'never done anything,' as one liberal put it, 'but mismanage the Travellers' Club'.[43] Poulett Thomson, the Vice President, had the confidence of the Manchester free traders, and more financial knowledge than his well-born colleagues; but his experience of the House of Commons was small.

A ministry so inexperienced was bound to make some mistakes at the start. The cabinet succeeded in very little during their first three months except in confirming that they were not revolutionaries. They showed more aptitude for repression at this stage than for anything else. The governing class applauded Melbourne's harsh treatment of the labourers involved in the agricultural revolt, though, incredible as this may seem, there were some doubts in London whether enough sentences of transportation had been secured.[44] Cobbett claimed in July 1831 that the whigs had instituted more political prosecutions of the press in seven months than the tories had in seven years. O'Connell was arrested in January in connexion with his agitation for repeal of the Union. The first fourteen counts of the indictment charged him with contravening the 1829 Act suppressing the Association. In February he offered to let judgment go against him by default on these counts provided that the remainder were withdrawn. The government, for whom his surrender was a triumph, agreed.

Financial reform proved more difficult than repression. Economy had been an excellent opposition battle cry; but, coming into office when upheavals on the continent had created something of a war scare, the whigs inevitably disappointed those who had expected great reductions in expenditure. Liverpool and Wellington had between them removed the most obvious abuses. Moreover, retrenchment was not popular in circles where Grey was particularly anxious to obtain support. He needed the king's favour; he would soon have lost it by slashing the Civil List pensions. The whig magnates, after years in opposition, were clamorous for their slices of the loaf. It was not the moment for reducing the rations.

An attempt to remove unpopular taxes met with equally little success. The budget, which was introduced on 11 February, proved a fiasco, and had to be much modified during its passage through the House. Althorp offended the city and the fund-holders by proposing a tax on transfers of real and funded property, and the country gentlemen by withdrawing the proposal. His duty on raw cotton drew protests from Manchester. The alteration of the coal duties was not thought entirely disinterested. It was said to have increased Durham's income by £36,000 a year.[45]

The government's misfortunes deepened the impression that their

Reform would fail. In *Crotchet Castle* Peacock made the Reverend Doctor Folliott sceptical of Brougham's Reform plans. Folliott predicted, on learning of Brougham's accession to office:

He will make a speech of seven hours' duration; and this will be its quintessence: that, seeing the exceeding difficulty of putting salt on the bird's tail, it will be expedient to consider the best method of throwing dust in the bird's eyes.[46]

By the end of February the cabinet looked less likely than ever to seize the initiative with a bold and effective scheme. Even the cautious Peel hinted in a debate on 18 February that the ministerial Reform was likely to prove as big an anti-climax as retrenchment.[47] After the budget the opposition were indeed afraid that Grey might not last long enough to dispose of the Reform issue for them. On 26 February *The Times* attacked Grey and called for the reconstruction of the government. By the end of the month Brooks's Club, the surest barometer of whig morale, was a scene of 'general despondency' according to Le Marchant;[48] and consols were lower than they had been after the cancellation of the city visit in the previous November.

Wellington and Peel were in no shape to unite and galvanize the opposition. The illusion that they had only to wait for the ministry to collapse thus held an almost irresistible attraction for them. They had lost Lyndhurst. Needing money and failing to keep the Lord Chancellorship, he had accepted the Chief Barony of the Exchequer from Grey. No one knew just how far this judgeship would keep Lyndhurst out of politics; but it was generally thought that he could hardly take a leading part in opposition while he held it. In any case his appetite for office under the whigs had naturally damaged his prestige among the tories. Wellington disliked opposition activity which had for him the horrible taint of faction. Moreover his speech of 2 November had curtailed both his prestige and his freedom of manoeuvre.

The real obstacle to a reunified opposition was, however, Peel. He had no sooner left office than he hinted that he might retire into private life. His trouble was a distaste, not so much for politics, as for his former political associates. He blocked attempts at reunion between the ex-ministers and the ultra tories. Towards the end of February various ultras in both Houses made overtures to the Wellington camp. But neither Knatchbull nor Vyvyan was identified with these efforts.[49] As no one wanted to bring down the government at this stage, others besides Peel thought reunion far from urgent. In the Commons the rift remained almost as wide as ever.

Peel meant to use his time in the wilderness to cut himself free not only from the ultras, but from Wellington too. He had refused to join the latter's political house party at Stratfield Saye in January. He wanted to combine and lead the moderates; and a powerful coalition on these lines seemed within his grasp once Reform should be settled. His personal ascendancy in the Commons was unrivalled now that Brougham had been removed. On 21 February the government were saved from defeat on the West India sugar question solely by his intervention. 'I do not know how long this will last,' Greville noted on 25 February; 'but it must end in Peel's being Prime Minister.' Peel was not the only one in that month to see the mirage of a great government of the centre.

A week or two after the government was formed Grey said to Durham, as they were walking down the steps of the House of Lords, 'I wish you would take our Reform Bill in hand'.[50] As Russell was not yet in the cabinet, Durham was the inevitable choice for chairman of the committee preparing the Bill. Apart from his relationship to the premier he was the only cabinet minister who had been active as a reformer since the end of the war. Russell was naturally asked to join him; and these two coopted Graham and Duncannon.[51] At this stage Durham looked on Graham as his protégé. He had wanted high office for Graham who had seemed likely to provide him with 'a kind of pocket vote' in cabinet, as Brougham called it. Graham was to prove somewhat more independent, and a great deal less radical, than had been expected. But as his other early mentor in the cabinet was Althorp, his views had not yet begun to diverge seriously from Durham's.[52] If Graham were the only other cabinet minister on the committee, Durham would be in a strong position as chairman. Duncannon probably owed his selection chiefly to his contacts with the O'Connellites whose support for the Bill would be badly needed. He was Althorp's first cousin and had been Melbourne's brother-in-law. This committee of four met regularly at Durham's house in Cleveland Row.[53] Their instructions from the cabinet were to prepare:

the outline of a measure . . . large enough to satisfy public opinion and to afford sure ground of resistance to further innovation, yet so based on property, and on existing franchises and territorial divisions, as to run no risk of overthrowing the [existing] form of government.[54]

These instructions pointed towards a comprehensive measure based
on large-scale disfranchisement of rotten boroughs. In Table 3 the
committee's recommendations are set out and compared with the
corresponding provisions in both the original Bill and the Act. The
scheme for England and Wales with which the committee started
came from Russell. He produced it 'in a short time': it contained, as
he wrote later, 'hardly anything new'.[55] In its main features it followed
the general run of Reform plans. Seats were to be taken from rotten
boroughs and given to counties and unenfranchised towns. A nominally uniform borough voting qualification was to be established and
copyholders and leaseholders were to be added to the county electorate. The electoral machinery was to be improved. In counties a
polling place was to be provided for each district. The outlines of a
system for registering both county and borough voters were devised
by Graham. Duncannon had the chief say where Ireland was concerned. The committee took advice on its Scottish proposals from
Cockburn, the Solicitor General for Scotland.

Russell proposed to take both Members from fifty boroughs (the
Schedule A boroughs as they became in the Bill) and one Member
from fifty more (Schedule B). The committee originally thought that
this meant taking both Members from boroughs with less than 1400
inhabitants and one from those with less than 3000. Durham checked
the 1821 census, however, and concluded that, if this extent of disfranchisement were to be achieved, the lines should be drawn at 2000
and 4000 inhabitants. These latter figures appeared in the committee's
report and were accepted by the cabinet. More will be said of them
later.

The borough qualification gave the committee the most trouble.
Russell started by suggesting votes in the old boroughs for householders rated at £10 per year, and in the new for those rated at £15
or £20.[56] These figures were in line with previous proposals. They
represented contemporary estimates of the minimum property needed
to give a voter 'independence'. In 1820, when proposing that Grampound's two seats should go to Leeds, Russell had put forward a £5
rental franchise. In 1821 he had altered this to a £10 rental; and the
House of Commons had further increased it to £20. A £20 rental
was the jury qualification outside London, under Peel's 1825 Jury
Act.

There was a case for giving the new boroughs a higher voting
qualification than the old. The higher figure would do something to

TABLE 3
COMMITTEE PROPOSALS, BILL, AND ACT
(England and Wales)

	Committee's proposals	First Bill on introduction March 1831	Reform Act, June 1832
REDISTRIBUTION OF SEATS:			
Counties	Counties with more than 150,000 inhabitants to gain two further Members, and to be divided into two constituencies.	Two Members for each Riding of Yorkshire; 26 other English counties to be divided into two double-Member constituencies; Isle of Wight to be given a Member.	As in First Bill. Add: 7 English counties to gain third Member; 3 Welsh counties to gain second Member.
Boroughs	To lose both Members if below 2000 inhabitants; to lose one Member if below 4000 inhabitants. Unrepresented towns to gain Members if over 10,000 inhabitants.	Weymouth (see Table I p. 20) loses two Members out of four; 60 Schedule A boroughs lose 119 Members; 47 Schedule B boroughs lose 47 Members; 11 unrepresented boroughs gain two Members each (22); 21 unrepresented boroughs gain one Member each (21).	Weymouth, as in First Bill; 56 Schedule A boroughs lose 111 Members; 30 Schedule B boroughs lose 30 Members. Schedules A and B composed according to the number of houses in each borough and the amount of tax paid there. 22 unrepresented boroughs gain two Members each (44); 21 unrepresented boroughs gain one Member each (21).

Counties	(1) 40-sh. freeholders to remain; (2) add £10 per year copyholders (see n. iii below); (3) add £50 per year leaseholders.	As in committee's proposals. Lease in (3) to be for 21 years at least.	(1) & (2) as in committee's proposals. Add: (3) £50 lease-holders if lease for 20 years at least (4) £10 leaseholders if lease for 60 years at least; (5) £50 tenants-at-will if occupiers.
Boroughs	(1) Existing electors to retain votes if resident. (2) Occupiers of houses worth at least £20 per year to gain votes.	(1) As in committee's proposals. (2) As in committee's proposals, substituting £10 for £20.	As in First Bill. Add to (1): rights of freemen extended to future freemen, provided right was (a) acquired through birth or servitude (apprenticeship), (b) if acquired through birth, derived from qualification existing before 1 Mar. 1831.
METHOD OF VOTING:	Secret Ballot to be adopted	Open voting to remain	As in First Bill
MAXIMUM DURATION OF A PARLIAMENT:	To be reduced from seven to five years	To remain at seven years	As in First Bill

NOTES

(i) The introduction of a registration system, the increase in the number of polling places, and the shortening of the poll to two days were common to all stages.

(ii) The Table is not intended to show all the intermediate changes to the Bill. Nor do the figures included reveal how far the Schedules were altered in composition as the Bill progressed (see Chapters 5 and 6).

(iii) Copyhold was a tenure of medieval origin 'by copy of the court roll according to the customs of the manor'. By 1830 it resembled freehold, to which it has been assimilated since 1925.

(iv) The numbers of voters in the various categories are shown in Table 5, p. 312.

ensure the independence of the voters in the new London constituencies. The old boroughs needed the lower qualification in that they would include all the constituencies with the smallest populations, and potentially the fewest voters. Moreover they contained existing voters who would keep their votes provided they were resident, whatever the qualification named. The committee soon opted, however, for a uniform qualification of £10 annual value in all boroughs. They were influenced probably by the political difficulty of imposing a higher qualification on the very places where the Reform agitation was most intense.

At this point Durham asserted his radicalism by proposing to include a secret ballot in the scheme. Secret voting was highly controversial.[57] Outside the ranks of the intellectuals many people thought it sneaking and un-English. When combined with a limited suffrage it also had the disadvantage of withdrawing from the non-voter his only means of influencing the voters. The advocates of ballot had made great strides in the last six months, however; and it had become something of a radical battle cry. It was specifically demanded in 280 of the 645 petitions which reached[58] the Commons between 5 November 1830 and 4 March 1831. The radicals needed a safe way of showing that they were democratic. Advocating a very wide diffusion of voting rights was not safe: advocating ballot was. Ballot served as a means of uniting middle-class reformers with those of the working class.[59] It was still difficult in most places to induce the two groups to combine. By including ballot in his proposals a middle-class radical could convince working-class reformers that he meant business: even if he did not want all working-class people to have votes, he was the enemy of aristocratic domination. At the inaugural meeting of the Liverpool Political Union in November 1830 the main speaker remarked: 'If we exclude the voting by ballot we must have universal suffrage and annual Parliaments.'[60]

Durham was a convinced radical. He was also vain and an egotist. He wanted the committee's report to be, not merely radical, but unmistakably his own production rather than Russell's. He had already tried to insert the radical formula for triennial parliaments into the scheme, and had been obliged to compromise on quinquennial.[61] It was far more important to him to insert ballot. He won the committee round, but at the cost of a major concession. Russell insisted that, if ballot were to be recommended, the borough qualification must be raised to £20 in order to confine the voters to those who were beyond the reach of bribes. He held the view, which was common at this time, that secret voting would increase electoral corruption, since it would enable the voter to take bribes from both sides with impunity, and would make bribery charges harder to investigate.[62] Russell may have thought too that, if the great proprietors were to lose a traditional means of influence over the voters, voting must be confined to persons of some property.[63]

The cabinet soon rejected quinquennial parliaments and ballot. Secret voting would probably have weakened the political position of the aristocracy in the 1830s, though much less than most aristocrats feared. The ministers' own fears about ballot were not the only reason for dropping it nor perhaps the decisive one. It had too many enemies in key places. The king loathed it. So did many peers.[64] The proposals which Grey and Althorp took to Brighton on 30 January were thus based on a £20 franchise in the boroughs and open voting.[65] Althorp was by now under popular pressure to give the date on which the Reform Bill would be introduced. On 3 February he announced that Russell would submit it to the Commons on 1 March.[66] On 4 February the king gave his formal consent to the proposals.[67]

The compromise of £20[68] and ballot embodied in the committee's report was absurd. All previous discussions of the borough franchise question had been concerned with new boroughs, where there would be a good number of voters whatever the qualification. If the committee had been thinking about the £20 qualification in relation to the Schedule B boroughs they would have realized that it was too high. Statesmen less irresponsible than Durham, and less confident than Russell,[69] would have obtained some statistical information before deciding what to recommend.

As it was, this information came to hand after the committee had reported. On 21 December a reforming MP had moved for a return of the number of £10 and £20 houses in parliamentary boroughs. The figures which the Office of Taxes produced in answer to this enquiry came into the minister's hands around 9 February. They showed that eight of the boroughs which were to keep one Member contained fewer than ten houses valued at £20 and above, and that more than half of them contained fewer than thirty such houses. The tables established indeed that many of the places in Schedule B would be short of voters even with a £10 franchise, and with the help of those who would keep their present voting rights.[70]

These figures were not an accurate guide. They were discovered some weeks later to have exaggerated the scarcity of voters, since many houses were assessed below their true value.[71] On the other hand, it was easy in using them not to allow for the proportion of qualifying houses occupied by women, and therefore not providing voters. The figures served to highlight the defects of the £20 franchise and to arm the cabinet ministers who criticized it. Grey had an old-fashioned whig's dislike of creating boroughs small enough to fall under government control. Brougham had too sharp a political nose to allow the creation of what would look like new nomination boroughs.[72] Melbourne was 'for a low figure. Unless we have a large basis to work upon,' he said, 'we shall do nothing.'[73] The Attorney General suggested to Russell that enlarging borough boundaries might help to provide more voters. The cabinet agreed. It was decided that no borough should fall below 300 electors, and that the boundaries of the less populous boroughs should be enlarged until that figure was reached. Such was the origin of what Professor Gash has called the ruralized boroughs.[74] This decision was not enough. It was clear that the qualifying level must be lowered[75] also. The king had already given his approval should this change be required; and in the middle of February the cabinet adopted a uniform borough qualification of £10.

The ideas of the ministers on Reform cannot be compressed into a single, internally consistent theory. The Huskissonites did not see the Bill in the same light as did a reformer of long standing such as Russell. On secret ballot there was a sharp division, Althorp being bold, while Grey and some of the other peers showed a caution characteristic of elderly noblemen. Not all the cabinet even shared the basic whig disposition to welcome the 'march of mind' and extend civil liberties. Richmond did not cease to be an ultra tory when he turned reformer. Moreover the statesmen of the time seldom asked themselves whether their ideas were entirely compatible with each other. Rigorous theoretical analysis enjoyed little popularity either in council or debate. An extreme distrust of theory was expected from all except radical politicians.

The cabinet wanted, while modifying the electoral system, to leave the general structure of politics as it was. Perhaps it is misleading to state as an objective what was in fact an assumption. It was assumed that the reformed system should be based, as the unreformed had been, on the representation of communities. There was to be a minimum number of voters for a constituency and the larger English counties were to be divided. The cabinet did not regard these features of their scheme as constituting even the first step towards a system of single-Member constituencies each containing a standard number of voters. They assumed that there would still be ways into the Commons for gentlemen who shrank from the noise of the hustings, and that the various interests in land, trade and industry would still find representation. Their Act would end dictation by the borough owner and would give the local landlords their proper weight. These changes were meant, not to diminish deference, but to increase it.

The ideas outlined in the last paragraph would have been compatible with a wide suffrage, for some constituencies at least. If the poor were given votes they would no doubt become the target for radical demagogues. But it was acknowledged to be from the lower classes that the aristocracy received the greatest deference.[76] Moreover, an enlargement of the electorate much greater than the one produced by the Bill might not have had a markedly democratic effect because the demand for a democratic arrangement of constituencies was still comparatively weak. The Chartist cry for 'equal electoral districts' and the radical slogan 'one vote, one value' lay in the future.

The cabinet would have broken their next tenet, however, if they had distributed the vote widely among the working class. They did not think a man fit to vote unless he had enough property to be in some measure independent. The long leaseholder could be enfranchised since in theory a landlord could not give orders to a man who had the protection of a lease. The same theory laid down in contrast that the tenant-at-will, being obliged to obey his landlord, was unfit to vote. Whig magnates had no wish to march crowds of ignorant tenants to the poll.

The whig view by which these apparently conflicting principles were reconciled was that the right kind of deference flourished best among men of some property and education. Such men deferred to the local magnate in the only way that was still entirely unobjectionable: they accepted his advice and leadership in politics, not because they had no alternative, but because they knew enough to recognize his superior knowledge. The borough electorate of £10 householders could thus be held to combine all the virtues, the voters being at once propertied, deferential, and independent.[77] Lower-class bigotry and ignorance would be excluded. In the whig phraseology of the time, votes were to go far more freely to the people than to the populace, the first term denoting the middle class, the second the working class.[78]

None the less, working-class support for the Bill would be needed if it were to reach the statute book. It would have been unwise to draw the line between voters and non-voters to correspond exactly with that between middle and working class. The £10 householder line produced no such correspondence. The cabinet realised that their nominally uniform borough qualification would be anything but uniform in practice. What proportion of householders it enfranchised would depend on house prices and living habits in each borough. In London it would give more artisans the vote and establish something approaching household suffrage. In some other places, by contrast, it would leave a good part even of the middle-class unenfranchised. The ministers defended these discrepancies by the argument that the £10 clause gave votes most freely where the level of education was highest, and where people were best informed on political issues. It was equally true that it gave the most votes where there was the greatest and most dangerous demand for them. The boroughs were intended to be uniform in one essential point only. In all of them the electorate was to consist of voters who were either men of some property or amenable to the wishes of great proprietors. In all of them as many voters as possible were to exhibit both these characteristics.

The cabinet aimed to recast the system so as to restore its popularity among the middle class without weakening the facilities which it provided for the ruling few. They hoped indeed to strengthen those facilities. Their county arrangements in particular were designed with that object. Their Bill was meant to end agitation and yet to leave the most important levers of power in aristocratic hands. Unpopular aristocratic privileges would be replaced by acceptable ones. The Bill, Grey wrote to Princess Lieven, 'takes from [the peerage] a power which makes them odious, and substitutes for it an influence which connects them with the people'.[79]

It was not merely a matter of letting the middle class into the outer defences while still barring them from the citadel itself. Once given the privileges of entry they were to become part of the garrison. The Bill was founded on the belief that when the middle class had been allowed a subordinate share of power they would side with the aristocracy and help to keep the working class in order. Remove the grievances of middle-class people against those above them and the danger of an alliance between middle and working classes would disappear. The new voters would not be anxious to admit others to the electoral privileges which they had won. An increase in wealth had prepared the middle class for a radical assertion of their rights; but in the longer run, provided that their claims were met, it would give them the cautious and conservative outlook of property owners. These were the calculations which underlay Brougham's rhetoric about the sober judgement of the middle ranks of society. Agitations which lacked middle-class leadership were not likely to come to much. No striking originality marked the conception behind the Reform Bill. The process of adapting institutions and seducing the insurgents which was to stand the British governing class in such good stead had begun before 1831. The originality lay in the boldness with which this technique was now to be applied.

The notion that middle-class people would be content not only with a subordinate place, but with borough arrangements which would not even give them all votes, may seem like wishful thinking. Yet it had a firm basis. The Bill gave the middle-class man a prospect of what he wanted most. It promised him, not so much a share of power, as a symbol of his importance. He wanted, not to destroy the aristocrats, but to be courted by them. 'When the aristocracy find,' said the *Morning Chronicle*, 'that their influence is dependent on the good opinion of others, instead of separating themselves from the people, and living in a world of their own, they will be obliged to display a kindliness of feeling towards the people.'[80]

The middle class might be seduced by the Bill into conservatism: they might be willing to remain subordinates. But how subordinate would the event show them to be? Having joined the establishment might they not come to control it? The risk here was small. The ministers had no wish to remove the greatest obstacles to middle-class ambition; nor were these removable by a Reform Act. In the days before joint stock acts and limited liability most business men had to give their whole attention to running their businesses. A Reform Act which gave MPs demanding constituents, and therefore more work, was not likely to send a host of industrialists to Westminster.

The merchants and manufacturers who dominated the politics of the big cities were chary of giving a seat to one of their own number. Apart from personal jealousies there would be a suspicion that such a Member might favour his own trade or interest at the expense of the others in which the city was involved. As a Liverpool speaker said in May 1831, 'there were so many conflicting interests on which a resident of the town would be so likely to have a bias that it was most essential ... that they should not have as a representative a gentleman who was altogether one of themselves'.[81] Besides, if nearly half the cabinet have been at Eton, an old Etonian may be thought the right man for dealing with them. Althorp told the Commons in December 1831 that when the Reform Act had been passed MPs 'would continue to be selected from the same classes ... but with this beneficial change, that they would then be acting under the influence of their constituents'.[82] The cabinet had good reasons for thinking that a Bill to restore the aristocracy's popularity need not give the middle class even the prospect of domination.

If the Bill were to preserve the essentials of aristocratic power it must be 'final': in the words of the instruction to the committee, it must 'afford sure ground of resistance to further innovation'. By a final measure the ministers meant one which would settle the question of the electoral system at least for their time. As Sydney Smith put it, the Bill should set Reform at rest for thirty or forty years; 'and this is an eternity in politics,' he added.[83]

It was easier to justify the wide scope of the Bill by arguing that only a large measure could be final than by an admission that the political unions would not have supported anything less. The finality argument may thus have been a little overworked. None the less, the cabinet were concerned to achieve finality. They believed that a Reform on this scale went to the limit of safety and that a further large change would be dangerously democratic. Like the rest of the governing class they held the convenient view that the perpetuation of their own power was in the interests of all.

Constitutional stability was held to be essential in producing the atmosphere of confidence on which the economic health of the country depended. The wealthy would find an uncontrolled movement towards democracy disastrously alarming. To their thinking it would entail unbalanced budgets, repudiation of the public debt, and a taxation policy of 'soaking the rich'. Despairing of their country they might even start investing their capital abroad.[84] The mere fear of a further Reform Act might be enough in itself to destroy commercial confidence, and so cause stagnation and unemployment. In 1831, as in many later agitations, there was much insistence on the danger to prosperity inherent in radical change or threats of change.

Professor D. C. Moore has lately questioned how far the Bill was, or was ever thought to be, a concession by the aristocracy.[85] A lifelong reformer such as Russell clearly saw himself, not as conceding, but as strengthening aristocratic influence. Melbourne, on the other hand, put a higher value on what was being surrendered. But this does not mean that Melbourne saw the Bill as a gratuitous concession. If inaction is believed to involve losing the whole, to promote a change which is aimed, on a low estimate, at keeping three-quarters does not imply an intention of conceding a great deal. The aristocracy may not have done as well out of the change as its authors planned. But a very small Reform, or none at all, would—or, at least, might—have involved the aristocrats in far larger losses and concessions than any which they incurred through the Reform Act. Lady Elizabeth Belgrave's comment, when the government's scheme was first published, probably indicates the predominant reaction among the whig borough owners. Lady Elizabeth was the Marquess of Stafford's younger daughter and had married the heir to the Grosvenor interest. 'This will clip the aristocracy,' she wrote to her mother, 'but a good deal must be sacrificed to save the rest.'[86]

A Bill that was to settle the question had to be accepted as fair. The cabinet's scheme contained no obviously partisan provisions. The tories were losing their rotten boroughs: adding further needless injuries would have been both unjust and impolitic. Parts of the original Bill were indeed distinctly high-minded. The House was to be reduced in numbers because the addition of a hundred Members through the Union with Ireland was held to have made it inconveniently large for debate.

Some of the high-mindedness disappeared during the tactical shifts of the parliamentary struggle. Over one point, however, the cabinet strove to be fair at every stage. They were anxious not to disturb the existing balance between the landlord and the manufacturing interests. The seats available from the abolition of the rotten boroughs went, as Table 3 (pp. 138–9) shows, partly to the manufacturing towns of the midlands and north of England, and partly to the counties. The Bill was designed to abolish the government interest which had long been shrinking. Otherwise the intention was to leave the great interests as they were.

This account suggests that the cabinet's views on the Bill differed widely from those of most reformers in the country. The difference was not essentially a matter of how many votes to create. Some reformers would certainly have gone farther than the cabinet. But the divergence here can be over-emphasized, since there were doubts even among the radicals about going below household suffrage in the existing state of education. The difference concerned, not the content of the Reform Bill, but the aim behind it. The cabinet meant to keep the existing governmental system as far as possible: the reformers wanted a new system. The cabinet wanted Reform in order to make the measures of the previous decade more acceptable: the reformers wanted it in order to sweep those measures away. Politically Grey was as far from Attwood as from Wellington. He differed openly from the duke about method. Between him and Attwood there was a latent difference of aim. Unlike Wellington he knew that Reform need not change the basis of the system. Unlike Attwood he knew that, if the basis stayed unchanged, nothing much else would change.

The scope of the Bill astounded contemporaries.[87] Compared to the 1830 proposals for giving two Members each to Manchester, Birmingham and Leeds, this was a very sweeping measure. It seems to have been assumed among the opposition that Brougham's plan of November 1830 represented the most far-reaching solution which the cabinet were likely to consider. This plan had been comparatively bold in creating borough voters, but very limited in abolishing boroughs.[88]

The opposition assumption was a notable piece of wishful thinking. In the first place it rested on the belief, for which there was no reliable evidence, that Brougham was the strongest reformer in the cabinet. He was, in fact, the only cabinet minister who tried to save some rotten boroughs. He argued that Schedules A and B would leave no seat for 'a clever young lawyer'. ('However, like a clever old lawyer, now that the measure is resolved upon,' Hobhouse noted, 'he takes care to have it given out he originated it.') Secondly, there was a crucial difference of type between the schemes which Brougham had propounded in opposition and the cabinet's plan. The former were designed essentially to catch votes and therefore involved sparing all but the most rotten boroughs. The cabinet, by contrast, were devising a governmental system with the expectation that their proposals would go into effect. Their scheme would be worse than useless unless it were large enough to endure.[89]

The opposition thought Grey a far more moderate reformer than he was. They did not realize that he had remained reticent on Reform during most of 1830, not from lack of zeal, but to avoid offending the ultra tories or provoking the kind of panic and repression which he had seen in the 1790s and in 1819. Between 2 November and the fall of the Wellington government he warned Graham that the plan of taking one seat from each of the rotten boroughs was no longer sufficient. He later told the Lords that his first few months in office had expanded his plans still further.[90] There is every reason to believe this. Several incidents during these months reinforced the case for Reform, as it was understood, not merely by the cabinet, but by any member of the governing class who was not a diehard defender of the existing system. The government had only just been installed when polling opened in the Liverpool by-election caused by Huskisson's death. This struggle highlighted the defects of a large freeman constituency. It cost over £100,000 to poll 4400 voters. The bribery was shameless. Three pilots who arrived from sea on the last day were said to have received £150 each for their votes. John Gladstone, who had been Canning's chairman when the latter sat for Liverpool, wrote in the following March that the winning candidate had paid £82,450, with some bills still unsettled. 'Insanity indeed,' he commented. 'What can call more loudly for Reform?'[91]

The advent of a reforming government raised expectations. The duke's declaration and its sequel had given the existing political unions new life, and had led to the formation of new ones in Liverpool and Manchester. The new railway between those two places ran past the tiny borough of Newton. Thousands of Mancunians now saw a place little larger than a village which returned two Members, while Manchester had none.[92] As the agitation grew, the chance of stilling it with a small concession diminished. There were fresh signs in December of revolt against the borough system, and indeed against the whole aristocracy. A by-election demonstration was mounted against the Duke of Devonshire's nominee for Knaresborough.[93] The duke announced that he would never interfere at Knaresborough again. Stanley was defeated at Preston by the radical, Henry Hunt, when he sought re-election on gaining office, despite his family's great influence in the borough.

France [Doherty's *Voice of the People* commented][94] has hurled despotism to the dust ... Belgium is free; and Poland—long oppressed and plundered Poland—has asserted her independence. Even Ireland is emancipated. And shall England sit still under the blighting domination of her boroughmongers? ... The intelligence and the spirit of the age forbid it.... 'The unwashed mechanics' of Preston have struck the first blow at.... usurped power and unconstitutional influence, in choosing as their representative the consistent and intrepid advocate of popular rights in the room of a scion of nobility....

Tell us not that the people have no power but in the field—no authority but with the pike or the pistol. Tell us not that they must wait to be led on to the conflict for freedom by the wealthy and the influential. The Catholics of Ireland have taught us how to control and to command governments without battle and without blood. . . . The gallant artisans of Paris have shown us the way to victory without the aid of the proud and pampered . . . aristocrat.

If the aristocrats were to regain their popularity something more than a half measure would be needed.

The cabinet knew by January that they must outbid Peel to succeed. To produce a mild Bill which he could modify and adopt as his own would play into his hands. The only way to check-mate him was to produce one sweeping enough to enlist strong support in the country. Then he ought to recognize that even if he defeated the measure and drove the government out he would be too unpopular to take their place. It was a mistake to infer from the ministry's early failures that they would be as ineffective on Reform as on everything else. The cabinet were acquiring the boldness of desperation. A sweeping Reform was their last chance of popularity at a stroke.

Although the expectations of a moderate Bill were foolish, it would have taken a very wise man to predict a scheme as sweeping as the one published on 1 March. Historians have been nearly as puzzled by its boldness as were contemporaries. It has been suggested that the cabinet were swept along by the committee of four. There is not much in this theory. The committee were certainly more whole-hearted in their support for Reform than were most of their colleagues. But they did not work in isolation. Grey and Althorp were in touch with all their discussions;[95] and Althorp's ideas were as sweeping as any initiated from Cleveland Row. He told Russell at an early stage that disfranchising 100 seats represented his minimum.[96] Moreover, the committee were scarcely capable of dragging the cabinet along. Where the most powerful ministers disliked anything in the committee scheme they had no difficulty in securing an alteration. Finally, when all allowance has been made for ballot and quinquennial parliaments, it may be questioned whether the committee's scheme would have proved more sweeping than the Bill as first published. The dislike of small boroughs which Grey, Brougham and Melbourne shared may well have been as radical in effect as any proposal which emerged from the committee.

The cabinet believed that a sweeping measure would give them the best chance of staying in power. As partisans they would have had an equally powerful motive for boldness when they looked farther ahead. The more drastic they made their Bill the more tory boroughs it was likely to destroy. But to attribute its scope to motives of party advantage would be a distortion. The underlings may well have thought in this way. Grey and Althorp did not. Their dislike of office was genuine. The mistake underlying the theory that such men were driven on by hope of party advantage has been mentioned already. The suggestion is mistaken, not because it makes them out as more selfish than they were (though it may incidentally do so), but because it misrepresents how they saw their own dominant interests. They wanted, not so much office and official salaries, as social peace and security for property. 'I always thought,' Russell told Melbourne after the 1837 election, 'that the whig party, as a party, would be destroyed by the Reform Bill.'[97] It is unlikely that Russell had foreseen quite as much as he claimed, but equally unlikely that he had expected great gains for the whig party from the Bill.

The most important explanation of the cabinet's boldness is the simplest. They brought in a sweeping Bill because the events of 1830 had told them that it was now an urgent task to sweep away the electoral system. The opposition leaders were astonished because they knew little and understood nothing about the impact of these events on their opponents. The cabinet were not acting in the face of obviously overwhelming pressure. Indeed the overt demand for Reform had comparatively little to do with their determination to make an end of the rotten boroughs. They were responding to signs of trouble which looked ominous to a whig. Politicians whose views and experiences were anything but whiggish might miss the signs or read them differently. The county elections which had so shocked the whig leaders made a smaller and a very different impression on Wellington and his colleagues. The fact that he had neither fought a contested election, nor sat for a county, blunted even Peel's perceptiveness.

Grey and his colleagues were convinced that any attempt to retain the system as it stood would provoke an explosion. The risks of refusing a substantial reconstruction seemed to them greater, and far more immediate, than those of conceding it. They saw no reason to wait in the hope that the demand for reform would die down, and a moderate measure become more acceptable. They realized that the demand originated in a social change, and that the longer it was baulked the more dangerous it would grow. A country which had been subject to a rapid growth in political information and awareness required some alteration in its political arrangements. 'A great change has taken place,' Grey told the Knight of Kerry,

in all parts of Europe since the end of the war in the distribution of property, and unless a corresponding change be made in the legal mode by which that property can act upon the governments, revolutions must necessarily follow. This change requires a greater influence to be yielded to the middle classes, who have made wonderful advances both in property and intelligence.[98]

In the face of a popular movement in which the middle classes were prominent the two front benches reacted in opposite ways. The whigs tended to assume that it was genuine. Wellington and his colleagues looked always for signs that it was being manipulated and for ways in which it might be repressed. Wellington regarded a surrender to agitation as a disaster. To the whigs the disaster lay in delaying until surrender or repression had become the only possibilities.[99] In their view Catholic emancipation would have done far more good if it had been conceded earlier. They meant to prevent a similar delay over Reform. The ex-cabinet had been in charge of the system for a long time and they valued it highly enough to defend it against strong attack. The whigs had been many years in opposition. They understood little about operating the system and thought it worthless. They did not know much about their ship: they had not been on the bridge until recently. Their inexperienced efforts to steer her were not turning out well. They were naturally far more ready than the last crew to acknowledge that she had sprung a leak and was going to sink.

The cabinet thus had several good reasons for introducing a sweeping Bill. It would probably have been less sweeping, however, but for a miscalculation. Grey suffered from one illusion almost as serious as those of the opposition; and it helps to explain the scope of his Reform. He believed that there would be majorities in both Houses for a drastic solution. He thus expected the Bill to be passed in a matter of weeks. He might never have sponsored it had he foreseen that its passage would entail fifteen months of intense agitation, which would include both an election on democratic lines and threats to swamp the House of Lords. He knew that its provisions were anything but democratic: indeed he called it, soon after its introduction, 'the most aristocratic measure that ever was proposed in Parliament'.[100] He did not know that putting it on the statute book would entail the use of democratic means. A Bill which was to give great numbers of people their first taste of insurgent politics could not be altogether aristocratic in tendency, however canny the drafting.[101] This miscalculation was so important that it must be examined in some detail.

Grey assured the king repeatedly that there were parliamentary majorities for the Bill. 'If what we shall have to propose shall obtain His Majesty's sanction,' he told Taylor, the king's secretary, on 13 January, 'I should have little fear of carrying it through Parliament.' 'There were indications in some quarters,' he reported on 4 February, 'of a strong opposition to the question of Reform, but . . . if we are not greatly deceived in our estimate of numbers in the House of Commons, the result is not much to be feared.' 'With the assurance of your Majesty's support,' he wrote four days later, 'Earl Grey is very sanguine in his hopes of being able to carry this important measure successfully through Parliament.'[102]

It looks at first glance as if Grey was deliberately deceiving the king. At the very time at which he was assuring William of his majority, and so discounting the need for a dissolution, his entourage were speculating on the chances of defeat in the Commons on the basis that a defeat would mean an election.[103] Charles Wood, the Prime Minister's son-in-law and secretary, went beyond speculation. At the end of January he told Creevey that, provided the king's support were assured, 'Grey is determined to fight it out to a dissolution of Parliament if his plan is beat in the Commons'.[104] Furthermore, Grey asked Anglesey on the day on which the Bill was disclosed to the Commons: 'If we are beaten could you face a dissolution under the present circumstances in Ireland?'[105]

In the light of this evidence Grey's assurances to the king might be explained by his fear that if he did not give them William IV would refuse leave to introduce the Bill. William was violently averse to a dissolution, as his ministers knew, largely because of the convulsions which it might bring in Ireland. He also hated any proposal which was clearly foredoomed in the Lords: hence his objection to secret ballot. Holding these views, he was politically too inexperienced to question most of what Grey told him. Grey thus had a strong motive for reassuring the king and in the royal closet he probably made himself sound more confident than he felt. Yet the theory that he was deliberately deceiving the king is impossible to accept. He was deceived far more than deceiving. The day before he wrote to Anglesey he told Princess Lieven that the government's calculations 'give us a majority of about 70'. He prudently qualified this by adding that, where a Bill such as this was concerned, no calculations were 'much to be relied on'. Even when qualified the prediction was remarkable, since both sides of the House, according to Croker, were then giving the opposition an anti-Reform majority of about sixty.[106]

Grey was not a rogue; and apart from this it would have been short-sighted to deceive the king deliberately on so crucial a point. He was not lying when he told the king in January 1832 that 'if he could have foreseen, or contemplated, the persevering and irreconcilable opposition which is given to the Bill in the House of Lords . . . he would have humbly declined the trust with which your Majesty was pleased to honour him'.[107] It is not even certain that the king would have refused to face the prospect of a dissolution had it been put squarely before him at the first stage. The factor which made him agree to dissolve in April was present in February also. If Grey were refused a dissolution and resigned, no other government could be formed.

The decisive evidence about Grey's attitude lies not in any assurances which he gave the king, however, but in his failure at this stage to prepare either for a dissolution or for increasing the reformers' strength in the Lords. When on 19 March he realized at last that the Commons might reject the Bill on second reading his reaction was near to panic. The truth is probably that he relied on the fear of a dissolution to prevent the need for one. The hints from his entourage that he was ready to dissolve prove no more than that he wanted people to believe in this readiness. Provided that enough MPs believed in it, enough of them would vote for the Bill to remove the need for a dissolution, and thus the need to prepare the king for one. As February wore on Grey's confidence ebbed a little, but not enough for him to sound out the king. He failed to see that in the long term MPs would not believe government talk about a dissolution without firm evidence that the king had agreed to dissolve. It is thus true to say that Grey agreed to a sweeping Reform Bill without realizing the cost. It was unrealistic to suppose that such a Bill could be passed so quickly that no impulse would be given to democratic change.[108]

Grey's overestimate of his parliamentary strength is not hard to explain. He suffered almost as badly as Wellington from prime ministerial isolation. He had neither time nor energy to attend the Commons debates.[109] He and his cabinet colleagues made it a rule not to frequent Brooks's Club, where they feared that they might be led into indiscretion.[110] 'Lord Grey had not a bad temper,' Melbourne told Queen Victoria, 'but [he] flew into a passion when you first told him anything.'[111] It would have been bitter for Grey to recognize that he could not ensure the safety of the aristocracy whatever kind of Bill he introduced, because a measure large enough to be final could be carried only by a vast agitation. He would not have liked to be told that certain tories encouraged him to expect their support for his Bill only because they were satisfied it would be moderate and therefore ineffective.

The cabinet's insistence that the contents of their measure should be kept a complete secret made it hard to assess promises of support realistically. Some of those giving the promises were reformers in a mild sense only. They favoured a moderate measure which should abolish a few boroughs while leaving intact those for which they sat. They were so convinced that the government's Bill would be moderate that the hopes they expressed of being able to support it were mostly worthless. The House certainly contained a substantial Reform majority, in the sense that most MPs wanted some kind of Reform; but this was not good evidence that there would a majority for the cabinet's sweeping Bill. An enormous misunderstanding arose. The more that various tories expressed confidence in the new government from a belief that Grey's Bill would be moderate the more they convinced Grey that it need not be moderate at all, and that he could command a majority for something sweeping.

The new objective of checkmating Peel had overlaid the old one of producing a Bill acceptable to the moderates. The cabinet failed to see that no Bill could be devised to make these two objectives compatible with each other. They probably relied too heavily on tory conversions to Reform. E. J. Littleton advised 'that, by an extensive enfranchisement of new places and by a division of counties, the tory proprietors might be won over, through a disclosure of so many new views of personal interest'.[112]

This was sound advice. But it can easily have given Grey an over-optimistic impression of how many opponents he could hope to convert. Littleton did not know that a Bill was being prepared which was liable to stun or enrage tory proprietors until they became incapable of fine calculations about 'personal interest'. It is also likely that the cabinet exaggerated the importance of ballot.[113] Some ministers may have thought that they could count on the support of the moderates

in both Houses provided that they excluded the ballot proposal from
the Bill.

The government whips had even less experience of office than the
cabinet. Moreover it is not certain that Ellice, the chief whip, told
Grey all he knew. Ellice had radical inclinations. His attitude was thus
somewhat different from that of Grey and the cabinet mandarins.
Unlike them he did not object to an election and a creation of peers.
If the cabinet and the king learned before 1 March what they would
have to do to collect the necessary majorities for the Bill they might
drop it altogether. After that date it could not be dropped. After
offering half a million people votes the ministry would not be able to
withdraw the offer.[114] Ellice who knew a great deal about the popular
Reform movement must have realized this. He thus had a strong motive
for preventing the ministers and the king from learning until 1 March
how slim the Bill's parliamentary chances were. There seems to be no
direct evidence that he concealed information from Grey. But it is a
reasonable inference that he was tempted to do so and that he laid no
great stress on the gloomier parliamentary forecasts.

Some of the keener and better informed reformers in the cabinet
may have been in much the same position. They may have known
that the moderates in the Commons were not the only people who
regarded the cabinet as timid and ineffective: a great many reformers
outside Parliament also held this view. A measure which shocked the
parliamentary moderates into opposition might well shock radical
reformers throughout the country into support. These ministers
wanted a sweeping measure proposed. If they guessed that their
chances of a Commons majority were poor, they would have kept
this pessimistic forecast, and all that it entailed, to themselves. They
would not have forced their more timid colleagues to see that the
cabinet was committing itself both to dissolving Parliament and to
coercing the peers. They would have concluded that splitting the
cabinet by airing disagreeable hypotheses was no part of their duty,
and that this political Rubicon was best crossed in fog.

Grey's illusions were not confined to a miscalculation about the
parliamentary support for his Bill. His whole notion that it might be
passed without any popular upheaval was unrealistic. If it had become
law in the summer of 1831 there would have been great pressure for
household suffrage, triennial parliaments, and secret ballot. Inevitably
the radicals would have concluded that the second stage of their programme need be no harder to achieve than the first. During fifteen

months of agitation the demand for the Bill gathered strength: so did
the reaction against further change. In 1831, as at other times, there
was no way of enacting the great Reform without arousing in-
ordinate hopes.

Another drawback about preparing the Bill in complete secrecy was
that very few people could be consulted about the propositions and
information on which it was based. Neither Durham's committee nor
the cabinet foresaw all the pitfalls involved in deciding which places
were to lose or gain members. No one among those privy to the Bill's
contents had a grasp of the particularly intractable problem presented
by the disfranchisement schedules. These schedules were based on the
proposition that the chance of freeing a borough from nomination
depended essentially on its size. Any borough too small to be freed by
an infusion of ten pounders would be disfranchised. This theory proved
defective: in some boroughs independence was not as closely related
to size as the authors of the Bill had supposed. Moreover invoking the
theory increased the difficulty of defending the single Member arrangements in Schedule B.[115] If a borough could be freed it should keep
both members. If it could not be freed it should lose both.

Few disputed, however, that disfranchisement must depend largely
on size. The real difficulty lay in measuring this. The criterion of size
adopted by the committee was the only reliable one then to hand,
namely, the population figures in the 1821 census. The cabinet maintained when the question was debated that, out of date as this census
was, it had been supplemented by their own enquiries and answered
their requirements. They refused to delay until the 1831 figures were
ready. The latter had been collected after the publication of the Bill
had given officials in the boroughs marked for disfranchisement a
strong inducement to falsify the returns.

It was far from obvious what should be the area under judgement
when the population of a borough was assessed. When the Bill was in
preparation the cabinet had barely recognized this difficulty, far less
solved it.[116] Schedules A and B were drawn up on the assumptions that
the area ought to be that of the borough, and that the 1821 returns
showed the population then living within the borough area. Neither
assumption was justified. As to the first, many borough boundaries
were outdated and artificial. Some had been curtailed by partisan
decisions of the House of Commons. It would have been unfair to
use these boundaries everywhere as the criterion which decided whether

a borough kept its MPs. It would also have been impracticable. 'Where the right of voting is that of burgage tenure,' Thomas Drummond wrote some months later in his Boundary Commission instructions, 'it not infrequently happens that . . . the boundary of the borough is either entirely lost, or so little known that its position cannot be assigned with any degree of certainty.'[117]

Secondly, the census figures often did not show the population within the borough area. The assumption that they did rested on a misunderstanding about the 1821 returns. These commonly gave a population figure for 'borough and parish'. In some cases this was the figure for the whole of the parish in which the borough lay. In many, by contrast, it referred merely to that part of the parish which comprised the borough; and in a few it was confined to the part of a particular parish in which part of the borough lay. Calne could be regarded as in the first class. The 'borough and parish' population of 4549 came within a hundred of the figure given in a footnote as the one for the 'entire parish'.[118] Leominster came in the second. The population of the 'borough and parish' was stated to be 3651, a footnote giving that of the 'entire parish' as 4646. Malmesbury was in the third class. The borough lay in parts of three parishes. The 'borough and parish' return referred solely to the sector of the borough in the parish of Malmesbury, which was one of the three.

By following the 'borough and parish' figures the ministers therefore made such mistakes as to put Leominster into Schedule B, while regarding Calne as a borough of more than 4000 inhabitants and so leaving it with both its Members. If they had studied the footnotes to the 1821 returns, in conjunction with the supplementary information which they had elicited from Returning Officers, they would have been warned against the inconsistencies in the 'borough and parish' entries. Thus the Returning Officer of Calne told them that he could not estimate what the population of the borough had been in 1821, but that it was about 2000 at present.[119] He added that the borough covered only 885 of the 8000 odd acres in the parish. This should have made clear that, while there could be doubt about how to classify Leominster and Calne, there could be none about the need to put both boroughs in the same category. These remarks would almost certainly have to be published, along with all the other statements from Returning Officers. Lansdowne, who controlled[120] Calne, was also Lord President of the Council, so that a decision which seemed to favour that borough could hardly remain uncriticized.

A mistake such as this in the schedules was at least comparatively simple to correct. Other difficulties were deeper-seated. The device of extending borough boundaries to make up the number of voters did not originate with the Durham committee and it combined awkwardly with the committee's ideas on disfranchisement. The test of population which determined whether a borough escaped the disfranchising schedules bore no direct relation to the number of electors obtainable within either the existing borough boundaries or extended boundaries. It was thus possible for one borough to be brought into the schedules although its prospective electorate was larger than that of another which escaped. A few nights of debate would show that this possibility was not merely theoretical. Moreover, the opposition, and some doubtful reformers, would find great attractions in enlarging boroughs to include rural areas. It would occur to them that, if such enlargements were to be taken a step or two farther, the need for Schedules A and B would be entirely removed.[121]

The cabinet were right to keep the Bill secret despite the disadvantages of doing so. If the opposition had known its provisions in advance they might have managed to strangle it at birth. As the procedure for a Bill then stood, the House had first to give leave for it to be introduced. Its opponents could divide against it at this stage though this was unusual. The opposition leaders met at Peel's on 20 February and decided not to oppose introduction. They would reserve their strength for the second reading division. Lowther's letter to his father on the previous day gives the argument for these tactics. 'Many would vote for the introduction of the Bill,' he wrote, 'to clear their consciences towards their constituents, that will disapprove and be opposed to all the details.'[122]

Lord Granville Somerset was particularly hostile to an early division.[123] He sat for an English county and therefore had to respect his constituents' views. But the decision was more or less unanimous. Wellington appears to have agreed with it;[124] and Peel must be presumed to have done so too. In his new role as a moderate he could not have agreed in advance to oppose the first stage. It is likely that on 20 February he did not even pledge his own vote against the second reading. He said afterwards in debate that he had made his mind to 'assent to' a moderate bill.[125] This does not prove that his views coincided with Granville Somerset's. He may possibly have wanted freedom to decide about a division when he had heard Russell's speech. The

evidence suggests, however, not that it was his policy to keep the
decision open, but that like everyone else he afterwards wished it had
been.

The secret was well kept. Documents were copied by Durham's
wife and eldest daughter. Drafting was not complete by 1 March. It
was in the hands of two lawyers of impeccable whiggery, the auditors
of leading whig noblemen.[126] The discretion of this pair was exceeded
only by their incompetence as parliamentary draftsmen. There was a
last-minute leakage; but it did no harm. 'Almost at the last hour,' Le
Marchant records, 'Lord Lowther contrived to learn some of the
particulars of the plan, but they appeared so improbable that no one
believed him when he mentioned them.'[127]

The opposition may be forgiven for disbelieving Lowther, for the
handful of ministerialists who were given an inkling of the plan were
almost as sceptical. Brougham asked one of his brothers who was a
radical MP: 'What should you say if we intended to disfranchise half
the rotten boroughs, or to leave them only one Member each?' 'Oh,
that is quite romantic,' James Brougham replied, 'you will never be
able to do that.' When first told what was in the Bill, Stanley 'burst
into an incredulous laugh', while Burdett and Hobhouse, the radical
MPs for Westminster, 'greatly doubted', according to Brougham's
account, 'if we did not go too far'.[128]

To clear the way for the Bill the Commons met on Saturday, 26
February, the sitting being entirely devoted to receiving Reform
petitions. Althorp presented 'about a hundred', including a group from
Manchester carrying in all 12,000 signatures, and one from Bristol
with about the same number. The Leeds petition contained 17,000
names, Edinburgh's nearly 22,000.[129] On 1 March nearly every seat
in the House was reserved by midday. A large crowd collected in
Palace Yard during the afternoon. At six o'clock Russell, looking
'very pale and subdued',[130] rose to introduce the Bill.

5

THE BILL IN THE COMMONS (I):
A DREADFUL RACE

Le vin est tiré—il faut le boire. (quoted by Holland to Grey,
21 April 1831)

Russell was small in voice and physique, and no natural orator. He
began with a historical and constitutional argument, and stayed long
enough in the middle ages to 'call forth,' in Le Marchant's words, 'a
slight degree of languor and impatience' from his audience. After this
the announcement of Schedule A 'came with an absolutely electrifying
shock'. When 'Lord John . . . read the long list of boroughs to be
either wholly or partially disfranchised,' J. C. Hobhouse wrote,

there was a sort of wild ironical laughter, mixed with expressions of delight
from the ex-ministers, who seemed to think themselves sure of recovering
their places again immediately. Our own friends were not so well pleased.
Baring Wall, turning to me, said, 'They are mad! They are mad!' and others
made use of similar exclamations. . . . Lord John seemed rather to play with the
fears of his audience; and, after detailing some clauses which seemed to complete
the scheme, smiled and paused, and said, 'More yet'. This 'more', so well as
I recollect, was Schedule B.

The reformers watched Peel. They thought that if he rose at the
end of Russell's speech and moved to refuse leave to introduce the
Bill he might be able to divide the House that night and secure a
substantial majority. If he waited this majority would melt away: for
once the plan became generally known it should arouse such popular
support that the doubtfuls would not dare to vote against it. To kill
the Bill Peel would have to act at once.

Peel was too wise to join in the jeers. He realized that the Bill had
destroyed his hopes of leading a government of the centre. It would
confine the tories to the wilderness, and him to the tories. He was
appalled and showed it. According to Althorp 'he turned black in the
face'.[1] 'As the plan was unfolded,' Le Marchant wrote, Peel 'looked

F

more and more cast down, and at last he held his hands before his face as if unable to control his emotions.' He made no move to follow Russell or the seconder. Sir Robert Inglis, the ultra-tory MP for Oxford University, embarked on a learned oration and the House streamed into the lobby. The chance had gone.

Peel's mistake did not affect events as decisively as the opposition afterwards made out. They were determined to maintain that the irresistible Reform movement did not begin until half a million men had been offered votes. Though an attempt to divide the House at once would have been sound tactics it might well have failed. The ministers would have done everything possible to keep the debate going. It is questionable therefore whether Peel had much of a chance on 1 March to stop the Bill.[2] He certainly had no chance to stop a sweeping Reform.

Peel was a ready and experienced parliamentarian, adept at seizing any tactical opportunity however small. It is not certain why on this one occasion he missed his moment. The tories knew that he had been trying to cut loose from them and distrusted him accordingly. He may have thought them too distrustful, and too disunited, to follow him if he made a sudden assault. Some of the arguments against immediate rejection which had carried the day on 20 February still applied even after Russell's speech.[3] More probably Peel did nothing simply because he was shaken by the Bill. It must have been a bitter and disabling shock for him when he realized that the cabinet had forced him back into the arms of the tory diehards.

Bulletins were scribbled to the peers in the cabinet to tell them how the Bill was being received. Le Marchant sent regular notes to Brougham who had Melbourne and Richmond dining with him. One note announced that Russell was nearing the end of his speech. When the next arrived Brougham held it unopened, and asked the company to take a glass of wine, 'that we may with proper nerve read the fatal missive'. Then, reading that the debate was still going on, he flourished the note round his head, and shouted ' "Victory! " ' . . . , and so we took another glass to congratulate ourselves upon our good fortune'.[4]

It soon became clear, however, that victory was some way off. The cabinet had expected a majority for their Bill if only it could be fairly launched.[5] The first three nights of the debate did not leave this expectation intact. 'We all huddled away [on the first night],' wrote J. C. Hobhouse, ' . . . the anti-reformers chuckling with delight at what they supposed was a suicidal project, and the friends of ministers in a sort of wonderment.' Le Marchant 'spoke to several staunch reformers and found them wavering. They were like men taking breath immediately after an explosion'. There is some conflict of evidence about Russell's reception at the end of his speech. If he was cheered at all it was only by the radicals.[6]

A whig banker, the patron of Midhurst, which was in Schedule A, said that Russell's speech 'made his hair stand on end'. 'It's true,' he told Howick, 'I lose my borough; but I had no notion you would have been so honest and wise at the same time.'[7] Hudson Gurney, who was also reckoned a ministerialist of sorts and whose seat was to be abolished, told Le Marchant: 'I consider it an honour to the age for any administration to have proposed this Bill, not that there is a chance of these men carrying it. Only Oliver Cromwell could do that.' Detonating enough explosive to shatter both sets of front-line trenches was doubtless magnificent. But was it politics?

On the second night Wetherell, the ultra tory, made a 'long, rambling, and amusing' speech against the Bill. 'He sat down,' in Greville's words, 'with such loud and long cheering as everybody agreed they had never heard before in the House of Commons, and which was taken not so much as a test of the merits of the speech as of an indication of the disposition of the majority of the House.'

'Everybody enquires,' Greville had written the day before, 'what line Peel will take, and though each party is confident of success . . . , it is thought to depend mainly upon the course he adopts and the sentiments he expresses.' On the third night Peel attacked the Bill strongly and pledged his vote against the second reading. He may have been influenced by bitterness against the men who had ruined his hopes, or by the ever present fear that moderation on his part would bring fresh charges of betrayal. But it is unlikely that such considerations determined his course. Almost all his political life had been spent in helping to operate the old governmental system. He thought it a good instrument of government for Britain, indeed the only one which could be made to work. He was outraged by what he regarded as an irresponsible decision to destroy it.

Alexander Baring also spoke against the Bill on the third night. He was something of a whig and the anti-reformers had not counted on him. The night did not produce any effective government statement to lessen the effect of these two speeches. 'Palmerston spoke ill and feebly,' Ellenborough noted, 'the House not attending to him.' Lansdowne heard this third night's debate. Like Grey he had believed the Commons to contain a majority for the Bill. He now knew better. The next day he wrote to tell Grey of his

decided conviction ... that the Bill will not pass, except under a degree of apprehension excited from without which one can hardly wish to see.... I think, therefore [Lansdowne continued], no time should be lost in considering how this state of things is to be met. It will be a very nice question for you to determine ... what interval of delay should be allowed before the next stage.[8]

Grey answered that he personally felt committed to the Bill 'without the possibility of retreat', but that if Lansdowne had doubts about proceeding with it they should be raised in cabinet.

Lansdowne had recognized the stark truth three days too late. The only chance of the Bill passing in that House of Commons lay in the effect on MPs of an overwhelming popular demand for it. His aristocratic colleagues were as alarmed as he was at the prospect of forcing it through by such means. But they found the alternative of postponing it or whittling it away more alarming still. Even if they had been wrong to introduce such a sweeping Bill they could not abandon it now. Nor could they allow it to be defeated. If it sank their political reputations would go with it; and it would be succeeded by a far more revolutionary measure of Reform. It was deplorable to succeed by agitation. But there was no other means of success and it would be fatal to fail. The degree of external pressure which would be needed in the next few weeks to collect a majority was disquieting. But if there were no majority there would have to be an election, and this implied a still higher degree of external pressure.

Brougham at least lost no time in arousing the country. He told Le Marchant the outline of the plan directly Russell rose. A report was handed to the editor of the *Courier* who was in waiting. It was printed at once and sent off to the provinces by express. The Bill was rapturously received in the large towns. On 5 March the *Manchester Guardian* reported: 'All parties seem pleased with it to a degree we could hardly have conceived possible.' The meeting of the Birmingham Union on 7 March, which was attended by about 15,000 people, expressed its gratitude to the king and his ministers and petitioned for their measure.

In London the success of the popular campaign was more doubtful for a day or two. The Lord Mayor, who was a whig, held a Common Council on 4 March at Brougham's request. Though this 'passed some flaming resolutions' it was 'very thinly attended'.[9] The Westminster reformers met the same day at the Crown and Anchor Tavern in the Strand. Their reaction to the Bill provided the test case of its general acceptability. They were fervent advocates of secret ballot. Moreover the condition about residence would deprive a good many of them of their votes. On the other hand, even apart from the preservation of the resident 'ancient right' voters, the £10 level gave something very near household suffrage in Westminster. In the event the constituency of 16,000 was reduced on balance by about a quarter.

The moving spirit for this, as for many other Westminster meetings, was Francis Place, the radical master tailor. Place possessed the organizing skill of a successful shopkeeper and much experience in appealing to the London craftsmen.[10] Before the meeting he secured the support of the organizing committee for resolutions in favour of triennial parliaments and ballot. As soon as proceedings began, however, J. C. Hobhouse jumped on to the table and urged that no resolution should be put except that of confidence in the ministry. His suggestion was approved unanimously.[11]

For the moment the scale of the Bill and, above all, the disfranchisement schedules swept away all doubts. Brougham, who had wanted to cut these down, admitted at the end of his life: 'It was Schedule A that finally carried the Bill.' R. S. Rintoul, the radical editor of the *Spectator,* found the slogan to fit the mood of these weeks: 'the Bill, the whole Bill, and nothing but the Bill.'[12] Most supporters of the ballot consoled themselves with the thought that it would not take a reformed Parliament long to adopt their proposal.[13] Joseph Hume commended the cabinet for refusing to encumber their Bill with ballot. In the first week after Russell's speech Henry Hunt said that, 'as far as the present measure went, it had his support'. Richard Carlile praised the Bill in the *Prompter;* and William Cobbett did the same in his influential *Political Register.*[14] Carlile wrote from the gaol to which the whigs had consigned him for his supposed part in the labourers' revolt. Cobbett was awaiting trial on similar charges; and he had said in the *Register* the week before that he would not support any measure which excluded ballot. The reaction of another leader whom the government were prosecuting was still more important. On 8 March O'Connell announced that, although he had some objections to the Bill, he would give it 'his most decided support'.[15] This represented a crucial accession of strength to the ministers, not only in Ireland but in the House of Commons as well.

The opposition could make no headway with the public. It was impossible to whip up tory party spirit against a whig measure. In the constituencies many tories were as eager for the Bill as were the whigs. Opposition spokesmen tried to make play with the disfranchisement of existing voters and the preponderance which the Bill was thought to give to the middle class. But they did not have much success.[16] There were very few places where a great many people were disfranchised. Fewer than 80,000 are thought to have lost their votes when the Bill became law.[17] But some of these would have gained a vote elsewhere in compensation. A number of the dispossessed out-voters at Bridgnorth, for instance, lived in Birmingham and must have qualified as ten pounders there. Disfranchisement apart, those who tried to work up popular feeling against the Bill had an impossible job. Any argument which came from an owner or defender of rotten boroughs was suspect; nor could the old system be made to look respectable. The man in the street would not believe that the proper functioning of government depended on the survival of grossly corrupt anomalies. 'Can the people ever be taught,' Sydney Smith asked, 'that it is right they should be bought and sold?'[18]

The success of the Bill with middle-class people was complete from the start. It promised them what they wanted, to have their place in the political system and yet to be protected from wild radical schemes. On the other hand it would be easy to exaggerate the volume of working-class support either at this stage or later. Neither this Reform nor any other could altogether heal the deepest split among reformers. The workers were in a dilemma. The Bill aroused a debate among them which lasted for the whole fifteen months of its passage.[19] Its supporters argued that this was the most sweeping measure which any government could carry. It would end the old system and lead to household suffrage. 'If the precedent be once set of altering the constitution,' wrote William Carpenter from the King's Bench prison in October 1831, 'the same arguments urged in favour of the first change will be irresistible when urged in favour of subsequent changes.'[20] By standing aside, Carpenter argued, and allowing the Bill to be defeated, the workers would gain nothing. The result of those tactics would be a repressive tory government, 'and all the ... edifying scenes of 1793 and 1819 enacted over again'. A defeat of that kind for the Bill might indeed lead to revolution and civil war, with 'the calamity ... augmented by the working classes and the middle classes being arrayed against each other'. The reply was that the Bill brought no benefit to the working class who had no interest in helping middle-class people to gain votes. Indeed, if working men helped to turn the Bill into law they would be adding to the strength and numbers of their oppressors.

It is hard to comment on this debate without showing traces either of what Dr E. P. Thompson has called 'the enormous condescension of posterity', or of the sentimental fallacy that intolerable conditions produce moral grandeur. Not all of the arguments used on either side stated the workers' insoluble problem in realistic terms. Thus the pro-Bill men argued that once the middle class had the vote they would in gratitude enfranchise the workers, to whose efforts they owed their own triumph. This was naïve. But expectations no less absurd circulated among the governing class. Althorp hoped, for instance, that in the reformed House governments would be able to dispense with whips.[21]

It is even harder to judge which side commanded the greater support among politically alert working-class people. The balance changed with each incident in the history of the Bill. Few working-class leaders took the same line throughout the crisis. At crucial points many of their followers must have been divided in mind. The high peaks for working-class support came at the beginning and the end—in March 1831 and May 1832.

At most times the pro-Bill men seem to have been in the majority. The principal working-class organization in London during the first phase of the struggle began in March 1831 as the Metropolitan Trades' Union, and was reconstituted in May as the 'National Union of the Working Classes and Others'.[22] It met weekly at the Blackfriars Rotunda. Here the doctrines of Thomas Paine were mixed with those of Robert Owen and with the 'primitive socialist theory'[23] of Thomas Hodgskin: a number of the leaders had been prominent in the London Mechanics' Institute and the British Association for Promoting Cooperative Knowledge. In this early phase the National Union judged the Bill to be inadequate, but acceptable as a first step. Henry Hetherington was the only prominent member to oppose it consistently. He was the most influential publisher of unstamped newspapers, that is, of papers with a working-class circulation which were sold cheaply because the newspaper stamp duty had not been paid on them. The *Poor Man's Guardian* which he started in July 1831 carried the best reports of National Union proceedings.[24] Hetherington was thus in an influential position. But the nature and extent of his influence need careful appraisal. Opposition to the Bill was not as widespread among the working class as his papers suggested.

Two of the leading working-class papers in the provinces said that the Bill, though inadequate, deserved support. James Bronterre O'Brien, who was then editing the *Midland Representative*, took this line. Though not 'warm' for the Bill, he was prepared to 'labour' for it. John Doherty's *Voice of the People,* published in Manchester, was cool at first, but became warmer as signs of the Bill's popularity multiplied:

5 March 1831: Though [the Bill] bears more of a popular character than we were led to expect from the present administration, yet there is not one clause ... framed for the benefit of the workman. ... Something, however, will be obtained from the borough-mongers, if the Bill is not suffered to be frittered away ... The way will. ... be paved for other and more useful reforms.

26 March: The entire nation has spoken out ... demanding a change in the system. ... If the ministers continue to act as they have begun, they will not only immortalize themselves, but secure a triumph to their country, the benefits of which it would be difficult adequately to estimate.

18 June (reporting Doherty at Manchester): The Bill will be one grand step towards the point we aim at—the universal establishment of political liberty.

No simple social analysis will explain working-class alignments for and against the Bill. It is probably true that in London the artisans tended to support the Bill, if only because some of them could expect votes under it. Working for the Bill came naturally, as Hetherington's *Penny Papers* put it in March 1831, to 'superior mechanics, who can afford to wash themselves clean and spare a holiday any day of the week'.[25] But to say that the London artisans agitated for the Bill, while those below them were indifferent to it, would be to exaggerate this tendency grossly. An opposite trend is also discernible, in that it was the more sophisticated working-class people who were inclined to hold aloof from the Bill and the less sophisticated who saw it as a deliverance. Every section of the working class was divided during the whole period that the Bill was before Parliament.

The agitation varied greatly in intensity and effectiveness from place to place. In the opening phase, as always, Birmingham was at the top of the scale. The Scottish lowlands, which had known the unreformed system in its most extreme form, perhaps came next.

At the foot were the Tyne and Wear where the strikes in the coal pits over-shadowed Reform. Manchester and Leeds fell between these extremes. In Manchester class conflicts were too acute to permit unity among the Reformers. In Leeds a big strike and the movement for factory reform not only increased these conflicts, but diverted interest to some degree from the Bill.

The patchiness of the agitation, in both geographical and class terms, detracted little from its effect. Its intensity staggered the politicians on both sides. They had known nothing like it, though it was to be surpassed later, notably in May 1832. Accounts of the Bill's reception from radical sources are suspect, since the radicals included experienced publicists, adept at exaggerating the fires which they had stoked. The most revealing comments came from the opposition. While they disputed every claim to support which the reformers made, they admitted privately how far the 'mania' or 'frenzy' for the Bill had spread.

County meetings provided the most important expressions of demand for the Bill. Twenty-three counties had met to petition for it by 8 April.[26] Its popularity was both mirrored and increased by the support of most of the London and provincial papers. The Birmingham Union had press extracts read aloud at its meetings. Crowds would collect in certain streets during the dinner hour and in the evening to hear reports of the previous day's debates. Artisans in country places tramped miles after work to hear the news. Six or seven farm hands or miners clubbed together to buy a paper at half price when it was a day or two old; and one of them would read it aloud to the group. By such means working people, meeting in open places, or the village ale-house, or round a single candle in a shed, learned about the great Bill which was to make life easier.

This popular approval was duly reflected in a swing to the Bill in the Commons. Independents in open seats realized that a vote against the Bill meant expense and possibly defeat in the next election. A dissolution might not be imminent; but their constituents would remember such a vote for years. Other Members seeing these apprehensions began to make their plans on the assumption that the Bill would become law, and reflected that a known anti-reformer would enter the reformed era at a disadvantage. When the opening debate was over, a junior minister (F. T. Baring) noted in his journal that on 2 March the reformers had been unwilling

to speak out ... the cheers of the House were nearly three to one against. ...
From [the third night] we gradually rose till the last ... when evidently the
whole appearance of the contest was changed; our friends were in spirits, the
opposition dejected, and having every appearance of a losing party.[27]

The opposition whips calculated on 3 March that they had a majority
of 113 against the Bill, with 53 still doubtful. On 11 March Hardinge
made out a majority of 37 against the second reading, supposing that
all the doubtfuls then remaining voted with the government. Three
days later the Marquess of Graham predicted to Ellenborough that
the second reading would be carried. 'The man who would not give
East Retford to Birmingham,' Croker reported to Hertford on 15
March, 'would now jump at a compromise which should take one
Member from each borough in the Kingdom.'[28] On 18 March
Ellenborough noted that Hardinge's lists showed an opposition
majority of two 'supposing all the doubtfuls to vote for the second
reading; but he has much doubt,' Ellenborough added, 'whether the
shabby ones who stay away will not convert this into a small majority
on the other side.'

Despite the trend, external pressure could hardly be expected to
turn a majority against the Bill into a sizeable one for it. In the first
place, its powerful action naturally produced powerful reactions.
Among the governing class an MP was expected to maintain a certain
independence not merely of the government, but of his constituents
as well. He must stick to his own views, disregarding the temptations
both of an official salary and of vulgar applause. The fear of being
thought afraid was thus apt to prevent a stampede from the unpopular
lobby. Moreover the astonishing popularity of the Bill with the
radicals made it daily more suspect to tory MPs. The people supported
the Bill in the belief that it made fundamental changes in the governmental system. The independents in Parliament would support it only
if they were sure that it did not make such changes. Charles Wood,
writing to Yorkshire on 3 March to persuade his father 'to get up
meetings and petitions ... in all quarters', described the Bill as 'an
efficient, substantial, anti-democratic, pro-property measure'.[29] By
mid-March a property owner who feared democracy needed a cool
head to be as confident as Wood. The doubtfuls believed that what
Cobbett liked must be dangerous. At any rate a victory for Cobbett
would be thought a defeat for the aristocracy. Like Joseph Chamberlain's radical programme, and the 1909 budget, the Bill became a
symbol of popular power. In such situations the fact that the symbolic

popular victory would leave the propertied classes in control is apt to be overlooked.

Secondly, the government could not bring the pressure to bear with sufficient urgency. The only weapon which would have given them a firm majority on the second reading was the one which they did not wield—the certainty that if defeated they would dissolve. Every opposition Member knew that a majority against the Bill meant prolonging a crisis which was damaging trade and intensifying unrest in industry and agriculture. But those troubles would be the ministry's fault for introducing the Bill. Every MP with constituents knew that a vote against the Bill meant expense at the next election whenever it came, and perhaps a risk of being unseated. But some of the doubtfuls were not long-sighted; and this was all speculation. There were many accidents in politics. If the king were only firm enough to refuse a dissolution he would give the opposition a little time and something might turn up for them. It was very hard to keep an agitation going for long at the highest intensity. 'A war and many things may arise in the course of time,' Lowther told his father on 19 March, 'to catch public attention.'[30]

From the start William IV had done all he could to show that his government enjoyed his support. Stanley had been put into a Windsor seat when defeated at Preston. Grey was now allowed to disclose that he had *carte blanche* in replacing those members of the Royal Household who had resigned after Russell's speech. But this was not enough. Everyone knew that the king liked his ministers and meant to be fair to them. He would be generous in affording them all the usual facilities; but that did not mean that he would let them dissolve. Apart from this the state of the Civil List and of the supply votes suggested that the cabinet were not quite so ready for a dissolution as their underlings made out.

The opposition leaders were in trouble too. They were already involved in a dispute on tactics which was to be with them throughout the passage of the Bill. Which gave the better chance of defeating it— a pitched battle or skirmishes? On 13 March Lord Wharncliffe tried and failed to persuade Peel to leave the second reading unopposed and to bleed the Bill to death in committee. Wharncliffe had been one of the Members for Yorkshire for many years. He understood the strength of the demand for the Bill better than any other opposition peer. He had not been in Wellington's government and so had no awkward association with the speech of 2 November 1830. The advantages of Fabian tactics were clear. They would allow time for the agitation to die down. A parliamentarian of Peel's ability might be able to amend the Bill to devastating effect without ever giving the government a pretext for dissolving.

The opposition could no longer hope for a decisive majority in a second-reading division. A small majority against the Bill would simply invite a dissolution. It would force the government to demand one; and, as it would not suggest that the opposition were strong and united, the king would be given no encouragement to refuse the demand. The resulting election would almost certainly reduce the opposition's strength.[31] A small majority for the Bill on second reading might be almost as bad for the opposition leaders, since it would demoralize their supporters and cast doubt on their ability to collect majorities for their amendments.

The difficulty about the moves which Wharncliffe suggested was that the conditions necessary for their success did not exist. His tactics required leaders whose freedom of action was unimpaired, and in whose determination to fight the Bill the party had complete confidence. They involved disregarding Wellington's declaration against Reform on 2 November and Peel's against the second reading on 3 March. They did not take into account that the slightest sign of compromise from Peel would have been greeted as a betrayal, to say nothing of his personal disinclination for 'ratting' again.

A Fabian campaign presupposed a united and disciplined party. There was no such party in March 1831. It is incorrect to refer to the ultra tories as being part of Peel's following at all at that time. He did not claim their allegiance, and was cautious about approaching their leaders. It is equally wrong to refer to the ultras as a single group. They were single only in their distrust of Peel. On the Bill they were hopelessly divided from each other. Those who followed Knatchbull and Vyvyan were not thorough going anti-reformers. They were inclined to follow defeating the Bill on second reading with a resolution in favour of moderate Reform. Wetherell's group were diehards. When Peel admitted in his speech on 3 March 'that he would consent to some Reform, Wetherell looked grave and desisted from cheering'.[32] One day early in April there were three tory meetings in progress at the same moment—at Peel's, Wetherell's, and Vyvyan's.

It was impossible, therefore, to achieve agreement among the opposition on anything save the most straight-forward plan. The only course open to Peel and his friends was to muster the largest vote they could against the second reading. Peel refused to endorse the Knatchbull–Vyvyan plan for a resolution. He considered trying to put the second reading off until after Easter in the hope that the agitation would have died down a little by then. But this came to nothing and the debate remained fixed for the original date, 21 March. Greville met a tory friend on 17 March who thought the Bill 'sure to be carried' and 'complained bitterly of the bad tactics and want of union of the party, and especially of Peel's inactivity and backwardness'. But on the very next day the cabinet showed that the opposition had no monopoly of bad tactics.

Althorp brought forward a revised scale of timber duties on 18 March. The issue was one of 'colonial preference', as it was later to be called. The preferential system for timber, which he was proposing to modify, was well supported in the House; and any tampering with it aroused strong feelings. He risked defeat on these duties[33] and he had planned to postpone this division until after the second reading of the Reform Bill. On the other hand he was under pressure both in the House and out of it not to leave the powerful timber and shipping interests in uncertainty any longer.[34] More generally, he was in a hurry to clear away the debris of his budget. The sugar duties were due to expire, for instance, on 5 April.

The cabinet eventually found what seemed to be a way out of this difficulty. They took advantage of improved revenue returns to revise the timber proposals and make them far more attractive. No alteration was to be made in the duties during the present year and there would be no increase in duty on any kind of timber thereafter. There were merely to be reductions in the Baltic rates until they came nearer to those on Canadian timber. The new plan emboldened Althorp to hold the timber debate before Reform. The opposition might find some difficulty in rejecting a scale in which the change was not only a reduction, but one that they would probably have made themselves if still in office. They were to be given no time to discuss their line. The concession was not announced until Althorp's speech opening the debate.

The scheme seemed to succeed at first. Convinced that there would be no division on the first night, Althorp allowed some of his followers to leave the House. He underrated both the bitterness of his opponents and their parliamentary dexterity.[35] They exploited the protectionists' dislike of his proposals, and yet contrived, by moving the chairman out of the chair, to avoid a direct vote against them. The cabinet's manoeuvre looked tricky and unfair. The various protectionist interests were for once united. The regular opposition combined with 'the saints', the West India interest, and the Canadian timber and Atlantic shipping interests, to beat the ministry by 236 to 190.[36]

The defeat probably did little in itself to impair the government's chances on Reform. But it frightened Grey. He had refused to face the question of a dissolution in good time. Obliged to face it in haste, at the last minute, he made a false move. Writing the next morning, 19 March, to Taylor, the king's secretary, he explained that while he still expected 'a considerable majority' on the second reading, the timber division made him doubt whether the Bill could be carried through the committee stage without mutilation. 'One material point,' he went on, 'will be the propriety of advising His Majesty to dissolve Parliament; and it is upon this point particularly that I shall be much obliged to you to inform me, with as little delay as possible, what you think is the state of His Majesty's feelings.'

The cabinet met in the evening of 19 March and decided that, as they still had a reasonable chance of a majority on the second reading, they would go on as if nothing had happened. They had no alternative. The state of parliamentary business and the king's known scruples put an immediate election almost out of the question. There was a connection between these two obstacles, because a dissolution would mean abandoning the new Civil List, about which the king was naturally anxious. Springing a demand to dissolve on him at the last moment would be simply inviting a refusal.

Grey wrote again to Taylor on the following morning telling him of the cabinet's decision. 'It may perhaps be as well,' he added,

not to say anything to the king on the subject of dissolution. Indeed what I wrote to you yesterday was only for the purpose of learning from you what you thought would be the probable effect of making such a proposition to him; but I believe I omitted, in the hurry in which I wrote, to express my wish that you should not bring this matter directly before him till you heard from me.

This omission was unfortunate because Taylor had shown Grey's first letter to the king before he received the second. William at once wrote to Grey refusing to dissolve 'in the present excited state of the United Kingdom, particularly of Ireland'. On 21 March he repeated his objections in a longer letter, Taylor warning the Prime Minister that they would 'prove final and conclusive'.

Grey tried to ensure that this refusal remained a secret; but he seems to have failed. Reports of the king's firmness were all over London, and in the opposition papers by 21 March. In view of the state of parliamentary business they were easy to believe. They may have been no more than clever guessing; but it is far more likely that there had been a leakage from Windsor. The court was full of violent and indiscreet anti-reformers, such as Earl Howe, the queen's chamberlain. Three members of the Household were indeed shortly to be turned out of their places for voting against the second reading. In these circumstances it would have been surprising if the secret had been kept. Lady Howe's brother, Lord Brudenell, was offering large bets by 21 March that the king had refused to dissolve.[37] Grey's enquiry aggravated his original mistake of failing to prepare the king in January for a dissolution. Uncertainty on whether he could dissolve if defeated had been dangerous; a conviction that he could not, spreading among such 'doubtfuls' as the Knatchbull–Vyvyan group of ultras, might be fatal.

This group met to decide their second-reading tactics on the morning of 21 March. Their admiration for the whigs and for Reform had not survived the publication of the Bill. Its provisions went far beyond anything which they had wanted or expected when they ousted Wellington.[38] A strong rumour that the king had refused a dissolution brought them some relief at last. To their leaders, who were county Members, the risk of an immediate election was not merely a worry, as it was to every doubtful, but an all-important preoccupation. It was almost certainly this risk which had made the group hesitate so long about opposing the Bill. They were now assured from sources which they trusted that the risk was non-existent. The issue of the *Standard*, the ultra evening paper, which appeared a few hours after their meeting, contained a particularly confident statement to that effect. They decided that they would vote against the second reading, but that Vyvyan, who was to move the rejection, should include a promise of moderate Reform in his speech.[39] Grey reported this decision at once to Taylor. If Vyvyan's manoeuvre should give the opposition a majority, he wrote, 'I cannot answer for the consequences'.

It is no wonder that Grey was anxious. Several tories, including Admiral Sotheron, the veteran Member for Nottinghamshire, went back on their promises to the government when the rumour about the king removed the fear of dissolution. Some kind of Reform was likely to be enacted somehow, whether the Bill were defeated or not. But that did not provide much consolation. Grey wanted a safe Reform, and one passed by a whig cabinet without riot and outrage. A second-reading defeat would make this very hard to achieve.

The second-reading debate lasted for only two nights, the House being impatient to divide. There was heavy betting: at the end the opposition were generally expected to win by a vote or two.[40] At three minutes to three on the morning of 23 March the Speaker put the question, the two sides roaring Aye and No with equal confidence. It was then the practice for one of them, in this case the anti-reforming Noes, to go into the lobby, the other being counted in the House. The Noes seemed endless as they filed out; and the reformers almost despaired. But the tellers, moving along the benches and counting out loud, reached 290, and hope revived. The Ayes began to call the numbers with them. There was a shout at 300, and another a moment later when the count ended at 302.

The Noes trickled back from the lobby each bringing a different report of their numbers—303, 310, 309, 307. At last Charles Wood jumped on a bench and shouted 'They are only three hundred and one'; and, as the tellers pushed their way through the crowd towards the table, the two for the government were seen to be in the winning position on the right. There was a wild outburst of cheering, and then silence while Duncannon read the numbers—Ayes 302, Noes 301. 'Then again the shouts broke out,' wrote the whig Macaulay,

and many of us shed tears. I could scarcely refrain. . . . We shook hands, and clapped each other on the back, and went out laughing, crying, and huzzaing into the lobby. And no sooner were the outer doors opened than another shout answered that within the House. All the passages, and the stairs into the waiting rooms, were thronged with people who had waited till four in the morning to know the issue. We passed through a narrow lane between two thick masses of them; and all the way down they were shouting and waving their hats . . . I called a cabriolet, and the first thing the driver asked was, 'Is the Bill carried?' 'Yes, by one.' 'Thank God for it, Sir.'[41]

'A dreadful race,' Graham wrote to Durham, 'won by an accident at last.'[42] He was referring to the report that Henry Bulwer had been intending to vote with the opposition and had missed the division by mistake.[43] The government's victory was ascribed to the lucky chance of Bulwer's absence combined with the last-minute conversions of Sir Andrew Agnew and John Calcraft. No particular air of mystery or intrigue surrounds Agnew's vote. He was a new Member and a moderate reformer.[44] He had made the usual parade of his independence on the hustings when elected, but had said that he was inclined to support Wellington. He had not voted in the 15 November division, and had not yet made his maiden speech. He seems to have been undecided how to vote until the last.

Where Calcraft and Bulwer were concerned luck was reinforced by Ellice's cunning. The latter's skill came into play in that the closeness of the division was anything but an accident. The agitation for the Bill meant that a number of MPs wanted to see the government defeated, but feared to damage their political prospects by voting with the opposition. A squad had thus come into existence who would not oppose the second reading unless they believed their votes to be needed to give the opposition a majority. In these circumstances something near to a tie was inevitable and it became crucially important for Ellice to conceal from the doubtfuls that the Ayes had drawn level with the Noes.

He knew of Calcraft's change of mind some time before the division but managed to keep it secret. Whether he had done anything to ease this conversion is not known. Calcraft was a whig by origin who had served as Paymaster General under Wellington. He had spoken against the Bill on 4 March. He sat for Wareham of which he was also the patron. It was in Schedule A and he was said to have been brought over by some promise of a reprieve for it. More probably he was moved by the hope of increased influence in the county if he joined the popular side. In the general election a few weeks later he became one of the Members for Dorset. In September 1831, convinced that both sides despised him, he killed himself.

What happened to Henry Bulwer's vote is also obscure. He was a young and ambitious liberal sitting for the Schedule B borough of Wilton. His patron, the Earl of Pembroke, was an anti-reformer who lived abroad. Bulwer was reported on 5 March as having deserted to the opposition. In April he voted for the Bill, left Wilton, and won a seat for Coventry as a reformer. He explained during his election campaign that he had abstained on the second reading because, although he had told Lord Pembroke that he wished to vote for the Bill, he had not received the latter's decision on whether he might do so.[45] His reforming colleague in the Coventry election was Ellice. It is practically certain that Bulwer's absence from the lobby was not the

accident which it was made to appear. He may have been encouraged
to abstain by Ellice's assurance that, if he did so, he would not have
difficulty in finding a Reform seat.

TABLE 4

SECOND READING, 23 MARCH 1831

	For the Bill	Against
ENGLAND		
Members for counties	51	25
Members for boroughs then in Schedule A	29	77
Members for boroughs then in Schedule B	31	58
Members for boroughs not then in either Schedule	111	65
Members for Weymouth (due to lose two of its four Members)	1	3
Members for universities	2	2
	225	230
WALES		
Members for counties	6	5
Members for boroughs	7	5
	13	10
SCOTLAND		
Members for counties	10	15
Members for burghs	3	10
	13	25
IRELAND		
Members for counties	38	20
Members for boroughs	13	15
Member for Trinity College, Dublin	–	1
	51	36
TOTAL	302	301

Source: *Parl. Deb.* iii.806–824.

Table 4 gives the general pattern of the voting. There was a considerable difference between this division and the one on Parnell's amendment. The ultra tories who had been united in ousting Wellington were divided on the Bill. Forty-five MPs, nearly two-thirds of whom were ultra tories, voted against Wellington in November but against the Bill in March. On the other hand a substantial group of ultras voted for the second reading. Thus some 25 of the Members voting for it had voted against Catholic Emancipation in 1829.[46] Twenty-eight MPs voted for Wellington in November but for the Bill in March. The salient feature of this latter group was distaste for opposition. They included, for instance, the Marquess of Donegall's Member for Belfast. The marquess wished to be a duke, and his eldest son, the Earl of Belfast (nicknamed Stickfast), had been allowed to remain vice-chamberlain of the Household despite the upheaval in November. The family were a remnant of the old 'party of the Crown'. They still followed the practice which had built up their fortunes, of voting for the government of the day whatever its politics.

The substantial majority for the Bill in the Irish seats reflected O'Connell's support. He had no attachment to either side. The Wellington cabinet had coupled Emancipation with the humiliating requirement that he should be re-elected for Clare after the Act had been passed. On the other hand the whigs were still prosecuting him, though he must have realized that now he had declared for the Bill they wanted to let him off as lightly as they could. They had not yet published their Irish Reform Bill; but he probably knew enough about it to be dissatisfied with it. What sent the O'Connellites into the government lobby was their knowledge that any Reform Bill which opened the Irish boroughs must work in their favour.

The erosion of opposition strength over several weeks and the last-minute losses of the government meant that both sides suffered from broken promises. More than twenty Members voted for the second reading despite promises the other way. Discreditable explanations circulated in anti-Reform quarters for some of these late conversions. The MPs concerned, it was suggested, could not face the prospect of riots, or that of losing their seats. The Earl of Mount Charles was said to have been bought over by an undertaking from his rich uncle that his debts would be paid if he voted Aye.[47] Most of the late converts to the Bill were not as selfish as opposition gossip suggested. Nor were they notably public-spirited. To vote for the abolition of the family borough believing that it was sure to be abolished anyway, and disliking to enter the reformed era as an anti-reformer, was prudent rather than altruistic. Some Members and patrons had second thoughts from studying the proposed system more closely. 'Lord Chesterfield amongst others,' Princess Lieven told Grey on 14 March, 'has just discovered that the Bill increases his influence; and he is now somewhat embarrassed at having promised his support to the Duke of Wellington.'[48]

We cannot tell of a given county MP whether he was impelled to support the Bill chiefly by fear of disturbances and of a slump if it were lost, or fear of not being re-elected if he voted against it. Either way it was the popular agitation which affected him; and this did more than anything else to give the reformers their last fifty votes. It naturally had the greatest effect on those in open seats. During the Emancipation debates in 1829 Peel listed the counties and towns which had constituencies open enough to make the Members concerned peculiarly responsive to public opinion. In March 1831 sixty-nine of the MPs for these places voted for the second reading, and only fifteen against it.[49] C. W. Wynn, who had resigned from the Secretaryship at War over the Bill, and spoken against it on 4 March, voted for it. He told his brother that he did so partly to prevent expensive contests in the constituencies with which he was concerned, and partly because he saw a reaction against the Bill beginning and therefore wanted a dissolution postponed for 'six weeks or two months'.[50]

It is a mistake to suppose that a single factor will explain the way in which any 'doubtful' voted. They were all influenced by a whole range of conflicting fears and beliefs about their own interests and those of the public. They all knew that the old system was hated, but feared that the new might prove unworkable. They were all afraid of the disorder which might follow the loss of the Bill, but were afraid also of showing that fear. They all shrank from such a sweeping change, but had some hope of a stake in the new system.

Each 'doubtful' weighed the risks differently. One believed that the king had refused to dissolve and looked no farther. The next was sceptical of that story and saw that, even if it were true, defeating the Bill would lead to an election in the end. No two of them had the same political experience: no two were subject to the same pressures. Some had exacting constituents, others exacting patrons. For some the balance was tipped by personal connexions, for others by party spirit. The second reading division broke political alliances and divided families. One of Earl Grosvenor's Members for Stockbridge voted for the Bill, the other against it. The Earl of Harrowby's sons, who both sat for the family corporation borough, voted on opposite sides. Lord Francis Leveson-Gower voted against the Bill although his father, the Marquess of Stafford, supported it with all the rest of the great family 'interest'. Lord Carrington's son and heir, who sat for Buckinghamshire, voted for the Bill and received this letter from his borough-owning father:

My Dear Bob,
After your vote … last night it would be as well for you not to come to Whitehall (i.e. Lord Carrington's house) for some time, as I might be tempted to use language which you would never forget, and which I myself might never forgive myself.

Your aff. father,
C.[51]

The votes of the Members for the Schedule A borough of Wootton Bassett (Wilts) may illustrate a few of the cross-currents. Thomas Hyde Villiers voted for the second reading, Viscount Mahon against it. Neither vote is easily explicable in terms of electoral interests. Villiers had a considerable interest in the survival of Wootton Bassett, of which his father, the Earl of Clarendon, was one of the patrons. Mahon's family had no interest in the borough; and, on the supposition that the Bill or something like it would pass in the end, he was throwing away a chance of a county seat by opposing it. If he had kept his popularity by a Reform vote he would have stood well to be one of the additional Members for Kent.

Villiers was a Canningite. He had personal experience of the expense and worry in which the borough system could involve a politician, since in 1826–7 he had survived a petition and an election committee to keep his first seat. He saw the defects of the Bill, and indeed wrote a pamphlet about them. Perhaps he also saw the necessity for it. But his support for it may not have been wholly disinterested. He held the post of Agent for Newfoundland, and was liable to need the government's good offices to retain this. He was an aspirant for office, and became Secretary of the Board of Control in May 1831. Mahon was a new Member of ultra-tory antecedents. His father, Earl Stanhope, had been a furious critic of Wellington a year earlier, and was to end by voting for the Bill. But Mahon was a connexion of Lord Granville Somerset. It was probably his party ties which determined his vote.

The Duke of Devonshire spoke to a county meeting at Derby on 22 March. His remarks show as clearly as anyone's why there was a majority for the Bill. 'The members of the aristocracy,' he said,

have been sometimes considered in an unfavourable light by the people. For much of this they are indebted to the manner in which the present constitution of Parliament has enabled them to interfere and dictate in the representation. It is time that they should be relieved from privileges detrimental to all parties. It is time for them to descend from their false positions. . . . Let them stand on their own merits; and I have no fear that the people of England will be unjust to the aristocracy of England, united by mutual kind feelings and good offices, and not by close boroughs and mock representation. I should be sorry to think my connection with my countrymen stronger through my burgage tenures at Knaresborough than through the cordial and independent body . . . I now see before me—the yeomen of the County of Derby. Those burgage tenures . . . I hope to be very shortly called upon to resign.[52]

The Duke of Devonshire was right. Trying to hang on to boroughs such as Knaresborough was foolish if it entailed risking the loss of Derbyshire.

Grey now knew that he must be ready for a dissolution as soon as the committee stage began.[53] Parts of the army estimates were voted the night after the second-reading division, and parts of the naval estimates on 25 March. By 30 March all the preparations were in train, and the House was adjourned over Easter until 12 April. A general recognition that the ministers were ready to dissolve might still relieve them from the necessity of dissolving. A belief that the king had given permission for a dissolution would be still more efficacious. Any fresh demonstration of royal support was therefore worth having. Grey spoke to the king at a levee on 23 March; and the Household officers who had voted with the Noes were dismissed. 'This is something like,' wrote Creevey.[54]

An opposition effort to stiffen the king's resistance to dissolution was less successful. Wharncliffe realized that William was bound to allow one in the end unless he saw some way of obtaining an alternative government. The opposition could form a government provided they would declare for moderate Reform. Wharncliffe therefore persisted in a plan which he had originally proposed when the Bill was only two days old:[55] he would stage a debate in the Lords in which the tories would disclose their new-found moderation and the fitness for office that went with it.

Wellington was embarrassed by Wharncliffe's plan; and until the second reading was over he succeeded in having it postponed. He was unwilling to embrace moderate Reform himself; and he knew that most of the ultra-tory peers, with whom he was on the point of re-union, would feel as he did. But Wharncliffe, as he proved more than once in the succeeding twelve months, was not easy to dissuade. He made his motion in a long speech on 28 March. He attacked the Bill, but admitted that 'an effective and proper measure of Reform' was 'quite necessary'. He ended by warning the king that 'if Parliament should now be dissolved ... it would place the House of Lords in a most dangerous situation'.[56]

The scheme failed. It required for success that all the opposition peers should be moderate Canningites like Wharncliffe himself. Eldon and Sidmouth tried to suppress the debate on the ground that a discussion of a Bill still in the Commons was irregular. Wharncliffe's announcements on moderate Reform, so far from making the tories look ready for office, merely exposed their divisions.

Both sides spent the Easter recess in devising amendments. The government's most important one concerned the part of the Bill which not only reduced the House from 658 to 596, but made an even more drastic cut in the number from English constituencies. An attack on this unpopular feature had been announced already. General Gascoyne, a veteran ultra tory sitting for Liverpool, had given notice of an instruction to the committee that each part of the kingdom should retain the proportionate share in the representation which it had derived from the Acts of Union.[57] The cabinet set about meeting this threat by halving the proposed reduction, and bringing the new House up to 627 Members. All but two of the 31 seats reprieved were in England. It was also decided that if Althorp were hard pressed he could agree not to make any reduction in seats. This fitted in well with the alterations which were needed in the schedules. It was easier for Althorp and Russell to take the boroughs which resembled Calne out of Schedule B than to put Calne itself into it.[58] The process of correcting the Bill's faults was less remote and high-principled than the original drafting had been. Most of the changes which the government introduced during 1831 were adapted to catch much needed votes.

Peel opened his attack on Schedules A and B three days after the second reading. He was particularly well placed to do so, since the Ministers had compounded the blunder of apparently favouring one of themselves at Calne by treating him unfairly at Tamworth. Althorp and Russell agreed at once to make the necessary changes. When the House reassembled, Russell announced that five boroughs would be transferred from Schedule A to B, while seven would be removed from Schedule B and allowed to keep both Members.

The ministers had at last addressed themselves to finding acceptable criteria on which to base disfranchisement. It was clear by now that, as the population yardstick for every case, the parish was of no more use than the borough. Some boroughs lay in very large or populous parishes. The parish which included the borough of Clitheroe formed part of the industrial area of Lancashire. It had contained a population of 84,000 in 1821, that of the borough itself being a mere 3200. The cabinet therefore adopted as their criterion the population of the town. In disfranchisement 'it was intended', Althorp said on 13 April, 'to take the population of all parishes into account which were chiefly town parishes'. 'Where the township was part of the borough,' Russell announced five days later, 'and depended on it, both ought to form but one place for the return of representatives'.[59]

This was a sensible decision; but it committed the ministers to making a controversial judgment on every borough that was near either of the disfranchising lines. The 1821 returns were concerned primarily with parishes and boroughs, not with towns. Petitions and memorials sometimes gave the information needed. Truro was removed from Schedule B when a local act was cited, defining the town and its boundaries and establishing that these had contained a population of 6000 in 1821.[60] In general, however, the definition of a 'town parish' was a matter of uncertainty. In April the Speaker ruled that consideration of the schedules must precede the votes on the disfranchising clauses themselves. The committee stage of the Bill now looked like a long business. Meanwhile Althorp and Russell took what advantage they could from these uncertainties. In making the numbers up to 627 they reprieved Northallerton from Schedule B, on the ground that the parish in which it lay contained a population of more than 4000. This 'town parish' extended some sixteen miles beyond the borough limits. Northallerton was controlled by opponents of the Bill, so that the opposition were unlikely to complain at the change. When Croker cited it as a precedent for reprieving Clitheroe, Althorp told him that he was making no case for the latter: he was merely showing that Northallerton ought perhaps to have been kept in Schedule B.[61]

The cabinet were helped in reprieving boroughs by the extent to which the 1st of March had improved the flow of information from the places under sentence. The Borough Bailiff of Reigate had written a few weeks earlier that Reigate Borough and Reigate 'Foreign' were 'as distinct as two several parishes in all respects'. Schedule A reminded him that they shared a single parish church. He deposed this in a memorial and Reigate was transferred to Schedule B.

The minimum population for acquiring a borough Member was 10,000. It was easy to pick out some more places which came above this minimum, and for which a case could be made on the grounds that they were 'centres of manufacturing capital and skill', and that their interests were not represented elsewhere. In this way Bury, Halifax, Oldham, the Potteries, Rochdale, Salford, Wakefield, and Whitby, were selected to receive a Member each. Counties had been given two more Members if their populations exceeded 150,000. Seven counties came between that figure and 100,000. It was now decided to give each of these seven one additional Member.

Palmerston persuaded his colleagues to consider more sweeping modifications which might win over the doubtfuls and so make it unnecessary to dissolve.[62] He may have been influenced towards moderation by the probability that he would lose his own seat for Cambridge University if there were an immediate election. He wanted to curtail or abolish Schedule B. He had no success.[63] The cabinet dared not withdraw from 'the whole Bill'. Faced by criticisms of the £10 clause Russell harked back to his original idea of various borough franchises. He proposed to make the £10 franchise depend on poor-rate assessments, and in the London boroughs to raise the qualification above £10. These two restrictive changes were to be balanced by conceding a form of household suffrage in boroughs which had enjoyed a scot-and-lot or potwalloper franchise.[64] The cabinet rejected these proposals too. It was doubtful whether there were parliamentary votes to be gained from such a package, while the restrictions in it would certainly annoy the political unions.

Among the opposition, the overwhelming threat presented by the Bill gave an impulse to the painful process of reunion. Peel, who held for the moment the more important position, was much less effective than Wellington in re-establishing relations with the ultras. Wellington had the easier task, because the main body of ultra peers were at least united among themselves in detesting the Bill. But Peel's failure was

largely his own fault. His manner was stiff except to his close friends.
The cotton spinner's son never felt wholly at ease in the patrician
circles which still dominated high politics. Even Hardinge who was a
friend and colleague confessed at this time that Peel's 'manners and
general bearing disqualified him for a parliamentary leader'.[65]

Peel knew that, though the ultras were obliged to seek reunion now,
they still distrusted him. He could hardly bear to combine with the
group with whom he felt no sympathy, and from whom he had so
recently planned to escape. He 'treats all the tory party with arrogance
and insolence', Mrs Arbuthnot recorded on 29 March, and

affects to consider himself as an individual and not the leader of the party and
has hitherto positively rejected all the advances of the ultra tories. . . . Yesterday,
when Mr Herries went to him, deputed by Wetherell and Ld Stormont to
express their desire and that of their party to be led and directed by him, all he
repeated twenty times over was: 'these are the fellows who turned us out
three months ago'.

The ultras were naturally chilled by this attitude: a majority objected
to enlisting under Peel when the possibility was discussed on 17 April.

In the end, however, the various opposition leaders concocted a
device which all groups would support. It took the form of an amendment to the motion for going into committee. In a variation of
Gascoyne's original 'instruction', it forbade any reduction in the
number of Members for England and Wales.[66] Gascoyne was to remain
the mover, his seconder being another ultra. The amendment was
cunningly drafted for attracting a majority. It appealed to ultra tories
on no-popery grounds, and to the large class of Members who hated
O'Connell, since adding to Irish representation at England's expense
probably meant increasing the influence of Catholics and repealers.
It was popular with keen tory partisans, because in a reformed House
the tories were likely to be stronger in England than in either Scotland
or Ireland. County Members could explain to the freeholders that the
extra English seats were likely to go to counties to strengthen the
landed interest. It had the advantage over Gascoyne's original version
that, while it played on all the fears about revolutionary Irish agitators,
a Scottish or Irish Member voting for it was not precluding an addition
to his country's representation.[67]

The announcement after the recess that the ministers would not
insist on any reduction in the numbers of the House naturally raised
a doubt whether they meant to risk their whole future, and that of

their Bill, rather than accept the amendment in its revised form. Some doubtfuls may have agreed to support the amendment in the expectation that Grey would continue with the Bill even if it were carried.[68] But it is extremely unlikely that Peel expected this. Accepting defeat from Gascoyne would involve far more than merely maintaining the numbers. It would oblige the cabinet either to abandon the additional Members for Scotland and Ireland, and so lose votes from those countries, or to face the humiliation of actually increasing the House by eight. Neither of these courses could be thought consonant with the scheme as Russell had expounded it on 1 March. Peel was thus joining in provoking a crisis in the hope that the king was still firm against dissolution. If he looked beyond the king's prospective refusal to dissolve he probably hoped that the cabinet would find resigning too risky when it came to the pinch. They could not be sure that they were the only possible government and, as such, irreplaceable. They might well stay in office and end by withdrawing the Bill in order to modify it.

The opposition had discussed a number of plans which carried less danger of dissolution. But they were all subject to one of two decisive objections. On some of them the government might have surrendered without a division: on the others the opposition might have been in a minority. Peel was on a falling tide. After the second reading there were many tales of defection to the government. He did not want a walk-over with Althorp and Russell agreeing to the alteration proposed. He wanted to prove that he had a majority.

The leader of a united party would not have needed to take the risk which this kind of amendment entailed. There were signs that the Bill was losing some of its initial popularity. Hunt had turned against it. On 7 April he told an audience at Manchester:

When Sir Robert Peel charged them [the ministers] with going to make a democratical House of Commons ... they said 'No, we are going to keep the power out of the hands of the rabble' .... Their policy ... was to get one million of the middle classes, the little shopkeepers and those people, to join the higher classes, in order to raise yeomanry corps and keep up standing armies, and thus unite together to keep their hands still in the pockets of the seven millions.[69]

Peel knew, and indeed exaggerated, all the advantages of caution and delay. 'Give us another month,' he wrote to Croker on 15 April, 'and there is an end of the Bill. ... One month hence, if the Bill is still in suspense, there will be an enforced natural union between aristocracy and disfranchised population against . . . the new voters.'[70] Yet two or three days after writing this he agreed to provoke an immediate crisis.[71] He had little alternative. The considerations which had told against Wharncliffe's plan for the second reading applied with as much force as ever. The opposition were far too disunited to vote at full strength for an agreed series of erosive amendments.

The debate on Gascoyne's amendment lasted two nights and the opposition looked like winning all the way.[72] After the first night Grey told the king and Taylor that the cabinet expected to win, but that if they did not they would probably ask to dissolve. His letter was hardly calculated to secure a favourable reaction as it also contained a warning that the Irish disturbances had become serious enough for the government to need further powers of coercion. The king replied at once that he was still unwilling to dissolve and that the state of Ireland confirmed him in this.

The division was taken at 4.30 a.m. on 20 April. The opposition did not obtain all the votes they had expected. One or two Scottish Members deserted them, and one of their supporters went away so drunk that his friends could not bring him back to vote.[73] But they won by 299 to 291. The numbers were heard in silence.

The cabinet met a few hours after the division. They were almost as worried as William IV about the risk of electoral disorder in Ireland. Because of this they hesitated to recommend a dissolution. If they insisted on an election, and it greatly intensified Irish unrest, neither the king nor the peers would forgive them, however large a majority they might have gained in the Commons. Anglesey, the Lord Lieutenant of Ireland, coupled his demands for further coercive powers with assurances that an election would not involve unacceptable risks. He was such a warm advocate of decisive Reform measures that these assurances were somewhat suspect. None the less they were reasonable. It was in O'Connell's interest to help the government. That meant doing all he could to keep the election peaceful in Ireland. Making trouble at the critical time for a Reform ministry was no more his game in April than it had been in March. Despite his incessant complaints about the Irish Reform Bill he wanted to see it on the statute book.

The government prosecution of O'Connell was still a difficulty. The ministers had found it a ticklish business to convince him of their goodwill and to ensure that he would be out of prison during the election period; but they were confident by now that they had attained both objects. Some of them would have liked to drop the prosecution against him altogether. But Stanley had made clear that he would resign if it were dropped.[74] A resignation on such grounds would have started a parliamentary uproar. Besides, Stanley could not be spared.

O'Connell was due to come up for judgment on the very day of the Gascoyne division. On 3 April Grey intimated to him (through Burdett) that he might 'move for an arrest of judgment, notwithstanding the condition imposed upon him by the court, without, as I believe, any right so to do'.[75] By 12 April Stanley was expecting O'Connell to 'move an arrest of judgment by which means his sentence may be deferred'.[76] When 20 April came the Crown obtained a postponement until early in May. Meanwhile in London the cabinet were deciding on dissolution.[77] The cabinet minute recommending it assured the king that 'from the best information' about Ireland which the ministers 'could collect . . . the measure which they recommended would be perfectly consistent with the public safety'.

Grey presented this minute at an audience granted the same afternoon. It was a levee day and the remainder of the cabinet waited in an ante-room ready to tender their resignations if the advice should be rejected. The king slept on the problem, and wrote on the following morning granting permission. He made plain that he did so because he could not risk leaving the country without a government. He told his ministers that he would have refused, and let them resign, had there been any prospect of forming another administration strong enough to withstand the demand for the whole Bill.

The king may have been influenced by an audience which the Lord Chamberlain, the Duke of Devonshire, obtained early on 21 April. Devonshire stated his 'intense conviction' that dissolution could alone save the state.[78] This opinion, coming from a borough owner who stood to lose a good deal in a revolution, probably made some impression. In any case William's conversion is not difficult to explain. As Grey and Durham had told him some weeks earlier, great public excitement was unavoidable whatever he decided; but if there were an election it would have a safe and constitutional outlet, whereas if there were not it would be directed against the throne and its occupant. No one capable of facing facts could have decided differently.[79] The Duke of Devonshire's sister Lady Granville, who was in Paris, asked pertinently: 'Is it true that the king will not dissolve, and that if beat Earl Grey bolts, and then what, where, who? And how will the country bear it? And shall you all soon come swimming over in a long boat—*émigrés*?'[80]

As soon as the king's letter was received the cabinet met and decided how to cope with the election in Ireland: they must obtain powers of martial law for Anglesey from the outgoing Parliament. Within a few hours, however, the king's decision became common knowledge and the prospect of either House doing anything further for the government disappeared. The bolder men of the opposition came to the fore, determined to prevent a dissolution if they could. In the Lords Wharncliffe gave notice for the next day of a motion praying the king not to dissolve. A technical objection was discovered to the Civil List Bill; but this turned out to be surmountable. In the Commons there was straightforward obstruction. Holmes, the opposition whip, told Ellenborough that he would 'have a good attendance . . . of men ready for anything tonight'. The adjournment of the House was carried by a majority of 22 before the report on the ordnance estimates had been received.

The cabinet seem to have been prepared for some such development. They had deferred their decision about the timing of the dissolution until the evening of 21 April, when most of them would be dining at Durham's in Cleveland Row. As soon as he saw that the ordnance estimates would not be passed Althorp sent Howick and Wood to Cleveland Row to recommend that it should take place at once. The dinner party accepted this advice. They had little doubt that they would gain in the election. They could therefore rely on an Indemnity Act from the next Parliament to cover acts of martial law in Ireland or any ordnance expenditure which had not been voted. Grey wrote to the king asking for a council next day at noon. In the morning someone discovered that there were precedents for using the previous year's ordnance surplus instead of the current vote. The opposition in the Commons were check-mated; but the peers could still give trouble.

Very late on 21, or early on 22, April a parliamentary official warned ministers that the opposition leaders in the Lords were searching the journals for precedents for delaying a prorogation. Wellington and his friends aimed to make time in which to pass Wharncliffe's motion. If Parliament were prorogued by commission they could do this, because by custom the peers might finish any business on hand before admitting the Commissioners. A collision with an opposition majority in the Lords, before the Bill had even reached there, was not what Grey wanted. The cabinet were therefore summoned at once; and it was decided that when Grey and Brougham had their audience before the council they should counter the duke by asking the king to prorogue in person. Brougham wrote later that, when the cabinet seemed inclined to demur at this request, and to discuss it further, he put an end to these hesitations by asking Richmond, who had fought in the Peninsular War, 'whether he had ever seen a council of war held on the field just before going into action'. 'By God, never,' Richmond answered, 'neither I nor anyone else.'[81]

The king who was a simple and excitable old sailor proved easy to persuade. He had been angered by Wharncliffe's notice which he took to be an interference with the prerogative. He pointed out, however, that it would take some hours to prepare for the ceremony: a military escort would be needed, for instance, to accompany the royal carriage. The Lord Chancellor replied that anticipating the royal commands he had ordered up a troop of the Horse Guards already. The king was taken aback by this liberty which he called 'high treason'.[82] But he soon entered into the spirit of the occasion, replying, it is said, to Grey's apologies for haste: 'Never mind that; I am always at single anchor.'[83]

Meanwhile ministers and officials scurried about on urgent errands. Someone went off to fetch the crown from the Tower. Durham drove in the Chancellor's carriage to summon the Master of the Horse. He found Lord Albemarle making a late breakfast, and asked him to have the king's carriages prepared instantly. Lord Albemarle replied that he would give the order directly he had finished his toast. He was told that this delay could not be allowed. 'Lord bless me,' he exclaimed, 'is there revolution?' 'Not at this moment,' said the minister; 'but there will be if you stay to finish your breakfast.'[84]

It was then reported that the tails and manes of the horses took five hours to plait. The king is supposed to have rejoined that if the state coach were not ready in time he would go in a hackney coach.[85] The speech was approved, the council held, and circulars sent from the Treasury informing the peers that the king would come to the House to prorogue soon after three o'clock.

Both Houses met about an hour before then. In the Commons Vyvyan attacked the Bill and the ministry in a passionate harangue punctuated by the discharge of saluting guns as the king approached. A struggle for the last word followed. 'The calls for Peel, Burdett,

Althorp, and Chair now were heard in wild confusion,' J. C. Hobhouse wrote,

half the House left their seats, and the opposition seemed perfectly frantic: . . . Peel stormed: the Speaker was equally furious: Lord Althorp stood silent and quite unmoved. . . . After some more shouting and screaming . . . Peel was heard. His speech . . . was such as completely unmasked him. All his candour, all his moderation, all his trimming, shifty policy disappeared; and he displayed his real vexation and true feelings of disappointment and rage in an harangue of sound and fury, signifying nothing but his own despair and hatred of those who had overreached him by calculating on the good sense of the people and the firmness of the king with more accuracy than himself. The Black Rod cut short his oration just as he seemed about to fall into a fit. . . . But Peel was not the only over-excited performer on that day; for Sir Henry Hardinge crossed the House and said [to the ministers]: 'the next time you hear those guns they will be shotted and take off some of your heads.'

The proceedings in the Lords were still more disorderly. The opposition were bent on passing Wharncliffe's motion, and the government on obstructing it. As soon as Wharncliffe started speaking Richmond rose to order and proposed that the peers should take their proper places by rank. He succeeded in provoking a quarrel and so consuming time. Londonderry had to be held back by four or five peers from offering his opponents violence. Brougham now produced a diversion in his turn by rushing back into the House and exclaiming against the doctrine 'that the Sovereign has not the right to dissolve his Parliament whenever he sees fit . . . , more particularly when the House of Commons have considered it proper to take the unprecedented step of refusing the supplies to His Majesty'. He was hooted, but went on speaking until he heard the guns.[86] Wharncliffe's motion was never put, though he contrived to bring it on, and so have it recorded in the journals.

The king robed hastily, put the crown on his head though there had been no coronation, and entered the chamber in time to cut short a final outburst of vituperative eloquence from the tory Earl of Mansfield. A friend told Greville

that in his life he never saw such a scene; and as he looked at the king upon the throne with the crown loose upon his head, and the tall, grim figure of Lord Grey close beside him, with the sword of state in his hand, it was as if the king had got his executioner by his side; and the whole picture looked strikingly typical of his and our future destinies.

6

THE BILL IN THE COMMONS (II):
THE REFORMERS' HIGH TIDE

Royalty and physical strength combined must carry all before them.
(Peel to Henry Hobhouse, 9 May 1831)

Most people in political circles expected substantial Reform gains from the election. Just after the dissolution the ministers were said to count on a majority of 58 in the new House.[1] A *Times* estimate, intended to hearten reformers, put this prospective majority between 70 and 103.[2] Some of the anti-Reform county Members, who had been rebuked in county meetings since 1 March, would retire at once and be replaced by supporters of the Bill. Grey would also gain by using the ministerial influence which those now opposing the Bill had held in 1830. On 23 April Lord Kenyon, an ultra tory who was an opposition whip in the Lords, wrote privately: 'We don't despair of the next House of Commons being better than the last, though government influence being used against us is not so well.'[3]

The opposition expected to offset such losses from at least one quarter. There were signs that a number of Schedule A and B boroughs were willing to be rescued from patrons intent on their abolition. Some of the 'close boroughs', Ellenborough noted on 24 April, 'rebel and require Members who will not disfranchise'. The ministers' worries were not concerned entirely with close seats. They feared that their excited followers might aim too high and embark on contests which would end in well-publicized and expensive defeats. Five days after the dissolution Stanley 'presumed' that the prudent Reform strategy in Liverpool lay in 'not attempting to oust Gascoyne'.[4] Until the dissolution Althorp had shared the representation of Northampton-shire with an anti-reformer; and Graham had been in the same position in Cumberland. Both were anxious to avoid a contest and discouraged any attempt to capture the second seat. Althorp had even written this to the anti-reformer concerned.[5] Graham, on learning that he might be

G

given a reforming cattle dealer named Blamire as a colleague, protested: 'Am I to carry Blamire on my back?' These warnings had no
effect. The Liverpool reformers were determined to challenge Gascoyne. A second whig was forced on Althorp at the last moment,
being proposed without warning by a Northampton shoemaker.
'Take care,' Graham was told, 'that Blamire hasn't to carry thee.'[6]

On 29 April, when news of the first return was published in London,
the opposition still had some hope. The government had captured the
second seat for Dover against the influence which Wellington wielded
as Lord Warden of the Cinque Ports; and there was a report that Lord
Lowther had abandoned his candidature for Cumberland. But the
Dover result gave no great surprise, while the news from Cumberland
was obviously unreliable. On the other side of the account, the second
Reform candidate had retired in Worcestershire, where the anti-
reformers clearly commanded large funds; and the sitting Members,
who had served the duke as President of the Board of Trade and Joint
Secretary of the Treasury, were reported to have secured the government borough of Harwich. Their success in building up their personal
interests indicated that in at least one corporation borough the voters
had no self-sacrificing zeal for the Bill. 'The liberal patron,' *The
Times* pronounced in some alarm,

must not be bearded by his insurgent vassal. . . . Should the borough-guards
prove too troublesome to be otherwise dealt with, a fresh dissolution of
Parliament . . . must be had recourse to without scruple; and *at all risks*, even
that of requiring a bill of indemnity for ministers, no writ should be directed
to certain descriptions of close boroughs, but a Parliament be assembled
representing those places where election was not a wretched mockery and
farce.

The news on the following day, April 30, killed the opposition's
hopes. The morning papers announced that the only opponent of the
Bill among the four London Members had retired after a single day's
polling. In the counties, where the elections were not due to start for
some days, the reformers were already confident of some notable
triumphs. Leicestershire and Essex each had one anti-Reform
Member. The first had withdrawn: the second was challenged. One
Oxfordshire Member had been driven out because, though he had
voted for the second reading, he had supported Gascoyne.[7] The other,
an outright opponent of the Bill, was in danger. The Oxfordshire
reformers had two strong candidates in the field; and the freeholders

were promising, not merely to vote for the latter, but to make no claim for the expense of doing so. In Hampshire the reformers planned to capture both seats and were first in the field. After two false starts a second Reform candidate had been found for Worcestershire in the person of Althorp's brother and heir.

The strength of the Reform hurricane in the counties was still more evident from the extent to which the strongest were bending before it.[8] Knatchbull had announced himself a reformer. 'Give us but time,' he had told the Kent freeholders; 'and an efficient, safe, and satisfactory measure of Reform may be arranged.'[9] The most startling county reports on 30 April came from Cumberland. They left no doubt that the Lonsdale interest there was crumbling. It was not certain that Lord Lowther could collect enough support even to announce himself as a candidate for the county. In Carlisle his family faced defeat, their sitting Member being reported to suffer from 'a politic indisposition'.

Little comfort came for the anti-reformers that morning from either open or close boroughs. A whig who had not opposed Gascoyne had lost Southwark to one of Brougham's brothers. Liverpool was not impressed by Gascoyne's efforts for Protestantism. Sir Manasseh Lopes's nephew and heir, who had succeeded in March to Westbury, and his uncle's other possessions, thought popularity the better part of valour. His borough had just been reprieved from Schedule B. It was to greet the new era by returning two reformers, of whom he would be one. Six members of Banbury corporation had undergone similar heart-searchings and were pledged to support a Reform candidate against the patron's nominee. During 30 April it became known that the reformers had won the contests in the two Hertfordshire boroughs. The Earl of Verulam's eldest son had lost his seat for St Albans and the Member supported by the Salisbury interest had been beaten at Hertford. On 21 April the anti-Reform member for Bristol had told the Commons how he would denounce the Bill to his constituents.[10] He had now been advised to withdraw before he even reached the city. It was eight days since the dissolution had been announced and no more than a handful of results were known. Yet the ministers were already assured of a triumph beyond anyone's expectations, most of all their own.

The government's early successes were infectious. Once a large majority for the Bill was certain, the heart went out of the opposition, candidates and magnates alike. A large majority meant that the Bill would pass. There would be another election as soon as it became law. No one relished spending heavily in order to hold a seat for a few months, and then facing a reformed constituency as the man who had tried to stop them gaining the vote. Assuming that the Bill was going to pass, fighting to preserve the family interest no longer made sense where the opposition were concerned. It was the interest in the future constituency, not in the present one, which mattered now.

The first week of May revealed the scale of the government's victory in the open constituencies. Gascoyne had represented Liverpool since 1796. He was rejected there now after a mere ten hours of polling. The Duke of Northumberland's Member for that county conceded defeat long before nomination day, despite his patron's long purse. The Duke of Newcastle's candidate was beaten at Newark, and the Marquess of Exeter's at Stamford. A vote for Gascoyne's amendment was thought almost as heinous as one against the second reading. For most candidates in open constituencies there was no recipe for success except complete support for the Bill. Lord Strathavon had voted for it on both second reading and Gascoyne's amendment. This was enough to alienate the leading anti-Reform interests in Huntingdonshire, but not enough to reassure the freeholders. They asked him for an outright pro-Bill pledge. He refused and was defeated. One of the Members for Coventry, who had cast both votes for the Bill, made the same refusal and suffered the same fate.

The government ended with a majority of 130 to 140. Numerically they gained the most in the open boroughs of England and Wales. By the calculation in Hansard the opposition lost two-thirds of the 60 seats of this kind which they had held in the old Parliament. In terms of prestige what mattered most was the startling success of the Bill's supporters in the English counties. Of the 82 English county Members, 27 had voted against the second reading, and 34 for Gascoyne's amendment. Only six of this band survived in the new House.[11] Three of these six sat for counties where the reformers had captured the other seat. The only counties in which the opposition defended their position with complete success were Shropshire, a strongly tory county where they held both seats, and Buckinghamshire, where the reformers made a foredoomed attempt, much resented by the government, to oust Chandos. The candidate concerned in this venture was in his seventieth year and, as an advocate for purity of election, was not prepared to spend money. His committee and that of the sitting reformer declined to coalesce.

The opposition gained slightly in the English and Welsh close
boroughs. They picked up the second Queenborough seat, for instance. A struggle had been going on there for years between the
resident voters and the government interest. In 1831 the residents won
a barren victory by defeating the government which had put the
borough in Schedule A. The Barings had been represented at Thetford
by a supporter of the Bill. The borough was in Schedule B at this
stage of the struggle; and its electors, as the Duke of Grafton reported
to Grey, were 'not over-fond' of this schedule. An adjustment was
made. They were given another Baring, this time one who opposed
the Bill.

The opposition's small gains in constituencies such as Queenborough and Thetford were offset by their losses in the Scottish
burghs. In Ireland they lost more in counties and open boroughs than
they gained in close seats. Most of the revolts in Schedule A and B
boroughs came to nothing. All three of the constituencies which
Ellenborough noted on 24 April as rebelling against reforming patrons
had elected reformers by 3 May. A patron in this position might be
able to make a switch which involved no loss to the government.
He would require the election of a government supporter. But he
would avoid reimposing on the angry electors the very man who,
as their representative, had voted to disfranchise them. Thus the
Marquess of Cleveland removed J. J. Hope-Vere from Ilchester,
putting another reformer into the vacancy. Cleveland's subscription
to election funds ensured that the retiring member would be found a
seat.[12] A whig nobleman controlled four seats in the Isle of Wight as
a trustee. He hired these to Ellice, although, as Greville noted, it might
have been more proper to lease them to someone who was not engaged
in abolishing them. Hope-Vere was elected for one of these seats.

The opposition comforted themselves by attributing their defeat to
the intimidation of their candidates and voters, coupled with the
reformers' improper use of the king's name. Intimidation was a feature
of all elections in this period. Observers did not regard this one as
especially violent. Greville thought that it had 'gone off very peace-
ably'. Moreover, a good deal of the disorder does not seem to have
affected the results.[13] The two anti-reformers sitting for Malmesbury
stayed away while the corporation re-elected them and the crowd
had to be content with burning them in effigy. Although there was
widespread rioting in Scotland, with anti-Reform voters kidnapped or

pelted, it did not bring the reformers many seats. In Edinburgh the Lord Provost narrowly escaped being thrown over the North Bridge.[14] But he and his hardy henchmen had done their work by then and elected an anti-reformer.

The pattern of violence in 1831 was unusual, however, in being one-sided.[15] Virtually all the intimidation was exercised by reformers. It is impossible to believe that fear of physical ill-treatment had no effect in deterring opponents of the Bill. It probably contributed to the opposition's serious shortage of candidates.[16] In the larger close boroughs, where an angry populace surrounded the privileged few, the risks for anti-reformers were formidable. At Wigan, for instance, where the government gained a seat, a son of one of the borough's patrons received fatal injuries from the crowd, while an anti-Reform candidate was stripped of his clothes.

There was also some justification for the charge that the reformers made an unfair use of the king's name. The dissolution brought William IV to the brief zenith of his popularity. He had safeguarded the Bill by dissolving; and it was mistakenly inferred from this that he must be an ardent reformer. The electors were exhorted, in a play on his name, to 'vote for the two Bills'. It may be doubted, however, whether all this owed much to exploitation by politicians. The outburst of enthusiasm for the 'royal reformer' was spontaneous; and politicians were not the only people to respond to it. Within a few days of the dissolution the Theatre Royal, Drury Lane, was advertising the inclusion of 'God Save the King' in the programme, and putting on 'Alfred the Great, or the Patriot King', with Macready in the name part.[17]

Neither fears of intimidation nor the effect of the king's name begin to explain the reformers' success. The most important explanation for this was the one which the opposition could not mention in public: it lay in the very great popularity of the Bill. This affected every type of seat. It is a mistake to draw too marked a contrast between government gains which resulted from a realignment of interests and those directly attributable to support for the Bill among the mass of voters. Where important magnates turned reformer it was generally popular pressure which had helped to convert them. The agitation for the Bill convinced them that resistance would endanger the institutions of the country, not to speak of their county interests.

Apart from making their two specific charges, the opposition suggested that the election gave a foretaste of the revolutionary regime which the Bill would establish.[18] Certain features of the campaigning were thought especially alarming. 'It is not the least appalling symptom of the spirit of the time,' wrote Richard Ryder, 'that the tenants have not seldom declined to vote with their landlords.'[19] Old-fashioned members of the governing class also objected to a county Member being judged solely by his attitude to one measure. They thought it wrong to disregard long devotion to local interests merely because a Member's allegiance to Reform was suspect, and equally wrong to elect Long-Wellesley, Wellington's disreputable nephew, for Essex as a reformer, when his debts obliged him to stay at Calais throughout the contest.[20]

The reformers' success was widely interpreted as a victory, and an earnest of future victories, for dissent over the Church. The dissenting deputies raised a fund to return Russell for Devonshire.[21] Surviving pollbooks, in so far as they show the contrast between the voting of dissenting ministers and that of the Anglican clergy, suggest that Reform candidates commonly derived substantial support from dissent. In the contests for the county and borough of Northampton, for instance, Althorp received 19 votes from dissenting ministers, his colleague 20, and the Reform candidates for the borough 6 each. No opponent of the Bill received any. But the Anglican clergy were not ranged against the Bill with equal unanimity. Of the 239 clergymen voting in Northamptonshire, 62 voted for Althorp and 49 for Milton. In Aylesbury, where the pollbook gives occupations for the town voters only, the Reform candidates each received two votes from clergymen, the anti-reformer none. At Tewkesbury the anti-reformer gained 17 clerical votes, the leading reformer four. Just under a third of the clergy voting in the Cambridge University election supported Palmerston and his reforming colleague. Many of those who voted for Reform candidates wanted to see the Church reformed and the last disabilities removed from dissenters. But the election provided no evidence of a serious attack on the English Church in the sense of an intention to disestablish and disendow it.

The fear that the shocks of 1831 might be a portent for future earthquakes, whether in Church or state, proved mistaken. No subsequent election was at all like it. Much that was done in 1831 represented the response to a unique situation rather than any permanent change in electoral habits. County voters were as much inclined as ever to reward a Member's good service. In 1831 this inclination was overlaid by determination to safeguard the Bill. It soon reappeared. Robert Palmer had sat for Berkshire since 1825. Having voted for Gascoyne's amendment, he was obliged to withdraw his candidature for re-election. The freeholders found no fault with him apart from his opposition to the Bill. When a vacancy occurred in one of the county seats a year later he was returned at the by-election unopposed. He then continued to sit for the county until 1859.[22]

Apart from this, frightened contemporaries naturally exaggerated the extent to which the election ran counter to tradition. The crisis brought in some innovations. There was no precedent for the reformers' popular subscription, the Loyal and Patriotic Fund, which received contributions from many parts of the country.[23] Coalitions between Reform candidates, perhaps with a single committee serving both, were also effected on an unprecedented scale.[24] On 29 April the freemen of Sandwich achieved a startling reversal of the usual procedure by actually treating the Reform candidate to refreshments. These were substantial, but not enormous, new departures. The Loyal and Patriotic Fund, which received about £12,000 in all, was not large enough to affect the issue of more than a few contests.[25] The reformers' most ambitious attempt at central organization, Place's Parliamentary Candidates Society, was a failure.

Much that went on during the election was thoroughly old-fashioned. Two anti-reformers were returned for Sudbury, where the freemen took advantage of the excitement to raise the price of a vote. Four candidates canvassed Shaftesbury. All were reformers, the winning pair being Lord Grosvenor's nominees and the others the champions of the independent interest. Reforming magnates were found to be as insouciant and difficult to organize as their opponents. E. B. Portman was sure to carry one Dorset seat for the government. He was reported to have sent £3000 to each side in the county to give the contest for the second seat 'a fair start and no favour'.[26]

Most voters were no more levellers than they were republicans. Indeed there was probably less anti-aristocratic feeling in this election than there had been in 1830. The magnates who had espoused Reform had become popular beyond their wildest hopes. Anglesey's family reversed their defeat in Carnarvon borough. The Duke of Devonshire's Members had little trouble at Knaresborough. The champion of the independent interest re-appeared in the town. But 'the inhabitants', in the words of *The Times*, 'had reason to suspect that he was not a thorough reformer' and he soon left.[27] The Grosvenor interest might not have been challenged at Shaftesbury had not Lord Grosvenor's agents issued notices to quit after the 1830 contest.

In 1831 the reformers were trying, not to overthrow established interests, but to bar the House of Commons to opponents of the Bill until it had been passed. Reformers commonly boasted during the election of the royal and aristocratic support which their cause enjoyed. 'If you find the richest, the oldest, the noblest families in the country, headed by the king himself, willing to try the experiment,' asked a Reform pamphleteer, 'if those who have most to lose appear to have least to fear, is this not rather a strong argument in favour of reform?'[28]

Aristocratic influence and prestige combined with popular pressure to produce a Reform compound which the historian cannot break down into its elements. The government gain at Dover, in the first result to be announced, sent to the Commons a naval captain attached to the Queen's Household who was an earl's grandson and a great-grandson of the Duke of Grafton. One of his cousins was married to the Duke of Bedford's eldest son. The turbulent shoemaker who represented the popular voice in the Northamptonshire election did not make the proceedings less aristocratic. The candidate whom he nominated was Earl Fitzwilliam's son and heir, Viscount Milton. Nor were aristocratic influences overborne in that county, whatever Richard Ryder might say. Fifteen Northamptonshire freeholders voted from the Parish of Aldwinkle and four from the neighbouring parish of Lowick. In the first the predominant landowner was a whig, in the second a tory. Milton received fifteen votes from Aldwinkle, but none from Lowick.[29]

The anti-reformers' jeremiads, however ill-founded, had some effect. They exploited fears which were beginning to spread in the governing class during the election. In winning on the hustings the cabinet were losing their most cautious supporters. John Gladstone's letters to his son William illustrate this process:

4 March 1831: I think well of the Reform measures as a whole, but they will require in some respects to be modified.

6 May 1831: We shall now have constituents instructing and laying down rules for their representatives and political unions dictating to the constituents .... Lord Grey will soon, I think, have to look to his 'order', when he may try in vain to protect it from the storm he has so industriously created.[30]

Many elderly moderates would have agreed with John Gladstone. The most prominent representative of this type was William IV.

The popular notion of the king as the Reform champion had no foundation. He had never entirely believed in the Bill, perhaps because he knew too little about middle-class opinion to realize the necessity for it. He had become alarmed as soon as he saw that it would not pass without a dissolution. Grey's assurances about a majority for it in the last House of Commons had proved mistaken; and its chances in the Lords looked equally poor. The king thought that the opposition peers had been enraged rather than overawed by the election. A clash on Reform between the two Houses had always been his chief dread. This now seemed near.

William IV therefore wrote to Grey two days after he had sanctioned the dissolution pressing for such 'modifications' in the Bill as should be 'calculated to conciliate' its opponents. He argued that the ministry would be strong enough after the election to make concessions. They should delay the Bill until the new census figures were available and employ the interval to 'remodel' it. On the next day Palmerston wrote in a similar vein from Cambridge where the university voters were in process of rejecting him. 'I have scarcely met six people,' he told Grey, 'who approve of our Bill.'[31] On 27 April there was an 'illumination' in London to celebrate the dissolution; and some anti-Reform grandees who did not put candles in their windows had them broken. The mob frightened the queen by surrounding her coach.

These incidents increased the king's anxiety to make a stand against the onrush of radicalism and he kept up the pressure for modification throughout May. The principal issues were whether to raise the borough qualification above £10 and whether to curtail the disfranchising schedules. These points were raised in a cabinet meeting on 29 May and discussed again on 8 June. It was decided not to make any important modification in the Bill. After the first meeting Althorp wrote to Durham who was away ill:

Lord Grey spoke very decisively against making any alteration in the franchise .... His expressions were so strong that they silenced Palmerston; and Lansdowne admitted that it was too late to make any change. I should say that with the exception of Palmerston all present agreed that a very probable consequence of attempting to conciliate the House of Lords by concession would be to lose the House of Commons; and Lansdowne expressly said that this would be absurd in the highest degree.[32]

The king did not kick against this decision. He still had confidence in his ministers and made every effort to show it. While he was demanding these modifications he rebuked Howe, the queen's chamberlain, for signing two petitions against the Bill and he gave Grey a supernumerary Garter. He could not ignore the force of Grey's arguments. On 24 June Russell, looking very confident this time, reintroduced the Bill.

Some attempt must now be made to summarize the most important arguments used in Parliament for and against the Bill. The parliamentary debates represented a discussion within the governing class to which other classes were allowed to listen. Of course, there could be no complete correspondence between arguments used publicly and views held privately. But there was some frank parliamentary speaking, particularly in the Lords.

It was not seriously disputed that a Reform Bill of some sort had been necessary when Grey formed his government. Except for Wetherell and a few ultra tories everyone recognized that an anti-Reform administration had become an impossibility by then. But the opposition had no truck with the view that it was social and economic changes which had necessitated the Bill. They maintained that the old system had been adaptable to such changes. Everyone had accepted it until the spring of 1830. Its unpopularity by November had been created by the irresponsible and office-hungry whigs, whose attacks on the constitution had unfortunately coincided with a trade depression and with revolutions in Paris and Brussels. This part of the opposition's case was unconvincing, though the suspicion that the whigs had introduced the Bill for reasons of party advantage gave it a certain force for tory partisans. Moderate people realized, however, that most of the cabinet had done very little to discredit the old system during 1830 whereas on 2 November Wellington had done a great deal. Moreover, there must have been something unstable about a system which required for its continuance that no one should attack it, and that there should be neither fluctuations in the economy nor disturbances in Europe.[33]

Admitting the necessity of some Reform involved arguing that the government's best course would have been to introduce a moderate Bill. Peel and most of the opposition front bench in the Commons took this line, and so had to explain why they had not introduced such a Bill themselves. Peel justified his failure to do so on the ground that no moderate Reform could have been final. He had declined to sponsor one, he said, because: 'I was unwilling to open a door which I saw no prospect of being able to close.'[34]

Even Peel had some difficulty in convincing his hearers that the whigs should be blamed for rejecting a solution which he had himself rejected. His speeches implied that the right policy in face of the agitation was to make the smallest possible change at the last possible moment. This argument has been mentioned in connexion with the July revolution and the 1830 election. The Reform agitation, it ran, had been aroused by temporary circumstances. Grey's surgery was the wrong treatment. The fever should have been allowed to die down, a mild dose of Reform being administered during convalescence. The government's contention was more convincing. They argued that a moderate measure might have succeeded if produced quickly. It was the long delay during 1830 which had made their sweeping Bill unavoidable.

Moreover, finality in the sense of preventing the recurrence of a Reform agitation was agreed to be an all-important objective. It was all very well for Peel to say that he would have supported a moderate Reform 'founded on safe principles'.[35] How could a Reform be safe if it were certain to lead quickly to something more sweeping? Peel's case for a measure which admittedly could not be final therefore involved arguing that the government's Bill would prove equally impermanent. Few Parliamentarians outside the opposition's devoted partisans rated its finality quite as low as that.

The imperative necessity for a Reform Bill to settle the question provided a rock-like foundation for the government's case. That case was strong even if all their expectations about the new voters were discounted. Relying on ten pounders might be disastrous in the end. Clinging to the rotten boroughs would be disastrous at once. It was better to grant Reform and endure unstable governments than to refuse it and be left with an unstable system. The cabinet's most powerful argument was that of Wellington in 1828–9. The cost of refusing the concession looked so high that granting it could scarcely be more costly on the worst forecast.

It was not possible for government speakers to keep this point before their hearers all the time. As the period before 1 March 1831 receded, the dangers of refusing any substantial Reform faded a little from people's minds. The argument could be shifted to the drawbacks of the new system; and it could be implied that there must have been a way to avoid incurring these. This shift brought the opposition onto far better debating ground. They demanded to know how the re-formed House would improve on the unreformed in composition and in the policies which it would adopt. This question naturally em-barrassed the government and they did not give a convincing reply. Ministers could not admit that the new House was designed to be as like the old one as possible in outlook and class composition, and that they did not expect it to adopt any drastic policy changes. An answer on these lines would have displeased the Birmingham Union. Att-wood's efforts would have slackened had he realized that the reformed House would be as hostile to his currency policies as the unreformed had been.

By contrast, the opposition were free to prophecy every kind of disaster from the Bill. It would destroy the mixed or balanced system whereby aristocratic and popular elements provided checks to each other. It would lead to clashes between Lords and Commons. It would make the country impossible to govern because, once all seats were under popular control, no government would command stable support. The anti-reformers' picture of the uses to which the ten pounder would put his vote presented inconsistencies. He was depicted alternately as persecuting the poor and as wishing to enfranchise them. There were similar inconsistencies in the opposition account of how governments would fare under the Act. One picture was of govern-mental weakness and instability: Reform would produce a succession of weak and short-lived ministries, since constituents would not allow their MP to support a government unless it pandered to their particular local interests. This was based on the continuance of a more or less traditional pattern of politics. The other picture was more apocalyptic. It showed governments as powerful at least in destruction: they would despoil the rich ruthlessly at the behest of the new voters. However inconsistent these prophecies might be with each other, they carried a certain conviction. The hearer was as unclear as the speakers about the political habits and interests which the new system might engender. He was free to adopt whichever picture of ruin corresponded most closely to his own fears.

The opposition leaders suffered from certain difficulties in pro-phesying doom. They maintained that to abolish rotten boroughs was to deprive governments of a much needed facility. This was a front bencher's argument. It had little appeal to those who had not them-selves faced the responsibilities of government. It was also difficult for

Peel to say exactly why he distrusted the new voters. He must have realized that he would soon be asking for their votes. The issue underlying the parliamentary debate was whether the poachers would be reliable as unpaid assistant gamekeepers. It was equally awkward for the opposition to accuse anyone of being a poacher, and for the government to disclose the subordinate nature of the poachers' future role.

One aspect of these opposition prophecies has been somewhat misunderstood. If the wilder predictions about the abolition of the monarchy and the peerage are discounted,[36] most of what was foretold eventually came about, in the sense that a democratic regime was established in Britain within a century of the Act being passed. This has led to the suggestion that the prophecies were essentially correct, although they exaggerated the speed with which the results predicted would follow. This suggestion obscures the fact that the essence of the prophecies lay in the time-scale. The opposition were predicting, not merely that the Act would usher in a democratic regime, but that this regime would apply to the Britain which they knew. A few diehards apart, they would have conceded that improved education and communications might eventually make possible, and even safe, further enlargements of the electorate. What they feared was the confusion which might follow if the enlargements were made before these improvements even came into sight.

The predictions went farther than this. The opposition foretold that the new system would fail to produce even the shortest interval of stability. The ministers had started down the slide that led to anarchy. Each concession would elicit a fresh demand; and each demand would be harder to resist than the last. 'Others will outbid you,' Peel told the ministers when the debate began, 'not now, but at no remote period. They . . . will quote your precedent for the concession, and will carry your principles to their legitimate and natural consequences.'[37] The result of the Act reaching the statute book, Peel added in July 1832,

would be that apprehensions would prevail for the security of property—apprehensions which were likely to affect considerably . . . the productive powers of the country—and that the political excitement would continue as rife, and the political unions as flourishing and as noisy, as ever.[38]

Strip the debating points away: add private admissions to public statements; and it may seem that no great difference remains between the views of one side in Parliament and those of the other. Both sides recognized the need for a Reform measure. Both dreaded that when the Act was passed disillusionment would set in almost at once. Agitation, it was feared, would then be renewed by political unions of formidable strength and experience until another step was taken towards manhood suffrage. Many easy hopes had disappeared by June 1831. The whigs now shared most of their opponents' forebodings. The cabinet still thought their £10 line defensible; but they recognized it to be even more arbitrary and anomalous than they had originally supposed. They no longer felt sure of achieving 'finality' for their time. Grey and his colleagues had all along known that resisting the Reform agitation would be too dangerous. They now knew that intensifying it with a sweeping Bill was far from safe. Wellington and Peel still preferred to rely on borough owners rather than on ten pounders. But they knew the shortcomings of each tory borough owner and his MPs more intimately with every month that passed.

Nonetheless the division between supporters and opponents of the Bill went to the roots of politics. It was not only that the tory bred in the government party refused to destroy a system which formed part of his life. Many tories were outside this tradition: they had never held office and did not aspire to it. In essence much of the opposition to the Bill was a protest against the new and apparently unstable England of mechanics' institutes and Brougham's 'godless academy'.[39] The squire who looked for deference and no longer found it blamed this on the new fad for education and on the middle class of the growing towns. He refused to bring the constitution into line with these changes. He would not acknowledge their permanence and his defeat. If he could recognize facts at all he knew that the unreformed system no longer worked usefully. He knew that he was voting for something already broken beyond repair. This knowledge did not lessen his opposition to the Bill. His protest was not a matter of reason. The same could be said about some of the support for the Bill among the governing class. Its authors believed that recent advances in political knowledge had equipped the new electors to vote wisely; and there were some facts to back this belief. But these facts were not the real foundation for the Bill. Like many other liberal reforms it was based as much on indignation as on any assessment of the facts. To do nothing towards enabling men to rise from ignorance, and then to use that ignorance as an argument for keeping those men powerless, struck Russell and Althorp as monstrous injustice. They would accept great risks rather than allow the last word to proponents of that argument.[40]

Among the governing class complete and sustained approval for the Bill came largely from people who had some inclination to welcome the 'march of mind', and who shared the whigs' general belief in bold but carefully limited concession.[41] Those who held this belief regarded the ministers as setting up a barrier against further change. Those who did not hold it saw them as inviting further change. Nearly all the reform schemes of the 1830s raised the same question. Would state support for education tame the working class and reconcile them to their lot, or give them dangerous thoughts and make them discontented? Would it teach men how to subvert society, or how to rise in it? Would its tendency be to disrupt institutions, or to ensure that they developed in a civilized way? Would reforming the Irish Church purify and thus strengthen it? Or would it be weakened when its property and arrangements were no longer seen as sacred?

As usual, disagreement was less complete between the front benches than the back because the front benches tended to see the problem in a governmental setting which took the edge off ideological differences. Melbourne agreed with most of what the opposition leaders said. He hated arousing expectations which he knew could not be fulfilled. A jotting in an early notebook shows his reluctance to disrupt political habits. 'Nothing,' he wrote, 'can justify a man in unsettling the minds of others, weakening the force of reverence, authority, and example, except a conviction . . . clear and strong respecting the consequences of continuing in the faith of his fathers.' Another early jotting deals with the dangers of disillusionment: 'Great reason against Reform that it will be found not to be attended with any of the benefits expected from it, and then more and more will be required.'[42]

Melbourne relished his privileges and was comforted to think popular government a fraud. He was franker than his colleagues in admitting the advantages of the unreformed system. He told Greville in March 1832 that he did not see how the government was to be carried on without the rotten boroughs. He knew that by 1831 there was no solution for the aristocracy which would allow them to keep all their privileges in entire safety. They must either sacrifice a little with a reasonable expectation that this would secure them the rest, or hang on everywhere and so risk losing everything. He expected the new system to fail. He was certain that the old could not be saved. 'I was not very much for it [the Bill],' he told Queen Victoria in 1839,

'I saw it was unavoidable.'[43] He was not entirely pessimistic about the reformed system, however. He distrusted all political prophecies, even his own prophecies of doom. 'A remedy may possibly present itself,' he told Greville, 'it may work in practice.'

These were arguments about the case for or against introducing the Bill. In theory the case for or against opposing it to the end was distinct. One was an argument about the justification for offering the vote to half a million men, the other about the feasibility of withdrawing that offer once made. Even someone who thought that a sweeping Reform had been avoidable until 1 March might conclude that it had become unavoidable since then. There was thus something to be said for the opposition confining their protest largely to the second reading. Peel seemed to hint in his first speech after the election that he would not resist for long. 'If necessities were so pressing as to demand it,' he told his constituents at Tamworth on 18 May, 'there was no dishonour . . . in relinquishing opinions or measures and adopting others more suited to the altered circumstances of the country.'[44]

It might be honourable to relinquish out-of-date opinions; but the honour of sticking to them when they were a bar to office was a good deal more obvious. Peel's speech was badly received by opposition MPs.[45] It was soon clear that their concern was not how far the Bill should be opposed, but how it could be opposed successfully. They were not in the mood for conciliation. In their view the cabinet should have foreseen—in all probability had foreseen—the fantastic expectations which their Bill would generate. The opposition benches were not inclined to make things easy for the men by whom they had just been routed. A government which had won a large majority by unloosing a Reform agitation on this scale seemed to deserve anything but help.[46] That the agitation was supremely dangerous Peel's colleagues and followers had no doubt.

There has been no single violation of property in France [Ellenborough noted in March 1831], nor has it been threatened with force. There has been no invasion of personal liberty. Yet through *mere agitation* the most opulent bankers and merchants in France are become bankrupts. The operatives are unemployed and the taxes have fallen off at the rate of 4 millions a year. If such have been the consequences of agitation in France what would they be here, in a country the state of which is so delicate and artificial, where *confidence* is as necessary to the working of the whole system as water to the working of the steam engine.[47]

Buying popularity by promising half a million votes had been bad enough; but the election was the last straw. Nothing could justify 'teaching the people', in Peel's words, 'to associate loyalty to their king with hostility to the constitution of Parliament'.[48] To their opponents the cabinet seemed to value their own continuance in office more than the maintenance of law and order. They had apparently been indifferent to the disorder which their election was bound to entail because they calculated that it would be directed against anti-reformers, and that there would not be quite enough of it to provoke a reaction against the Bill.

In December 1831 a writer in *Blackwood's* looked back at the election. 'The strength of government', he pronounced,

the protection of property, the authority of the law . . . consist . . . in the habits of obedience, order, and submission to which the people have been trained . . . the moral awe in which the lower classes have been educated, the veneration with which they have been accustomed to regard the institutions of their country.

Since the Bill had been introduced, the article continued, these institutions had been 'attacked with relentless severity'. The lower classes had been 'urged in the leading ministerial journals to receive the anti-Reform candidates on the hustings with showers of stones'. It was surprising 'not that there is so much, but that there has been so little, conflagration and anarchy in the country'.[49]

The most criminal aspect of the election in opposition eyes was what appeared a disgraceful intrigue by which O'Connell had been allowed to go free. The Law Officers had given their opinion that the prosecution against him must lapse once the law under which it had been brought expired with the dissolution. The government maintained that they had neither received nor anticipated this ruling when they decided to dissolve. Their disclaimer was greeted with scepticism on the opposition benches. It was held there that ending the prosecution, and thus buying O'Connell's continued support for the Bill, had constituted one of the cabinet's more powerful motives for dissolving.[50]

The events of May and June 1831 were not calculated to lessen this resentment. Opponents of the Bill scrutinized reports of Reform meetings, and gave the most sinister interpretations to any extravagant phrases of the romantic era which the speakers might have used. During this phase stories were current in opposition circles of servants who would 'only hire themselves for six months', from a belief that they would no longer have to work once the Reform Bill had been passed.[51] It was indeed clear that the Bill had awoken disturbing desires beneath the surface of society. On 3 June some 25 people were killed in a collision between strikers and troops at Merthyr Tydfil. Professor Gwyn Williams has described the attitude of the Merthyr rioters as follows:

What emerges above everything else ... is an obsessive concern with personal dignity, with 'fair play', with justice. What they were rebelling against, in the last resort, was humiliation. That is why their masters and their magistrates found it so hard to find out what they actually *wanted*. They wanted nothing that those masters could give them, because they wanted everything. They wanted a renovation of all things. They wanted Reform.[52]

To their opponents the government had committed the unpardonable crime of raising hopes which could not possibly be satisfied.

The problem for the opposition in the Commons was to give their friends in the Lords the best possible chance to defeat the Bill. One idea for lessening its chances with the peers was to send it on with all its imperfections retained and heightened. The opposition leaders soon rejected this. The decision on how many clauses, and places in the schedules, to contest in committee was more difficult. Peel favoured shortening the committee stage by taking 'only the great points'.[53] He hoped by avoiding obstruction to win the respect of the majority, and so to dissuade them from voting blindly for everything in the Bill; and he thought it more likely to be rejected in the Lords if it went there fairly soon. The government would have fresh chances with every week that passed to nullify Wellington's majority by converting peers or creating them. Moreover the opposition peers might flinch from voting against the Bill if it did not reach them until late in the year. They would need nerve to provoke the reformers' frenzy during the distress inseparable from a severe winter.

After Peel's remarks at Tamworth the opposition were understandably distrustful of his advice; and the arguments for fighting a prolonged campaign borough by borough prevailed. The Bill was as likely to reach the Lords too early as too late. The peers might be best placed to kill it if it came to them after a stout fight in the Commons, and late enough for the emergence of some signs that it had become less popular. The expected 'reaction' was a long time coming. But the Reform fever must abate soon. People of property would wake up to the danger of a radical House of Commons. Let the Manchester politicians talk a few months longer and the farmers must realize that Reform would mean the end of the corn laws. If the Bill survived its second reading in the Lords the opposition peers would need to know which clauses to delete or amend. They would be given the best guidance if the opposition in the Commons divided constantly and so discovered the features of the Bill for which the government could not muster their usual majority. Despite the changes made in April, and incorporated into the new Bill, the schedules still presented some tempting targets. Moreover, it would be difficult to prevent a debate on a condemned borough if its Members were insistent on starting one. In 1831 there was no difficulty in carrying out a policy of delay and obstruction. Closure procedures did not even become an issue in the House of Commons until the 1870s. An opposition which wanted time had merely to take it.

The committee stage therefore presented many difficulties for the ministry. But they had one indispensable asset for it, a large and determined majority. The reformers on the back benches were if anything angrier than their opponents and more unyielding than their own leaders. The mutual recriminations between the party of change and that of resistance do not vary much from age to age. The government benches thought the opposition factious and corrupt. Nothing could justify trying to upset a Reform government when no other could be formed, or clinging to rotten boroughs at the risk of revolution. The government's supporters were incensed, in the midst of their efforts to allay the storm, at being charged with arousing it. The opposition, one reformer told the Commons, had failed to grasp that Reform was the lightning conductor, not the lightning.[54] The storm would never have become dangerous if the opposition had seen that the Bill was bound to be passed and had allowed it to be passed quickly.

The reformers' determination was made less effective by a certain indiscipline. Like all ministries of the time, the government counted among its supporters many Members who were independent by conviction and parliamentary habit. A majority of 136 on the second reading (7 July) seemed to put the ministers beyond danger of a serious defeat and so to make minor deviations permissible. Ten of the sixteen amendments tabled by 21 July came from those who had voted for the second reading. Viscount Milton, for instance, was inclined to sit a little loose even to a government which he greatly admired. Two days after the second reading he gave notice of several amendments to the Bill. Steady ministerialists were particularly galled by Milton's aberrations because he owed his seat for Northamptonshire to Althorp's money; and he was apt to move his amendments from a seat near Althorp's on the front bench.

He is an excessively proud, conceited, eccentric man [E. J. Littleton noted in his diary], conceiving himself to be . . . , to use a phrase of his own in the House of Commons, 'one of those who inhabit a more elevated region, where they look down with contempt on the Thompsons and Johnsons in the vale below', and thus, unconscious of mischief, considers himself exempt from the ordinary rules and obligations of party men towards their leaders. . . . With this disposition he has a long lank countenance and a solemn puritanical air.

There was a touch of the martyr about Milton's persistence. Russell and Graham, meeting him at dinner on 10 July, rallied him, according to Littleton, 'saying "Cartwright [the anti-Reform candidate for Northamptonshire] would have been a better Member for us". [They] then proposed jocosely Mr Cartwright's health, which we all drank in playful earnestness amidst most malicious laughter.' The next day, however, Milton explained his amendments at length to Althorp's meeting of Reform Members; and he moved them when the time came. He made many speeches in committee, including one in which he begged his fellow reformers not to waste time by speaking. After giving the opposition much comfort he eventually received a remonstrance from Brougham. This drove him into the country, protesting that 'he could not listen tongue-tied to proceedings of which he disapproved'.[55]

The O'Connellites were perhaps the most troublesome group in the government's majority. They had some provocation to be. They were treated as aliens and inferiors and scarcely allowed to influence the terms of the Irish Reform Bill. Stanley sneered at O'Connell even when announcing that the prosecution had been dropped. The new Irish Arms Bill, devised by Stanley and introduced on 2 July, struck Althorp as 'one of the most tyrannical measures I ever heard proposed'.[56] In August O'Connell and his followers staged a revolt on the Irish yeomanry question. But in this Parliament as in the last they preferred the Irish Reform they were being given to none at all. The Arms Bill was withdrawn and the yeomanry plan shelved to appease them; and they stuck to the government after a fashion.

Pressure from constituents and from the political unions did something to keep the majority in line. Alderman Thompson, one of the City of London Members, was obliged to appear before the Livery for voting against ministers on the borough of Appleby. He apologized and promised to vote for the whole Bill in future. But many MPs were unwilling to take orders from their constituents; and few had constituents as watchful and near at hand as Thompson's. The reformers outside the House were seldom as effective as that. Indeed they were now in the difficulty which was to become familiar to the Irish nationalists later in the century. As long as the establishment are not frightened they say that no concession is needed: there is no strong demand for it. When they become frightened they say that in the face of such disturbance to concede would be disgraceful and unsafe. 'If we hold no meetings,' Attwood told the Birmingham Union in May 1832, '[the anti-reformers] say we are indifferent. If we hold small meetings they say we are insignificant. If we hold large meetings they say we wish to intimidate them.'[57]

Constituents were moreover apt to condemn all amendments except one to the clause which left them under-represented. The Potteries were to receive one Member. E. J. Littleton was obliged by an embarrassing promise to his Staffordshire supporters to propose changing this to two.[58] His amendment was defeated by 101; but it had displayed yet another vulnerable point in the Bill to the anti-reformers in the Lords.

Most reformers in the country knew nothing of House of Commons procedure and were inclined to attribute delays in passing the Bill to the government's lack of zeal. Althorp was sandwiched between political unionists who had assumed after the election that the Bill was as good as passed, and MPs who were wedded to a parliamentary timetable quite unsuited to measures of this scope and complexity. On 21 July, when the Bill had already been six days in committee, he secured an understanding to reserve about eight hours a day for it on four days a week. This was the best bargain open to the government: even if the House had agreed to a more drastic arrangement they would not have adhered to it. By engendering resentment and the will to obstruct, it might have hindered progress.

Most of the later attempts to gain more time did not succeed. The House was not to sit on Monday 1 August because of the opening of the new London Bridge. Althorp therefore insisted that the Bill should be taken on the preceding Saturday in compensation, though Saturdays were normally reserved for petitions. He had his way, but only after discussions and a division which wasted as much time as was gained. When Coventry and Birmingham sent petitions asking the House to hurry on with the Bill the Speaker ruled them out of order as disrespectful. Prodded by his Middlesex constituents, Hume proposed on 27 August that the committee sittings should start at midday. His motion merely wasted several hours.

Finally, the ministers were plagued by the defects of the Bill itself. They were not experienced enough always to be wary on technical points and they had few officials on whom to rely. Their draftsmen were so hard pressed that a ministerial amendment might not be ready by the time a particular clause was reached. They fell into 'serapes', as Althorp called them, on both the principal points in the Bill, the £10 qualification in boroughs and the disfranchisement schedules. When the Bill appeared on 25 June it contained the new proviso that a ten pounder did not qualify unless he paid his rent at half-yearly or longer intervals. This was a concession to the section of the cabinet who still hankered after a higher borough qualification. Althorp and Russell had agreed to it not knowing that in some places quite substantial rents were paid in quarterly, or even in weekly, instalments. It was attacked at once by *The Times* and the political unions as a retreat from the ten pound clause; and Althorp abandoned it, sensibly but ingloriously, before the second-reading debate had even begun.[59]

The residual difficulties presented by the disfranchising schedules took far longer to resolve. Four changes were made when the Bill was reintroduced. With a large majority behind them the cabinet no longer shrank from increasing disfranchisement; and Downton and St Germans were moved from Schedule B to A. The sole interest at Downton belonged to the Earl of Radnor, whose whiggish views were tinged with radicalism. He had spoken to Russell about the extreme difficulty of making the borough independent of himself. To give it the necessary electors would entail merging it with Fordingbridge, a larger place in the next county. St Germans was a straggling Cornish fishing village. The borough comprised 40 acres, and the town 50, in a parish of over 9000 acres. The existing male population of the borough was only 247. It had started in Schedule B because the 1821 census had given the parish a population of 2404. This figure was shown for the 'borough and parish' in the return, probably because the borough was not large enough to maintain overseers of the poor distinct from the parish overseers.

As a counterpoise to these disfranchisements Penryn and Sandwich were removed from Schedule B, the former being enlarged by union with Falmouth, the latter with Deal and Walmer. The first of these decisions, on Downton, raised the whole question of whether a borough's survival should depend on what electorate it could be given by enlargement. The second, on St Germans, added another principle to those already enunciated, namely, that the numbers of a surrounding parish were not relevant in lessening disfranchisement unless the borough accounted for a substantial proportion of them. The third provided precedents for proposing the reprieve of any borough where there was a neighbouring town inviting a marriage. Those trying to erode Schedules A and B had a wide choice of openings.

They chose the wrong one. Croker was the ex-minister most intent on fighting borough by borough. His aptitude for detail was not tempered by a sense of proportion. He had become convinced that the design of the two schedules was directed principally towards allowing Calne to keep two Members. 'Calne,' he said, 'is the keystone of the arch.' Downton, in his account, had been transferred to Schedule A in order to prevent the precedent of Calne from keeping the tory borough of St Germans where it was.[60] This kind of farrago was a great help to the government. They had plenty of trouble as fresh information made them waver, or change their minds, over yet more boroughs. But they remained in control of the disfranchising schedules. Russell wrote years later that on the schedules Croker had been 'a formidable adversary. . . . But . . . , even where the particular point on which he insisted was not mistaken, his exaggerations of its importance were repulsive to the House of Commons'.[61]

The government were also helped as usual by unresolved disagreements opposite. Peel continued to act as if taking 'only the great points' were the policy of the party although most of those on the opposition benches clearly wanted to fight the Bill in detail. As a result the opposition missed the full advantages of obstruction without gaining those of a constructive and reasonable approach.

After the election as before it, Peel was largely responsible for this disunity. The role of leader of the opposition in the Commons was still so ill-defined that it was possible for him to take a very restricted view of his authority. He objected, for instance, to the despatch of attendance notes in his name. He alienated the ultra tories before the new Parliament had even met. His Tamworth speech made them suspicious that he might surrender on the Bill; and he threw cold water on a scheme for a reunion dinner of the whole party although it had Wellington's approval.[62]

This continued discouragement of the ultras was deliberate. Peel's grudge against them had not weakened. Where they were concerned he was, as Mrs Arbuthnot said, 'a determined hater'. He also had dispassionate reasons for his policy, which was to combine with the ultras (or anyone else) against the Bill, but to avoid reforging a general party connexion with them. A complete alliance would not now enable him to stop the Bill; it would merely involve him in obligations which might be disastrous once the Bill was passed. The ultra-tory Members were not the allies with whom he wished to enter the reformed era. He stood for government and against fanaticism. Their outlook was the reverse of that. After 1829 he had a sharp distaste for such allies.[63]

The ultra problem is not the only explanation of Peel's negative and chilling leadership in 1831. He had little stomach for the fight against the Bill. This may indeed partly explain his inclination to take 'only the great points' in committee. He was not a diehard by nature. His distaste for his role subjected him to a strain which made him erratic and secretive and increased the habitual coldness of his manner. He gave his associates no encouragement to speak in debate and was apt to get up and correct them when they sat down. 'His dinners only do harm,' Ellenborough was told in July, 'his manner [as a host] is not conciliatory.' He could indulge these faults without any fear of being supplanted, for however his party might groan about him he was indispensable to them. Each speech which he made against the Bill confirmed his pre-eminence in debate.[64]

There's that fellow in the Commons [Wellington told Lady Salisbury in November 1831], one can't go on without him; but he's so vacillating and crotchetty that there's no getting on with him. I did pretty well with him when we were in office; but I can't manage him now at all. He is a wonderful fellow—has a most correct judgment—talents almost equal to those of Pitt; but he spoils all by his timidity and indecision.[65]

The government were blessed with a Leader of the House who possessed all the qualifications which Peel lacked. 'It was Althorp,' according to Hardinge, who 'carried the Bill.'[66] There is no reason to dispute this judgement from a leading opponent. In July 1831, when it looked as if Althorp might be removed from the Commons any day on succeeding to his father's earldom, the latter's pulse rate became

important political news. In March 1832 Althorp was asked to take a
peerage as no one else had much hope of steering the Bill through
committee in the Lords. The scheme fell through because no successor
could be found to lead the Commons.[67]

   Althorp had agreed to join the government only because Grey
would not take office without him. Asked what office he would like,
he replied that he would be Chancellor of the Exchequer and lead the
House. 'Lead the Commons,' said Grey in astonishment, 'but you
know you can't speak.' 'I know that,' Althorp replied, 'but I can be
of more use to you in that capacity than in any other.' 'He became,'
wrote Greville, who recorded this exchange, 'the very best leader of
the . . . Commons that any party ever had.'[68]

   Grey's surprise is understandable. 'There is a better speaker than
Althorp,' a whig wrote in November 1830, 'in every vestry in
England.'[69] Castlereagh's career showed, however, that a poor speaker
could be a successful leader. The position required either commanding
eloquence or none at all. It was possible to lead, as Canning had done,
by dominating the House. It was equally possible to do so by plodding
carefully in a way that did not hurt anyone's self-esteem. Althorp had
all the qualifications needed by a leader of the second type. He belonged to the inmost whig circles; but his outlook and friendships
made him acceptable to the radicals. The county Members trusted
him as one of themselves. He was a great aristocrat, but had the manner
of a squire. He had no temptation to be sarcastic. He was extremely
likeable, and cleverer than he looked. No one supposed that he had
either wanted office or needed its emoluments. He was not an aspirant
for the premiership. He thus had a reputation for integrity such as is
attainable only by a leader without political ambitions.

There stood Althorp [Littleton wrote after a party meeting in March 1832],
with his stout, honest face, and farmer-like figure, habited in ill-made black[70]
clothes, his trousers rucked up in a heap round his legs, one coat flap turned
round and exposing his posterior, and the pocket of the other crammed full
of papers—his hat held awkwardly in one hand and his large snuff box in the
other . . . while he briefly and bluntly told his plain, unsophisticated tale with
his usual correct feeling and stout sense.

   In the debates on the Bill Althorp owed something to his colleagues'
efforts, and still more to the defects of his ablest opponents. Despite
his rather frail health, Russell did sterling work at every stage of the
Bill's passage. Stanley spoke splendidly on great occasions; so did

Macaulay from the back benches. Peel's shortcomings were not made good by the other opposition leaders. Croker was disliked and distrusted. Sugden and Wetherell came under suspicion as lawyers. The first was moreover self-made and a tedious debater, the second a clown. Wetherell's only lucid interval, as the Speaker had once remarked, was the gap which opened during his speeches between his waistcoat and trousers.[71] Even so, they were not negligible opponents; and it was not an invulnerable Bill.

The Reform Bill committee required, not eloquence, but strong health, good judgement and temper, and detailed knowledge. Above all, it required a determination proof against any discouragement, since if the Bill were defeated in the Lords, as seemed increasingly likely, all the work in the Commons would have to be done again. Althorp's knowledge of the Bill, Brougham wrote, 'was almost supernatural. The others knew it so ill, and got into such scrapes when opposed to . . . Croker . . . that it became necessary to prevent them from speaking, or, as it was then called, "to put on the muzzle"; and Althorp really did the whole'.[72] As the committee wore on most reformers became reconciled to sitting muzzled while Althorp put the government's case without ornament on point after point. On the night of 25 August he spoke forty times. When he unmuzzled them they responded gaily. 'When I came to the House [for the debate on the new London boroughs],' J. C. Hobhouse recorded, 'Lord Althorp called me to him, and said, "Now, master, you must take off your muzzle tonight". I told him that I had not heard any speech except Peel's. "That will do," said he.' Hobhouse made a strong speech for these boroughs, though he did not in the least approve of them.

Even more important than Althorp's knowledge of the Bill was his name throughout the House for fairness. He did not close his mind before the debate began. While this sometimes led him into scrapes it also contributed to his hold on the House. Members knew that he would not insist on any clause unless he was satisfied that there was a good case for it. Peel and Croker 'spoke rather well of Ld. Althorp', Ellenborough noted in July 1831, '. . . he puts points shortly and clearly, and then sits down. When his points are good he adheres firmly to them. When they are bad he gives them up at once'. A less defective Bill might have been forced through by more masterful methods. But with the Reform Bill as it was when it entered committee, a refusal to listen to criticism would have been disastrous.

Althorp 'once', according to Hardinge,

in answer to a most able and argumentative speech of Croker, . . . rose and merely observed 'that he had made some calculations which he considered as entirely conclusive in refutation of the Right Honourable gentleman's arguments; but unfortunately he had mislaid them, so that he could only say that if the House would be guided by his advice they would reject the amendment'—which they did accordingly.

'There was no standing,' Hardinge added, 'against such influence as this.'[73]

The committee stage was due to begin on 12 July. On the previous night Peel outraged his followers by leaving a debate on the wine duties, although he had not spoken and there was to be a division for which an opposition whip had been sent out by his authority. He seems to have taken offence at a remark made in debate. Someone was sent to beg him to return; but he had gone to bed.

This incident left the opposition seething and uncontrolled. On 12 July just before midnight their wild men defied Peel, who soon went home, by embarking on obstructive adjournment motions. The government defeated seven of these, keeping their numbers above 180 all night while the opposition figure fell to less than 30. At 7.30 a.m. Althorp had his way and the House went into committee *pro forma*. The opposition had made a bad start. The government majority could well lose a night's sleep to show their mettle and their opponents' factious incompetence.

The government followed this up with decisive successes in the four opening committee divisions. Their numbers in these never fell below 285 and their lowest majority was 97. On 19 July, however, when the battle over Schedule A was just beginning the opposition agreed on a plan for tightening their organization. That night they did well on their amendment to transfer Appleby to Schedule B. The government majority was down to 74; and two nights later when the transfer of Downton came up it fell to 30. On 26 July St Germans was kept in Schedule A by a majority of only 48 and ministerial embarrassments over parish and borough boundaries reached a climax with the question of Saltash.

The 1821 census showed a population of 1548 in Saltash borough, and a further 1325 as living in the parish of St Stephen by Saltash. The circular of enquiry sent out in December 1830 did not elicit any useful information on the parish/borough problem from the Returning Officer of Saltash.[74] The cabinet, inferring mistakenly from the census that the parish of St Stephen and the borough were separate from each other, put Saltash in Schedule A. After the Bill had been published it was discovered that the two entities were not separate: the parish included the borough. It was thus possible to claim that the true population of Saltash at the 1821 census had been 2873, and that it ought to be in Schedule B. Although this claim looked plausible in July 1831 it did not survive investigation later in the year by the Boundary Commissioners. The peculiarity of Saltash was that the borough had little connexion with the other places inside the parish boundary. It had been put into Schedule A for the wrong reason. But this was the right place for it, and the one to which it had returned before the Bill became law.[75]

The opposition entered the Saltash debate knowing more than the government. They realized that, although they had a case of sorts for transfer to Schedule B, it was not a strong one: they were not planning to divide. When Croker moved for transfer, however, Althorp 'muttered a very indistinct opinion' that 'the case was one of doubt': he would 'leave it to the House to decide'. 'On which a division immediately ensuing,' Littleton recorded, 'no one knew what he was to do. The Attorney General, the Secretary at War, two of the Lords of the Treasury voted against the government, and ... Ellice ... went home in a rage, saying he would be dragged through the dirt no longer.'[76]

For once, Althorp's open-mindedness had led him astray. He had failed, not only to warn his followers that he might allow a transfer, but even to make clear, when one was actually proposed, that he meant to vote for it. Saltash was transferred to Schedule B by 231 to 150. Fewer than thirty reformers voted with Althorp and Russell in the majority. Schedule A was completed and passed that night.

The ministerial embarrassments in Schedule B were similar though less acute. It was finally passed on 2 August. The case of Sudbury was debated for the second time that night after Althorp had postponed it for three days. It was kept in the Schedule by a majority of only 49. The crux was whether the hamlet of Ballingdon formed part of a Sudbury parish though it lay in the next county. If Ballingdon were included the population would exceed 2000. Althorp was prevented from reprieving the borough by learning at the last minute of a local Paving and Lighting Act in which the limits of Sudbury were described as excluding Ballingdon. Although, in the struggle for finality, seventeen boroughs had been moved from their original positions, the disfranchising schedules still had a provisional air. It seemed as if nothing but a miracle or a massive creation of Reform peers would bring them unscathed through the Lords.

The enfranchising Schedules injured fewer vested interests and gave less scope for technical error. The first division in Schedule C, though nominally on Greenwich, was taken as a trial of strength on the new London boroughs as a whole. The opposition regarded these eight metropolitan Members as the most democratic point in the Bill and one of the most vulnerable. But the Reform benches were not easily shaken when the case was watertight and the leadership firm; and they were showing greater stamina than their opponents. The ministers had a majority of 107.

After that the government's only bad divisions in the borough schedules came on the boundaries of Whitehaven (Schedule D), and on their refusal of a Member for Merthyr Tydfil. Their majorities in these cases were 44 and 41. In both they showed doubt about their own proposals. The difficulty with Whitehaven was to prevent it from becoming a nomination seat under the Lowthers. The ministers' remedy was to enlarge its boundaries. No convincing case of gerrymandering could be made against them as they had produced a similar enlargement to prevent Huddersfield, also in Schedule D, from falling totally under the whig Ramsdens. But on Whitehaven, as so often, they forfeited support by producing their solution very late.

The county arrangements included three vulnerable features. The first of these to be debated, the division of the larger counties into two constituencies, represented one of the cabinet's efforts to compensate the landed interest for the loss of the rotten boroughs. 'The intention of the framers of the Reform Bill,' Graham said later, 'was that in the counties property and not numbers should have influence.' The cabinet hoped that dividing the counties would leave the local landed magnates in control except perhaps in the divisions which included big cities.[77] The example of Yorkshire suggested that an undivided four-Member county would be too expensive a constituency for a local squire. There would be too great a risk of contests for him, and too many voters now that the county electorate was being enlarged; and those who came from the other side of the county would not know him. He would be ousted by politicians of national reputation—by candidates resting on 'mere popularity' as Althorp called them—who might even be 'strangers' to the county.[78]

The government were never in great danger of defeat on the division proposal. But it was an awkward one for them in that they might need some votes from opponents of the Bill in order to collect a majority on it. Their radical supporters disliked it. So did those who wanted the county Member to retain all his prestige. It could be feared 'as a precedent', in Peel's words, 'for a departmental division of the country'. If there were a sufficiently formidable revolt among government supporters the opposition's attitude would become uncertain. They would be reluctant to prevent a ministerial defeat by voting for any clause, even for one of which they approved.

Peel spoke for the proposal, however, when it was debated on 11 August.[79] He then spoiled the effect of this stand for principle by leaving the House before the vote. Littleton bullied the radicals into voting for the division scheme by threats of reprisals.[80] The government had a majority of 109, though nearly fifty of their regular supporters, including more than a dozen Members for English counties, voted against them.

The cabinet were far more vulnerable on the borough freeholder and tenant-at-will questions, since their policy on these involved standing up to the landlords. The borough freeholder problem originated in the fact that the reformed system, like the unreformed, would leave counties and boroughs entangled with each other. The pattern of a series of constituencies, each of which is geographically entirely separate from the others, is a modern one in Britain. In 1831 it was possible to vote in both county and borough elections by virtue of a single piece of property. The forty-shilling freeholder had a county vote even if his qualifying freehold lay in a parliamentary borough. Sixteen of the cities and towns which were counties of themselves provided the only exceptions to this. In six of these the freeholders were borough voters. In a further nine they had neither borough nor county votes.

Some ultra tories had turned to Reform chiefly in the hope of ridding the counties of town voters; and the attempt to limit the number of borough freeholders who were to vote in the counties formed an essential feature of the Bill.[81] Two principles on which there was wide agreement underlay the scheme of limitation. First, where a borough freehold was occupied by its owner and worth £10 a year or more it must give him a borough vote. A freeholder of this kind was to be, in effect, an ordinary £10 borough voter. Secondly, the borough freeholder could not be allowed any longer to gain both a borough and a county vote from a single freehold. Nor must he be deprived of his vote altogether. He must either be given a borough vote or be allowed to go on voting in the county.

The difficulty came with the freeholders who did not occupy their holdings or who owned freeholds which were worth less than £10 a year. It would be contrary to the principle of the Bill to allow free-holders who had no residence qualification to vote for the boroughs. If all the freeholders were made borough voters, some small boroughs would become subject to influence or even nomination from great landlords. A batch of voters such as would have no decisive influence in a county constituency might give a landlord control of a small borough. Moreover, the Bill represented an attempt, not merely to hold the balance fairly between land and trade, but to prevent too sharp a separation between the two interests. They were not to be left confronting each other in hostility. To remove all the freeholders from the counties would make the latter too exclusively agricultural and the frontier between the interests too sharp, and would thus be objectionable to many reformers. So far from being given influence in the small boroughs, the landlords should not be left in undisputed control of their counties.[82]

It was commonly thought in Reform circles that no exclusively agricultural constituency could vote freely. 'The man who cultivates the land,' the *Morning Chronicle* pronounced in December 1831,

is, and always was, a slave. . . . It is only where a man is surrounded by others that he feels himself secure and confident. . . . In towns, therefore, men dare to profess their own opinions. But a tenant knows well that his landlord has a hundred ways of harassing him. . . . If a nobleman do not prove altogether a monster, he may count with certainty on the votes of his tenants.[83]

During the 1831 election *The Times*, commenting on the sluggishness of the Northamptonshire reformers, remarked: 'A large amount of booby-ism must be reckoned on where agricultural habits and characteristics prevail.'[84] The tradition that 'town air makes free', which the reformers here echoed, was one of the oldest in Europe. There was a hard basis of fact to it, as the 1831 Northamptonshire pollbook illustrates. If the votes of each town and village from which over thirty freeholders polled are abstracted, the leading anti-reformer heads the poll.[85]

Unlimited favours to the county landlords would not have been acceptable, therefore, to keen reformers. The creation of the new boroughs and of the ten-pound borough vote had removed a great many town freeholders from the counties. Many landlords would enjoy increased borough influence in the reformed system. If the landlords tried to add to these gains, and to ensure their ascendancy in the counties by ridding the latter of all town votes, they would merely make themselves unpopular and jeopardize the finality of the settlement. It was a mistake, in Russell's words, to hold the squires 'up to the jealousy of all other classes'.[86]

If all these votes were cast in the counties, on the other hand, there would be protests, in which some reforming Members would join, that town interests were trenching unfairly on the rural landlord's preserves. It was not possible to leave the balance of interests just as it had been. The Bill would make too great a disturbance for that.

We are not to argue of the future from the past, [Peel wrote]; a new spirit has arisen. Town property gives a facility for the creation of little freeholds which has not yet been called into action, but which infallibly will be if the Reform Bill is to pass.[87]

The clause in the Bill abolishing the requirement that the freehold voter be assessed to the land tax could be assumed to increase town influence in the counties. It would strike the landed interest as invidious to keep in the county constituency precisely those electors whose qualifications were deemed insufficient for a borough vote. There would be particular objection to combining a provision for bringing ten pounders to the desired number by eating into rural areas with one whereby masses of town voters were to be left to the counties. The MP who was a landlord and a reluctant reformer would see the counties as the best bulwark against urban radicalism. He would not take easily to flooding the new county constituencies with what he regarded as the off-scourings of the boroughs.

Until the debates of August began the ministerial balancing act between land and trade had enjoyed some success, in that the opposition's accusations of unfairness had tended to cancel each other. The Bill, Scarlett complained in March, gave 'too decided a preponderancy to the land'. Alexander Baring made the opposite criticism in July. Under the new system, he prophesied, 'the field of coal would beat the field of barley'.[88] The borough freeholder problem provided the ministerial tight-rope walkers with their hardest test. In view of the various claims and fears of the town interests and the county landlords the very low forty-shilling freehold qualification was an embarrass-

H

ment. The probable effects of the various solutions were impossible
to foresee. No one knew how many of the freeholds in new or enlarged boroughs would belong, in any true sense, to town interests,
and how many to the landed interest. It was clear only that the pro-
portions would not be the same in any two boroughs. In a borough
of the market town type a freeholder might be as much a part of the
landed interest as any rural tenant. But this would not be true of the
freeholders in Manchester. The issue was of symbolic importance, as
affecting town and country interests. But there was substance to it
also, as a glance at the outcome will show. In 1864–5 the county
electorate of England and Wales numbered just over 540,000. About
100,000 of these votes depended on qualifying property in boroughs.[89]

The borough freeholder clause, as it stood when the debates on the
question began, represented a compromise weighted in favour of the
county landlords.[90] A forty-shilling freeholder in a borough was not
to have a county vote if he 'or any other person' qualified by means of
that freehold for a borough vote. Thus the only freeholders qualifying
to vote in counties through borough property were to be those whose
freeholds were not occupied by a male adult or were worth less than
£10 a year. When the Bill was drafted ultra-tory support had been
all important; and the proposal about the borough freeholders may
have reflected concern about this support.[91] But it may have resulted
from inadvertence or from a desire to prevent, wherever possible,
instances of a single property conferring votes on two people. Whatever their reasons, the cabinet had started by going as far as their
principles would allow to preserve the county seats for the rural
landlords. They had withdrawn the maximum number of town
voters from the counties short of withdrawing them all.

This compromise was not well conceived and Althorp quickly
abandoned it. It would have deprived the borough freeholder who was
a landlord of a county vote merely because his freehold had given his
tenant a borough vote. Where the tenants renting parts of a freehold
included a male occupier at or above the £10 line, the freeholder
would have no vote for the county. It was not thought proper in
1831 to disfranchise landlords by this kind of side wind. *The Times*
criticized the clause as an 'inadvertency' on 20 May. When a reforming
Member, following the lead of *The Times*, gave notice of a simple
amendment to delete 'or-any-other-person' from the clause, he was
apparently told by Althorp that the government meant to introduce
this amendment themselves.[92]

The public announcement of this intention was bound to raise vehement protests so that Althorp was in no hurry to make it. He wanted to dispose of the tenant-at-will question, on which he faced possible defeat, before he revealed that he was ready to increase very substantially the number of borough freeholders who were to vote in the counties. It would be a mistake to give the agricultural landlords of the country interest the impression, just before the tenant-at-will debate, that their point of view meant nothing to the government. The tenant-at-will amendment would be debated before the borough freeholder clause was reached, so that there was a chance of deferring controversy on the latter until Althorp judged the time to be ripe.

Any such hopes were destroyed by Sugden. On 12 August he braved a barrage of interruptions to point out that the borough freeholder clause as it stood virtually disfranchised borough freeholders who were landlords.[93] He presented the government with a dilemma. The would-be author of the amendment to remove 'or-any-other-person' from the borough freeholder clause had been answered by another reformer. The latter had given notice on 11 August of an amendment to remove all borough freeholders from the counties.[94] Sugden was obliging the government to choose, publicly and at once, between these two amendments. They must either provoke trouble and give the counties more borough freeholders, or accept humiliation and give them none. The author of the first amendment made matters worse on 13 August by telling the House that the government had agreed to make the change which he wanted.

On 14 August the cabinet endorsed the amendment to which Althorp had virtually committed them. The change was to be limited to freeholders. It was not to apply to the borough copyholder, since a man in this latter category had no county vote under the old system and thus no vested interest. Althorp was authorized to summon a party meeting and explain what was intended. He was to say, in Holland's words, that the cabinet's 'reason for altering our former determination was a persuasion that we should hardly be able to carry a provision so injurious to the rights of persons connected with town population'.[95]

Althorp did not manage to keep this decision secret until the right moment. He made several speeches without mentioning it when the cities and towns which were counties of themselves came under debate on 17 August. But the borough freeholder problem formed the chief

topic of discussion and eventually Sugden asked the government once
again what they meant to do about borough freeholders who were landlords. Althorp then outlined the change which the cabinet had sanctioned. That announcement, Sugden replied, represented 'a root-and-
branch cutting up of the power of the aristocracy, and of the influence
of land on the return of county Members'. The ministers' 'changing
and shifting' on issues such as this, he added, showed that they had
introduced their measure 'without due inquiry'.[96] Althorp had been
obliged to make his statement at the worst possible time. The tenant-
at-will debate was due on the following day. Apart from this, a discussion on the cities and towns which were counties of themselves
highlighted the county squires' objections to the change. The six of
these places where the freeholders now held borough votes illustrated
the feasibility of the system for which the squires were pressing. The
government's majority on the cities which were counties of themselves
was only 40.

On 18 August the government suffered their one committee defeat.
They had known for some months that an amendment would be
proposed to give substantial tenants-at-will county votes.[97] More than
one possible mover was mentioned for the proposal. It rested eventually in the hands of the Marquess of Chandos and was to apply to
the occupiers of holdings worth £50 or more a year. The cabinet
decided on 22 July that they would resist it in the Commons but
accept defeat on it. They hoped that its mildly democratic flavour
might make it unacceptable to the Lords.[98]

Chandos's amendment was carried by 232 to 148. The bulk of his
support came from the landlords;[99] but some radicals voted with him
too. The government never had any hope of reversing this vote.
Their case against the clause appealed only to those believers in the
Bill's finality who feared that enfranchising a group obviously dependent on landlords meant provoking a further Reform or a ballot act.[100]
Some landlords were too reckless to have such fears, the radicals too
democratic. The tory Marquess of Londonderry conveyed to Le
Marchant a few days afterwards that 'the tories now saw their only
chance of defeating the Bill was by making it too democratical for
Lord Grey to adopt it'.[101]

The radicals had no liking for the voter who was dependent on his
landlord. But this was outweighed for some of them by their dislike
of finality. They did not want the Bill to be unobjectionable. They
wanted it to work outrageously enough to make an overwhelming

case for ballot or for a further Reform. They saw advantage in giving the landlords a good deal of rope. Peel and his friends were not believers in finality. They thought that a new Reform Act was on the way and that giving the vote now to some tenants would make little difference to the speed with which it came. The addition to the county electorate was considerable. In 1864–5 tenants-at-will accounted for over 116,000 of the 540,000 qualifications to vote in English and Welsh counties.[102]

The cabinet were attacked by *The Times* for conceding too much to the landlords. A leader in that paper announced that the division of counties and the Chandos clause taken together constituted a serious weakening of the Bill. The ministers did not adopt such a gloomy view.[103] Their defeat on the tenants-at-will helped them to solve their borough freeholder problem. In trying to hold the balance between town and country they were concerned, not so much with the effect of each clause, as with that of the Bill seen as a whole. The fact that Chandos had added to the influence of the county landlords provided a cast-iron case for allowing some town votes in counties as a counterweight. On 20 August Althorp secured the adoption of his revised borough freeholder clause with little opposition. The tenor of the discussion had changed greatly since 17 August. A prominent reformer now argued that even the revised clause did not leave enough borough freeholders with county votes. Four days later the ministers defeated a last attempt to keep all borough freeholders in the boroughs by 225 to 136. In that debate Russell conveniently forgot that the revised clause had been produced before the Chandos debate, and attributed the revision to the need to counter the effects of the tenant-at-will.[104] A speech by Althorp on 26 August was characterized by a similar lapse of memory.[105]

The government were not hard pressed in any further committee divisions. Peel, who hated being separated from his family, left London for a fortnight at the end of August.[106] The committee stage ended at about 7 p.m. on 7 September after consuming forty nights of debate. The report stage took three nights. In the course of it the ministry made a last adjustment to their Schedules by giving Wales two more Members and adding Ashton-under-Lyne and Stroud to Schedule D as a counterpoise. After a further three nights for the 'third reading' debate, the Bill was finally passed early on 22 September by 345 to 236.[107] The government were estimated to have lost 22, and the opposition to have gained 8, since the second reading. Later on the same day Russell, accompanied by more than a hundred Members, brought the Bill up to the Lords. Nothing was said by the opposition peers. Althorp thought this ominous. It showed, he told his father, 'very good discipline and entire agreement on the part of the enemy'.[108]

7

THE BILL IN THE LORDS (I):
THE WHISPER OF A FACTION

It is easy for a peer to be a statesmen if the trouble of the life be not too much for him. (Trollope, *Phineas Finn*)

The attitudes which had determined the course of the struggle in the Commons were operative during the opening phase in the Lords also. In both Houses the Bill's opponents began with a certain tactical advantage, since the government, having overestimated their parliamentary support, lacked any power to coerce the doubtfuls. In both the opposition leaders rejected attrition and used this advantage to mount an outright attack on the Bill. In both this decision was dictated, partly by the leader's conviction and inclination, but also by his weak hold on his followers and by their disorganization. Its adoption was made easier in both by a certain disregard for the force of popular enthusiasm for the Bill.

The cabinet ceased to believe before the dissolution that the House of Lords already contained a majority for the Bill.[1] But they still hoped that popular pressure might cow the opposition into allowing the second reading without a division, or that, if this failed, a majority could be scraped up somehow by the autumn. Grey wrote on 18 May about the Lords: 'I hope that what has taken place in the late elections may have its effect on the prudence of that body.'[2] These hopes were not confined to the government. Some observers did not share the king's view that the Bill as it stood was doomed to defeat. 'It is probable the peers will trot round as they did upon the Catholic question,' Greville noted in the same month.[3] Creations on a modest scale were planned, not so much to provide a majority in themselves, as to help in converting the doubtfuls by showing that the king was still behind his ministers and the Bill.

Holland was urging a token creation on Grey as early as 21 April. His arguments were reinforced when the election of the sixteen

Scottish representative peers turned out badly for the government; and five reformers were promoted to the Lords in a batch in June. No permanent addition to the peerage was entailed: three Scottish peers, and one Irish, and a peer's oldest son, received baronies of the United Kingdom.

Early in July the opposition, hoping that taking the coronation oath might add to the king's scruples about assenting to revolutionary legislation, pressed for the coronation to take place without delay. Fearing the exertion, and wishing to save the expense, the king had been anxious to postpone or even avoid the ceremony; but the ministry now advised him that it must be held. This gave Grey the chance of another, and rather bigger, creation. He obtained the king's sanction to the largest batch of coronation peerages which the precedent of 1821 could be stretched to cover, and thus added fifteen more votes to the government's strength.[4]

Useful as these additions were they do not seem to have made a great impression on the doubtfuls. They avoided the drawbacks of a massive creation. These are described below. It is enough to say here that they were very great. But the hope of gaining the advantages while avoiding the drawbacks proved vain. The king's sanction for the June and September lists was not regarded as evidence that he would allow the entirely different scale of creation needed to ensure the passage of the Bill. The five reformers of the June batch were well qualified for seats in the Lords in the normal course; and everyone had expected peers at the coronation. After many years of tory creations the whigs were clearly entitled to start redressing the balance. It was the problem of March in the Commons over again. No one doubted that the king would give the cabinet all normal facilities. But that degree of support did not entail creating enough peers for a majority, just as in March it had not entailed allowing a dissolution.

The effect of massive support for the Bill in Commons and country was equally weak. The proportion who could be overawed by a popular movement was smaller in the Upper House than in the Lower, while the proportion who reacted against any such movement was larger. The dissolution seemed to the doubtfuls in the Lords reckless and almost unconstitutional. It repelled two peers for each one who was impressed by the majority which it had produced. The election might have shown that it was unwise for MPs to defy the government. A peer was more happily placed for a display of independence. Alarm at Reform mobs had little effect except among those noblemen whose country seats lay near great towns. Many opposition and doubtful peers regarded the possibility of disorder if the Bill were rejected as a bogey raised by the government. Moreover the fear of being thought afraid was even more powerful among the peers than in the Commons. Their principles forbade them to yield to threats, especially to threats in which they did not believe. The government's attempts to show that the king would allow a large creation were unconvincing; and no other threat counted.

The government were active in personal canvassing. Anglesey was confident of securing the Earl of Harrington on the ground that he had once succeeded in the harder task of persuading that noble dandy to part with his whiskers and beard. But Harrington did not vote for the Bill. The use of patronage gained some support. The Marquess of Downshire was clinched, for instance, with the ribbon of St Patrick given in the coronation honours.[5] Most of the Irish nobility were notably exacting, however. 'Northland professes to be with us,' Grey told Holland on 2 June,

but wants to be an earl, and rather intimates that he will not come if he is not. Ditto Ld. *O'Neill* who wants to be a marquess; & that is the case with nearly the whole Irish peerage, who, thinking that we are in distress, press their claims without mercy. Amongst them *Lord Donegall*, who applies for a dukedom.[6]

Northland was given his earldom in the coronation list.

The problems presented by Donegall and O'Neill were more complex. Neither was a whig;[7] but both had ties with the ministry. Donegall's have been mentioned already. His son and heir, the Earl of Belfast, had been allowed to keep a household office in November 1830. O'Neill's brother, who sat for County Antrim on the family interest, had voted throughout for the Bill. Each nobleman was given a Lord Lieutenancy and O'Neill was offered a marquessate. It might be thought that the government had met all the reasonable claims of these two, and that, patronage apart, political consistency in O'Neill's case, and a binding obligation in Donegall's, would have ensured their votes for the Bill. But unreasonableness and inconsistency lay lightly on some Irish magnates; and their attitude towards obligations could be flexible. O'Neill demanded a special remainder of the marquessate to his brother. Donegall indicated that two Lord Lieutenancies were due to him. As his second he coveted Antrim which had gone to O'Neill. It would clearly require the dukedom to assuage this insult and ensure his support for the Bill. A special remainder and a dukedom for doubtful supporters of tory leanings were more than Grey would stomach. In straits though he was he refused. When it came to October Donegall voted for the Bill and O'Neill abstained.

By the end of August the cabinet had no doubt of the weakness of their position; and Brougham and Holland were pressing Grey for a creation large enough to secure a majority. This proposal entailed daunting difficulties. There was, first, the problem of securing the king's consent to an exercise of the prerogative for which only one precedent existed dating from Queen Anne's reign. Secondly, while plenty of ill-qualified people wanted to be ennobled, many of those best qualified wanted not to be. Sir Clifford Constable, MP, not only applied himself but had a statement on the size of his income sent by his steward.[8] He had, however, voted more or less consistently against the Bill. On the other hand when Lord George Cavendish was given an earldom in the coronation list, Devonshire told Grey of his

very great regret at the probable shortening of William Cavendish's career in the House of Commons and his representation of Derbyshire. . . . Had I been consulted I should without opposing have considered that I was making another sacrifice in support of your administration.[9]

Devonshire's objection is understandable. William Cavendish needed to stay for some time in the House of Commons for the sake both of his own political career and of the family interest in Derbyshire, which could not be maintained at full strength unless a prominent and capable Cavendish were available to sit for the county. He was the grandson and heir of Lord George and also stood in line of succession to the Dukedom. Lord George was 77 and Devonshire 41. To say that the earldom would 'probably shorten' William Cavendish's time in the Commons was thus no overstatement. In the event his grandfather's death removed him from the Commons in 1834 whereas he did not succeed to the dukedom until 1858.

As Lord Chamberlain Devonshire was expected to make sacrifices: noblemen not in office might be less amenable.[10] It was accepted that a new creation, however large, must be composed entirely of the wealthy and well-connected, and must make the smallest possible permanent addition to the peerage. The 'peerables' were thus largely confined to rich and respectable reformers who fell into one of three categories. These were, first, the heirs to peerages, secondly, Scottish and Irish peers (since their promotion would enlarge only the House of

Lords and not the peerage as a whole), and thirdly, commoners whose peerages would die with them, 'barrens' as Holland called them. None of the categories overflowed with willing and unobjectionable candidates. It would have been easier for Asquith to make 300 peers in 1911 than for Grey to make 50 in 1831.

Thirdly, no MP sitting for a popular seat could be regarded as a 'peerable'. Even supposing that the family would allow the heir who was a county Member to be 'called up', a by-election was unlikely to suit the government's book. A Reform candidate who was acceptable personally, who could afford enough money to carry the seat, and who was willing to spend that for a tenure of a few months, might be hard to find. The cabinet could not afford a clutch of by-election defeats.[11]

Finally, there was the problem of how many peers to create. It would be disastrous to make too few and be defeated. Yet to ensure against all risks would require a creation larger than either the king or aristocratic opinion would sanction. There were two reasons for this enormous margin of error. The first was the care taken by the opposition to conceal their strength. Wellington restrained his followers from rushing into the division lobby and disclosing their numbers on such secondary matters as relations with Portugal. A peer holding another's proxy had to enter it in a register in the House before he could cast the proxy vote. At the end of August the duke had not entered any of his proxies. The second uncertainty concerned the effect of a large creation on wavering government supporters. Those peers who found the Bill rather sweeping would probably regard swamping the House of Lords as next to a revolution. A potential vote for the Bill would thus be lost, or even turned into one against it.

In face of these difficulties the cabinet agreed on 5 September to try the effect of the coronation batch of peers and to leave open the question of any larger creation.[12] Postponing such a creation until the need for it had been proved was thought to be the only way of ensuring sufficiently massive support for it. Althorp argued that 'the crisis which, by preventing the conduct of public affairs, would justify a large creation of peers . . . had not yet arrived'. Defeat would justify the measure: the expectation of defeat did not.

The fact that this doctrine almost certainly entailed the loss of the Bill, and a delay while the Commons passed its successor, became partly obscured by the usual wishful thinking. A rumour was circulating that, when the Bill was brought up to the Lords, Wellington would propose delaying consideration of it. A division on this proposal would have been ideal for the government. The opposition could not have secured a majority for it without both revealing their numbers and strengthening their opponents' case for a creation. Wellington learned on 15 or 16 September that the government hoped for a vote when the Bill arrived and, as has been related, he did not oblige them. The leakage of the cabinet's wishes was of minor importance in guiding him. The rumour about his plans seems to have been baseless from the start. There is no evidence that he had ever intended to allow a division before the second reading.

Encouraged by the rumour about a delaying proposal, the ministers virtually left open the question of what they would do if defeated on the second reading. The discussion on 5 September had made clear that a move to create peers would divide them even if it were made after they had been put in a minority. Lansdowne, who was a prominent opponent of a creation, let his supporters know in confidence that, if the majority against the second reading were substantial, the government would resign. This news aroused indignation. Macaulay, when Lansdowne told him, protested 'with as much strength of expression as was suited to the nature of our connection and to his age and rank'.[13]

The back benchers in the Commons who had voted for the Bill held what was in effect a protest meeting on 21 September. Resignation was condemned roundly. E. J. Littleton, who was one of the organizers, noted: 'Much strong language talked, especially about the chance of ministers *resigning* if beaten—which all considered would be treason to the king, treason to the people, and a betrayal of their supporters.' But the back benchers were no more ready for a massive dose of peers than were the cabinet. Hume's resolution demanding a sufficient creation should the Bill be defeated was rejected as too revolutionary at this stage. It was merely agreed to reconvene the meeting at noon on the day after an adverse division in the Lords.

No one suggested resignation as a tactical move in September 1831. The idea of obliging the opposition to try to form a government, in order to show everyone that they were incapable of doing so, was not mooted.[14] A letter of 2 September from Stanley to Grey suggests that those who talked of resignation were chiefly concerned with avoiding the charge of clinging improperly to office.[15] The protesting back benchers objected, on the ground that it was despicably weak to propose the Bill and then to abandon it. It was months before the reformers in the country could be accustomed to the idea that resignation might be necessary. In October 1831 the political unions would have seen it simply as a betrayal. 'Government is afraid of the people breaking loose,' Parkes told Grote on 4 October, 'it is impossible if they but stick to the helm.'[16]

The spectacle of a cabinet pledged to enact a measure, and yet as unwilling as their followers to sanction the only means of enacting it, is a familiar one. Grey's position was somewhat like Asquith's in the case of Irish Home Rule. Both led parties which would not face up to the conditions that had to be fulfilled if their policies were to be enacted. The reformers wanted the Bill passed without either a sufficient creation of peers or the government's temporary resignation. The liberals of 1912 wanted Ulster put under Dublin without any Ulstermen being coerced, still less shot. Grey like Asquith shared his followers' distaste for facing the facts. To a second generation peer of his type diluting the peerage by a massive creation was peculiarly abhorrent. But there was a great difference between the two cases. Grey's difficulties, unlike Asquith's, were temporary. In 1912 there was no prospect that a majority of electors would come to sanction putting Belfast under Dublin by force. In 1831 there was every prospect that the reformers would come to demand peers.

Among the opposition leaders in the Lords Ellenborough and Wharncliffe opposed a head-on collision and supported amending in committee. Ellenborough's aim, as recorded in his diary on 7 July, was, by a series of amendments, to

place the ministers in the position of being obliged to take what will satisfy half the reformers, or to throw away the whole. . . . I wish to divide the reformers, drawing to the side of the H. of Lords all the most respectable.

Supposing, [he recorded on 20 July] that we should throw it [the Bill] out, there would be a clamour against us aided by the ministers, the press, and the king's name, under cover of which peers enough would be created, and we should have the whole Bill forced down our throats.

Ellenborough's colleagues agreed with his aim, but saw great objections to his tactics. His was a minority view from the start. The opposition's chance of success in inserting amendments during committee was no better now than it had been in April when the same tactics had been rejected by the leaders in the Commons. It was as hard as ever for anti-reformers to agree on a method of improving the Bill. Moreover Wellington was not sure of his majority for committee amendments. In the first place he was sensitive, as always, to ultra-tory pressure. The ultras in the Lords were more hostile to Reform than were their counterparts in the Commons; and they might well be so outraged by a 'surrender' on the second reading as to withhold their cooperation in committee. Secondly, his superiority was greatest in proxies. The rules of procedure did not allow these to be used in committee; and most of the proxy voters concerned were too old or feeble to attend in person. Finally, a number of opposition peers who would come for the second reading could not be kept in London in November even to stop a revolution. The duke judged his force to be fitter for a brief battle than for a siege.

The disadvantages of rejection on second reading were far less obvious. The crucial question was one of numbers. All the cabinet's notions of a creation in case of defeat assumed that the majority against the Bill would be small. 'Persons conversant in lists,' Holland noted in his journal on 27 September, 'pretend that the Bill will be beat by nine without bishops and some say (preposterously, I think) by 17 when they are added.'

Wellington, by contrast, expected to defeat the government by at least 40. He had no fear of peers being created straight after the division if his majority were of anything like that size. He knew by mid-August that some ministerial peers objected violently to a creation and that one or two eldest sons had refused to be called up.[17] By the last week of September he was sure both that he could inflict a heavy reverse on the government and that they would not reply to it either by a creation or by resigning. Like many of his followers he was not afraid of the riots which were likely to follow rejection. Unlike the other opposition leaders he was convinced by mid-September of a 'very prevailing change of opinion in the country upon . . . the Bill'.[18] His great object was to gain time and allow this reaction to gather momentum, by forcing the ministers to introduce a new Bill and so to do all the work in the Commons again. Even if the reaction went little further something might turn up at last to divert attention from the Bill. 'In this interval,' Wellington wrote in October, 'the country may manifest an important change of opinion, or providence may otherwise save us from the misfortunes impending.'[19] Sydney Smith compared the duke's efforts against Reform to the attempts of a certain Mrs Partington to sweep back the Atlantic in the great storm of 1824.[20] In fact, however, 'Mrs Partington' was keeping his feet dry in the hope that the tide would soon turn.

The duke was justified in distrusting the suggestions that the loss of the Bill would be a signal for serious disorder. They came largely from ardent reformers whose testimony, Melbourne told Sir Herbert Taylor, 'though by no means to be rejected, must be received with some allowance'.[21] On the other hand anyone less optimistic than Wellington would have discounted just as heavily the evidence that the Bill's popularity had begun to wane. This evidence amounted to no more than that some Reform meetings in September, notably those in Westminster and on Penenden Heath in Kent, were comparatively ill-attended.[22] That might be a symptom less of apathy than of confidence that the Bill was now safe. To a dispassionate eye nothing about it had become unpopular except perhaps its conservative clauses.

Wellington's appreciation of the position thus showed his characteristic mixture of shrewdness and political short sight. He knew the opposition peers' strength and their limitations. He understood the cabinet's hesitations about peer-making, but not the pressure for the Bill to which they would be subjected; for he still did not grasp the force of the Reform movement. He thought that the ministers themselves did not wish to carry their Bill: 'They must know,' he told Ellenborough in July, 'it puts an end to aristocracy.' It should have been clear that, whatever the ministers wanted, they had been governed less since 1 March by their inclinations than by what their followers obliged them to do. Nor was time on the opposition's side as certainly as Wellington supposed. Delay might allow the reaction to gather strength. It would also educate the reformers in the governmental tactic of resignation, and force Grey and the king to face up to peer-making.

Neither Wellington's misjudgments nor the government's had much effect on the decision at this stage. The Reform MPs were not yet ready either for a creation or for the government to resign. The shadow cabinet would probably have decided to oppose the second reading even if their leader had appreciated to the full the weight of Reform opinion. The opposition did not all have Wellington's integrity. It was possible to approve of his tactics for reasons different from his. A diehard line was advocated by some on the ground that any considerable delay in the passage of the Bill would bring widespread disorder, and that this would in turn produce a demand for repressive government in the tory style. Every month by which the crisis was prolonged would increase unemployment and make it harder for the government to control the radicals.

In August 1831 *Blackwood's* looked ahead to a time when

the horrible stagnation ... of internal trade ... will have come to such a pass as to command attention in all quarters to something much more interesting, as well as important, than *any* Reform. By that time ... there will be war by land and war by sea; and there will be a bit of a dust at Manchester or elsewhere and it will be laid in blood.[23]

In public the opposition said that people were too apathetic about the Bill to riot when it was rejected. The writer in *Blackwood's* revealed another view. At least one anti-reformer not merely expected rioting, but welcomed it. He is unlikely to have been the only person to entertain such thoughts. He was unusual only in being indiscreet enough to publish them.

The formal decision to divide against the second reading was taken at a dinner of leading opposition peers at the duke's on 21 September. Wharncliffe suggested announcing during the debate that if the Bill were rejected its opponents would move an Address to the king in favour of moderate Reform. This proposal found no support. The discussion of it was curtailed by the arrival of Eldon and Kenyon, loquaciously drunk after dining with Cumberland. Wharncliffe revived his scheme at a further dinner on 1 October when it was fully discussed. As in March, the object of this proposed moderate Reform pledge was to win support and show the king that the opponents of the Bill could form a government. The proposal was rejected again, though those present, by choosing Wharncliffe to move the amendment, showed that they did not want to appear as the opponents of any Reform. There were great objections to any Reform formula. It would embarrass the duke in view of what he had said on 2 November 1830. It might split the party. No two opposition peers agreed on how much Reform was admissible; and, although this type of declaration was calculated to encourage the king to send for the opposition, it was also liable to be a nuisance to them when he had done so.

Two leading tory statesmen, Harrowby and Lyndhurst, attended neither dinner. After much speculation on their intentions both of them spoke and voted against the Bill. Harrowby had retired in 1827 after a long ministerial career. He was a liberal of the older school and had been Pitt's intimate friend. In a world in which placemen and parties still lay under some suspicion he commanded respect as a disinterested elder statesman. His decision on Reform was recognized to be unaffected by place-seeking or partisanship. He was a lifelong friend of the Church and very influential with the bishops. Most of the thirty voters on the episcopal bench were doubtfuls. They feared that if the Bill were passed it would strengthen their radical foes, but that if it were rejected with their votes turning the scale popular anger would fall largely on them.

Harrowby had been abroad until August 1831. In the last week of September he decided to oppose the second reading. Most of the considerations which had influenced the opposition leaders to do so applied in a slightly different form with him too. He thought the Bill disastrous; and he had not been in England long enough to appreciate the strength of feeling for it. Being 68 and in uncertain health he lacked the stamina for a wrangle in committee. He said in debate that he had tried his hand at amendments but found that no changes which he could devise bettered the Bill materially.[24] His decision was almost certainly affected by the Reform meeting and the duke's first dinner, both held on 21 September. He was reported at the dinner as hesitating to oppose because he feared 'being left without a government'.[25] The meeting of Reform MPs must have removed that fear: after it no one could suppose that Grey would resign if defeated. Apart from this, once the duke and his dinner guests had committed the opposition against the second reading the 'independent' fringe were more or less obliged to follow and ensure the success of the policy. The smaller the majority against the Bill the likelier a creation of peers,[26] while its passage by a narrow margin, because Harrowby and his friends would not vote against it, would preclude any hope of effective cooperation from the diehards in committee. Harrowby's decision delighted the opposition leaders. 'It will keep the bishops steady,' wrote Holmes, the whip.[27]

Lyndhurst, who was the only opposition speaker capable of answering Brougham in debate, received an invitation to the first dinner, but dined that evening with Grey and Holland at Holland House. The government had hopes of his voice and vote. Contemporaries regarded Lyndhurst as an opportunist whose political line was always, in Greville's words, that 'which appeared most conducive to his own interest'.[28] Lady Lyndhurst told her friends that her lord was under no obligations to the tories. It was thought that he must have expectations of still higher judicial office from the whigs. After the debate Lady Bathurst wrote:

Her Ladyship's language had latterly been so Reform like (I mean quite in the political sense) that many people supposed she wd insist upon his voting for the 2d reading. This I confess I *thought* . . . most improbable; but the bad state of health of one of the Chief Justices made one not wish to risk a large bet upon it! I suppose the said C. Justice is better for Ld. Lyndhurst quite went out of his way to attack the Premier.[29]

Despite all the speculation, and the judgeship which Lyndhurst had accepted from the whigs, it is questionable whether he ever wavered in his allegiance to the opposition. He had told an opposition meeting in July that he was with them; and he wrote to Wellington on 20 September: 'If we have a fair prospect of success we ought to divide upon the second reading.'[30] His appetite for high office was certainly sharp as his later manoeuvres showed. But attachment to the whigs did not offer the best chance of satisfying it. They had the advantage of being in power; but they were already supplied with a Lord Chancellor.

There were no eleventh-hour developments to arrest the growing strength and confidence of the opposition. Grey was prostrated for some days by the death on 24 September of his grandson, Durham's elder son Charles Lambton. 'Why did the blow fall on this heavenly boy,' he wrote to Princess Lieven, 'whilst I and so many others who would be no loss to the world are spared? I can think of nothing else and am quite unnerved for the battle that I have to fight.'[31] Even if Grey had been undistracted, news of opposition gains would never have induced him to put in hand a last-minute creation. Indeed it had the opposite effect. In the end Holmes showed Ellice the opposition list to prove that a small creation would not give the government a majority. 'Lord Grey,' Ellenborough recorded, 'when he understood what our members would be, said it relieved his mind very much, for no one now could ask him to make peers.'

Nor were the final demonstrations of support for the Bill over-whelming enough to frighten opposition peers. On the first day of the debate Attwood held a meeting on Newhall Hill where even anti-reformers gave the attendance as 15,000.[32] Brougham presented eighty petitions to the Lords that day, and Grey more than forty. On the other hand 800 merchants, bankers, and traders of the City of London petitioned the Lords against the Bill;[33] and in the Dorset by-election where polling was in progress throughout the debate Viscount Ashley, the tory candidate, seemed likely to succeed, though the reformers had won both seats in the general election.

The second-reading debate began on 3 October and lasted for five nights. 'By all accounts,' wrote Greville, 'it was a magnificent display and incomparably superior to that in the House of Commons.' This superiority is not hard to explain. Both sides strained every nerve, believing that some votes depended on the debate. Both deployed practically their whole debating strength. As the division would probably finish the business nothing need be kept in reserve. There were comparatively few poor speeches. Unlike most MPs, peers did not have to please patrons or constituents. They felt little pressure either to be reticent or to spout unnecessarily. With few exceptions their speakers both had minds of their own and spoke them. Moreover the Lords contained in Grey and Harrowby the only surviving exponents of a fine rhetorical style. In the Commons years of increasing business had swept away the classical eloquence of Fox's time.

The peers in the cabinet outshone their predecessors in speaking power. Grey who made the opening and closing speeches was a far better speaker than Wellington on an issue of this kind. If the government had a chance of avoiding defeat it lay in the ascendancy which they were generally expected to establish during the debate. All hope of this ascendancy was extinguished by Harrowby, who made the speech of his life against the Bill on the second night. His detached position gave him an exceptional opportunity. As he had not served in the last cabinet Wellington's remarks of 2 November did not embarrass him. He was free to say that the government should have introduced a moderate Reform Bill. Van Buren, then the American Minister in London, thought this the ablest anti-Reform speech which he had heard in either House. To it, Lady Bathurst told a friend, 'we undoubtedly owe many votes'. 'Harrowby's was the most effective, as well as the best, speech,' George Villiers wrote to his sister, 'because he was the least liable to suspicion of sinister motive.'[34]

The climax on the last night was the duel between Brougham and Lyndhurst. Galleries had been built for the debate and the chamber was crowded to suffocation. When Brougham rose soon after nine the temperature had reached 85°. Sustained and inflamed by tumblers of mulled port he delivered for over three hours, in Littleton's words, 'one of the most splendid speeches conceivable—flaming with wit and irony and eloquence, and nerved with argument and admonition to a degree that made one tremble'. Brougham's speech included a powerful reply to Harrowby. But this, besides being long-deferred, included a personal attack which was thought in bad taste. He spoke to the press reporters as much as his fellow peers. Neither he nor any other lawyer was likely to affect votes.

Lyndhurst answered Brougham in severe and masterly fashion. The Archbishop of Canterbury then spoke shortly against the Bill on behalf of the bench. Grey replied between four and five in the morning. He had been roused by Lyndhurst; and even opponents admitted the power of this reply.[35] The MPs behind the throne could scarcely be restrained from cheering. Brougham was by now so drunk that he had difficulty in putting the question. The opposition had a majority of 41. Most of them heard the numbers in silence.[36]

The Bill's opponents had achieved 'a great triumph', as Althorp admitted in the Commons.[37] All the whigs and many radicals agreed that to create peers in reply to such a majority was 'out of the question'. Grey used that phrase to the king: so did the young radical, George Grote, in writing to Parkes.[38] The group in the cabinet who had pressed for a creation in case of defeat now dropped the plan. Althorp, for instance, told his father: 'A majority of 41 is not to be coped with. I think the reasonable part of the country would not support us in making fifty peers.'[39]

On 10 October Viscount Ebrington's motion of confidence in the ministry, reasserting the 'firm adherence' of the Commons 'to the principle and leading provisions' of the Bill, was debated and passed by a majority of 131.[40] Althorp, who was the only speaker from the government front bench, declared: 'Unless I felt a reasonable hope that a measure as efficient . . . might be secured by our continuance in office, I would not continue in office an hour.'[41] His statement had been approved by the cabinet, and was similar to those already made by Grey in the Lords during the debate. To show that the king approved of reintroducing the Bill, Grey went that day to Windsor and secured the removal of Earl Howe, the queen's chamberlain, who had voted against the second reading.

Though the cabinet were uncertain of their next step the hope of passing an equally efficient measure was not baseless. It seemed unlikely that the opposition could bring such numbers against the Bill again. They were anything but a united band of anti-reformers. Wharncliffe had declared for moderate Reform in moving the opposition amendment. The Archbishop of Canterbury had taken the same line; and his speech suggested that the bishops were unwilling to persist in an unpopular stand. Harrowby was a moderate by habit and temperament. When someone congratulated him on his part in the opposition's victory he had replied: 'I am not good for this prank a second time.'[42] His speech had been a plea for delay so that some compromise might be arranged. His policy was in essence the one which Wharncliffe had been advocating since March. These two now began to consult together. They were natural allies. Harrowby's eldest son was married to Wharncliffe's first cousin and Wharncliffe's eldest son to one of Harrowby's daughters. Harrowby supplied the prestige and power in debate which Wharncliffe had hitherto lacked.

For both Harrowby and Wellington the object of opposing the second reading had been to gain time. But, whereas Wellington meant to sit tight and await developments, Harrowby planned to use the interval won to produce agreement on a modified Reform. Wellington's position has been described already. The second reading vote, he told Ellenborough on 15 October, gave 'a delay for six months during which time a change might take place in the public mind'. The opposition hoped that the unnatural Reform coalition between middle and working class would soon break down. 'The alarm which has long prevailed among men of large property,' Ellenborough wrote in his diary for 19 November, 'will find its way down to persons of smaller property, and so gradually descend until the great mass of the proprietary classes combine against revolution under the mask of Reform.' Alternatively there was still some chance for Peel's 'enforced natural union between aristocracy and disfranchised population'.[43] The opposition triumph on the second reading had, however, done nothing to remove the drawback to Wellington's tactics. While these changes were a possible outcome of delay, its only certain outcome was a strong demand for a creation of peers.

Harrowby hoped that the Lords' vote would produce some popular reaction against the more sweeping provisions of the Bill. He and Wharncliffe meant to exploit the resulting demand for a compromise. Harrowby was not prepared to take the risks involved in a policy of waiting indefinitely. He had no mind to stand by while bishops' palaces were burned. Granting that the opposition's majority was liable to melt away there was much to be said for his tactics. But his hope that the Lords' vote would rally moderate opinion was unrealistic. Once again the opposition were incapable of adopting the only tactics which would have been effective. To follow up their second-reading victory with a compromise move backed by the whole party was beyond them. Nothing else would have made much impact on the government, the public, or even the king.

An immediate attempt to rally moderate opponents of the Bill was an essential part of Harrowby's scheme. He and Wharncliffe therefore at once revived the latter's proposal of a resolution for a modified Bill and notified the cabinet through Carlisle that this was to be moved. But both sides were discouraging and the scheme was dropped. The cabinet apparently told Harrowby that, to reassure Reformers in the country, they would be obliged to oppose a resolution if moved at once, but that concessions might be made when the excitement had died down. Wellington's success on the second reading had raised his hopes of avoiding any but the smallest Reform and thus increased his objection to a resolution pledging him to go farther. He told Ellen-borough on 8 October that no more was needed 'this year' than buying up Old Sarum and Gatton and transferring their seats to Leeds and Birmingham.

Harrowby and Wharncliffe were not deterred by the failure of their scheme for a resolution. One London paper with a comparatively large circulation took their line: the *Morning Herald* announced on 12 October that it had 'never joined in any cry for "the whole Bill"', and argued against a creation of peers. On that day Harrowby's son, Viscount Sandon, opened a correspondence with Stanley in which various possible modifications in the Bill were discussed;[44] and Wharn-cliffe took the opportunity of a Reform petition to tell the Lords that he would support a modified measure to settle the question. Harrowby and Haddington, a Scottish Canningite, made similar statements in the Lords the next day.

On 21 October Sandon defeated a radical Reformer in the Liverpool by-election after a campaign during which he supported modifications in the Bill. Wharncliffe now made contact with two groups who, while opponents or at least critics of the Bill, were particularly anxious for a settlement, the leading bankers and merchants of the City of London and the bishops. The vote in the Lords had been followed by an alarming demand for gold. The tory bankers wanted moderation more than ever. Many of them were prepared to swallow the Bill rather than see political uncertainties and the possibility of disorder

continue to hamper trade. The division had borne out all the bishops'
fears about the hatred to which voting against the Bill might expose
them. They had supplied Wellington's majority, in the sense that if
the 21 of them who voted against the second reading had been on the
other side the government would have won. Some of them, notably
the Bishop of London who had been absent from the division for
private reasons, now wished to disengage the Church from the
defence of the rotten boroughs. They were deeply interested in
preventing a creation of peers, since radical proposals about the
organization and property of the Church were unlikely to become law
while the tories kept their Lords majority. The Archbishop of Canterbury was no diehard. His immediate reaction to the division had been
to make a compromise move. He had already approached Peel
without success through Aberdeen.[45] He knew that there was as much
anxiety for a settlement in the City of London as among the bishops.
Horsley Palmer, the Governor of the Bank of England, was his wife's
brother-in-law.

On 24 October Horsley Palmer and Ward, lately an MP for the
City, began a series of meetings with Wharncliffe as a result of which
they agreed to launch a City declaration for a modified Bill. On the
following day Wharncliffe saw the Archbishop of Canterbury and
the Bishop of London. The negotiations with these two groups were
conducted in consultation with the government who were represented
in the business chiefly by Althorp.

Wharncliffe's idea was to demand concessions in the new Bill in
return for an undertaking that it should not be defeated in the Lords
on second reading. Early in November Stanley stayed at Lord Harrowby's in Staffordshire with Grey's consent; and on 11 November
Harrowby and Wharncliffe drew up a statement of the changes in the
Bill at which they aimed. Wharncliffe then returned to London and
saw Palmerston who had been one of the originators of the negotiation.
Finally, on 16 November he had a long discussion with Grey. The
'waverers' as they were soon nicknamed were under way. But the
reaction against the Bill on which they relied had not appeared.

Popular protests against the loss of the Bill showed the usual variation
in intensity. In Birmingham the bells were tolled all night after the
news had been received; and 100,000 people are said to have attended
Attwood's protest meeting. In Leeds, on the other hand, the tory-
radical tradition still had some effect; and even the liberal paper there

admitted the popular indignation to be 'deep' rather than 'loud'. In London the editions of the *Morning Chronicle* and the *Sun* giving the news appeared in mourning with deep black borders. On 12 October the metropolitan parishes, 70,000 strong, marched through the West End to present their Address in support of the ministry and the Bill to the king.

Serious riots broke out at Derby and Nottingham; and Nottingham Castle which belonged to the Duke of Newcastle was burned.[46] It lay very close to the town and Newcastle charged the whig magistrates of the Nottingham corporation with a disinclination to defend his property. As usual, local boundaries provided an alibi. The Nottingham magistrates pointed out that the Castle Liberty was outside their jurisdiction.

A carriage containing an anti-Reform peer and his daughter and son-in-law was attacked in Darlington. The occupants were lucky to escape alive. In London on 12 October Life Guards had to rescue the Marquess of Londonderry. The Bishop of Durham dared not show his face in the Palatinate. The Bishop of Exeter was advised to postpone a consecration. His palace was defended by coastguards, and on one occasion by yeomanry. It had become dangerous even to look like a bishop. Among those mistaken for anti-reforming bishops, and attacked, were a bishop who had voted for the Bill, the Roman Catholic Bishop of Cork, a dissenting minister, a reforming MP, and the two Law Officers. A clerical hatter in the Strand sold off his shovel hats for thirty shillings a dozen.[47]

The suspicion soon spread in the Reform movement that the cabinet were planning a long prorogation of Parliament in order to negotiate the passage of a modified Bill. A rumour which was as near the truth as this could not be scotched. Russell assured the Birmingham Union that 'the whisper of a faction' in the Lords 'would not prevail against the voice of the nation'.[48] But there was clearly no plan for drowning the whisper. A deputation of Westminster reformers, including Place, managed to make contact with the Prime Minister late at night on 12 October, though the least prepossessing member of the party had to be screened from Grey's patrician eyes.[49] They came away disappointed. The premier refused to commit himself, but gave the impression according to Place,

(1) that Parliament would be prorogued till after Christmas,
(2) that a more conciliatory Bill would be introduced,
(3) that no new peers would be made,

(4) that if the public made riots, they would be bayonetted, shot, and hanged.[50] Grey's open letter to Hobhouse a few days later promised a 'not less efficient' Bill, but did not say how it was to be passed.[51]

The vote in the Lords intensified the popular demand for Reform. A number of new political unions were formed. Leicester acquired one, for instance, on the Birmingham model.[52] This had enrolled 800 members by the time of its first public meeting on 2 November. Between the Lords' rejection of the Bill and the end of October, Attwood and his colleagues were said to have received fifty requests for their rules from would-be founders of political unions.

While the Lords' decision stimulated the growth of the political unions, it also presented the union leaders with problems of control. It was not possible to confine reformers to supporting the Bill when there was no longer a convincing prospect that it would be carried intact. It became harder than ever for leaders such as Attwood to keep the working class united with the bourgeoisie in the path of moderation. A gathering of 10,000 at Manchester on 12 October was flooded by radicals who chased the moderates from the ground and passed resolutions in favour of universal suffrage.[53] The Bolton Political Union held its first meeting on 31 October. At the second on 28 November there was a bitter split between moderates and extremists, the former walking out.[54] On November 17 a group of Leeds working men met at the Sir John Falstaff Inn, St Peter's Square, to inaugurate a radical political union dedicated to the attainment of manhood suffrage—a 'low union', in the phrase of the time. The principal supporters of the ministry and the Bill in Leeds had prepared an immediate ripost. On the same day, at the Cross Keys Tavern, Little Holbeck, 200 of them approved the rules for a union of the Birmingham type.[55]

The union leaders were thus faced not only with the appalling difficulty of maintaining the agitation at full strength for months more[56] but with the imminent threat of splits. If they took a moderate, middle-class line and stuck to the Bill they were liable either to be outvoted or to lose their working-class support by secession to a low union. If they turned to the full radical programme they would scare off the substantial middle-class element which provided their leaders and their money. Either way they would lose their effectiveness. A check to a popular movement naturally intensifies any extremist threat to the moderate leaders. When the suspicion grows for any reason that a Redmond or a Dr Martin Luther King cannot deliver the goods, the Sinn Feiners and the advocates of Black Power are sure to make gains.

The problem came to a crisis over the proposal for a 'National Guard' on the lines of the one which had played a part in Paris during the July revolution.[57] The news of the Nottingham and Derby riots brought this suggestion to the fore. If peers were not to be created at once, the *Globe* said on 12 October:

> it will be necessary for the middle classes to take steps to protect property. . . .
> Armed associations of householders must be formed. Let them be called loyal
> associations, national guards, or by what name we will, some such organization
> will be necessary, should the Reform Bill be long delayed; or we shall have to
> choose between an increase in the military force and military government on
> the one hand, and the violence of the mob on the other.

At least one working-class leader had anticipated such a proposal. 'It is in contemplation among the "middlemen",' the *Poor Man's Guardian* warned its readers on 8 October,

> to establish a National Guard, seeing how successful and immediate a power
> it has been in France to suppress the people and to protect the established
> institutions of property. Friends, . . . such a guard would ensure your political
> thraldom unless you have a counter-force. . . . You too must form your
> millions into a guard . . . a 'Popular Guard'. Keep yourselves prepared . . .
> lay by as much as possible out of your scanty earnings for the purchase of a
> musket and accoutrements.

Divisive though the national guard proposals might be, the *Morning Chronicle* took them up, and, being friendlier than the *Globe* to the radicals, did so with less of a repressive, middle-class twist. On 26 October the *Chronicle* called for a National Guard which would unite 'the most respectable and efficient of the middle and labouring classes'. On the following day *The Times* demanded the formation of 'Conservative Guards' who were to be drawn from 'the whole mass of householders'. They 'should be drilled occasionally and taught the use of the firelock'.[58]

The pleas for conservative guards might have died away had it not been for the Bristol riots which broke out on 29 October and raged for three days. Bristol was a turbulent port containing all the ingredients for a riot. The corporation was self-elected and of the weakest kind. Although it had contained a tory majority since 1812 the mayor was a reformer who had presided in the previous year at

the Bristol meeting welcoming the July revolution.[59] Neither side
had confidence in him. The local anti-reformers thought him a
trimmer. To the Bristol Political Union he personified a corrupt
oligarchy.

The riots were occasioned by the arrival of Wetherell, the Recorder
of Bristol, for a Gaol Delivery. The corporation knew that this visit
meant trouble. The Commons debates on the Bill had made Wetherell
anathema to reformers and on 13 October he had recharged this
enmity by championing the Duke of Newcastle, and trying to censure
the government, over the riots at Nottingham and Derby. A deputation from the magistrates therefore came to London to see whether
the Recorder's visit could be postponed. Wetherell declined to take
the responsibility for interfering with the usual judicial procedure. He
referred his visitors to the Home Secretary. Melbourne saw them
twice and decided that the Gaol Delivery could not be deferred.
Wetherell and Bristol's two MPs attended at the second of these
interviews.[60]

One of the Members, Edward Protheroe, who had close relations
with the Bristol Political Union, argued against relying on the army
and made a proposal which suggests that he at least was more intent
on a victory for Reform than on preventing disorder.

I stated [he wrote] that, if we could be secured from thieves and adventurers
from other places, I could with the aid of friends [the Union] keep all in
perfect order. I offered ... to attend Wetherell, and to do all this, provided
I might be allowed to enable the people of Bristol, thus constrained, to express
in some measure their strong and unalterable disapprobation of Sir Charles
Wetherell's political conduct, that we might all be insured from the insidious
conduct of the tories, who, *if the people are quiet,* would say there is a reaction
against the Bill.[61]

Protheroe's offer was declined and Melbourne undertook that by 29
October the Bristol magistrates should be able to call on a military
force.

By 26 October three troops of regular cavalry, comprising 93
mounted men, had arrived in the Bristol area, their orders being 'to
obey the commands of the magistrates' of the city.[62] The Bristol
Political Union, to whom the magistrates had appealed for help,
publicly denounced this reliance on the army. 'If the magistracy of the
city,' the Union's poster read, 'feel themselves incompetent to preserve
the public peace without being supported by the military they should

resign their offices.'[63] A few days earlier an attempt to use the seamen in the port in a peace-keeping role had been frustrated by the anti-corporation party.[64] The magistrates now failed to enrol the special constables they needed and were obliged to resort to paid constables. Meanwhile the Bristol press announced the arrival of the regular cavalry and it became clear that this force, though possibly provocative, was far from large.[65]

Wetherell reached the Mansion House safely on 29 October. But a riot developed outside in Queen's Square. The sessions were postponed and he escaped over the roof. Next morning the Mansion House was stormed and sacked and the mobs increased until they were some thousands strong. The military commander, Lieutenant Colonel Brereton, failed to obtain support from the magistrates and withdrew two of his troops from the city. An appeal from the Political Union had no effect on the rioters. By daylight on 31 October two sides of Queen's Square, including the Custom House and Excise Office, together with the Bishop's Palace and several gaols and toll houses, had been pillaged and burned.

Brereton was court-martialled for his performance in the riots and shot himself before the case had ended. He seems to have been con-vinced beyond reason that the civil authorities would not uphold him in strong measures. Had he been more resolute and less humane he could perhaps have prevented the rioters from gaining control on 30 October. But this would have been difficult. His troops were tired and most Bristol people still resented their presence. Major Mackworth, a staff officer who was in Bristol on leave, advised, in his own words, 'that the cavalry should refresh during the night ... painful as it was to leave the city at the mercy of the mob'.[66] If Brereton had withdrawn his men, but kept them within the city, they might have been overrun in their quarters. If he had attacked and been worsted, the mob, as he later argued, 'flushed with their victory would have ... fired the shipping'.[67] His men had to open fire even to make good their with-drawal.

On the evening of 30 October about two hundred Bristol house-holders gathered in the Council House. The vice-president of the Political Union was asked, in Mackworth's words, 'whether he would get his Union together and try to save the town. He said he could not answer for it if the soldiers were employed'. Mackworth, 'much disgusted and disheartened' at the 'party spirit' displayed, told the meeting that it was plain to him there would be no union or energy among them until danger compelled it. . . . The burning and plundering a few private houses, which would inevitably follow the unchecked destruction of public property, would alone, and that soon, rouse the inhabitants of Bristol to a sense of their common danger.[68]

This prophecy was soon fulfilled. On the following day (31 October) the troops were welcomed by all peaceable inhabitants. The rioters were exhausted, many being incapably drunk. Some, having broached the cellars, had been burned to death when buildings were fired. At dawn Mackworth persuaded Brereton to charge with the only cavalry troop still in the city, just as the mob were starting on the still un-burned side of Queen's Square. The charge succeeded and the other two troops were summoned back to the city and brought into action. The streets were finally cleared at midday when cavalry reinforce-ments arrived from Gloucester. Many more were wounded than killed in the cavalry charges, though some rioters were driven back without hope of escape into burning buildings. The number of casualties in the riots was never known. It probably exceeded 400. Charles Kingsley, then a schoolboy in Clifton, saw, and did not forget, the charred corpse fragments in Queen's Square.[69]

The Reform press quickly pointed the moral of the riot. 'There might probably be organized in Bristol and Clifton,' said the *Globe* on 1 November,

15,000 men, all sincerely desirous of the preservation of tranquillity. . . . We believe . . . to the organization of the people we must come. It may be gall and wormwood to the tory lords; . . . an organized nation may be as terrible in their eyes as in those of the lovers of disorder. The defence of the public peace and property must cease to be at their mercy. The people must not be left unarmed because their enemies dread their bayonets.

'It is now obvious,' *The Times* pronounced on the same day,

that the regular troops and peace officers are not . . . sufficient . . . on occasions of sudden and very general emergency. We say then to our fellow subjects—organize and arm.

On 1 November, the Council of the Birmingham Union appointed a committee to draw up a scheme for organizing the Union on semi-military lines. This was a risky move. Some of those who advocated national or civic guards hoped that the government would give these formations an official status. But Attwood had no assurance of the cabinet's approval. He told his followers that it was necessary to prepare against Grey's fall and to organize the Union for action 'whilst the present ministry are in power'. He may have thought that, as he could not stop the movement for a civic guard in Birmingham, the least dangerous answer was to lead it. The formation of an entirely middle-class guard, enlisted specifically to defend property, would have endangered the cooperation between middle and working classes on which he depended.[70] A 'popular guard' with a working-class bias might have been equally dangerous to him.

Even in Birmingham the Political Union was not securely established as the prime mover in Reform activities. The Town Meeting held on 20 October to protest against the Lords' decision was largely a whig affair and Attwood played no part in it. A vote of thanks to him and to the council of the Union, proposed towards the end of that meeting, was withdrawn 'on the remonstrance of Mr Parkes who said . . . it would create disunion'. Attwood and his colleagues were thus looking for every opportunity to assert their importance and to consolidate their hold on the Birmingham Reform movement. When the national guard band-waggon appeared they decided to climb aboard.

The plan which the committee produced was discussed in the Council on 7 November. According to the *Morning Chronicle* it was favourably received. It ensured, the *Chronicle* reported, 'that if riots should occur in Birmingham ten or fifteen thousand men will, in the short space of two hours or less, be prepared irresistibly to vindicate the law and restore the peace and security of the town'.[71] Attwood later claimed that the scheme had not been one for arming the Union: if individual members bought arms that was their affair. His statement may be accepted; but an armed union was not far from a drilled union organized on military lines most members of which owned arms. On 3 November an anonymous informant drew Melbourne's 'attention to one part of [the] plan, which is "that subscriptions be entered into to provide muskets for those who are unable to purchase them".' Birmingham was not the only place where such ideas were under discussion. The Blackburn Political Union were said to be involved in a scheme for an armed meeting.[72] On 12 November the *Morning Chronicle* published an offer by a certain Colonel Macerone to supply bayonets at ten shillings each for fixing to fowling pieces or pistols.[73] The price of arms was rising. No one knew how many of the frightened householders who bought them meant to put them at the service of a union.[74]

It was soon clear that the plans for military organization were arousing opposition and alarm. Most middle-class people were shocked by the idea of private armies. At the same time enlisting in formations on the Birmingham model had little appeal for the workers. The working man, as the *Examiner* said,[75] could afford neither the arms nor the time needed for drilling, so that the guards might be not merely conservative but repressive. The *Birmingham Journal*, though very sympathetic to Attwood, opposed the project of guards from the start.[76] The chief military figure among the radicals, Colonel W. F. P. Napier, refused to take the lead in recommending a national guard.[77] *The Times* had begun to retreat by 9 November. On 16 November it explained away its guards proposal still further and remarked of the political unions that 'even as transitory excrescences upon the commonwealth' they could 'be no otherwise justified than by the depth of the emergency which produces them'. On that day Grey asked Melbourne to take the Law Officers' opinion on whether the semi-military organization of political unions was legal.[78]

Meanwhile Attwood was also in retreat. On 15 November he explained that 'the Council had never once discussed the question of arming the Union'.[79] He managed to defer a decision on the organization plan for a further week. These proceedings were reported in *The Times* and *Morning Chronicle* on 18 November. By that date the government knew that if they banned the military organization of political unions they would be strongly supported. If such a ban were to be imposed, however, it must be published before 22 November, because on that date the Birmingham Political Union were liable to adopt their committee's plan.

Events in London caused Melbourne still greater concern. On 5 October the National Union of the Working Classes adopted a petition to the Lords for manhood suffrage, annual Parliaments, and the abolition of the property qualification for MPs, and added: 'as a peaceable means to this end we pray your right honourable House to pass the Bill now pending'.[80] The Lords' vote inclined the Rotunda men against the Bill and brought Place into the field. On 12 October the National Union resolved that it would 'not be satisfied with any future measure for improving the representation which does not recognize the just right of every man to the elective franchise'.[81]

On the same evening the first meetings were held under Place's scheme for a London political union which should 'amalgamate as much as possible all classes without distinction'. It was to be constructed 'on the plan of the Birmingham Union omitting only . . . the particular views of Mr Attwood respecting the currency'.[82] The inaugural meeting was arranged for 31 October. Sir Francis Burdett, one of Westminster's MPs, agreed to be chairman; and Place persuaded him that the union would need

a much more general object than merely 'supporting the King and his ministers', which seemed to be all that Sir Francis desired to have done. It was necessary that we should make our declaration such . . . as would induce the better sort of the working people to join us.[83]

Place entertained great hopes for the National Political Union, as his creation was to be called. London's strong craft tradition did not make for a deep cleavage between middle and working class. The inaugural meeting did not go well, however. To Place's disgust a powerful contingent from the Rotunda had a resolution passed that at least half of the union's council should be working men. This provoked the middle-class group of Westminster reformers into forming their own union, in which they would confine 'their objects to supporting the . . . Bill and preserving the peace of the city'.[84] Burdett resigned the chairmanship of Place's union in anger a few weeks later. By the end of the year Place was far from the 100,000 members at which he had aimed. But he and his friends had a membership of about 6000, as compared with 3000 in the National Union of the Working Classes.

The Rotunda leaders did not confine themselves to trying to capture Place's union. They also did their best to put it in the shade. On 24 October, in the aftermath of the Lords' vote, they adopted a class system, with class leaders and an average of 25 members per class. A mass meeting was announced in White Conduit Fields for 7 November. The notice about it called 'upon our fellow labourers in all parts of the Kingdom to re-echo these principles [manhood suffrage, ballot, abolition of the peerage] on the same day, in public meetings throughout the country'.[85] A working-class speaker boasted at this time that 104 towns had low unions. The invitation to demonstrate on 7 November was particularly directed to the working-class union in Manchester, which maintained 27 branches.[86] Place might call his union 'National'; but when it came to links with the provinces his rivals had the advantage. Unlike him, they paid little attention to the laws against corresponding societies.[87]

It was suggested that each man should come to White Conduit Fields armed with a twenty-inch stave. Place bought one of these staves 'as a curiosity' for fourpence. He judged that a blow with it 'would break a man's arm or fracture his skull'. A move towards arming by a low union was apt to provoke a response from its rivals. At an inaugural meeting on 4 November of a National Political Union branch in Cripplegate the chairman said that 'they had also met for the purpose of forming . . . a Conservative Guard'.

On 5 November Melbourne secured the postponement of the White Conduit Fields meeting by telling the leaders that they would be prosecuted for treason if they persisted.[88] Some of the inhibitions concerning the arms and organization issue which characterized the Attwoodites were appearing in the National Union. On 9 November a motion for public drilling was dropped.[89] Meanwhile the Manchester leaders asked for more time in which to organize the simultaneous meetings of the working-class unions. It was proposed to hold these on 21 November; and they were later postponed to 28 November.

This was the background against which the government had been negotiating with the waverers and which soon put an end to the negotiation. The new developments undoubtedly entailed some reaction against Reform. People of property began to realize the dangers involved in change and to forget those involved in the refusal to change. The first French revolution returned to many minds. The cabinet were led to adopt a more conservative position. Some cabinet ministers realized how dependent they were on the support of the 'respectable' unions, and were still ready to defend many of the activities of Attwood and his followers. Brougham, as he told Holland, spoke to the king 'forcibly' on 13 November about the

utter impossibility of keeping down the plunderers . . . if the middle classes were adverse to government and disposed to be the allies of the mob or even neutral and indifferent in the hour of tumult. . . . The unions [Brougham added], even at Birmingham and elsewhere, were composed and composing of those who must stand between us and the plundering mobs of Hunt and Bristol.[90]

No minister could possibly defend the Birmingham Union's organization plan, however. Indeed the Law Officers pronounced the

I

plan to be illegal. Moreover the proposals for a National Guard had stimulated a counter-threat, not only from working-class leaders, but from those who opposed the Bill. The possibility of armed clashes between the political unions and their opponents could no longer be ruled out. On 31 October the *Morning Post* had warned anti-reformers that they might need to form themselves 'into associations, . . . on a principle of military hierarchy', and to become 'capable of resorting to arms'. If the political unions went ahead with drilling and arming it would 'be found that there are . . . even yet thousands of stout hearts and unflinching arms in England ready to be uplifted in defence of . . . Church and . . . aristocracy'.[91]

The ministers were under considerable pressure from the king to move against the unions;[92] and they knew that this was the one issue on which Wellington might succeed in displacing them. His letter advising the king to suppress the Birmingham Union had been passed to Grey. The duke admitted later that this letter had been meant as a hint that he was ready to form a government.[93]

All this did not impel the cabinet to negotiate on the Bill with a view to modifications. It had the opposite effect. They intended to issue a proclamation that unions organized on military lines were illegal. But if they were to do this they must at the same time reassure reformers that the Bill was not to be whittled away.[94] A long prorogation was by now so thoroughly identified by the public with a reduced Bill that the only way of giving this reassurance was to announce the early reassembly of Parliament. The possibility that dealing with the unions would require legislation also pointed to an early date.

On 19 November the cabinet decided to recall Parliament for 6 December and to issue the proclamation against the military organization of unions. The first of these decisions was carried by eight votes to three. Grey, Richmond and Palmerston voted for a January date but deferred to the majority.[95] In this crisis, as in April over dissolution, the decisive voice against yielding or delay was Melbourne's. His scepticism about prophecies of disorder which reached the Home Office from friends of the Bill had not diminished. But to his thinking a January date would convince the unions that the Bill was to be seriously modified, and so make a clash with them inevitable. He was engaged in the urgent and delicate operation of suppressing their military plans without provoking such a clash. Early reassembly represented an indispensable move in this operation. Melbourne had only just managed to stop the White Conduit Fields meeting. His

information about the plans of the Rotunda leaders, and of their opposite numbers in Lancashire, was very full. As far as London was
concerned, he could check the reports in the unstamped press against
those of a police spy. Not all the reports on the postponed meetings
had reached him by 19 November; but he already knew a good deal.
The Birmingham Union's plan was bad enough in itself. The thought
that it might be copied by all the low unions was far worse. 'Other
classes,' as the Law Officers wrote of the plan, 'may foresee danger to
themselves from the existence of such an association, and may organize
and arm themselves in the same manner to check its movements.'[96]
Attwood's army looked like provoking both the anti-reformers and
the Rotunda radicals.

For the Home Secretary an immediate move to bring the unions
under control took precedence over all other considerations. Melbourne did not like the Bill; but he knew that it must be passed as it
stood. 'It is a very dangerous way of dealing with a nation,' he had
told Sir Herbert Taylor a few weeks before, 'to attempt to retract that
which you have once offered to concede.'[97] A report which he received on the day of the proclamation must have confirmed Melbourne
in this view. A police spy wrote that on 21 November the NUWC
leaders had told some 575 union members and sympathizers in the
Rotunda about 'the necessity of all the working classes to immediately
arm themselves and form by their union a guard to themselves'. The
reckless William Benbow had added, on the organization of the
union into classes, that the best class leaders would be soldiers, since
they could teach their classes 'to march or the use of the firelock'.[98]

Parkes was in Birmingham on the day of the cabinet meeting, at
Althorp's request, to warn Attwood of the forthcoming proclamation.[99] His hint was effective. The news that Parliament was to be
recalled in a fortnight restored the government's standing among
reformers and persuaded the Council of the Birmingham Union to
anticipate the proclamation and abandon the semi-military scheme.
They dropped it on 22 November just as the proclamation was
published.

Palmerston, who was extremely angry at the cabinet's decision,
implied that the majority had voted in ignorance of how far the
conversations with Wharncliffe had progressed.[100] There does not
seem to have been much substance in this.[101] Grey's conversation
with Wharncliffe had been in 'the strictest confidence'; but it was
agreed that the Prime Minister might 'state generally to the cabinet

the grounds on which . . . it might be possible to obtain the consent of the House of Lords to a new Bill'.[102] Greville, who took the waverers' line, lamented that the moderates in the cabinet were often absent. On this occasion, however, the four absentees would not have affected the outcome. Lansdowne and Stanley would have voted for January, Durham and Graham for December.[103] The majority were no more ill-informed than usual; and their objections to a long negotiation were well founded. It may be surmised, for instance, that Parkes would have jibbed at the task of restraining Attwood unless he had received some assurance that Althorp would stand out if necessary for the December date.

The waverers' efforts now languished. Wharncliffe sent his detailed demands for modifications to Grey on 23 November. Three days later the cabinet decided that most of them were unacceptable. On 29 November there was a second interview at which Wharncliffe found the premier so unyielding that he broke off the negotiation. With the ministers reconstructing their Bill in haste, for introduction early in December, there was clearly no chance of reaching agreement. The end of the talks was hastened by the collapse of the plan for a moderate declaration from the City. A meeting on 22 November revealed that the 'aristocratic' bankers were unwilling to offend ultra-tory customers. The declaration was attacked by Henry Drummond and Coutts Trotter.[104] Drummond, among his various eccentricities, favoured a Reform Bill 'as efficacious as that now proposed' which would none the less preserve the rotten boroughs.[105] A final meeting on 10 December suggested by Lord Chandos, at which he, Wharncliffe and Harrowby met Grey, Brougham and Althorp, came to nothing. Althorp according to Chandos 'sat saying nothing, with his hands in his pockets, and then, after an hour, went away to Fish-mongers' Hall'.[106] Brougham did not arrive until the conference was nearly over.

When it was clear that the waverers' negotiation would fail, the diehard tories said that the government had never wanted any other outcome. The cabinet certainly emerged from the failure with some advantages gained. They knew which minor concessions might win them votes. They had brought the king nearer to a creation by showing him that their opponents could not be conciliated. The split in the opposition had been made more obvious, if not deeper. But the die-hard account oversimplifies the motives predominant in the cabinet when the conversations began. For the ministers the drawbacks of an abortive attempt at conciliation were almost as great as its advantages. They must have known that it could not be kept secret, and that once revealed it might cost them their popularity with the unions. The three who composed the minority in the cabinet vote on 19 November were clearly prepared to take large risks to keep a negotiation alive. Nor was the inducement of splitting the opposition as overwhelming as the tory diehards made out. As the majority against the second reading clearly could not be assembled again, the split existed in essentials before the waverers began.

The truth seems to have been that some of the cabinet, including the Prime Minister himself, wanted the negotiation to succeed and believed that it might, and that the rest, in so far as they realized what was happening, had no case for vetoing it. The only alternative policy was a large creation; and even those ministers least sympathetic to the waverers were not yet ready for that. Around the middle of November the anti-waverer group gained in strength and attained control. On 14 November Althorp told his father that Parliament would not reassemble until January.[107] The balance was tipped back to an earlier date during the next three days by a growing conviction that the political unions could and should be prevented from organizing on military lines,[108] and that issuing this prohibition involved announcing a December date for the reassembly. The ministers' daily increasing fear[109] that their meetings with the waverers would be reported in the press was scarcely less important as a propellant towards December. Rumours of the negotiation were going round the city by 19 November and *The Times* referred to it two days later.

In a letter to Harrowby on the day of the cabinet decision Wharncliffe unwittingly showed why the ministers had to blight the negotiation. After referring to the rumours in the City he wrote:

As to the government I have no fear of their drawing back; for even if our negotiation was to go off entirely, the very entering into it, and the sanction they have given to the proposed declaration from the City, will for ever estrange the radicals and violent people from them; and they have now no choice but to depend upon us for support.[110]

Wharncliffe was wrong. The cabinet still had the chance to draw back on 19 November. But it was their last chance.

The negotiation was thus foredoomed whatever the original degree of cabinet support for it. The modifications which the waverers demanded were reasonable in that they left the main principles of the

Bill untouched. But such adjustments as tampering with the £10 clause, dropping the new London boroughs, extinguishing Schedule B, and taking town householders out of the counties were too important to be made inconspicuously. The waverers might be right in maintaining that Schedules B and D ran counter to the historic principle of representing communities. According to them long lists of single-Member constituencies opened the way to the democratic horrors of 'equal electoral districts', since the double-Member arrangement was the bulwark against apportioning seats by population. Schedules B and D could not be eliminated, however, without an entire recasting of the Bill. The waverers also asked that the order of the Schedules should be reversed, so as to make enfranchisement precede disfranchisement. This would carry an implication which hardly any reformer could accept. It would suggest that abolishing the rotten boroughs was not intrinsically desirable: they had to go solely because of the need to give seats to growing towns while keeping the House to a reasonable size.[111] Yielding to the Lords' majority on any of these points after a division would be one thing, surrendering without a fight quite another. A government that did not dare even to admit that it was negotiating on them was not likely to give them up quietly.

Moreover each side wondered how much it would gain from an agreement. The government were doubtful of the waverers' ability to guarantee the passage of the second reading.[112] Wharncliffe did not pretend to speak for Wellington and the other opposition leaders, though Wellington was in fact friendly towards his efforts at this early stage. Even Harrowby was not prepared to endorse everything in the memorandum of 23 November and insisted that Grey should be told of his reservations. There was a chance that the duke's majority would crumble; but that did not depend on an agreement with the waverers. As discussions went forward both sides began to suspect that better terms might be obtainable by fighting for each point in committee than by prior agreement.

The waverers could not expect support from keen opposition partisans. The reaction of the latter was to wait and let the rift between the government and the radicals widen. The hopes of the writer in *Blackwood's* looked like being fulfilled provided that the Bill could be blocked a little longer. Southey commented on the Manchester meeting of 12 October: 'The whigs called the meeting; the radicals had their own way at it; and both have done what the conservative party would have wished them to do.' 'One great good,' *Blackwood's* pronounced in December,

has already resulted from the noble stand made by the peers against the flood of democracy; ... it has made the mask drop from the faces of the radical faction, and put an end to that boasted union of reformers in support of the Bill.... We always said that this union was mere hypocrisy.... The event has justified our prediction.[113]

Both sides wanted the struggle to go on, the anti-reformers in the hope of defeating the Bill, the reformers in the hope of hurrying it into law. Backing a modified Bill meant abandoning the hope of outright victory. The 'hard liners' on either side were not willing to do that.

It was the upper-class moderates, therefore, on whom the waverers relied. There were many such people and each day's bad news deepened their conviction of the dangers of extremism. Yet it proved impossible to drum up much support outside Parliament for a modified Bill. Wharncliffe elicited a moderate resolution from Liverpool, where the Canningite tories were strong and the freemen naturally feared being swamped by ten pounders. Elsewhere the moderates reacted as the majority of the cabinet had done. They were as fearful of radicalism as the waverer leaders could wish. In the aftermath of the Bristol riots the tone of politics was scared and apprehensive. A cholera epidemic had been raging on the continent for some months and early in November reports from Sunderland told every newspaper reader that it had spread to Britain. There were many burnings in the agricultural districts[114] and renewed strikes in the north. The prospect of political uncertainty continuing to hamper trade throughout a grim winter was very disturbing. But these fears did not increase the backing for a modified Bill. Moderate people wanted a quick settlement of the Reform question. By mid-November a modified Bill looked like anything but a quick or peaceful method of resolving the crisis. The moderates' mounting fear of radicalism increased, not their willingness to see the Bill whittled down, but their alarm at the disorder which whittling down would invite.

The cabinet had learnt from the waverers which concessions might lessen opposition. They now spent some hectic weeks trying to insert as many of these into the new Bill as they could without detracting from its efficiency, or otherwise infuriating reformers in the Commons and outside. Even after the negotiation with the waverers had failed time was wasted in the effort to square various circles. Virtually every modification proposal made since March came up for a final urgent review. An attempt by Althorp and Russell to eliminate Schedules B and D dragged on throughout November but came to nothing.[115] Transferring the town freeholders from county to borough, which Russell favoured and Althorp opposed, was also rejected. It scarcely seemed a vote catcher. Wharncliffe had been loud on his dislike of these voters in the counties, but silent about his willingness to have them in the boroughs. For the reformers E. J. Littleton warned Russell that separating boroughs and counties by putting the town freeholder into the borough would divide the Commons into the two warring interest groups of industry and agriculture.[116] There were long discussions about the division of counties, on which the waverers had for once lived up to their nickname.[117] It was clear that the division scheme would not have the markedly aristocratic effect originally intended, and equally that cancelling it would not have one either. In the end the divisions were retained. At one of these cabinet meetings, as Holland recorded,

Richmond suggested ... extending the right of representation to colonies, whose Members, without appearing so, would be, he said, a sure counter-action to the force of popular clamour ... on the House of Commons. But so large and new a principle was most reasonably objected to at this stage.

These problems had to be solved by 5 p.m. on 12 December when Russell was due to expound the new Bill to the Commons. Nine of the reports about particular boroughs needed for compiling the disfranchising schedules were received only on the morning of 12 December;[118] and at 5 o'clock Russell was still working on them. He began his speech half an hour late, none of his colleagues knowing, when he rose, exactly which boroughs were reprieved and which condemned.

Despite this haste the changes in the Bill were a neat blend of aristocratic and popular elements. The freeman franchise was preserved, subject to the residence qualification, in perpetuity, and not merely as in the former Bill during existing lives. But to prevent mass creations by tory corporations for electoral purposes freemen admitted since 1 March 1831 would qualify for the vote only if their freedoms were derived from birth or servitude, as opposed to purchase.[119] The £10 clause was simplified and so slightly extended in operation. But the requirement that the householder should be a ratepayer and not in arrears with his rates was made more specific and thus slightly more restrictive.[120] The cabinet do not seem to have realized how greatly the rate-paying clause would facilitate bribery. But they might still have adopted it if they had realized this. They needed the clause in order to reassure the doubtfuls. It was intended, in Grey's words to the waverer leaders, to guarantee 'the respectability of the franchise'.[121]

The principal concession to moderate critics of the Bill was made by redrawing the schedules. The opposition had objected to disfranchisement being based on population and on the use of the 1821, instead of the 1831, census. On the latter point the ministers had replied that the population figures in the 1831 census were compiled after the announcement of the Bill's contents had put a premium on falsifying certain returns. The criterion for disfranchisement was now changed to a formula based on the number of houses in the borough and the amount of assessed taxes paid.[122] The figures for houses were taken from the 1831 census. Unlike population figures these could be checked.

Apart from the reshuffling of boroughs which this change entailed, the attempt to reduce the numbers of the House was abandoned. Theories on the ideal size for a deliberative assembly had now to yield to tactical needs. Eleven of the 23 seats thus provided were used to reduce Schedule B to 30, and ten to give second Members to some of the towns formerly in Schedule D. By these means the new single-Member constituencies were reduced from 69 to 49. (The Act in its final form, is summarized in Table 5, pp. 310–13) Although fewer seats were abolished the radicals were not given cause to complain. Eight out of the ten towns receiving a second seat were in the north midlands or north; and these new Members in the 'popular interest' would outweigh those from Schedule B. Filling up the numbers of the House also solaced the no-popery squad in that it increased England's representation in proportion to that of Ireland. The O'Connellites were not pleased.[123] But they had no strength in the Lords; and their votes in the Commons were not as valuable as they had been in March.

The final concession to waverers and conservatives, which may be mentioned here though it was not published for some weeks, concerned the method of enlarging boroughs in order to give them enough constituents. Littleton recorded the following conversation about these new enlargements in his diary for 21 December:

Littleton: 'Perhaps your new plan, by making boroughs more rural, will please the peers and country gentlemen better than your former plan of creating town constituencies. I suspect that was partly your object.'

Althorp: 'Perhaps it was. Having secured the great and leading principles we are at liberty, and it is our duty, to shape the measure so as to ensure its success.'[124]

A number of boroughs were made rural to some effect. If those which had been enlarged before 1832 because of bribery are excluded, the Boundary Act more than trebled the area of the English boroughs.[125]

The changes announced on 12 December were very successful. Russell introduced them in a subdued tone. Peel was tempted by this into a bitter and exulting speech and congratulated the House on the escape from the last Bill which his party and the Lords had secured. He had mistaken the mood of his followers and there were signs of revolt. In the aftermath of the Bristol riots the opposition were as chastened as the government's supporters: polemics had lost much of their appeal. Chandos, Lord Clive, Sandon, and Wharncliffe's son Stuart-Wortley, all made conciliatory speeches. So did Warrender, 'caught', Littleton noted, 'by the two Members preserved to Honiton'.[126] Clive's father was a tory borough owner and his father-in-law and brother-in-law tory dukes. His defection from the diehards was a matter of note.

The new Bill was equally well received in the country. The ultratory *Standard* regarded it as 'much less objectionable than the last'. In gaining the approval of former opponents the ministry had not lost that of staunch reformers. *The Times* pronounced the Bill to be 'satisfactory'. All the London Reform dailies except the *Morning Chronicle* approved of it. Hobhouse and Cobbett thought it an improvement. Durham and Place[127] seem to have been the only prominent objectors in politicians' circles. Durham objected violently to any form of conciliation. He had scarcely been consulted about the redrafting; and he was not the man to think other people's handiwork better than his own. When he recovered from his son's death he was sent to Belgium on a diplomatic mission, from which he did not return until 29 November. His influence in the cabinet was by now small; and on 30 November he exhausted the remains of his colleagues' patience by abusing Grey violently at a cabinet dinner. 'I doubt whether he knows anything about the alterations,' Althorp wrote of him after that scene, 'as he will not allow anybody to tell him what they are.'[128] Place was justifiably hostile to the new rate-paying clause.[129] Though critical, these two did not maintain, however, that the changes destroyed the Bill's efficiency.

After two nights of debate dominated by Macaulay and Stanley the second reading was passed early on 18 December by 324 to 162. The opposition vote had fallen by 69 since the second reading in July. Analysis of the lists tempered the government's rejoicing. Plenty of former opponents had abstained. But Warrender was the only one actually to reverse his vote. On 19 December Grey told Taylor that neither this triumphant division nor anything else which had happened since 8 October betokened a majority for the Bill in the Lords.

8

THE BILL IN THE LORDS (II):
'TO STOP THE DUKE'

What is the best test of a great general?—To know when to retreat and to dare to do it. (Wellington)

Changing the Bill so that it might pass the Lords had not worked. There remained changing the Lords so that they would pass the Bill. Three views emerged at the crucial cabinet meeting on 2 January. Durham at one extreme wanted a large creation of peers at once. At the other, the group who had been friendly to the waverers, comprising Richmond, Palmerston, Melbourne, Lansdowne, and more doubtfully Stanley, were still inclined against any move towards a creation. In the centre the majority favoured obtaining permission to create ten or twelve immediately with more to follow if needed. This line was based on the view that the imminent prospect of a large creation would at last bring the doubtfuls to their senses. The latter must come round, the argument ran, when it became evident that the government actually held permission to make enough peers. Then with luck the large creation would not be needed.

The centre view prevailed; and it was agreed that Grey should put it to the king on the following day. Brougham was absent from illness. The opponents of creation were over-ruled partly because Grey had at last deserted them, but still more because, assuming that a second rejection had to be avoided, there was no alternative, as Grey saw, to obtaining the king's promise of peer-making in case of need.

The king objected to an immediate, token creation on the ground that a half measure at this stage might merely irritate some of the doubtfuls into opposition. It might also, he thought, suggest that he and the cabinet neither meant to create enough nor even knew how many would be needed. Otherwise, greatly as he disliked the prospect of a creation, he did not bar one. His answer to Grey was much what it had been over dissolution in the previous April. In effect, he said that, seeing no prospect of an alternative government, he was in no position to refuse his ministers' demands. On 13 January a formal minute was drawn up in which the cabinet asked for power to make enough peers 'to secure the success of the Bill' on the understanding that this would be used only when all prospect of success by other means had disappeared.

On 15 January the king replied agreeing to the proposal, 'it being understood that the contemplated addition shall be deferred till it may appear certain that, without such addition, the strength of the government would be insufficient to bring the measure of parliamentary Reform to a successful issue'. The letter went on to attach

the positive and irrevocable condition that the *creations of new peers* shall, under no circumstances, exceed the three ... already agreed ... ; that the other additions shall be made by calling up eldest sons, or collateral heirs of peerages where no direct heirs are likely to succeed ... ; that if these sources should prove insufficient (which, however, His Majesty can hardly conceive possible) recourse may be had to the Scotch and Irish peerage for promotion to the English peerage.

The king professed himself satisfied from inspecting the lists of possible peers that his conditions would not embarrass the government.

The news that the king would not object to a creation spread quickly;[1] and the waverer leaders were confirmed in their determination not to allow the Bill to be rejected again. Wharncliffe accepted that the cabinet had a pledge which they could almost certainly bring into effect if faced with the imminent prospect of another second reading defeat. He did not think it likely, however, that they had been given anything near to *carte blanche*. It is not easy even now to define the extent of the king's pledge. The circumstances which would imperil 'the success of the Bill' were not described; nor was it stated whether the king or the cabinet was to judge whether they had arisen.[2] The king's remarks to Grey on the latter point were not entirely consistent with each other. He made reasonably clear that the insertion of amendments in committee would not be a ground for creation unless the principles of the Bill were affected. On the other hand he wrote in February leaving the 'consideration of the necessity' of making peers 'entirely' in the Prime Minister's hands.[3]

The pledge was not, in practice, unlimited as to numbers. The understanding on this subject may be summarized as follows. The bishops and others who had offered no longer to oppose the second reading were thought to have brought the opposition majority down to twenty. The king received the impression on 3 January that he was being asked for twenty-one creations. When he accepted the final cabinet minute he agreed to waive the numerical limit. But on 16 January Grey wrote that he hoped the number might 'not exceed, or at all events not greatly exceed', twenty-one. The king told Grey later that 'he would have placed a *positive* restriction' on numbers 'if he had considered it possible that an addition of fifty or sixty peers could ever be suggested to him'. Grey and Brougham agreed during the crisis in May that the king 'had never encouraged them to expect that he could consent' to fifty or sixty.[4]

This low estimate of the creations required shows once again how hard it may be for a Prime Minister to admit, or perhaps to face, the facts. Grey had been arguing for months that creation might lose the votes of the doubtful peers.[5] Yet the figure in his letter of 16 January was based on the assumption that it would not lose a single vote. Self-deception apart, it was extremely difficult for him to demand a promise of at least fifty peers. Nothing would have rallied support to the king like the knowledge that he was resisting a pledge to create such a number. Moreover the king's promise was for show even more than for use. The first objective was to scare the opposition into allowing the second reading to pass. Peers would not be needed unless this objective proved unattainable. It was reasonable to hope that the opposition would not learn how far Grey was from having *carte blanche* about numbers.

In the event ministers became aware as soon as the king's pledge was given that their figure for the creations needed might be too low.[6] The knowledge that the cabinet had permission to create caused a number of reforming peers great irritation. It may be questioned indeed whether a token creation would have caused more. Some of the doubtfuls were scared: still more were angered. Threats by reforming noblemen to oppose the Bill if any peers were made were reported in the press on 15 January. A week later the Duke of Portland was said to head a list of peers who would reverse their votes in case of a creation. According to *John Bull* twenty-four names were listed: others said forty. The list apparently included Radnor and Segrave, both of whom ranked as staunch supporters of the government.[7] Radnor was almost a radical. Segrave had received his peerage from Grey in the previous September.

Some of the cabinet doubted whether many of these recalcitrant peers would actually turn against the Bill when the new creations were announced.[8] It is impossible to say how far this scepticism was justified. Similarly there is no means of knowing how the king would have interpreted his pledge had the entire opposition maintained a diehard line against the Bill. It is reasonable to suppose that the cabinet would then have presented him, however reluctantly, with a much increased estimate of the peerages required, and that he would have agreed, with equal reluctance, to create the larger number. He was saved from this by the waverers.

Grey was not the only statesman to visit the king at Brighton early in January. Wharncliffe was also there, determined to do all he could to prevent a creation. He saw Taylor on 8 January and the king three days later. He said, in effect, that he and his friends were prepared to vote for the second reading of the Bill, but only if the cabinet showed some disposition to yield on subordinate points during the committee stage in the Lords. If the government resorted to a creation to force their Bill through unchanged, the waverers would vote against it as before. When this was reported to Grey he indicated that, while he and his colleagues would resist all amendments in the Lords, they would accept defeat on any that did not do serious injury to 'the principle and efficiency of the Bill'. The king was delighted to hear that there would be 'free and dispassionate discussion in committee of the points of detail at issue'.[9]

Wharncliffe may have had a hand in Portland's ultimatum. The waverers certainly did all they could to exploit such reactions. To make sure that both king and cabinet understood his position Wharncliffe told Taylor on 8 February that he and Harrowby should soon have collected enough followers to 'insure' the second reading, but that if peers were created the group would 'convert the support which they are now disposed to give to the second reading into the most uncompromising and bitter hostility to the government upon the whole measure and in every stage of it'. Melbourne asked Haddington how he could vote against the second reading, though thinking that it ought to be carried, merely because the government took steps to carry it. Haddington replied that, in the first place, one of his objects in voting for it was to amend the Bill; and a creation would rule out amendments. Secondly, he would help a government which resisted radical designs, not one which forwarded them.[10]

The king was well aware that by the terms of his pledge peermaking remained difficult except as a last resort. He had no intention of making it easier. He was sympathetic to the waverers. He had the greatest objection to a creation which he regarded as a surrender to the radicals and the political unions. He was very willing to see the Bill amended in the Lords, provided that no amendments were adopted of a kind to make the cabinet demand a creation. The belief that he would create peers strengthened the waverers' position with the opposition. The doubt whether he would create enough of them strengthened it with the government. This situation was acceptable to William IV and Sir Herbert Taylor.[11]

Despite this scarcely concealed royal favour the waverers were doubtful about restarting their operations and courting another failure. They were convinced that defeating the Bill again on second reading would be ruinous. With the large creation which would probably result, the opposition would lose all power to amend, not merely this Bill, but any other which a reforming House of Commons might send up. The right course according to this argument was for the moderates to vote for the second reading and ensure its passage, and for the whole opposition then to combine on a policy of careful amendment in committee. The waverers doubted with good reason, not the advantages of their scheme, but whether they were capable of carrying it through. It would involve, as the negotiations in November had not, a direct defiance of Wellington who was almost sure to want another majority against the second reading. For complete success it also required a united effort in committee by those who had voted against each other on the second reading.

At an interview with Wharncliffe on 19 January Wellington refused to countenance any compromise. That evening Harrowby, Wharncliffe and Haddington dined together and decided none the less to go ahead. By 25 January Harrowby had drafted a circular to opposition peers outlining waverer policy and asking for support. Wharncliffe wrote in explanation to Wellington on 31 January. The debate between waverers and diehards had begun.

The waverers' argument assumed that preventing a creation and amending the Bill were objects of paramount importance. It did not assume that the second would prove feasible. Harrowby maintained that the prevention of a creation would in itself justify allowing the second reading to pass even if the Bill then became law unamended. Nor did the argument assume that the government's power to create peers even for the second reading was proof against all chances. In

Harrowby's view, as the opposition could not form a government, another defeat for the Bill on second reading would be fatal to them whether Grey's application for peers were granted or refused. The ministry's resignation on a refusal would merely prove the opposition's impotence.

If the government resigned, Harrowby asked in his first circular,

what is to happen? Is it possible to form any Government which could stand for a week with the present House of Commons, and is there the least hope that a dissolution would materially mend the matter? To go on without some Reform Bill is evidently impossible. Neither the duke nor Peel will make themselves responsible for any bill. Can they, or either of them, be ministers upon any other terms? And, if not, who is there?[12]

Harrowby was acute and well-informed on the king's promise to create. He argued that even if the cabinet wanted to make peers to prevent minor defeats in committee they had no permission for this: they could not invoke the prerogative except to defend the essentials of the Bill. But supposing the worst case, namely a massive creation in reply to the first successful amendment, the opposition would still have gained an advantage from allowing the second reading, because the moderates who might have approved of peers to save the Bill itself would object to a creation to save every clause. Harrowby answered the charge that the waverers were splitting the party by pointing out that, if a diehard policy led to the government's resignation after a second-reading defeat, it would cause just as bad a split. Assuming that a new administration could be formed at all, a Reform measure would have to be introduced and this would be opposed by many ultra tories. Finally, collecting another majority large enough to resist any but a massive creation involved dragging the bishops into battle again. 'As a friend to the Church,' Harrowby wrote, 'I *dare* not be a party to this.'[13] A majority of a few votes against the second reading, such as a small creation would erase, was of no use whatever.

Peel produced the most subtle reply to Harrowby.[14] He assumed that the ministers would be able to make any number of peers to carry the second reading. This convenient assumption allowed him to deal solely with the probable results of a creation, and to ignore the problems which the government's resignation might bring to the anti-reformers. He was sceptical about the possibility of amending the Bill. The opposition, he argued, could decide only whether the Bill should pass by creation or by threat of creation. He preferred the former because it would bring a reaction in the long run. By the latter the cabinet would 'have gained the prize without incurring the odium and disgust of the crime'. Peel hinted that the whig-radical control of the Lords produced by a creation would not last. The new peers themselves might turn conservative. A successful threat to create would constitute a worse precedent than a creation.

This argument, like all Peel's reactions to the Reform crisis, evoked doubts of his sincerity. Critics hinted that he was thinking of his recent performance on Catholic Emancipation, and taking a diehard line for his own sake, not for the country's. Even colleagues admitted that his policy was influenced by partisan considerations. 'Some of our friends,' Hardinge explained to Mrs Arbuthnot on 18 January, 'having in short words *ratted* once on the Catholic question cannot afford to do so a second time'.[15] Hardinge was not criticizing the duke and Peel. Their policy had to take account of the fact that, unlike Harrowby, they were party leaders with a dangerous record of concession. They were not in a position to defy the ultra-tory peers and split the party. Dying hard, provided that it provoked a creation of peers and not the resignation of the government, would at least hold the party together; and the country needed a united conservative party. Wellington thought the waverers' efforts disruptive enough. But this was as nothing compared with the shattering effect which he would have produced by taking their line himself.

Whatever Peel's motives much of his argument was sound. In the event, amending the Bill proved impossibly difficult. A creation was not a recipe for radical supremacy in 1832. It would not have prevented the Lords from drifting towards conservatism throughout the 1830s. It was Peel's central contention which was weak. His argument assumed that the moderates would continue to object to a creation whatever the circumstances. It is possible that, as far as some Reform peers were concerned, this assumption was justified. But it can hardly have been true of any other group. The certainty of another rejection on second reading would have given the cabinet a case for creating such as no reasonable man could have disputed. It is at least arguable that the wrath of the moderates would then have fallen not so much on the cabinet for making peers as on the duke for forcing them to do so. The most deferential and doubtful reformer might have been brought to agree with the Earl of Essex, who told Littleton in December 1831 'that the king ought to stop at the first stand of hackney coaches in Piccadilly, and make all the coachmen in succession peers until the number was filled up'.

The waverers made one great mistake. They thought of the risk that the government might resign entirely in terms of the second reading. They assumed that, once in committee, Grey must choose between a creation if that were obtainable and acceptance of any amendments which the opposition managed to insert. To use modern terms, they did not think that he could make any feature of the Bill a question of confidence unless he expected defeat on it to lead to a creation of peers. They did not envisage that he might treat a committee defeat like one on the second reading and that, if the king would not allow it as a ground for peer-making, he might simply resign. Their neglect of this possibility is understandable. The reformers had been so unwilling to let the cabinet resign over the second-reading defeat in the previous year that they did not seem likely to approve of resignation for a mere amendment. But the situation was no longer that of October and inferences drawn from what happened then might be wrong.

Beneath the argument on tactics lay opposed views of the Reform movement. To Wellington Grey was an enemy: to Harrowby he represented a potential ally. The waverer leaders wanted to strengthen Grey against the radicals, just as Gladstone in 1886 wanted to strengthen Parnell against the Irish extremists.

By the end of February Harrowby and Wharncliffe had collected enough followers to make it likely that the second reading would be carried. The diehards put these conversions down to fright. There may have been something in this. Yet it is not usually the most timid who defy clamour in the press and appeals to party loyalty. Along with strong nerves the policy of another rejection demanded a certain capacity to disregard where the balance of the argument lay, for Harrowby presented his case far more ably than Wellington. The duke never put the diehard position as convincingly as Peel did. At times he seemed to imply against the weight of the evidence that, faced by another large majority against the second reading, the cabinet would have neither created peers nor resigned.[16] He had been ill over Christmas; and at this stage he was not only less convincing but less active than the waverer leaders.

It would be absurd, however, to label the whole body of diehards as irrational and the waverers as the reverse. The diehard case was quite strong, however badly Wellington stated it. Some opposition peers understood the arguments for dying hard better than the duke did. Others held all arguments of expediency to be beside the point. As they disapproved of the Bill they thought it their duty to vote Not Content, and, in Milner's phrase of 1909, to 'damn the consequences'. Wellington sympathized with this view. Dying hard on principle was not the only way of disregarding the various arguments summarized above. There were others; and plenty of peers on both sides adopted one of these. They followed Wellington because, right or wrong, he was their leader and they refused to join in disrupting the party, or Harrowby because they thought him disinterested and trusted his judgment. Some voted with Wellington because he had won at Waterloo, others with the waverers because Harrowby was a devoted churchman of exemplary private life. Some were put off wavering by resentment that Wharncliffe should bring himself forward as a leader or by some unintended slight.[17] Lord Grantham's inclination towards Wellington was attributed to the failure of the waverer leaders to call on him early in their operations.[18] All the conflicting considerations which had been operative among MPs in March applied now in the Lords. Frightened peers inclined towards the waverers. Those who were frightened of being thought frightened continued to die hard.

The waverers as they finally emerged in the division on the second reading were a miscellaneous group.[19] They naturally included a number of the leaders' friends and connexions. But their most obvious characteristic, if they are considered apart from their leaders,[20] is their political insignificance. A peer who wanted a future with the tories could not afford to revolt against the duke and enlist under a leader who had returned to politics for the duration of the crisis only.

A good many peers who wished the Bill to pass on second reading never became waverers. Many more shared this wish than were prepared to defy Wellington and act on it. The party stalwarts might hope that Harrowby would succeed; but they could do nothing for him. In April 1832, as in March 1831, the smallness of the majority for the second reading was no coincidence. Where so many peers, while wanting Harrowby to win, also wanted not to vote for him, he was unlikely to have many more votes than he needed. Lord Kenyon wrote to Harrowby on 6 February: 'I have difficulty in thinking I can bring myself to support the second reading of a Bill so utterly un- principled; ... yet could we but all nearly accord as to the needful amendments I am much inclined to think that course would ... give us the best chance of preventing much mischief.'[21] On 12 April, just before the second-reading division, Kenyon told his sister: 'I expect now we shall lose it by two or three; and I confess that . . . I think we had better lose it so than gain it by a very small majority.'[22]

The attitude which Kenyon represented was so widespread that a question arises: would Wellington have been obliged to allow the Bill a second reading in the end even if no waverer group had ever been formed? On this hypothesis all that the waverers achieved was to afford the diehards the luxury of a consistent line freed from its disadvantages, and to relieve Wellington from having to execute an embarrassing withdrawal. The hypothesis must be rejected. If the waverers had not acted the inducements for the duke to retreat would have increased. But they would never have equalled those to stand firm. A last-moment retreat, or even a tacit permission for others to do so, would have seemed almost impossibly difficult and disruptive. In April, as in January, most of the ultra-tory peers would have been outraged by a sign that the leaders meant to yield. Moreover the duke would not have been scared by the near prospect of winning: he was prepared for peers to be made or for the government to resign. His conduct in May does not suggest that he was convinced of his own inability to form a government. Nor does it seem likely, if a change by Wellington is ruled out, that any spontaneous, last-minute revolt from his leadership could have deprived him of his majority in time to stop a creation. Harrowby and Wharncliffe had complete confidence in the rightness of their policy and in their title to take the lead. They combined well with each other and possessed between them considerable influence. Yet it took them two months to rob the duke of enough followers to assure a majority for the second reading. The work would not have been done without leaders in a few days.

The activities of the waverers were all over the press by March and *The Times* thundered for peers. The cabinet were better able to disregard the thunder than they had been in November. Now that they had published their Bill and obtained the promise of peers it could at least be argued that they must be left to decide the timing of the *coup*. But Attwood and the other leaders of the 'high' unions, knowing that their followers could not be kept from violence if there were another check, kept begging that the second reading should be made safe.[23] In truth no practicable way could be found of making it safe, though Attwood could hardly be told this.

Creating fifty or sixty peers would entail serious trouble with the king and be riskier than relying on the waverers. A creation if no alternative had existed would have been one thing. A creation with the waverers at work to prove it unnecessary would be quite another.[24] The ministers were disillusioned and discouraged. They had dreamed of solving the Reform problem in a matter of weeks without upheaval. Even if the Bill passed the Lords safely it had been too long delayed to do the good which they had once expected of it. 'Damn Reform,' said Grey in February, 'I wish I had never touched it';[25] and Althorp admitted that he had removed his pistols from his bedroom for fear that with the means to hand he might commit suicide. A few weeks later he said to Hobhouse: 'I do not know whether I ought not to make matters easier by shooting myself.' This did not strike Hobhouse as a solution for the government's troubles. 'For God's sake,' he rejoined, 'shoot anybody else you like.'[26]

The Bill reached the report stage in the Commons, after twenty-two nights in committee, on 10 March. If there was to be a creation it could be delayed no longer. On that day Althorp wrote to Grey saying that if peers were not created he would have to resign. Brougham, Holland and Graham identified themselves with this demand, though it is doubtful whether any of them actually threatened to resign. The point is not of moment, since Althorp's resignation alone would have put an end to the government.

Grey knew that, while an unsuccessful creation would smash his government and his reputation, a failure on the second reading after his refusal to create would be more ruinous for him still. In the outbreak of violence sure to follow the loss of the Bill his life would not be safe. Yet his reply was unyielding. Althorp, he pointed out, was mistaken in regarding a creation before the second reading as an effective precaution against defeat. A majority as things stood was 'nearly certain'. 'Creating fifty or even sixty peers' would expose the government 'to a great risk of failure even on the second reading.' It might be necessary to create if troubles accumulated in committee; and such a creation, while difficult to execute, should not be impossible. Until then, Grey answered, 'I do not think anything would induce me to be a consenting party to a large creation'.[27] Grey thus produced his own threat of resignation to match Althorp's. If Althorp persisted he would not obtain peers: he would destroy the government and jeopardize the Bill.

Althorp and his associates surrendered. When Durham proposed a prompt creation in cabinet on 11 March no one voted with him. He had apparently intended to resign in case of failure. But he found that if he did Russell would go with him, whereupon he too decided that he could not destroy the ministry.[28] All now depended on the waverers. The Bill passed the Commons in the early hours of 24 March. Harrowby and Wharncliffe had agreed with Grey that they would use the opportunity of its introduction into the Lords to pledge their votes for the second reading.

On 26 March the House was full, though fewer MPs attended than in the previous September. Althorp and Russell brought the Bill up, looking, so Le Marchant says, 'more triumphant than they felt'. After a few words from Grey, Harrowby spoke for ten minutes. Wharncliffe followed. 'He was so nervous,' according to Le Marchant, 'that his voice failed him; and he would not have been heard but for the extreme stillness that prevailed. . . . Everyone seemed to keep his breath for suspense.' The Bishop of London then promised his vote for the second reading. He was far less embarrassed. Having neither attended the debate and division in October nor used his proxy he could not be charged with turning his coat. Grey made a judicious reply. No diehards spoke except Carnarvon, who opposed the Bill though a whig, and Wellington. The duke closed the discussion by 'promising,' in Greville's words, 'that if the Bill went into committee he would give his constant attendance and do all in his power to make it as safe a measure as possible. So finished this important evening much to the satisfaction of the moderate, and to the disgust of the violent party.'[29]

Though the cabinet were confident about the second reading[30] they had learned by experience to take precautions. On the next day they sent a minute to the king advising him that, if the Bill were rejected, 'it would be necessary . . . immediately to prorogue Parliament for a few days, and at the same time to make such an addition to the House of Lords as would afford a certainty of success in the progress of the measure'. The alternative was the ministry's 'immediate resignation'. In an audience on 1 April Grey made clear that to preserve public order the newspapers which announced the loss of the Bill should also announce peer-making. The king asked how many peers would be required. 'I answered,' Grey recorded, 'that I should be deceiving His Majesty if I stated that I thought a less number than fifty or sixty would be sufficient to insure success. This, he said, was a fearful number.'

The king refused to agree in advance to a creation as an immediate reply to defeat; and neither Grey's arguments in the audience nor further minutes on 3 and 7 April converted him. His pledge to create peers as a last resource was 'sacred', he said, subject to his 'consideration of the nature and extent of the addition'. But it did not apply until every expedient for reducing opposition had been tried. The right answer to rejection was to negotiate for an agreement on a modified Bill. The cabinet's proposal was moreover premature: the question of a creation could not be discussed properly until the defeat had occurred.

The king showed his resentment at the mistaken ministerial assurances which had been produced at each stage to overcome his doubts. He reminded the cabinet that they had begun work with 'a very erroneous estimate' of the parliamentary opposition which their Bill would encounter.[31] He objected to the revised lists of 'peerables' shown to him, noticing that a number of the most eligible eldest sons would not go upstairs. By maintaining his objection to any but eldest sons and collateral heirs he limited the approved names to forty. His refusal did not involve going back on his January promise though no one could have given it a more restrictive interpretation. The pledge applied to preventing a second-reading defeat, not to avenging one.

The cabinet had no intention of entering on the kind of negotiation which the king wanted. 'The king's letter . . . is very unsatisfactory,' Holland wrote to Grey on 6 April: 'nothing remains if we are beaten but resignation; for there is no time for parley and discussion.'[32] Meanwhile *The Times* speculated on the Prime Minister's fate should the Bill fall from his neglect to take the obvious precaution, and remarked that in ancient Rome the author of such a disaster would have been 'flung from the Tarpeian rock'.[33]

The second-reading debate began on 9 April, the division being taken after four nights at 6.30 a.m. on 14 April. Once again the gallery was full and a throng of MPs sat or lay round the throne and at the bar. Stanley and Graham were there on the last night, 'more anxious-looking', Hobhouse thought, 'than became cabinet ministers'. Grey was afraid that his troubles with the king would leak out and erode his majority as had happened in March 1831. But no one who had understood and accepted the waverer argument would have voted against the Bill again in the hope that the king would refuse to create. The government clearly could not accept a second defeat; and according to Harrowby their resignation would be as disastrous as new peers. In any case, there was no repetition of March 1831. The opposition do not seem to have known much this time when the division was taken. Ellenborough noted in his diary on 8 April: 'the king went out of town on Wednesday almost in a state of madness . . . the *wherefore* is not yet known'. The current rumour rather favoured the government and the waverers. It was that the king's pledge applied only to the second reading, and that he wanted the Bill pulled to pieces in committee.

The waverers were not steady troops; and the anxieties of their officers equalled those of the government. 'Nothing can equal the hot water we have been in,' Greville recorded on 11 April, 'defections threatened on every side, expectations thwarted and doubts arising, betting nearly even.' For the rank and file, however, the uncertainty had its agreeable side. The views and scruples of a number of obscure peers suddenly assumed momentous importance. The Earl of Coventry, for instance, seems to have found his wavering unexpectedly enjoyable. Kinnaird, in assuring the government whips that Coventry would vote for the Bill, added: 'I think it right, however, to tell you that he promised the other side yesterday.' 'I never before,' Coventry observed, 'was fully aware of the usefulness of indecision . . . I have received more invitations to dinner this week than I had for years.'[34]

The debate was naturally less interesting than that of October. The Duke of Buckingham gave notice of his own more moderate Reform Bill should the government's be rejected. His move was generally ridiculed. It was made far too late; and he did not command respect. Harrowby spoke well for the waverers and Ellenborough for the diehards. Grey opened and closed the debate with fine speeches. He had to clinch every doubtful vote by offering all possible inducements for sending the Bill to committee. He also knew, from the recent exchanges, that it would be very hard to persuade the king to make fifty or sixty peers for any but the most serious committee defeat. He therefore conceded that neither the precise number of boroughs in Schedule A nor the figure of £10 in the borough qualification formed part of the unalterable principle of the Bill.[35] He indicated that the government would submit the Lords' amendments to the Commons, and make peers only if there were 'a collision' between the Houses.[36] Jeffrey, writing to Cockburn, depicted the scene during this final speech: 'The candles had been renewed before dawn, and blazed on after the sun came fairly in at the high windows,

and produced a strange, but rather grand, effect on the red draperies
and furniture and dusky tapestry on the walls.'[37] The Bill was given a
second reading by 184 votes to 175. A few hours later a young man
in the coach from Manchester to London 'saw horses galloping and
carriages coming at a speed which would quickly have left behind
our coach if they had been going the same way. . . . They were chaises
with four horses in each chaise, having two or three men inside, and
they were throwing out placards from each window.' In this way John
Bright learned of 'the glorious triumph of popular principles even in
the House of Lords'.[38]

Congratulations poured in on Grey. They were deserved. His
repugnance to a creation had inclined him to the right decision. 'I
find everybody very well satisfied with the division,' Althorp told his
father on 16 April,

and . . . I perceive that if we had made a large creation of peers we should not
have been well supported in the House of Commons. For a great many people
who are among our staunchest men have expressed to me so much pleasure
at our having carried the second reading without a creation, that this, in addition to the flatness with which all allusions to it have been received in the House,
convinces me that it would have been an unpopular measure among our
supporters generally.[39]

The cabinet expected trouble in committee, however, unless the
opposition blundered.[40] They trembled as they faced a committee
stage without the help either of a majority or of Althorp. Their worst
problem in using a creation to stop the process of amendment was one
of timing. If they demanded peers too soon, or on an insufficient
pretext, they would meet with a refusal. But if they allowed the
whittling down to go on until their case was overwhelming they
might still be refused. The whittling-down process would disillusion
reformers in the country; and once disillusionment brought a reduction
in pressure for the Bill the king would judge it safe to stand out against
peers. The cabinet's difficulty was sharpened by the king's increasing
dislike of their doings. Apart from his resentment at their failure to
warn him that their Bill could run into serious parliamentary trouble,
he had grown to distrust their handling of foreign affairs. He thought
that in settling the Belgian question they had deferred too much to
France. This was the subject of a sharp royal protest just after the
second-reading division.

The committee stage had been postponed until after Easter to give time for discussion. The opposition began with a conference on 17 April between the diehards, represented by Lyndhurst and Ellenborough, and the waverers represented by Harrowby, Wharncliffe and Haddington. They were faced by a serious initial embarrassment in that if the House passed the first clause it would be committed to disfranchising all fifty-six boroughs in Schedule A. In discussion with the waverers before the second-reading debate the government had made a tentative offer to omit the figure of fixty-six from the clause. The opposition would then be enabled to agree to the principle of disfranchisement without being committed on its extent. The government would maintain their principle that disfranchisement should precede the enfranchising clauses.

The opposition meeting on 17 April welcomed this proposal and recommended accepting the two disfranchising clauses provided that the figures were omitted. But when Lyndhurst and Ellenborough reported their discussion to Wellington, Rosslyn, and Bathurst on 18 April they met with a veto. Wellington 'thought', in Ellenborough's account,

that although our friends would vote for the omission of fifty-six and thirty in the first and second clause [sic], they would not afterwards allow the clauses as amended to pass without a division, and that a breaking of the party upon the first division would induce many to stay away in the subsequent stages and so prevent our doing anything with effect.

This objection was felt by all to be good; and it was agreed that it should be brought under the notice of Ld. Harrowby and his friends, and that it should be urged upon them to vote for the postponement of the two clauses, the committee after the third clause proceeding at once to enfranchise.[41]

Later that day Lyndhurst and Ellenborough had their second meeting with the waverers.

The reasons for postponing the clauses of disfranchisement were explained [Ellenborough recorded] and deemed sufficient to require that course. It was felt that the passing of the clauses without a division after the omission of fifty-six and thirty would have placed us in a better position. Still the essential point was to keep the party together for ulterior operations.

It was decided therefore that we should all support the postponement of the clauses, and that Ld. Lyndhurst should make the motion, declaring at the same time his full adherence to the principle of disfranchisement, now sanctioned by the House, and his disposition to act upon it to some extent.

Ld. Harrowby still reserved the power of changing his opinion.[42]

Meanwhile the cabinet were trying to discover which modifications the political unions would regard as acceptable. Parkes was asked about a waverer proposal to restrict the borough vote by altering the qualification from £10 value to £10 rating. Grey's remarks in the second-reading debate had aroused suspicions and these overtures did not prosper. Charles Attwood of the Northern Political Union protested on 18 April against any raising of the borough qualification; and Cobbett publicly accused Parkes of failing to stick to the whole Bill.[43]

Palmerston and Wharncliffe met, at the former's request, on 20 April. Palmerston asked Wharncliffe to meet Grey. He said, in Wharncliffe's account:

Lord Grey has become convinced that he may now go farther, in endeavouring to meet those who are afraid of the extent of the measure, than he had hitherto thought he should be permitted to do by the feeling out of doors, and is anxious to have a friendly conversation with you ... to see if difficulties cannot be smoothened by it.

I answered [Wharncliffe goes on] that he must be aware that circumstances were now greatly altered, that we must now look to the cooperation of the Duke of Wellington and the tories to carry ... amendments, and that we were, in fact, in communication with them. That although personally, therefore, I could have no objection to such an interview, I felt that I was bound to do nothing of that kind without its being known and consented to by them.[44]

Lyndhurst advised Wharncliffe to see Grey and discover the government's intentions. Wellington, on the other hand, protested when Lyndhurst told him of the proposed interview. It had been arranged by then, however, and could not be stopped.

Wharncliffe met Grey, Brougham and Palmerston on 28 April. He told the ministers of the plan to postpone the disfranchising clauses. Grey said that he could not agree to postponement, and asked Wharncliffe to do everything possible to have the plan dropped. The accounts of how Wharncliffe replied to this are conflicting. In his own version, as recorded by Greville, he answered that he would try to stop the scheme, but 'that he knew the tories were much bent' on it. For himself, as Greville reports his words, 'he would support nothing calculated to interfere with the essential provisions of the Bill'. In Palmerston's account to Littleton, Wharncliffe answered that if postponement were proposed he would vote against it.[45]

The opening committee sitting had been arranged for 7 May. After a final meeting with Lyndhurst and Ellenborough on 5 May the waverers very reluctantly agreed to vote for postponement. One of them suggested that Grey should be warned of the decision. Lynd-hurst objected to this. The ultra tories, he said, had been made suspicious by Wharncliffe's interview with Grey and there must be no more communication. No warning was given. The cabinet remained ignor-ant until the end that the postponement plan had the backing of a united opposition. They dined at Holland House on 6 May, and 'agreed that any postponement of the first clause should be resisted to the utmost. It was thought,' Holland recorded, 'that in that resistance many of the waverers, and certainly Wharncliffe who acknowledged he dis-approved of such postponement, would join.'[46]

The postponement motion made peer-making or the resignation of the government inevitable. It gave the cabinet the best case for resigning which they could hope to have. With one exception the opposition leaders did not realize this. The waverers' blind spot here was as bad as ever. Harrowby was more perceptive than Wellington, Ellenborough and Aberdeen. He saw that the motion would have the wrong effect on the ministers. But he expected it to make them less conciliatory, not that it would drive them to resign. 'He thinks,' Ellenborough wrote, '[that] the government wish to be enabled to make concessions by our acquiescing in the principle of disfranchise-ment but [that] if we postpone the first clause they will be assailed by meetings and be obliged to be obstinate.'

Rumours about the king's growing alienation from his ministers help to explain this blindness. Once the second reading was over discussion centred on the risk of peer-making; and all sections of the opposition were encouraged by the signs that the king was disinclined to create peers during the committee stage. Amid these cheering signs it was easy to assume that if a creation were refused the ministry would submit.[47] Though the waverers had realized from an early stage that the opposition could not form a government, they still did not draw the conclusion that the whigs would exploit this weakness by resigning; and indeed the difficulties involved in this kind of resignation remained very great. Grey would be taking a formidable risk in resigning for a procedural question when the Bill was in its last stages. Even now his followers in the Reform movement might not be ready to see him leave office.

Moreover among the upper classes governments were expected to steer between the Scylla of clinging dishonourably to office and the Charybdis of deserting the king without good cause. Submitting to another second-reading defeat would have been wrong. Not submitting to reverses in committee might be thought equally wrong. Resigning at this stage could easily look like an attempt to gain party advantage by the discreditable method of leaving the king without a government.

Harrowby's mistake did not originate in tactical obtuseness, or even in failure to gauge the reactions of the reformers in the political unions. It arose essentially from his inability to understand the attitude of the whig leaders to office. The toils of office formed part of the tory way of life. To a statesman such as Harrowby, bred in the government party, the distaste of the whig magnates for official life was unimaginable. None of the tory leaders, except perhaps Lyndhurst, realized how tired Grey and Althorp were, or how much they wanted a chance to resign with honour.

Wellington probably did not take much stock of the waverers' dislike of postponement. There was little risk that they would refuse to cooperate from distaste for the tactics chosen. They were reasonable men who had aroused the hostility of most of the party and were anxious to do nothing to increase it. As in September 1831 they had a very strong inducement to come into line once the bulk of the party were committed to a plan. By abstaining on postponement they would either turn a large majority into a small one, thus leaving the operation at least as dangerous as it would have been if they had joined in it. Or they would goad the ultras to fury by depriving the opposition of a majority altogether. To keep the split in the party open by abstention would doom any scheme of amendments to failure; and it was of the first importance to the waverers that the amendments should succeed.

The ultra tories were a different story. The duke's remarks on 18 April show that he was still touched by the obsession which had led him astray on 2 November 1830. He and his colleagues had somehow to secure ultra support. The ultras under Eldon and Cumberland loathed the Bill and made no pretence of statesmanlike moderation. If their advice was flouted they would sulk. Their leaders were elderly men with little political future in a reformed system and practically no belief in the usefulness of amendments.[48] If they sulked, all attempts at amendment would fail. For securing ultra-tory support postponement was a masterstroke. Early in May Eldon and Cumberland indicated that they would support Wellington's amendments without requiring advance information about them provided that disfranchisement were postponed.[49] This was an almost irresistible offer.

Wellington's principal weapon was as clumsy as Grey's. Countering amendments by a creation presented the government with a problem: collecting a majority for any particular amendment was a still greater one for the duke. Amending the Bill looked as difficult as ever, even if the ultras did not interfere. Any change designed to make it less democratic was apt to lessen the likelihood that it would produce even a temporary settlement of the Reform question; and the more responsible of the opposition peers now wanted a settlement as much as anyone. Raising the qualification in the great towns would keep some dangerous people out of the electorate; but they were just the people, now that they had been offered votes, who would never rest until they had them. A proposal to lower the voting qualification in boroughs presented the opposition leaders with an even more difficult problem, since they were not agreed about the probable behaviour of working-class voters.

One view was based on the change in attitudes which the growth of industry was bringing. In an increasingly industrial country, the argument ran, the working-class voter could not be trusted to show proper respect for people of property. As *Blackwood's* indiscreetly remarked, if the lower orders of Britain had all belonged to the 'peasantry' Reform would have involved little danger: it was the industrial workers, according to *Blackwood's*, who were liable to be moved by 'turbulent and democratic principles'.[50] Wellington took this line. He did not want too large a working-class vote. 'We are all too ready,' he told Bathurst, 'to believe that the lower orders of the people in this country are the best. I admit that they were well inclined. But they have been educated, and read, and are corrupted by, the newspapers. Plunder is everywhere the object; and the lower we go, the stronger we find the desire to plunder.'[51]

Some of Wellington's colleagues, however, hankered after what was to become in several countries the great conservative device of the century, namely, giving votes to the working class to counteract middle-class influence. The deferential attitude of many poor men which unfitted them for the vote to a radical's way of thinking made them eminently suitable voters in the eyes of some tories.[52] The problem was to devise amendments which would enlarge, but also set a limit to, the working-class vote. As a radical remarked with some truth in 1835 during the debates on the Municipal Reform Bill, the tories wanted enough votes to bribe but not enough to make the system one of popular government.[53] These ideas could not be

translated into effective amendments. The first people to be brought
in by a lowering of the voting line would be artisans; yet these were
the very men on whom tory suspicions centred. To a tory eye the
unsettling effect of education was seen at its worst in this group. They
were unlikely to prove reliable voters.

More complicated ways of tinkering with the borough suffrage
would not remove the difficulty. Some regard had to be paid to the
principle that no one should receive the vote unless he was 'independent' and 'respectable'. The new voter must not be so poor that he
was bound to come under someone's dictation, nor so uneducated
that political issues meant nothing to him. These principles seemed to
the opposition leaders to preclude the creation of a borough electorate
whose deferential qualities could be guaranteed. Wellington's colleagues lacked the assurance and sleight of hand which Disraeli was
to command by 1867. The hope that the artisan voter might be as
timid as any member of the *bourgeoisie* had not yet been born. No one
guessed that the 'aristocrat of labour' might soon fear the unskilled
workers below him almost as much as he resented those above.

Agreement on a scheme of amendments would be out of the
question if all these issues, and each amendment proposed, had to be
discussed with ultra leaders who wanted to concede nothing. Moreover
the duke was a believer in secret planning by a small circle. If he were
not obliged to divulge his plans to the ultras and other groups, he had
a fair chance of taking the government by surprise.[54] Enticed by the
ultras' offer of a blank cheque on one condition, the opposition leaders
overlooked the dangers which this condition involved.

One leader, however, knew the risks. Lyndhurst made some remarks
to Disraeli a few years later which suggested that he had meant to
oust the government.[55] He had been convinced of their weakness for
some time. After the Russian–Dutch loan debate in the Commons on
26 January he had taken Ellenborough aside 'and said he thought
these fellows might be turned out provided it were known that an
administration could and would be formed if they went out'. He must
have realized how reluctant Wellington and Peel were to take office
and pass a Reform Bill; but they might be still more reluctant, when
the king had refused to make peers, to leave him powerless and
without a government.

Lyndhurst's motion to postpone disfranchisement was reckless.
There were no signs that the Bill had become significantly less popular.
An Edinburgh meeting on 24 April to petition the Lords to pass it had

attracted an attendance put at forty or fifty thousand. The political
unions would not accept a smaller Reform measure from the anti-
reformers. Indeed the ministers' defeat and resignation would at once
unleash a demand for a more radical Bill; and on 27 April Attwood's
council had drawn up resolutions for such a Bill in case of a ministerial
defeat.[56] But Lyndhurst had a certain irresponsibility and love of
mischief. His reputation, which had not stood high since his acceptance
of the Chief Barony,[57] had recently been lowered still further by a
scandal involving his wife.[58] A bold stroke if successful would re-
establish him with the party. Postponement was not a plot on his
part. The proposal seems to have emanated from the duke who was
talking of it as early as 15 April.[59] Lyndhurst merely saw its possibilities. He was both the most perceptive of the opposition leaders and
the least responsible.

What passed at the Grey–Wharncliffe conference on 28 April must
remain in doubt. Holland's account, largely taken from Wharncliffe's
minute, is probably the fairest. Although, according to Holland,
Wharncliffe did not declare

an intention of *voting* against it [the postponement motion], Palmerston and
the others understood him to say that he (and he should think Harrowby)
would resist it. By his [Wharncliffe's] own note ... Ld Grey distinctly declared that ... postponement ... would ... be *fatal* to the satisfactory termina-
tion of the business and that he never would consent to it.

'If this', Holland adds, 'was not ... to avow *totidem verbis* that, if the
majority decided to postpone the clause, he [Grey] should either
resign or insist on making peers, there is no meaning in words.'[60]

Holland's evidence is valuable; but his conclusion may be doubted.
At such a conference each party is apt to give the most convenient
interpretation to the statements made. Wharncliffe probably meant
that, in private, he would try to dissuade his tory colleagues from
moving postponement. The members of the government interpreted
his statement hopefully to mean that, if postponement were moved,
he would 'resist' it in the House. Grey probably meant that, if postponement were carried, he would—or at least might—obtain a creation
of peers or resign. Wharncliffe must have disliked acting as the
channel through which the opposition received the Prime Minister's
threats. His efforts at interpretation were no doubt equally hopeful.
He took Grey to mean merely that the government would protest
vigorously against postponement and divide the House against it. The

K

conference misled all concerned except for Lyndhurst. He probably guessed from it that postponement was an almost perfect formula for ousting the ministers. They would not realize how certain their defeat on the motion was, since they could be prevented from learning that the waverers would vote for it. They were therefore unlikely to take counter-measures. On the other hand, they would not submit to the defeat and the king would not create peers to avenge it. After 28 April an observer as clever and cynical as Lyndhurst would have known that the government were as good as out.

The debate on 7 May was short and tense. If anything more had been required to stiffen the government Lyndhurst's opening speech supplied this. Greville thought it 'very aggravating'.[61] The Commons had been counted out early in the evening; and Grey several times consulted Althorp below the bar. The cabinet were furious with the waverers. Yet they welcomed an immediate crisis which might release them from the difficulties of steering the Bill through committee. They quickly confirmed the decision to make the question one of confidence. Brougham, Holland and Grey did their best to make clear, despite the veiling imposed by the dignified language of the time, that if the government were defeated they would secure a creation of peers or resign. Some government supporters thought this stand rash.[62]

Among the opposition the contrast between front and back benches was reversed. The leaders were alarmed at last, while some of the back benchers supposed that Grey was bluffing. Others had not heard the government's warnings, or were obtuse enough not to understand them. Many peers, says Le Marchant, 'had only just come up from the country, and stepped from their carriages into the House to enquire what was going on. . . . The peers, with few exceptions—as usually happens when a question is imperfectly understood and the House is taken by surprise—voted according to party.'[63] The government were defeated by 151 to 116.

During the division Wellington, Lyndhurst, Ellenborough, Bathurst, Harrowby and Wharncliffe had a hurried consultation. They now realized that Grey meant to bring matters to a crisis; but they had no idea that his resignation was only hours away. They thought that ministerial strategy would be to promote the greatest possible agitation for a few days, and on the strength of that to obtain a creation or resign. To enable the king to resist peers they needed to prove that their postponement motion had not been designed to destroy the Bill.

They therefore put up Ellenborough to outline their scheme of amendments. This was an awkward assignment in a House which had just been told by a tory ex-minister 'that they ought to limit the disfranchisement to that . . . required by the enfranchisement; and it might be a question whether any disfranchisement at all, in the strict sense of the term, would be necessary'.[64] Ellenborough's announcement that he and his colleagues were ready to abolish all 113 seats in Schedule A 'fell', in his own words, 'like a bomb' among the ultra tories 'who had no idea of any such thing being proposed'. Grey replied, amid cheers, to the effect that it would have been more honest to detonate the bomb before the division, and the sitting ended.

The leading ministers collected in the Lord Chancellor's private room. In a mood compounded of anger, relief, and above all fatigue, they decided not to stay in office without a creation of fifty or sixty peers. A cabinet was summoned for eleven the next morning. At midnight Grey wrote to Taylor: 'the only point . . . to consider tomorrow would be whether we should propose a creation of peers or at once tender our resignations to His Majesty'.

The cabinet, Richmond alone dissenting,[65] resolved to demand a creation large enough 'to ensure the success of the Bill in all its essential principles'. This was agreed to mean creating fifty or sixty peers. Just before the opposition's plan became known Grey had favoured resigning without asking for peers in case of an important defeat early in the committee. But he was now aroused and his scruples had disappeared. The ministers demanded peers as a matter of principle and to protect their standing with the Reform movement. They expected the king to refuse; and for various reasons most of them hoped that he would. Grey and Althorp wanted a tory attempt at government to succeed and free them from office. Brougham and Durham wanted it to fail and return them to office in triumph. Hobhouse was told in a ministerial gathering the same day that 'if the tories had been paid for it they could not have acted more for the country and the character of the ministers'.[66]

Grey and Brougham left for Windsor as soon as the cabinet was over. They drove so hard leaving Hounslow that they ran into another carriage and broke its pole. They presented the cabinet minute asking for fifty or sixty peers, and were promised an answer the next morning. They then set off back to London, dined *en route* off mutton chops (to which the irrepressible Brougham insisted on adding kidneys),[67] and reported to the cabinet at 11 p.m.

Early the following morning (9 May) the cabinet learned that their resignations were accepted. The king came to London; and at a levee that afternoon he pressed Brougham and Richmond to stay in office. Both refused. Lyndhurst was then summoned, on the ground, by now somewhat quaint, that as a judge he would give impartial advice. He was asked to make overtures to anyone who might be capable of forming a government to pass an 'extensive' Reform bill.[68] When Althorp entered the Commons that evening to announce the resignation he was met with a storm of cheers. Though precluded by convention from giving details he referred openly to the king's refusal to make peers. Ebrington gave notice of a motion for the next day supporting the outgoing ministers; and Althorp's request that this should be postponed because it might embarrass the new government was refused. One hundred and eighty reforming MPs then met at Brooks's and decided on the terms of the motion.

On the morning of 10 May an administration to carry an 'extensive Reform', in the king's phrase, did not seem out of the question. Althorp thought Ebrington's motion imprudent, apart from trying to stop it as a matter of duty.[69] A majority for it, he argued, would merely invite a dissolution by which the whole labour of carrying the Bill to the present stage would be lost. Ebrington himself thought that he might be defeated. Duncannon and Ellice were equally pessimistic.[70] The more moderate Reform MPs might not relish the gesture against the incoming government which voting for the motion would involve. They would not mind which party put the Bill through its remaining stages. They simply required that someone should settle the question quickly. They would not want to force the incoming Prime Minister to dissolve. Finally, some of them might still doubt the justification for a large creation of peers.

Before Ebrington's motion even came on, however, Lyndhurst and his friends received a check from which they did not recover. Peel refused to serve in the projected government either as Prime Minister or otherwise. Few tories found the decision whether to accept office an easy one. They thought it both their duty and their interest to rescue the king and to take him, as Wellington put it, 'out of the hands of the radicals'.[71] But they did not want to be accused of deserting their principles to gain office. They could not serve their sovereign without taking large salaries for sponsoring the Bill which they had spent the last year in opposing.

For the duke duty to the king was paramount. To answer that call he did not hesitate to sacrifice his anti-Reform opinions, his last shred of popularity, and whatever reputation for political consistency emancipation had left him. His ideas were not only extremely old-fashioned by 1832: they also reflected his unique position. Eminence and unquestioned probity gave him some protection at least against the charge of office seeking. He thought that he owed a special duty to the crown. He had spent his life in serving it. To it he owed all his honours. 'I have eaten the king's salt,' he would say.[72] His decision to go with the king had about it a touch of that nobility which made Robert E. Lee go with Virginia in 1861. These two soldiers were loyalists who moved through the complexities of politics by the guidance of a single, simple allegiance. Each was bound to a bad and losing cause by his own integrity and the wild scheming of others. But Lee's decision had tragic consequences, whereas the duke's led merely to a brief farce.

Peel was not so well placed to overlook his past. Now, as so often during the Reform crisis, memories of emancipation affected him. 'He is still smarting,' Greville noted on 12 May, 'under Catholic question reminiscences.' No one could induce him, after only three years, to change sides a second time and sponsor another measure which he had always opposed. Being thin skinned for a politician he shrank from another storm of abuse. 'Some allowance must be made,' he told the Commons in his explanation on 18 May, 'for human failings.'[73] But it would be unfair to attribute too much to this sensitiveness. Peel's case for staying out was very strong. 'One of the greatest calamities that could befall the country,' he told Croker on 12 May, 'would be that utter want of confidence in the declarations of public men which must follow the adoption of the Bill . . . by me as a minister of the crown.'[74] At the time of the Clare election he had been a minister. He had advised adopting emancipation and had felt bound to stay in office and put the policy into action. He was under no such obligation now. He had approved of the postponement motion and encouraged it. But he held no responsibility for what had happened in the Lords.

Peel's refusal entailed Goulbourn's and confirmed Croker and Herries in their reluctance to join. Lyndhurst and the duke were thus left without anyone competent to control the Commons and with a very weak front bench there. Compared with this disaster Ebrington's majority of 80, a reduction of 51 on the October figure, was no great blow.[75] Taken together the debate and division were not encouraging, however. Althorp's avowal of the advice to create enough peers to safeguard the Bill had aroused thunderous cheering. In its final form the motion was strongly worded. No one who had voted for it could be expected to give the new ministry any support.

The next three days (11–13 May) were spent in a frantic search for a Prime Minister. Harrowby refused, as was expected. That left two possibilities—the duke and the Speaker, Manners Sutton. This latter solution was favoured, and may well have been initiated, by Peel. Sutton's asset was that, although a known anti-reformer, he was not committed against the Bill.

Lyndhurst caused confusion because in his efforts to find a premier of some sort he made what were virtually offers of the post to both Wellington and Sutton. However, the king came to London on 12 May and made clear that he chose Wellington. In the Lords the duke had every assurance of support even among the ultra tories. But he could not collect as much as a token front bench in the Commons. Alexander Baring and Sutton refused to serve under him because of his record as an opponent of any Reform. He was left with his two Peninsular generals, Hardinge and Murray. On the afternoon of 13 May he therefore handed the task to the Speaker to whom he offered his services. He explained that he was authorized to offer those of Baring also. Sutton would not make up his mind that day. He expounded his views to the duke and Lyndhurst for some three hours, at the end of which Lyndhurst, according to Greville, 'returned home, flung himself into a chair and said that "he could not endure to have anything to do with such a damned tiresome old bitch".' Nonetheless the formation of a Sutton–Wellington cabinet could now be assumed. The question was whether the majority of the House of Commons would accept it.

The political unions were making their utmost efforts to show their strength and so to persuade MPs that order could not be restored unless Grey were returned to office. The delay in forming the new administration gave the union leaders their chance. Although there were rumours of a warrant made out for Attwood's arrest it is extremely unlikely that they had a basis in fact. While there was no government in existence capable of making decisions, Attwood and Place could lay their plans, whether legal or illegal, in comparative safety.

It was a good time for putting pressure on Members. If the new government could not control the House there would be an election at once. Even if the dissolution did not come immediately it could not be more than a few months away, since a Reform Bill of some sort was now certain to be passed and its arrival on the statute book must be the signal for a new-style election. May 1832 thus represented a bad moment for making an unpopular stand. If the wavering MPs could be shown that there was still overwhelming approval for Grey and his Bill they would have little truck with the incoming government.

Attwood had expected a crisis early in the committee stage. He therefore held what turned out to be the largest of all his Newhall Hill meetings on 7 May. This gathering, which was attended by anything up to 200,000 people, was mistimed in that reports of it were not available in London when the vote on Lyndhurst's motion was taken. But Attwood and his council faced the crisis buoyed up by a recent and impressive demonstration of their strength. Moreover, they had learned a good deal since October 1831.

Place's National Political Union met some thousands strong on 9 May and petitioned the Commons to refuse supplies until the reformers had been reinstated in power. The next day the Common Council of the City of London adopted a similar petition and practically all the meetings followed suit.[76] The Manchester petition was signed by some 25,000 people in three hours on 10 May and was presented to the Commons on the following day.[77] The political unions came into their own at last: they grew in size and standing with every hour. Within a day of the news of Grey's resignation reaching Birmingham, Attwood announced the enrolment there of five hundred new members.[78] Reports in the London press made clear that many of the new recruits to unions were men of property.[79]

The May crisis marked the high point in cooperation between middle- and working-class reformers. Even in Manchester a treaty was made 'between the reform committee of last year and the political union of the working classes'. It was agreed, in the words of the *Manchester Guardian*, that at the meeting on 14 May,

the resolutions . . . should be passed unanimously, on the one side the acknowledgement being made of the right of every man to be represented in Parliament, and on the other the demand being at present confined to the Bill, and consequently a pledge given that no motion should be brought forward for any Reform on more radical principles.[80]

As a result, although Hunt's radical followers raised their voices at the meeting, no attempt was made to disrupt it.

It is extremely hard to estimate how intense the popular agitation was during the days of May, as they soon came to be known. The press is an unreliable indicator. Papers on both sides tended to play down the agitation. The editors who had opposed Grey naturally took the line that the new government would be launched without serious disturbance. Those who had supported him depicted the reformers as being peaceable both on principle and from a conviction that Sutton and Wellington could not possibly succeed.

Retrospective accounts of the crisis are suspect. Upper-class Victorians were apt to remember the days of May as a kind of nightmare. They could barely believe that when they had been young plans had been laid for an English civil war. On the other hand in the militant working-class tradition these plans became part of a romantic legend. Finally, much of the available information about the crisis comes from the archive to which Francis Place devoted his declining years. In it his own power and prescience receive the fullest recognition.

Even in this crisis the agitation was not quite so overwhelming as the leading agitators made out. A meeting in Leeds on 14 May was more turbulent than the one at Manchester. The tories and manhood suffrage radicals managed to demonstrate that Leeds was not entirely united behind the Bill.[81] On 12 May the *Poor Man's Guardian* advised its readers to 'stand at ease' and let the middle class fight their own battles. In London there was still disunity between the supporters of the Bill and the extremists. Place managed to prevent a suggested mass meeting on Hampstead Heath. According to his own account he did so because he was afraid of such a meeting passing out of his control: by giving the extremists a chance to proclaim that the Bill was not enough for them, it would advertise the division in working-class opinion.[82] This may not have been his most compelling reason for caution. Perhaps he feared that he could not assemble a London mass meeting large and enthusiastic enough to be formidable. Probably both these mischances were in his mind. To impress the politicians a London meeting had to be united as well as enormous; and Place believed that these requirements could not be met. A meeting in Regent's Park on 14 May at which Hume spoke was a comparative failure. 'There were not above 3 or 4000 assembled,' Lady Wharncliffe reported to her mother, 'nothing could be more *flat*.'[83]

Nonetheless this was the most intense burst of agitation which anyone observing it had ever known. Five Reform petitions were displayed for signature in Perth during the Reform struggle. For the first, in November 1830, 1200 signatures were collected in ten days. May 1832 was at the other end of the scale: 5300 Perth people signed then in a day and a half.[84]

Attwood gave the lead on tactics at a Newhall Hill meeting on 10 May. He adjured his followers to keep to lawful paths and to rely on the staunchness of the reformers in the Commons. If, however, the unions were 'compelled . . . in self defence' to take up arms 'Englishmen could not hesitate to use [arms] for the putting down of their enemies'. Attwood realized that if the moves to form a new government succeeded an attempt would be made to isolate and subdue the reformers in Birmingham. On the evening of 10 May he therefore sent a deputation to London, and asked Newcastle and Glasgow to send delegates to Birmingham.

Attwood held the council of his union to a middle line. He refused to mitigate his opposition to Wellington when he learned that the latter meant to pass an extensive Reform Bill. If the unions accepted the Bill from those hands, he said, 'there was an end of popular power in England; and the spirit of the people would be utterly broken'.[85] On the other hand he advised the council not to demand more than the Bill while there was a prospect that Grey would be quickly reinstated.

By midday on 12 May deputies had arrived in London not only from Birmingham but from a number of other places; and a meeting between them and the Londoners was held at a tavern in Covent Garden. 'The persons present were all men of substance,' Place wrote. 'Some were very rich men . . . . It was clearly understood that in the event of Lord Wellington . . . forming an administration . . . open resistance should at once be made, and in the meantime all that could be done should be done to prevent such an administration being formed.'[86]

For the present resistance was to be limited to a refusal to pay taxes until the Bill had been passed and to an attempt to promote a run on the banks. Neither proposal was new. Both fell within the letter of the law. The Quakers regularly subjected themselves to distraint for non-payment of Church rates.[87] Financially the witholding of direct taxes was not overwhelmingly important, since these represented only about one-twelfth of tax revenue.[88] But as a gesture of defiance it was effective and difficult to counter. Its effect depended on agreements that goods which had been distrained for non-payment would be neither handled by the auctioneers nor bought by the public. As early as 11 May a report of such agreements being made appeared in the *Morning Chronicle*. The auctioneers' zeal in the Reform cause was no doubt reinforced by their dependence on the goodwill of their reforming clients. Like withdrawing gold from the Bank of England, non-payment had the advantage of not inviting military reprisals. 'The Blues,' as *The Times* put it on 12 May, 'could make nothing of a charge against unbought feather beds in front of a broker's warehouse.'

Promoting or intensifying a run on the banks was a far bolder step.[89] Business activity, which was sluggish before the May crisis began, had been brought to a very low ebb by the news of Grey's resignation. 'Orders,' the *Manchester Guardian* reported on 12 May, 'were forthwith countermanded; buyers from a distance went, or were recalled, home without effecting their purchases; and a large number of our manufacturers and warehousemen state that, for anything they really have to do, they might just as well actually close their establishments.' A disturbance to trade on this scale was bound to engender fears for the stability of the banking system. Parkes and Place now calculated, despite some protests from their friends,[90] that if they could damage Wellington's chances they would be forgiven for adding to the alarm. Stopping the Bank's payments would be thought less of an evil than failing to stop the duke. By the morning of 13 May Place had placarded much of London with the slogan:

> To Stop the Duke
> Go for Gold[91]

The effect of such placards, in London and the provinces, has been much disputed. With the exception of Thomas Attwood, the witnesses before the Bank Charter Committee later in the year thought that the demand for gold arose largely, if not entirely, from fear.[92] The people who sold stock, and took the proceeds in sovereigns, mostly feared that the banks might soon stop payment. They, or the creditors by whom they were dunned, also wanted, in Place's words, to 'have some money by them in case of the worst'.[93] The withdrawals made solely in order to stop the duke seem to have been the exception. But they were not absolutely negligible. The man who was reported to have withdrawn 'about £20,000' from a London bank on 11 May, and to have gone straight to the Bank of England to demand sovereigns for his notes, may not have been thinking only of the precautions appropriate to troubled times.[94] Again, the fact that the run was directed primarily against the Bank of England, rather than the country banks, suggests that some of those concerned may have been affected by political motives.[95]

The politicians worried far more, however, about panicky depositors than about radical politicians at the bank counters. Political motives might soon lose their effect, whereas fear bred still worse fears. The man who thought of selling his stock in order to top the duke would not do so if prices plunged. He would risk a small loss to forward Reform, but not a large one. The man who was selling because he feared revolution and anarchy might do so at almost any price. An ex-governor of the Bank of England, commenting later on the days of May, remarked: 'When men are frightened they will submit to great disadvantage in order to realise their property.'[96]

This does not imply that devices such as Place's placard were ineffective. The placard may have intensified the scare. A depositor who believed that the reformers might create a run until his bank had to stop payment would be inclined to withdraw his money. Place did not need to persuade reformers to demand gold. It was enough to persuade nervous depositors that the reformers might do so. Place and his friends understood this well. They combined their advocacy of political withdrawals with stories of withdrawals in panic. A National Political Union meeting was told on 12 May of a 'tory lord' who, unwilling to withdraw gold from the Bank of England himself, had 'employed his various tradesmen' to make the withdrawals for him.[97] The one certainty, when all these claims and rumours are surveyed, is that the City of London, by now thoroughly frightened, wanted Grey's government re-established and the Reform question settled quickly. This was realized in political circles by 13 May and had its effect. How far Place's schemes contributed to the city's alarm will never be known.

Against this background the whig MPs assembled at Brooks's on Sunday 13 May to decide how to treat the incoming government. Ebrington wanted to move a resolution in the Commons 'that after the Duke of Wellington's recorded opinion on the Reform Bill no administration of which he forms a part can have the confidence of this House or the country'. After a long and lively discussion this was rejected. It was agreed, in John Campbell's words, 'to let the duke carry the Bill in the Lords and send it down again to the Commons, and then to accept it, and then to turn out the duke'.[98]

It might seem at first glance that the roaring of the reformers all over the country was barely heard by 13 May in Brooks's. Any such impression would be mistaken.[99] Now as always, whig politicians showed a reasonable scepticism about the political unions' claims. They were well practised in appraising the efforts of people who blew up the fire and then exaggerated its heat. They were equally practised in concealing their fears. But private diaries show that many of those at the meeting knew the strength of popular indignation against the duke, though they might keep their knowledge to themselves. 'The feeling of the majority,' Le Marchant records, 'was in favour of violent measures. The fact was that news was now pouring in from all parts of the country of the furious hatred that prevailed against Wellington.' Hobhouse disliked the decision of the meeting. 'I was afraid,' he noted, 'that if we relaxed the people would distrust us.' Ebrington did not accept the decision and persisted in his intention to move the resolution.

The opposition to the resolution was sustained by the whig country gentlemen. They hated to look factious and they were afraid of driving Sutton and Wellington to an immediate dissolution. The prospect of two elections within a year, one on the old system and the other on the new, was serious for a county Member. The factor which had told against Ebrington on 10 May told still more strongly now: an election would almost certainly mean a renewed majority for Reform but it would delay, and perhaps endanger, the Bill.

The advice which decided the issue came not from the country gentlemen, however, but from the ministers. Althorp and Stanley were adamant against the resolution. They were determined not to be branded as office seekers and almost equally determined not to be obliged to pilot the Bill once again through all its stages. As Althorp told his father, the result showed his influence to be 'complete'. Stanley brought all his eloquence and adroitness into play, jumping onto the table and defending the moderate course with a speech of astonishing violence. ('He went very near declaring the throne vacant', Le Marchant noted.) The majority disliked the decision, but thought it no moment for quarrelling with their leaders.

The next day (Monday, 14 May) Sutton consulted Fitzgerald and Peel who both advised him to accept the premiership. The duke soldiered on despite his doubts about Sutton's suitability. 'Many of our friends will not approve of the arrangement,' he wrote to Lyndhurst, 'however . . . I must take steps to reconcile them to it.'[100]

Early in the afternoon he received the Speaker's agreement. Sutton would try to form a government subject to a final word that night. In the Commons 'Hardinge stepped over to Lord Althorp before the debate began,' Le Marchant recorded, 'and told him that all the real difficulties against forming the administration were at an end.' Meanwhile the troops in London were confined to barracks. The Adjutant General had ordered that they should be 'held in readiness to turn out at a moment's notice in aid of the Civil Power, the horses to remain completely equipped, and not to be even unbridled, except in succession . . . whilst feeding'.[101]

The news reaching MPs that Monday was daunting. The *Morning Herald* reported that some of the soldiers in Birmingham had joined the Political Union.[102] According to an evening paper (*The Sun*) notice had been given, by the close of business on 12 May, to withdraw £16,000 from the Manchester Savings Bank. 'The whole country,' Littleton noted in his diary, 'in a state little short of insurrection.'

The Commons debate of 14 May was nominally concerned with the City Livery's petition against granting the new government supplies. The ministers designate were quickly overwhelmed by the whig onslaught. The House cheered every attack on them for deserting their anti-Reform convictions to gain office. Ebrington and Althorp described this desertion as an act of 'public immorality'. 'If others wish to have infamy and place,' said Macaulay, 'let the House of Commons at least have honour and Reform.' Russell referred to the new cabinet as one 'into which honour could not enter'. There was nothing insincere about these strictures; but the necessities of politics may have given them an edge. The whig leaders knew that they were risking their popularity by the decision in Brooks's to accept the Bill from its enemies. To safeguard their position with the Reform movement they had to show that they despised the men whom they would not oust. More serious, and less predictable, were two speeches from tory anti-reformers of high standing, Sir Robert Inglis and Davies Gilbert. Both declared that those who had opposed the Bill had no right to try to carry it. Eventually Baring, on whom most of this storm fell, took up a suggestion from Ebrington that the whigs might resume office on the guarantee of the anti-reformers in the Lords that they would allow the Bill to pass.[103]

When the Commons rose the leading tories drove to Apsley House and told Wellington that no new administration could be formed. Baring said that 'he would face a thousand devils rather than such a

House of Commons'.[104] The duke though surprised was prompt to recognize defeat. He had known for some days that only Rothschild's utmost efforts were preventing a serious fall in government stocks.[105] 'The king had better send for Lord Grey at once,' he said; 'he will have to do it at last; and it is not right to keep the country in agitation during the interval.'[106] It was agreed that when the duke gave the king this advice he should offer to withdraw personally from opposition to the Bill in the hope of sparing his sovereign the humiliation of peer-making.

Fear of an uprising was not the only impulse behind the rejection of a Wellington–Sutton government. Much of the anger in the Commons was spontaneous. The duke's attempt to rescue the king held no appeal for the whigs who were traditionally sceptical about monarchical pretensions. Independent tories such as Inglis and Davies Gilbert were equally unimpressed. They differed greatly in outlook from the official wing of the party. They did not approve of a leader turning his coat to become a placeman.

In other respects Inglis and Gilbert were in opposite camps. Inglis was a diehard, Gilbert a moderate who had voted latterly for the Bill. He was affected, though perhaps not decisively, by his knowledge of the unpopularity of a Wellington–Sutton government. To Inglis, who knew little of the ferment outside Parliament, Wellington was wrong to promise Reform: to Davies Gilbert he was wrong to think that his promise of Reform would prevent violence and discontent. More than ever it was the moderates like Gilbert who counted. The MP who knew enough about the Reform movement to want the Bill on the statute book knew that, if it were to bring peace, Grey must put it there.

Wellington surrendered his commission on the morning of 15 May. The whig ministers had never given up their seals of office. The king wrote at once to Grey, asking him to resume his ministerial duties and carry the Bill 'with such modifications as may meet the views of those who may still entertain any difference of opinion upon the subject'. Without even waiting for the cabinet to meet, Grey answered that the last week had made modification impossible. But, although the cabinet naturally insisted on the whole Bill, they were very willing to have it without a creation. To avoid the latter they needed to obtain and display the kind of guarantee from the tory peers that Ebrington had suggested. The chances of obtaining this seemed quite good. The tories' outlook had been changed by their new circumstances of acknowledged impotence. They realized that to yield on the second reading in order to avoid a creation, and then obstinately to invite one when the king had no power to refuse it, involved having the worst of both worlds. They now wanted to keep control of the Lords for use after the Bill had been passed. At the end of the previous week Hardinge had been talking privately about the possibility of a guaranteed passage for the Bill should the attempt to form a government fail.

The ministers thought it in their interest to pursue the idea. As always they dared not employ a creation, or even the threat of it, until they had proved that there was no other way of carrying the Bill. 'If we give any handle to the tories,' Althorp wrote on 16 May, 'to say that we are endeavouring to make the king give us a majority in the ... Lords for general party purposes, I think we shall be beaten.'[107] Bullying the king at once for a creation might also, Althorp said the next day, 'give Peel the excuse he is looking for to join the duke'.[108] To give time for the guarantee to be arranged the cabinet deferred any statement of the terms on which they would resume power until 18 May. Taylor wrote to the leading tory peers by the king's command, asking them to declare in the Lords on 17 May that they would no longer oppose the Bill.

When the Lords met no declarations were made, however. The king's eldest illegitimate son, the Earl of Munster,[109] had encouraged the opposition not to surrender by telling them that his father meant to resist Grey's demands. The duke and Lyndhurst had already promised the king privately, and in their personal capacities, not to oppose the Bill further. But the duke refused to repeat this in public. To do so, he said, would be to cooperate in the policy of peer-making. Apart from this scruple he and Lyndhurst opened the debate with explanations of their abortive ministry-making which were warlike enough to prevent any tory peer from hoisting a white flag. The ministry were flabbergasted. On the strength of the expected declarations Althorp had told the Commons that a solution reinstating the ministry and safeguarding the Bill was already in train. When he heard what had happened in the Lords he remarked that it was 'rather a bore' to have been so misled, but added happily: 'Now I shall have my shooting.' He was reminded that he might not need to withdraw to the country to hear gunfire.[110]

The *Morning Chronicle* of 18 May called for the announcement by 'this evening' that Grey had been reinstated with full powers, adding 'we are otherwise on the eve of the barricades'. The cabinet met at noon and agreed to demand that the king should at once authorize the making of sufficient peers 'in the event of any fresh obstacle arising which should, in the humble judgment of your Majesty's servants, render it necessary for the success of the Bill'. The loopholes were stopped at last. There was no mention of a limit on numbers; and the ministers, not the king, were to say whether the necessity had arisen. The minute added that the demand was made 'for the public safety'. This time no one dissented; and no one was foolhardy enough to hope for a refusal. 'I have never till within these 48 hours,' Lady Holland told her son that day, 'been seriously alarmed at the state of the country, always ascribing much to exaggeration and vapouring. But now it really appears there is, bona fide, an organization of the people amounting to a national guard, all ready, equipped, disciplined, and as *yet* obedient to their leaders.'[111] Lady Holland was not alone. Many years later Russell recalled the Days of May as 'the only time during my political life in which I have felt uneasy as to the result'.[112]

Grey and Brougham could not present the cabinet minute until after 4.30 p.m., though statements were due in both Houses at five. In great distress the king gave his unconditional consent for peers and agreed, apparently at Brougham's prompting, to put this in writing.[113] The two ministers drove straight to the Houses of Parliament which were wrapped in gloom and foreboding. Stanley was sent to the Commons to tell Althorp the good news; and Grey announced that he and his colleagues having 'sufficient security for passing the ... Bill ... unimpaired in all its principles and ... essential provisions ... would continue in their places'.[114] 'The most deafening cheers followed,' Le Marchant wrote;

all was now joy and congratulation. The throne was thronged by Members of the other House. They almost wrung my hand off. Everyone spoke to his neighbour as if some unexpected good fortune had happened to him. Men's hearts glowed within them and every selfish consideration was lost in a sense of the public good. Indeed the crisis had been such that private and public interests were identified. Few but the most furious partisans of the duke expected that private property could long survive a change of the administration.

Taylor wrote on his own authority to the leading opposition peers to tell them that the king's pledge was unlimited in numbers and could be invoked by the cabinet for the slightest check. 'I stated,' Taylor reported to Grey, 'that they therefore had before them the alternative of the . . . Bill with an addition to the peerage or the . . . Bill without it.'[115] Most of the Bill's opponents withdrew from the Lords until it had been passed.[116]

How much did the fears which Lady Holland expressed on 18 May help to keep Grey and his colleagues up to the mark? Assessing the effect of the popular agitation during the first phase of the crisis is difficult. For the second phase it becomes almost impossible. It can be argued that, once the House of Commons had rejected a Wellington–Sutton government on 14 May, the agitation ceased to have any considerable effect. It was the parliamentary situation, it might be said, not the ferment in the country, which compelled Grey to demand, and the king to concede, full authority to make peers. This contention cannot be sustained; but it serves to underline an irony in the later phase of the agitation. By 15 May the plans which Parkes and Place were completing had become politically irrelevant. They were formed on the supposition that Wellington would become Prime Minister or the power behind the government. After 14 May there was next to no chance that this would happen.

Parkes and Place had contacts with the ministry. They were thus able to garnish the news items available to any politician with confidential titbits cooked specially for the ministers. Place was in touch with Hobhouse, the Secretary at War, and with Melbourne's private secretary. Parkes sat with Durham until 2 a.m. on 14 May.[117] It is clear that the cabinet received a great deal of news about the agitation. It is not clear how much of it they believed, and how far it alarmed them.

It is not likely that after 14 May the whig leaders paid much attention to the reformers' actual plans for military action against the duke. It would be wrong to infer from this, however, that thereafter the agitation had little or no effect on the course of events. But for the pressure from the public, the cabinet's reluctance to humiliate the king openly might have kept them parleying with him long after 18 May.

The ministers must have been alarmed by the business stagnation and the run on the banks. On 18 May the *Morning Chronicle* mentioned 'a commercial house in Manchester' with average sales in May of £2000 a day. Its sales were given as £170 on 12 May and £155 on 14 May. 'The buyers will do no business,' the report continued, 'until the present political prospects alter.' On 1 May the Bank of England held 'between three and four millions' in gold coin, though its reserve was popularly supposed to be larger than this. Upwards of £1,600,000 was withdrawn in the ten days of the crisis.[118] This far exceeded any normal fluctuation in the reserve. Grey is said to have been visited on 18 May just before he saw the king by a representative of the Bank of England, who warned him that if good news could not be sent in that afternoon's mails the withdrawal of deposits and demand for gold all over the country would exhaust the Bank's reserves in four days.[119] The story is not worthy of much credit. But the cabinet may well have known that the figures popularly given for the Bank's reserves were too high.

The whigs were greatly impressed by the disciplined nature of the popular protest. 'The fearful part of it was the absence of riot,' Cockburn wrote of Scotland. 'All seemed reserved,' Sir Robert Heron commented about 18 May, 'for a tremendous explosion'.[120] In Lady Holland's words, the insurgents were 'as *yet* obedient to their leaders'. How long could this control last? The cabinet feared, not what Attwood would do with his army, but that he might lose command of it. He had pacified his followers so far by assuring them that Grey was back firmly in the saddle.[121] To prevent the 'tremendous explosion' this assurance had to be borne out by events.

If the Bill were delayed further, the stagnation of trade would bring increased unemployment, until outbreaks of violence became almost inevitable. Sir John Wrottesley, a whig Member for Staffordshire, told the Commons on 17 May that he had a 'very strong' petition for the Bill from Wolverhampton. The greater part of the dense population there, he said, 'depended upon their daily labour for their . . . bread. In consequence of the situation of public affairs a vast number of those people were thrown out of employment, and were in a state of the utmost destitution'. If the Bill were not passed quickly 'to put an end to . . . the want of confidence throughout the country' the people would be driven to acts of violence.[122] The cabinet knew, even better than the leading citizens of Wolverhampton, why Reform must not be delayed any longer. They are not likely to have overestimated the political unions, or the degree to which working-class people wanted the Bill to be passed. But they knew that if continuing political uncertainty intensified the trade recession they would be faced with disorder on a frightening scale.

Birmingham contained two troops of the Greys totalling 150 mounted men. To reinforce the rumour in the papers that the Greys would not act against the Birmingham Political Union[123] Place had passed similar information to the ministers about the troops in Weedon Barracks, Northamptonshire. It would be extremely difficult to move troops into the midlands from London and it was unlikely that any yeomanry force would be prepared to act against the reformers, in the Birmingham area or elsewhere. At Attwood's meeting on 16 May the reformers' armed force in Birmingham was put at 1500 men.[124] A government which failed to safeguard and speed the Bill, and so lost the confidence of the political unions, would have little authority anywhere, and none in Birmingham.

If the Bill were delayed, and the shooting started, where would it stop? The sale of arms had been brisk since the start of the National Guard controversy. By now a great many English people were armed; and through the activity of Home Office spies the members of the government knew as much about this as anyone.[125] An old labourer at Woodstock told a liberal canvasser in 1868 that arms had been stored in his father's cottage during the Reform crisis.[126] A radical manual on street fighting by Colonel Macerone, published a few months previously, had enjoyed a large sale.[127] Attwood and Place might plan to keep things 'as quiet as possible' in Place's phrase;[128] but England was an underpoliced country containing many unemployed and nearly desperate men. Over thirty years later the author of a treatise on the Progress of the Working Classes confessed 'to having had his sharpened pike by him in 1832, ready for a march on London if the Reform Bill had not passed'. He added that he had been 'but one of thousands of Manchester working men who were alike prepared for the dread hazard of civil war'.[129]

It is impossible to say how near Britain was to revolution and civil war during either phase of the May crisis. England escaped from violence in 1832 because the city of London, the commercial world, and more than half the House of Commons wanted the Reform Bill passed as quickly as possible by the only government from which the political unions would accept it. It can be argued that the struggle was certain to end in the reformers' favour before blood had been shed. Nothing could have kept the Reform ministry out of power for long. The parliamentary moderates were becoming more alarmed about the popular agitation with every day that passed. If Peel's record and principles had allowed him to take office he and Wellington would still have been ousted. The two of them might have formed a government. But an election would have gained them nothing—they would have been deserted directly they had tried to govern. MPs who turned against the duke on the threat of financial trouble would hardly have backed him in using force against the political unions. Nor can it be assumed that, faced with the need to use force to maintain his government in power, he would have used it. He knew that he could no more prevent the Bill from being passed than he could have saved the Protestant constitution in 1829. He had refused to risk a futile civil war then. Even to save the king he would probably have refused to embark on one now. If he had embarked, the Commons might have been in time to stop him. There was thus an absence of the will to resist in the citadels of power which corresponded to the dislike of unconstitutional methods felt by the leading agitators.

On the other hand it can be argued that Wellington might easily have lasted long enough to dissolve Parliament, and that during this interval the horrible cycle of insurrection and reprisal would have begun.[130] Equally if the cabinet and the king had delayed a day or two beyond 18 May there might have been fighting. In this connexion Attwood, Parkes and Place faced both ways. They were the reverse of revolutionary conspirators. They had no secrets: their plans were brought carefully to the notice of the relevant politicians. In the first phase they were trying, not to overthrow the governmental system, but by threatening its overthrow to persuade the whigs and independents to move against Wellington. Their aim was not to start a revolution, but to frighten the House of Commons into stopping one. In the second phase their aim was similar, except that they now tried to scare Grey's cabinet rather than the reformers in the House of Commons.

Place's distrust of the manhood suffrage radicals of the Rotunda was as great as Grey's. He explained to Hobhouse how essential it was that the reformers should not be forced to extremities. He thought

that the defeat of the duke when in power might be an instant destruction of the government in church and state, and the formation of a purely representative government, for which the people were by no means as well fitted as they ought to be, and it was most of all desirable they should be, before any such change were made. This revolution was therefore undesirable, not only on account of the present mischief... but of the future trouble and peril a premature revolution could not fail to produce.[131]

Attwood and Place thus resembled revolutionaries only in the sense that their plan might lead to revolutionary violence however much they hoped it would not. They meant to threaten a revolution, not to make one. But it would be wrong to regard their threat as a bluff. To call it that is to assume that if it had not worked they would have backed down. This assumption runs counter to what we know about them and their followers. They could not have avoided challenging the Sutton–Wellington government had it been formed. Probably they would not have tried to stop their machine: certainly they would not have succeeded.

Nor was the reformers' Birmingham army a mere matter of bluff that would have melted away the moment trouble had started. It was not an effective military force in the conventional sense. Finding a competent commander for it would have been a problem. Parkes and Place bragged about their contacts with army officers.[132] But Napier always said that he would have refused this command; and in view of his refusal over the National Guard project in the previous November, and of his distrust of the whigs, his statement may be accepted. He had no wish, in his own words, to cooperate 'in arms with a Birmingham attorney and a London tailor against the Duke of Wellington'.[133] Attwood might well have been left with Count Czapski. Count Chopski, as he was known, was presented to the Birmingham meeting of 7 May as a hero of the Polish struggle against the Czar. His qualifications to be Attwood's general were, and remain, obscure.[134]

There was thus a touch of comic opera about Attwood's army (as there was about Carson's Ulster Volunteers in 1914). Its chances against regular troops would have been poor. It was not intended for fighting regulars, still less for defeating them. Its function was to put Wellington in the position where he must give the order to fire on the reformers or concede defeat. The duke was reported to have predicted in October 1831 that the people would submit quietly to a firm government. 'If they won't', he added, 'there is a way to make them.'[135] This was the bluff most likely to be called. The radicals understood as well as we do how much Wellington and those who went with him dreaded civil war. Even if the duke were prepared to make the reformers quiet by opening fire, his followers would not be.

The expertise of Attwood and Place lay, not in military matters, but in the politics of agitation. Their calculations, like Carson's, smelled more of politics than of powder and shot. They relied, not on the intrinsic strength of Attwood's army, but on the political impossibility of opening fire on it. We may guess that essentially their calculation was sound. But in 1832, as always, it was full of peril.

The Bill went through committee in the Lords in only seven days. No amendments were accepted on points of substance. Nearly all of the opposition front bench had withdrawn from the House except Ellenborough;[136] and the cabinet had the better of the debates. Durham made an able defence of the new London boroughs.[137] 'Yesterday Grey . . . talked with me,' Creevey wrote on 2 June; 'he dwells upon the marvellous luck of Wellington's false move—upon the eternal difficulties he (Grey) would have been involved in had the opposition not brought it to a crisis when they did.'[138]

The third reading was carried on 4 June by 106 to 22. The king refused the cabinet's suggestion that he should regain some popularity by giving the royal assent in person. It was given by commission on 7 June. Thirty or forty MPs attended. There were very few peers present, none on the opposition benches. The ministry had apparently kept the time secret to avoid annoying their opponents still further by a triumphal display. The Clerk of the Crown had hardly pronounced 'Le Roi le veult' when an anonymous note was passed to him reading: 'It surely would have been more appropriate if you had said "Le canaille le veult".'[139]

TABLE 5
THE REFORMED HOUSE

	County seats	Borough seats	Univer- sity seats	TOTAL
ENGLAND				
Yorkshire	6			
26 four-Member counties (each divided into two constituencies)	104			
7 three-Member counties	21			
6 two-Member counties	12			
Isle of Wight	1			
City of London		4		
Weymouth (reduced from 4 Members)		2		
110 old two-Member boroughs		220		
4 old single-Member boroughs		4		
30 Schedule B boroughs (reduced to single-Member)		30		
22 new two-Member boroughs		44		
20 new single-Member boroughs		20		
2 universities, Oxford and Cambridge			4	
	144	324	4	472

	County seats	Borough seats	University seats	TOTAL
WALES				
3 two-Member counties	6			
9 single-Member counties	9			
13 single-Member borough constituencies formed by grouping boroughs		13		
	15	13		28
SCOTLAND				
27 single-Member counties	27			
3 single-Member constituencies, each formed from 2 counties	3			
Edinburgh, Glasgow (two-Member)		4		
Aberdeen, Dundee, Greenock, Paisley, Perth (single-Member)		5		
14 districts of burghs (constituencies formed by grouping burghs)		14		
	30	23		53
IRELAND				
32 two-Member counties	64			
6 two-Member boroughs		12		
27 single-Member boroughs		27		
Dublin University			2	
	64	39	2	105
TOTAL	253	399	6	658

THE ELECTORATE IN 1831 AND 1833
(figures rounded to thousands)

Notes

(1) *Plural voting.* Some electors were qualified to cast more than one vote. The figures for electors should be read with this in mind.

(2) *The registers.* The figures for 1833, while a little less unreliable than those for 1831, reflect the defects in the register. Some of these are outlined in Chapter 9, pp. 325–7.

England and Wales

		Counties		Boroughs	Total
1831	about	247,000	about	188,000	435,000
1833		370,000		282,000	653,000

The long-accepted total for 1831 has been reduced by John Cannon (*Parliamentary Reform, 1640–1832*, 1973, p. 259 and app. 4) to 366,000. The Act increased the electorate of England and Wales by 50 per cent according to the higher figure, by nearly 80 per cent according to Cannon's. By 1835–6 freeholders accounted for about 70 per cent of registered *county* voters, tenants-at-will 20 per cent, and copyholders and leaseholders together 10 per cent. The last two classes nowhere exceeded a sixth of the constituency. Tenants-at-will, however, approached or exceeded a third of the voters in 23 county constituencies (C. Seymour, *Electoral Reform in England and Wales, 1832–85*, 1915, ch. 4 and p. 533). In the *boroughs* the 'ancient right' voters numbered at the first registration:

Freemen	63,000
Other 'ancient right' voters	45,000
	108,000

By 1865 the freemen had declined to 42,000, and the others to 9000 (*Parl. Papers*, 1866, lvii.242).

The largest two-Member county constituency was the West Riding of Yorkshire with an electorate of over 18,000 at the first registration, the smallest Rutland with less than 1300 (*Parl. Papers*, 1833, xxvii.24-110). Among the two-Member boroughs Harwich and Totnes were the smallest with 214 and 217 registered voters, Westminster and Liverpool the largest with 11,600 and 11,300.

Scotland

		Counties		Burghs	Total
1831	about	3,000†		1,440*	say 4,500
1833		33,000		31,000	65,000

†Figures are given for each county in *Parl. Papers*, 1820, vii.276. For some 1831 figures see Jeffrey, *Parl. Deb.*, vii.528–30. Jeffrey said that there were about 2500 electors for Scottish counties, and that the other 500 qualifications represented plural voting.

*At first stage of elections: see Chapter 1, pp. 31–2. Jeffrey (op. cit.) gives 1440. *Parl. Papers*, 1830–1, x.38–9, produce a slightly lower total.

Ireland

	Counties	Boroughs	Total
1831	26,000‡	23,000§	49,000
1833	61,000‖	29,000‖	90,000

‡N.P. Leader's figure: see *Parl. Deb.*, xiii.580–5. The number registered was far greater than this (*Parl. Papers* 1830, xxix.462–3; 1831, xvi.197); but many of those registered were no longer entitled to vote.

§Leader's figure (op. cit.). See also *Parl. Papers*, 1830, xxxi.322.

‖*Parl. Papers*, 1834, ix.599–600. The totals obtainable from *Parl. Papers*, 1833, xxvii.291–310 are similar. The county figures given in 1866 (ibid., 1866, lvii. 847–57) appear less reliable. They were obtained, not from the published papers cited above, but from a search of the old registers. No figures were supplied for Cavan, Dublin and Limerick. Clare was credited with 12,524 electors in 1833, probably a mistake for 2524.

In 1833 Antrim, with 3500 voters registered, had the largest electorate of any Irish county, Sligo, with under 700 voters, the smallest. Dublin was the largest of the two-Member cities and boroughs, with over 7000 voters, Carrickfergus the largest of the single-Member with over 1000, and Lisburn the smallest of the latter with 90. Dublin University had an electorate of more than 2000 in 1833.

Population: census of 1831 (millions)

> England and Wales: just under 13·9
> Scotland: under 2·4
> Ireland: just under 7·8

9

IT MAY WORK

Our principle is . . . to give to the nation contentment, and to all future governments the support of the respectability, the wealth, and the intelligence of the country. (Grey, House of Lords, 3 October 1831)

The Reform Bill is a trick—it's nothing but swearing in special constables to keep the aristocrats safe in their monopoly. (George Eliot, *Felix Holt: the radical* speaker in ch. 30)

In the exaltation which followed the Days of May the whigs bestowed gracious words on their radical allies. Grey saw Attwood on 19 May, thanked him for his services, and asked if anything could be done for him to show the ministers' gratitude, an offer which Attwood wisely declined.[1] Even O'Connell was given a good mark for standing by the Bill at the last: 'He has behaved very well in this great emergency', Hobhouse recorded on 18 May. The honeymoon was short. By the end of the year relations had become embittered even by the standards of politics. Attwood was thought 'a coxcomb and a knave' by Grey, and was told by Melbourne that he deserved to be 'torn to pieces'.[2] In the case of the O'Connellites expressions of hostility were not confined to private remarks. The proceedings of the reformed House began with the mover of the Address referring to O'Connell as a 'bird of prey'.[3]

The whigs' bitterness against radicals and O'Connellites is understandable. It was a sign of disillusionment. The cabinet were no longer confident that they had achieved their aim of satisfying the middle classes while preserving the aristocracy's power. Their victory could not remove the fear that since March 1831 the whole basis of their Bill had been undermined. The long agitation culminating in the Days of May looked as if it might entail a radical House of Commons. Such a House would presumably make haste to pass a second Reform Act based on household suffrage, triennial parliaments and secret ballot. Monarchical and aristocratic government could scarcely survive another hammer blow such as that. Some cabinet ministers were as alarmed as Wellington at radical strength. 'You may think yourselves defeated,' Richmond is reported as saying to Wharncliffe in May 1832; 'but ours is the real defeat; we have created the monster which will turn upon us as well as you. Attwood and O'Connell will turn the scale in the end.'[4] 'I have also my fears about the elections,' Graham told Russell in the following December: 'The radicals will be stronger than we imagined; and the destructives will overpower the conservatives.'[5]

Some radicals believed these forebodings to be justified. John Stuart Mill looked forward in October 1831 to a time when 'the whole of the existing institutions of society are levelled with the ground'.[6] After the first reformed Parliament 'the ground will be cleared', he wrote. Even those who had warned the working class that the Bill would do nothing for them tended to come round during the Days of May, and prophesy the imminence of a further Reform. The *Poor Man's Guardian* announced on 26 May: 'We cannot think so ill of human nature as to think that those who will ... have gained their own freedom will not aid us to gain ours.'

Nonetheless, the radicals suffered from obvious weaknesses. They were heterogeneous and disunited. Cobbett had been abusing the utilitarians for years; and he quarrelled with Attwood during the opening stages of the 1832 election campaign. Moreover the favourite radical project, appropriation for lay uses of the Irish Church's surplus revenues, looked like a vote loser. 'All the Protestant feeling of the country', Grey predicted, would be ranged against taking revenue from an established Church and so favouring the Catholics.[7] When Durham was thinking of resigning in protest at the cabinet's rejection of lay appropriation, Barnes, the editor of *The Times*, warned him that this would be unpopular.[8] There were English votes to be held or won by standing up to the Church in order to help the dissenters.[9] But outside Ireland there were few to be won, and many to be lost, by helping Catholics.[10] The most experienced radicals were more cautious in their forecasts than young Mill. 'The elections have taken our last wind,' Parkes told Place in January 1833; 'Who the devil is to go on with this public work and his private duty? I can't.'[11]

The one safe prediction about the radicals' struggle for ascendancy was that it would subject the government to severe internal strains. Ministers like Richmond and Graham meant to stand or fall with the 'final' measure. They would rather see the tories in power than march with the radical 'party of movement.' On the other hand this was not the attitude of all their colleagues. It seemed likely, therefore, that the radical upsurge would split the ministry, and that this would strengthen the radicals still further. 'The radicals,' C. W. Wynn told his brother in November 1832, 'will drive a part of the whigs into the opposite ranks and swallow up the remainder.'[12]

When Wynn's prediction was made the campaign had already begun to go the other way. The pro-radical wing of the cabinet had lost the first battle. Stanley had secured cabinet agreement for an Irish Church Bill which barely recognized the principle of lay appropriation. (Even this recognition disappeared later during the Bill's passage through Parliament.) Moreover the first election for the reformed House in December 1832 was no great triumph for the radicals though it much increased their parliamentary strength. While the ministerialists with their radical and Irish allies emerged holding some 500 seats, whigs of various shades occupied over 300 of them.[13] In March 1833 Durham left the government with an earldom, and Stanley became a Secretary of State.

Yet Wynn's prophecy that the leading anti-radicals would be driven from the cabinet was sound. Despite its unpopularity in the country, lay appropriation commanded a majority in the House. In May 1834 Russell declared for it. In the resulting crisis Stanley, Graham, Ripon and Richmond left the ministry. Isolated by these defections Grey resigned a few weeks later over Irish coercion. He was succeeded by the more pliant Melbourne. In November 1834, when Althorp was removed to the Lords by his father's death, the new Prime Minister proposed Russell for the Leadership of the Commons. A government which had lost its anti-radicals, and in which the advocate of lay appropriation was to be advanced to second place, was too much for William IV. He dismissed them.[14]

The king's move failed. Peel, who became Prime Minister, could not face Parliament without a dissolution. The election of January 1835 increased his strength in the Commons to around 270. But the Reform coalition remained in a majority. Moreover within the coalition the radicals were now proportionately stronger. In April 1835 Melbourne formed his second government, insisting with unprecedented firmness on a pledge of parliamentary support from the Royal Household.[15] Russell duly became Leader of the Commons. The way was now open to complete the work of 1832 by reforming

the corporations. The Municipal Reform Act of 1835 was, thought
Creevey, 'a much greater blow to toryism than the Reform Bill
itself'.[16] The king and the Lords had been shown their place once
again. The party of movement seemed to be on the move.

They were not. 'The country,' Wellington told Greville in February
1835, 'is on its legs again.' It was the conservative reaction which was
on the move. In the 1837 election following the death of William IV
the conservatives reduced Melbourne's majority almost to nothing,
the radicals faring disastrously. O'Connell had turned out a bad
ally for the latter. Association with him brought them unpopularity; and he spent much of 1837 and 1838 in attacking the trade
unions.

Hard pressed for votes, Melbourne now made concessions to his
radical wing. In 1839 ballot was made an open question in the cabinet.
Two years later, in a bid for radical and anti-corn law support, a
small fixed duty on foreign corn was proposed instead of the sliding
scale.[17] But these gestures reflected the government's weakness, not
radical strength. Attwood resigned his seat in 1839, soured by the
continual rejection of his currency proposals. 'Seven years of bitter
experience of the reformed Parliament,' he told his Birmingham
constituents, 'have now convinced me that all my anticipations of
national benefit were vain.'[18] Grote, one of the ablest of the younger
radicals, retired eighteen months later, seeing no use in sustaining
'whig conservatism against the tory conservatism'.[19]

The collapse of the parliamentary radicals presaged that of Peel's
party. While the conservative party seemed the only bulwark against
radicalism, Peel and his followers had to stick to each other. When
the radical movement failed the compulsion for the conservatives to
stand together went too. Peel won a majority of about 80 in the 1841
election and led a notable conservative government. But the disruption
of his party was near even before the Irish potato blight ravaged the
corn laws. Disraeli's *Coningsby* was published in 1844. It contains in
Mr Rigby a malicious portrait of John Wilson Croker. Rigby is
depicted as a figure of fun whose jeremiads on the country's descent
to political ruin have become an intolerable bore. Ten years earlier
no one would have dared to laugh at such forebodings. By 1844
Wellington's prediction that the Reform Act would start a
revolution 'by the due course of the law'[20] had been proved wrong.
The reformed electorate was not radical enough to vote for its own
enlargement.

The radicals explained their failure largely in terms of the incompleteness of the Reform Act. Radical electors, they said, were powerless without the protection of the ballot, or were swamped by tory serfs enfranchised under the Chandos clause; and if any radical proposal reached the Lords the tory majority there lay ready to destroy it. These excuses, while not unfounded, were naturally the product of much exaggeration and suppression. The Chandos clause seems to have helped the tories in the counties. But its effect was seldom decisive since those it enfranchised were much like the bulk of the county electorate. Plenty of 'freeholders' were just as dependent on tory landlords as any tenant-at-will. A man might vote in right of a forty-shilling freehold, and yet hold the rest of his farm without even a lease to protect him.[21]

Open voting injured the radicals on balance. In most seats landlords were better placed to bully than radical mobs. But a great deal of the landlord influence exercised during the 1830s depended on deference rather than bullying and would have survived ballot. After the Reform Act as before it, many tenants were willing to leave the choice of MPs to the landlord. In their eyes he was as much part of the 'agricultural interest', and as deeply concerned to retain legislative protection for it and for its products, as they were themselves. There was some truth in the prediction with which the *Morning Post* heartened its tory readers when the election results were being announced in December 1832:

With the return of stable and regular government ... the tory party will gradually regain its political ascendancy ... simply because it has a great, manifest, and indestructible superiority over every rival party in its association with the historical glory of the nation, in its possession of large masses of property, and its insuperable connexion with the education, the intelligence, and the respectability of the country. . . . Neither vote by ballot, nor universal suffrage, nor both of these combined, would retard this restoration.

To ascribe the radicals' failure to the tory majority in the Lords was not entirely plausible. If the radicals' proposals had aroused widespread enthusiasm that obstacle would have been removable by a creation or the threat of one. The tory peers had the last word because enthusiasm on that scale was lacking: a creation was no longer practical politics.[22] The Chandos clause and open voting, and obstruction in the Lords, do not explain the radicals' loss of support in the press. The explanation of defeat that mattered was, as usual, the one which none of the defeated dared give. The trouble with the 'popular party', as they called themselves, was that they were not popular enough. The electors who sent the radical contingent to Parliament in December 1832 were voting, not for radicalism, but against the old toryism. Once that contingent started to press their views on the electorate most of their popularity disappeared. To a doctrinaire radical appropriating the surplus revenues of the Irish Church to lay purposes symbolized rational reform. To many voters it meant helping the papists.

The radicals failed because the Reform cabinet's original calculation about their Bill was sound. The poachers were successfully transformed into gamekeepers. Those new voters who were not men of substance often turned out to be amenable to the views of their richer neighbours. The reformed electorate was neither radical nor tory: it was conservative. Although by no means confined to people of property it was dominated by them. Middle-class people, once given the vote, wanted to conserve institutions which they had formerly been inclined to attack. Peel's achievement, symbolized by his Tamworth Manifesto of December 1834, was to bury ultra toryism and so to attract to his party hosts of these natural conservatives. The Manifesto gave them the assurances they wanted. In it Peel accepted the Reform Act as a permanent settlement, and laid the basis for a great anti-radical alliance.

Most of the new voters wanted, not to challenge the aristocracy, but to win recognition from it: once they had their rightful position they did not favour further adventures. Dr John Fife of Newcastle was one of the chief organizers of the Northern Political Union during the Reform agitation. He gained some prominence in April 1832 by announcing at a Newcastle meeting that he would pay no more taxes until the Bill had been passed. He resigned from the executive council of the Union later that year because he disagreed with the radical majority who wanted further Reform. Some years afterwards he was knighted for his success in dealing with the local chartists.[23]

The fears which had bound commercial men and industrialists to the *status quo* in the 1820s, and on which the expectation of the Act's finality had been based, were just as strong ten years later. Such men had seen enough of radical agitation, and of the disturbed trading conditions that went with it, in 1831–2. They had agitated to secure the Reform Bill. Some of them were to repeat the performance in order to repeal the corn laws. But they would not embark on an agitation, with all its risks, for ballot or triennial parliaments or household suffrage. Many of them operated on credit. 'Quiet times are good for all trade,' Edward Lytton Bulwer wrote in 1833: 'but agitated times are death to a man with a host of alarmed creditors. This makes the middle class, especially in London, a solid and compact body against such changes as seem only experiment.'[24]

After 1832 the middle classes not only remained as deferential as ever and as reluctant to engage in agitation. They also retained all their determination not to allow the workers a greater influence in politics. The reformed system might be a disappointment; but it was better than plunging towards democracy by means of another change. Before the Act was ten years old the fears of 1831 began to look foolish. Lord Hertford had concluded then that a nobleman's property was no longer safe from spoliation in Britain, and had therefore put half a million pounds in an American concern. He would have done better in consols. The concern failed and he lost the money.[25]

The whigs did not exactly welcome the rise of Peel's Conservative party.[26] Nevertheless its ascendancy coincided with their primary aim of preserving the political and social order. That aim entailed keeping the radicals from gaining too much power. It did not entail keeping Peel from power once he had thrown off the diehards who might provoke another explosion. To the whigs the Act was a success in that the existing order was conserved. It was unfortunate but of secondary importance that some of the work of conservation fell to the Conservatives.[27]

The radicals had no consolations. The brilliant young men of the 1820s had gravitated naturally to radicalism. It was equally natural that those who were undergraduates when the Bill was being passed should react against the reformers. Gladstone and his friends began their careers as Conservatives. The radicals' gradual realization of their weakness brought them up against the characteristic dilemma of a left-wing group. Were they to defy the whigs and make their protest, or curry favour with the whigs and creep into a small share of power? To keep the left wing united in face of this problem was as difficult in the 1830s as it has been since.

Although the Reform Acts of 1832 and 1884 were regarded as radical triumphs, both were followed by periods of Conservative ascendancy. This is no coincidence. In each case a sequence of action and reaction is discernible. Once the radicals seemed near power their partners became frightened. The alliance by which the Reform had been enacted failed to hold together; and the conservatives were the beneficiaries of this alarm and disruption. The opening chapters of this book depicted the tories in decline. From 1827 to 1830 they despised their opponents, quarrelled, and came to grief. From 1832 to 1835 they feared their opponents, maintained their unity, and prospered. When they thought themselves safe they had been in danger. Now that they thought themselves beaten they were safe.

In the short run, and as far as the new voters were concerned, the long agitation culminating in the Days of May detracted nothing from the conservative qualities which Grey had claimed for his Reform. For every man of property who learned in those fifteen months to be a radical there was at least one who became a frightened conservative. Indeed, where such people were concerned, the opposition's contention that delay would lessen the Bill's radical impact may have been correct. The radicalizing effect of the agitation lay lower down in society among those whom the Bill did not enfranchise. This process complemented the other. The more those below the £10 line were radicalized, the more those above it were frightened into conservatism. Could a House of Commons which was not radical by inclination be turned towards radical measures by outside pressure?

A measure drawing a line between voters and voteless was bound to increase the class consciousness of the latter. When a vast and prolonged agitation was added the result was a dramatic upsurge in working class aspirations. Trade union and cooperative activities had been considerable even before the stimulus of the political unions was applied. In 1834 they rose to a tragic climax with the Grand National Consolidated Trades Union, which in its few months of life enrolled perhaps half a million members.

It was some years, however, before working-class people realized how little they could expect from the reformed House. The disillusionment of those who had hoped that the new voters would reward their fellow reformers did not reach its height until the poor law was reorganized under the Act of 1834. Trading conditions helped to delay the reaction. The years from 1832 to 1836, being comparatively prosperous, exemplified the difficulty, remarked by Cobbett, of agitating men whose stomachs were full. The direct challenge to the

L

reformed system, in the form of Chartism, came with the slump that followed. The Charter, first published in February 1837, contained in its six points all the democratic proposals which the authors of the Reform Act had been determined not to concede: universal adult suffrage,[28] constituencies each containing an equal number of voters, secret ballot, annually elected parliaments, abolition of the property qualification for MPs, and payment of MPs. The movement was based on the three groups most aggrieved by the Act—the London Working Men's Association, the revived Birmingham Political Union, and the operatives of northern England in revolt against the new Poor Law. As MPs and voters would not incline towards radicalism they were to be pushed into it by 'moral', or even by physical, force. The Chartists had learned a good deal from the Reform agitation and still more from the behaviour of the reformed Parliament.[29]

The Anti-Corn Law League too had learned from that agitation. The League used the techniques of 1830–2 and improved on most of them; and some Leaguers saw the onslaught on the corn laws as the start of a renewed challenge to aristocratic government. Neither of these movements provided a serious threat to the 1832 settlement, however. By raising hopes which were then dashed, the authors of the Reform Act had unwittingly provided the drive behind the Chartist movement. By turning many middle-class people from insurgency they had ensured that the movement would fail.[30] The Anti-Corn Law League did not make a direct attack on the governmental system during its short career.

Nonetheless, the 1840s were not a tranquil decade in Britain. Sir Robert Peel's forebodings in 1847 were as grim as Lord Liverpool's nearly thirty years earlier. Chateaubriand, dining as French Ambassador at Lord Liverpool's, had 'praised to my host the solidity of the English monarchy, kept in balance by the even swing of liberty and power. The venerable peer . . . pointed to the City and said: "What sense of solidity can there be with these enormous towns? A sudden insurrection in London, and all is lost".'[31] In 1847 the Chief Secretary from the French Embassy dined as Peel's guest and had a similar exchange. He was asked by his host about 'the socialist writings of Louis Blanc . . . and . . . their influence in France. I expressed the hope', the Chief Secretary recorded, 'that such appeals to revolt against the inevitable conditions of civilized society would never find many dupes or victims.' Peel disagreed.

Such writings, [he argued] must not be judged by the effect which they may produce upon the fortunate ones . . . , upon those classes whose education or enlightenment can preserve them in comfort. . . . Our civilization has had the result of dooming numberless millions . . . to . . . perpetual labour, to profound ignorance, and to sufferings as difficult to remedy as they are undeserved. What ferments will not be produced in these cramped intelligences, in these embittered hearts, by such passionate invitations, to their hopes, to their desires, and to their revenge? The soil . . . of Europe is deeply undermined. Is England herself unassailable?[32]

It was Britain's escape from revolution in 1848, when most of the European capitals were convulsed, which brought a change of mood.[33] Lord Stanley of Alderley (E. J. Stanley) had once been Durham's radical henchman. When he lay dying in 1869 he heard a noise in the street, and asked whether the revolution had begun. His daughter who recorded the question seems to have thought it a little old-fashioned.[34]

The fear and resentment which the Reform Act had aroused at first were gradually replaced by a cooler appraisal of its working. Its authors were much blamed for the governmental instability which characterized the 1850s. In August 1854 at the end of the parliamentary session Greville ruefully recalled Wellington's question of 1831: when the rotten boroughs had been abolished, how was 'the king's government to be carried on?' During the confusion which followed the shattering of Peel's conservative party the question seemed highly pertinent. But the Act had not brought any great change in this. There had been little governmental stability between 1800 and 1812 or between 1827 and 1831. 'Governments were then only strong,' Bagehot wrote of the pre-Reform period, 'when public opinion was definite and decided; and when that is so they will be strong now.'[35]

While this was true, the 1832 Act led to nothing resembling the disciplined parties which give British governments stability nowadays even when the electoral tide is slack.[36] Its registration provisions had the unplanned side effect of stimulating party organization; and the new complexity in the pattern of interests increased this stimulus. But party organization as we know it originated in the 1860s and 1870s, and owed its rapid growth to the second Reform Act rather than the first. It did not become impossible to govern Britain in the decades after 1832. It merely remained extremely difficult.

Although the authors of the Act were sometimes blamed unfairly by the next generation, twenty years' working revealed large defects

in their scheme. In one matter they had left their work incomplete by
their own admission. Under the Succession to the Crown Act of 1707
no MP could accept any important ministerial office without first
vacating his seat and being re-elected. This rule was an anachronism;
but it had not done much harm hitherto. The by-elections resulting
from it had usually been a formality, since few would-be ministers had
occupied open seats. With the passage of the Reform Bill, however, it
could become a serious nuisance, as Grey and his colleagues admitted.
Contests were more likely in by-elections than in a general election
because in the latter many constituencies gave opportunities for an
agreement whereby the parties took one seat each. Party allegiances
were sometimes weaker than local grievances. Should the government
be unpopular at that time or in that place the new minister might well
be defeated. If he were, next to no machinery existed for finding him
another seat.

During the Reform debates several ministers suggested the repeal of
the law about vacating;[37] and on 1 June 1832 the Marquess of Northampton, a government supporter, announced a bill for that purpose.
But the bill languished, as did all attempts during the next few years
to revive it. E. J. Littleton's diary reveals one reason why there was no
enthusiasm for it among the ministerialists. 'I told Lord Northampton,'
Littleton recorded,

that I had once thought of bringing in such a bill, but that the view of party
interests had deterred me. It would only afford a facility to the tories to accept
of office . . . in case the king . . . should attempt to avail himself of any moment-
ary unpopularity of his minister to get back the tories. It was right that this
government should consult every art . . . to consolidate its own power. Let
the tories bring in such a bill if they pleased.[38]

Within a year, however, the tories were enjoying the government's
embarrassments over the 1707 law far too much to want it repealed.
There was immense difficulty in finding an Irish Secretary. 'The man
must be competent,' Greville wrote, 'and sure of re-election. Few are
the first and none the last.'[39] After three whigs had refused the post
E. J. Littleton accepted, despite the 'immense sacrifice' which a by-
election represented for him.[40] He was not a successful minister. His
indiscretion in the following year to O'Connell over the Coercion
Bill occasioned Grey's resignation.

The new Attorney General was out of the House for three months
in the spring of 1834. But, greatly as this old law damaged the whigs,

Littleton was right in thinking that it would be even more embarrassing to the tories. The by-election problem helped to persuade Peel in December 1834 to dissolve Parliament at once instead of meeting it with his new ministry. These difficulties did not disappear until the growth of party organizations after 1867 had made by-elections safer and facilitated the provision of alternative seats for ministers. The 1707 law remained unchanged until 1919 when it ceased to apply for the first nine months after an election. It was finally repealed in 1926.[41]

The authors of the Act also failed to solve the more complicated problem of the compound householder. The basic data for compiling the lists of £10 householders came from the rate books. Under an Act of 1819, and various local acts, parish vestries were allowed to direct that the rates on houses below a certain value should be paid, not by the occupier, but by the landlord.[42] The vestry saved in costs of collection, so that the landlord was allowed a rebate, which was nowhere more than 25 per cent. He recovered the rate with the rent. His name, and not the compound householder's, was entered in the rate book.

By the time that the final Bill was drafted in the autumn of 1831, the cabinet knew how difficult it was to put compounders on the register.[43] They felt no compulsion to overcome the difficulty. As was related in Chapter 7, they meant to appease their opponents by limiting the effect of the £10 franchise. This involved using the rate-paying clause to reduce the number of prospective voters. To give the compounder some semblance of fair play there was a clause in the Bill whereby he could tender payment of the rate in full himself and so be named in the rate book. The Court of Commons Pleas held this to mean that the occupier must claim every time a rate became due.[44] As there were often four, and sometimes six, rates a year this put the compounder at an enormous disadvantage by comparison with any other class of voter. The other borough voters were not required to take the initiative at all. The county voter initiated his claim; but once made it remained valid from year to year unless his qualifying property or residence was changed. By an Act of 1851 an effort was made to end the compounder's virtual disfranchisement. Only one claim was now needed each year for inclusion in the rate book; and if the tenant paid the rate he received the same discount as the landlord. The Act had little effect. The compounder was usually of modest means. A claim even once a year which he must not merely initiate but be prepared to defend in a revising barrister's court might be beyond him unless he had the help of a party agent.

In 1866, of the £10 compounders in parliamentary boroughs qualified to vote, 25,000 were on the register, and 70,000 off it. By then compounding difficulties were depriving more than one borough householder in ten of his vote. This disfranchisement was so uneven as to be utterly indefensible. Compounding was common in some cities and practically unknown in others. In the London boroughs created in 1832 the rates for nearly all houses of between £10 and £18 annual value were compounded. There was no uniformity even within a single constituency. In some parishes the overseers of the poor defied the law and listed the compounders on their own initiative. In 1866 all the compounders were said to be listed in Clerkenwell, none in Holborn.[45]

The whole registration system was inadequate, the exclusion of the majority of compounders being merely its most glaring single defect. It entailed endless complexities. In the counties there were 576 types of qualifying freehold, and over twelve hundred distinct qualifications in all.[46] A franchise law as intricate as this required a corps of officials for its administration. But the electorate would have grudged paying for these officials, and would not have trusted them to remain impartial. Indeed the corps could not have been recruited as there was then no tradition of professional administration in Britain. The overseers had the advantage that everyone was used to them and to their rate books. But in many places they were negligent. In eighty east Somerset parishes they failed entirely during the second registration season to make out and publish the voters' lists required by the Act. In north Shropshire one overseer in three was said to be unable to write.[47] The election agents of the parties soon learned to exploit this inefficiency and the complexities of the Act. Despite the efforts of the revising barristers, party machinations kept many bona fide electors off the register, and some dead men on it.

The open voting system helped an election agent to identify claims to vote emanating from potential opponents of his party. It was his duty to object to these. A trifling objection was always worth while. The claim might not be defended. If it was, no costs could be awarded against the objector until the Registration Act of 1843. Even then they were limited to a pound and were seldom awarded.[48] On the other hand it was not difficult to personate a dead voter; and detection might not mean failure. In one instance a vote was upheld although the 'voter' was said by his widow to have been dead for eight years.

No law could be devised with the machinery available which would both open the register to good voters and close it to bad ones. Every facility given to objectors was an obstacle to bona fide claimants. Thus the provision in the 1843 Act whereby objections could be made by post was widely exploited, especially by the Anti-Corn Law League. The capacity of the postal services was limited everywhere. Objections had to reach the claimant in time for him to appear before the revising barrister and defend his vote. But if a party official handed his objections in to the post office on the last day permitted, he could make it difficult to deliver all of them in time to allow the claimants to appear.[49]

A drastic interference with the forty-shilling freeholder would have been thought even more revolutionary than an attempt at adequate registration machinery. Yet this historic franchise, which combined a very low qualification with the absence of any residence requirement, invited the creation of faggot votes. The Splitting Act of 1696 which had been intended to prevent this was a dead letter as a result of various court decisions. A landowner who was prepared to forego a thousand a year in rent could thus turn five hundred of his dependants into forty-shilling freeholders and voters. If he wished to retain possession of the property concerned he could lease each parcel for forty shillings a year on the day on which he ceased to own it. This game had begun long before 1832. The Act intensified it because the division of counties and the new uncertainty about the balance of interests increased the proportion of county elections which were contested. During the 1840s the Anti-Corn Law League was an active creator of freeholds.

By the 1850s it was clear that the Act had not reduced electoral corruption. 'Bribery,' Samuel Warren wrote in his *Manual of Election Law*, 1852, 'is seen perhaps in fuller action at the moment than ever before.' It is not likely that the total amount of money paid corruptly at each election increased much after 1832. Limiting the poll to two days,[50] dividing the counties and providing several polling places within each division, and disfranchising the distant out-voters in the boroughs, had a considerable combined effect. These changes ended the colossal expenditures occasionally incurred in unreformed times on a single contest. The effect of the Act was to spread the sum spent over more constituencies and more people. Apart from the enlargement of the electorate the number of contests had been roughly doubled. This meant increased numbers demanding bribes. 'It was immaterial,' Melbourne thought, 'to the candidate whether he paid two thousand pounds to one owner or to two hundred vendors for the seat; [but] public decency was less infringed in the former case than in the latter.'[51]

In some places the new voters were soon as corrupt as any freeman. Despite the heightened political awareness which the Reform crisis had brought, many of them found a vote useful only as something to sell. An MP said about the electors of Canterbury that it 'would be paying too great a compliment to a considerable portion . . . to suppose that they had any particular political opinions'.[52] That remark was made, not about the pre-Reform era, but in 1853. Some voters had political views, or were at least firm in their allegiance to one party, but expected to be paid for voting for it. Others were so securely under some magnate's influence that they were not free to sell their votes however corrupt their inclinations. Ballot might have enabled these unfortunates to take money from one side or both. The evidence suggests that it would have done little to reduce corruption.[53] There was probably no way in 1832 of increasing the electorate without also increasing bribery. Similarly, a rise in the number of election contests was bound to increase the incidence of electoral violence. Though violent incidents were encouraged by open voting their roots lay in the manners of the time. In 1832, as always, many of those swept in to demand the vote proved unready to use it when the demand was prudently conceded.[54]

An account which ended by excusing Grey and his colleagues entirely for their failure to curb corruption would be too favourable.[55] In electoral morality they were little better than the other respectable members of the ruling class. They disliked the blatant buying of votes. They approved of the legitimate influence which depended on residence and personal services, as well as on local property, and disapproved of the illegitimate variety which was merely a matter of money or bullying. They hoped that their fellow magnates would behave discreetly and be content with influence of the legitimate kind. But they wanted the weight of property to tell in elections. They were not prepared to interfere on a large scale with the methods by which it told. They regarded the local landowner's son as a suitable candidate, and the adventurer new to the constituency with £5000 in his pocket as a deplorable one. But they recognized that a system designed to help the former could not be made to exclude the latter. Their efforts to reduce electoral corruption were half-hearted.

The Act's defects should be judged in the context of the crisis during which it was devised.[56] Its provisions were the outcome, not of a leisured attempt to build a faultless system, but of a severe parliamentary struggle. It contained clauses intended to appease critics and last-minute improvisations of all sorts. When alterations in the Boundary Bill had to be settled for the Report stage, for instance, Littleton and Drummond had great difficulty in finding Russell. They ran him to earth in a stable, and arranged the Bill 'with the groom's ink bottle and pen, and lying down on straw in one of the stalls'.[57] These pressures apart, Grey's cabinet lacked both the experience and the resources needed for tackling complicated administrative problems. Their political judgments by contrast proved largely sound. Their assumption that the essentials of their political world would survive the Act was justified. Althorp's prediction, quoted earlier, that MPs 'would continue to be selected from the same classes' proved right.[58] The number of Members belonging to the aristocracy showed little decline between 1831 and 1865.[59] To keep their seats the aristocrats were obliged in most constituencies to work harder and show more attention to public opinion.[60] The landowner had the increased time to give. Most commercial and industrial magnates had not.[61] It was almost as difficult as ever for one of them to enter the House. The abolition of seats which had been for hire offset the enfranchisement of commercial and industrial centres. Viscount Sandon who sat for Liverpool from 1831 to 1847 was preferred by the merchants there to one of their own number. He aroused no jealousies. Not being identified with any business in the city he could be trusted to use his influence impartially for all his mercantile supporters. Many Liverpool merchants thought an aristocrat best for dealing with an aristocratic government. Lord Sandon, as a Liverpool pamphleteer told his fellow-electors in 1832, 'has personal friends amongst those at the helm of affairs, which cannot but allow a freer and more easy intercourse than amongst strangers, and which has been highly serviceable to us'.[62]

The network of landlord influence became far more complicated after 1832; but it remained almost as strong. The magnates had not lost control. But in most places they were obliged to agree among themselves, and perhaps act with more consideration and restraint, in order to retain it. Provided they agreed the voters had little chance to vote: in the 1847 election there were no contests in nearly three-fifths of the constituencies. While control by an individual magnate became less common, it did not disappear. Professor Gash has estimated the number of boroughs which remained under some considerable degree of patronage after the Act. He distinguishes, though with difficulty, between 'proprietary' boroughs and those which were a little less dependent and fall into the 'family' class. He lists some seventy 'proprietary' seats.[63]

Alexander Baring's suggestion that the Act would dethrone the land and make industry supreme was scarcely borne out. Of course, the field of coal gradually beat the field of barley; but there is little or no evidence that the Act accelerated this process. It does not seem to have made any great contribution to the slow rise of the industrialists to political power. Althorp never altered his view that it gave too much influence to the landed interest.[64] He told Brougham in 1841 that it had helped to delay the repeal of the corn laws.[65] Gladstone expressed the same belief in the 1870s.[66]

It is more difficult to say whether the Act proved as 'final' as its authors intended. It could be argued that Sydney Smith's prediction about the Reform question being set at rest for thirty or forty years was exactly fulfilled. The next Reform Act was passed in 1867; and there was no Reform agitation formidable enough to make even the slightest impression on Parliament until 1866. Underlying the prediction was the view that, with the Reform Act on the statute book, Britain's progress to popular government would be orderly and slow. This also proved correct. Ballot and Irish Church disestablishment were not passed until after the 1867 Reform Act. The peers were not curbed, nor were MPs paid, until the present century. None of the Reform Acts were followed by the disturbances which the opposition predicted in 1831, and which might have accompanied a more rapid movement towards popular government.

Once rid of the rotten boroughs, the aristocracy survived through the railway age and beyond it. In five generations the immediate connexions of the first Earl Grey have included three Prime Ministers, five Viceroys of India, four Governors General of Canada, four Foreign Secretaries, two Chancellors of the Exchequer, four Secretaries of State for the Colonies or Dominions, and two First Lords of the Admiralty, to name only the highest posts.[67] In 1837 Thomas Arnold wrote:

I shared [during the Reform crisis] the common opinion as to the danger which threatened all our institutions from the force of an ultra-popular party. But the last six years have taught me ... that when an aristocracy is not thoroughly corrupted its strength is incalculable; and it acts through the relations of private life which are permanent, whereas the political excitement which opposes it must always be short-lived.[68]

The finality of the Act can be exaggerated, however. The period during which it set Reform completely at rest was not thirty-five years, but a mere sixteen. Though Britain escaped, the revolutions of 1848 convinced Russell, who was then Prime Minister, that a further Act was needed.[69] He presented a scheme to the Commons in 1852 and from then until 1867 Reform was always in the air. Moreover, while the political scene is evanescent, politicians are not. Bagehot pointed out that the 1832 Act lasted scarcely long enough to come into full effect. Until 1865 British politics were dominated by men who had formed their political habits in pre-Reform days. Gladstone and Disraeli, who had learned their politics in the 1830s, did not reach the premiership until the 1832 Act had been replaced.[70]

Some of the authors of the Act judged it more harshly than this. Grey wrote to Ellice about O'Connell in September 1837: 'If I had thought that the result of the Reform Bill was to be the raising of a new Rienzi, and to make his dictatorship and the democracy of the towns paramount to all the other interests of the state, I would have died before I would have proposed it.'[71] This did not represent a passing mood. In December 1841, while touring in the United States, Morpeth dined with an American judge. The constitution was pronounced 'an utter failure' by the other guests. 'They talk', Morpeth recorded, 'much as Lord Grey would talk of the present proceedings of the Reform Parliament.'[72]

Melbourne hated to think of what he had done in 1831 and 1832. He wrote to Russell in January 1839 about a modification of the corn law: 'We shall ... only carry it by the same means as we carried the Reform Bill; and I am not for being the instrument or amongst the instruments of another similar performance.' On another occasion Melbourne told Russell that if the Act 'was not absolutely necessary it was the foolishest thing ever done'.[73]

Russell was better satisfied than this with his handiwork. An obituary by him of Grey and Althorp appeared in January 1846. On the original reception of the Bill he wrote: 'The radicals deceived themselves when they supposed that so large a ruin must lead to a more uniform construction. The authors of the plan were alone justified by the event.'[74] Russell's view did not change when he decided that another Reform Act was needed. He told the queen in 1851 that the decision to retain some small boroughs had been sound. Their Members tempered extremes of opinion. In the repeal of the corn laws they had helped to counteract the counties: when it was important to keep up the army and navy estimates they neutralized the large towns.[75] Russell was critical of one feature in the Act, however. Introducing the Reform Bill of 1854, he said that the 1832 Act had 'tended ... to divide the country in a way in which it was not divided before; in short, into opposite camps according as the districts might be connected with land or trade'.[76] The greatest liberal of the next generation, whose judgment was unaffected by the guilt or self-justification of a participant, was as severe on the Act as Grey had been. Gladstone constantly maintained that the unreformed system had been superior to the one created in 1832.[77]

These are not the judgments of historians. They illustrate the truth of De Tocqueville's dictum that 'great successful revolutions, by effecting the disappearance of the causes which brought them about ... become themselves incomprehensible'.[78] Much the same might be written of successful reforms. As the Reform crisis receded, the conditions under which the Act had been launched became hard to discern, while its defects loomed large. No great effort to remember the political situation in 1830 and 1831 underlay the later judgments even of its authors.[79] Grey thought that the consequences of conceding Reform had been harmful. He did not keep in mind that the consequences of refusing it might have been disastrous. It did not occur to him that, even if he had foreseen all the results of his Bill from the first, he would still have been right to regard introducing it as the least dangerous course that he could take. Perhaps the judgment from the last century which comes closest to expressing what was done—and prevented—in 1832 is John Bright's: 'It was not a good Bill,' Bright said; 'but it was a great Bill when it passed.'[80]

The repentant authors of the Bill were inclined to think that they had gone too far. Today they may seem not to have gone far enough. The Bill, it might be argued, could have been made far more radical without any risk to the institutions of the country. In retrospect we may question even the need to postpone a more sweeping change until the educational standard had been raised. No doubt the provision of better schooling, together with the drive in the working class for self-improvement, had made Britain readier for a wide suffrage in 1867 than it had been in 1832. Basing the first Reform Act on household suffrage in the boroughs instead of the £10 rule would have increased the number of ignorant men who were given the vote. Yet it might have been the most effective method of extending education. It is no coincidence that the Education Act of 1870 followed so hard on the second Reform Act. It was not quite a case of making people voters because they were now better educated. They were given a better education because they were now voters.

Few of the radical proposals look revolutionary today. With the significant exception of annual parliaments even the points of the Charter are firmly enough embedded in our political system to be taken for granted. Reading what one radical said privately to another we can see how cautious they were. The fears of revolution which were to trouble E. J. Stanley on his deathbed had grown to full size many years earlier. 'We have quite as much reason,' he told Durham in December 1833, 'to fight against the wild notions of destruction amongst the radicals as [against] the senseless folly of the tories.'[81]

Our views about the mildness of the radicals are beside the point. The king and the opposition would not have allowed a more radical Bill to pass peacefully. A great change is not compatible with political stability if enough people refuse to accept it. After a long and peaceful political evolution this obvious truth is easily forgotten in England. The Act was well judged because reformers would not have accepted less as a settlement, and anti-reformers might not have accepted more without bloodshed. The means used to pass it were well judged, not because the 'independence' of the House of Lords benefited the country in the nineteenth century, but because the tories would not have accepted as an irreversible settlement an Act which had been forced on king and Lords by an avoidable creation of peers. In the bitterness caused by such a creation the system of government would have remained a leading political issue.

The fact that most of the gloomy prophecies about the Bill proved to be mistaken does not make them absurd. They were no more wrong, and no less reasonable, than later predictions that the 1867 Act would give the working class a permanent dominance in British politics. No one on either side foresaw just what effect the 1832 Act would have on the governmental system. In 1830, or indeed in 1860, no one could have predicted the process by which Britain has come to be governed by two centrally organized parties alternating in power. The reformers of 1832, though better prophets than their opponents, were not infallible. Many of the hopes aroused by the Act turned out to be dupes. Some of the fears were liars.

The conclusion that the authors of the Reform Act judged well for their purposes does not constitute the whole verdict in what Sir Winston Churchill called 'the grievous inquest of history'. Something must be said also about the purposes themselves and about the more distant effects of the change. Each book about the Act is coloured by the preoccupations of a particular time. Our criteria for success are not those of the whigs. They thought sometimes of popular education and of raising the living standards of the poor. We expect such preoccupations to be with a statesman always. They were inclined to assume without argument that the predominance of their own class was for the general good. We do not share this patrician assumption.

In some ways the new House was more oppressive than the old. This reflected the greater confidence which a broader basis of support provided, rather than exceptional harshness among the new voters. MPs had been convinced for years that the poor law must be reformed. But until 1832 governments had always shirked the issue. The Poor Law Amendment Act was harsher than anything which the old House would have dared to pass. On the other side of the account might be set the Factory Act of 1833 and the beginning in the same year of a state grant for education. It is impossible to say whether, on balance, working-class people were injured by the Reform Act.[82] Their own belief that they were is not conclusive evidence. The horrors of the new poor law were very real. But their effect was heightened by disillusionment. Miseries which might have been accepted in the 1820s seemed intolerable after the hopes of 1831.

Nor is it possible to make a valid comparison between the work of the reformed and the unreformed Houses. In trying to judge the effects of the Reform Act the inquirer is almost as apt as Grey or Gladstone to forget how it came to be passed. He compares the political system of 1825 with that of 1835. Finding the latter the more democratic in such and such ways, he concludes that in those ways the Act had a democratic tendency. But the political system of 1825 was collapsing by 1830. If there had been no Reform Act it would have been overturned by more or less revolutionary means. The comparison required therefore is one between the system of 1835 and what would have existed then had no Reform been conceded. But this comparison is too speculative to pursue. It is hard to imagine a refusal to concede Reform in 1831 and 1832.

Such questions as how far the Act increased middle-class influence, or had a democratic tendency, do not admit of clear-cut answers. It gave the middle class a new political status and made their influence more obvious. Equally it fixed them in a status in which they were acknowledged to be subordinate to the aristocracy. Once again the views of contemporaries must be treated with reserve. The fact that Attwood's hopes were dashed and his currency schemes neglected does not mean that his class gained nothing from the Act.

In so far as the Act confirmed and prolonged patrician power its effects were aristocratic. But it was a recognition of an altered social balance. The agitation which accompanied its passage diffused political awareness. It was a precedent for further changes. In these ways its tendency was democratic. It is difficult in the light of history to say which measures were radical in outcome and which conservative. The more sweeping the present reform the more it is liable, by forming new habits and vested interests, to delay the next. Any enactment which is at once sweeping enough to form such habits, and yet moderate enough to be accepted by those who have opposed it, is likely in thirty years time to be an obstacle to progress. No reformers can escape from this 'finality' when they come to legislate, whether they rejoice at it like the whigs of 1831, or are dismayed like modern men of the left.

Whether the authors of the Act unwittingly quickened Britain's progress to democracy cannot be determined. What can be said is that they helped to make this an orderly progress, uninterrupted by revolution or episodes of dictatorship. The Grey cabinet made some bad blunders at the start of their Reform career. Their committee's original scheme was faulty and they overestimated their parliamentary support. They thus became committed to a severe parliamentary campaign which they were by no means sure of winning. On at least three occasions—in April 1831, towards the end of that year, and in May 1832—they might have lost control of the Reform movement but for their opponents' mistakes.

When it mattered most, however, Grey and his colleagues did not go wrong. On the greatest Reform questions their judgment was shrewd and enlightened. They were liberal enough to see the sort of changes which were needed to rejuvenate the system. They had experience and confidence enough to put these in hand while there was still time. They realized that no mistake which they could make would be as serious as the mistake of doing little or nothing.

'The principle of my Reform,' Grey said in November 1830, 'is to prevent the necessity for revolution.'[83] The men who carried that principle into effect deserved to be honoured. In England the advantages of a peaceful political evolution, and the drawbacks of a revolutionary tradition, are easily overlooked. Violence has a high price in hatred, misery, and stagnation. Any political system may become ossified; but there is no ossifier like the memory of a revolution.[84] To enact the Reform Act by peaceful means was a great and beneficent feat of statesmanship.

NOTES AND REFERENCES

Chapter 1. The old system in decline

1. Stuart J. Reid, *Durham* (1906), i.130.
2. Preface to vol. xii: quoted in E. P. Thompson, *The Making of the English Working Class* (1963), p. 810.
3. *Parl. Deb.*, N.S., xvii,544. For the standard of parliamentary reporting in this era see A. Aspinall, *Essays Presented to Sir Lewis Namier*, Ed. R. Pares and A. J. P. Taylor (1956), pp. 227–57.
4. ibid., xxi,1070 (G. Wilbraham).
5 *Parl. Deb.*, 3rd ser., iii,87. See John Cannon, *Parliamentary Reform, 1640–1832* (1973), p. 186, n. 2.
6. *Croker*, i, 170.
7. Greville, *Diary*, 19 Sept. 1834. See also Le Marchant, *Althorp*, p. 210; *Parl. Deb.*, iii,316 (Russell).
8. *Three Diaries*, p. 118 (Le Marchant).
9. *The House of Commons, 1754–90*, Ed. Sir Lewis Namier and John Brooke (1964).
10. *Representative Government*, Chap. 4.
11. See D. Read, *The English Provinces* (1964), p. 4; J. Cannon, *Parliamentary Reform*, Ch. 3.
12. See *Blackwood's* xxviii (Nov. 1830), 724, 730–1, for a tory view on the political effect of these advances in technique.
13. Class terms, and indeed the whole notion of class, were new in the period with which this book deals. See A. Briggs, (1) 'Middle-Class Consciousness in English Politics, 1780–1846', *Past and Present*, no. 9 (1956), pp. 65–74; (2) 'The Language of Class in Early Nineteenth-Century England', in *Essays in Labour History*, Ed. A. Briggs & J. Saville (1960), pp. 43–73. These sweeping new terms were apt to obscure the differences within a class between one social group and another. But in this they were no more dangerous than the old categories. Talking of 'the lower orders' involved, as Francis Place complained, jumbling together 'the most skilled and the most prudent workmen with the most ignorant and imprudent labourers and paupers': Briggs, *Essays in Labour History*, p. 44, n. 4. The new classification was not accepted by all. Robert Owen (1771–1858), inspirer of the cooperative movement, condemned the distinction into upper, middle, and lower classes (*Crisis*, 4 Aug. 1832); William Carpenter told working men: 'the middle classes are not only *not* a class of persons having interests different

from your own. They are the *same* class; they are, generally speaking, working or labouring men' (*Poor Man's Guardian*, 19 Dec. 1831).

14. C. D. Yonge, *Liverpool* (1868), ii,298. See also S. Bamford, *Passages in the Life of a Radical*, Ed. W. H. Chaloner (1967), p. 7; *Morning Chronicle*, 10 Sept. 1829.

15. Among legislative changes were the 'Durham Act', 1763, 3 Geo. III c. 15, by which an honorary freeman needed twelve months' standing before he acquired a parliamentary vote; the Grenville Act, 1770, 10 Geo. III c. 16, establishing select committees to hear election petitions; Act of 1786, 26 Geo. III c. 100, requiring six months' residence as a qualification for scot-and-lot and potwalloper electors; Last Determination Act amended, 1788, 28 Geo. III c. 52, cl. 31, so that the House of Commons regained authority to reverse former election decisions; 1793 Act, 33 Geo. III c. 21, enfranchising Roman Catholic voters in Ireland; Act of Union, Ireland, 39 and 40 Geo. III c. 67. Four boroughs were 'sluiced' for corruption, the freeholders of the surrounding hundred being added to the borough electorate: New Shoreham 1771, Cricklade 1782, Aylesbury 1804, East Retford 1830. In 1821 Grampound was disfranchised for corruption, its two seats being given to Yorkshire. See also Ch. 4, n. 91.

16. The census figures were: 1801, 210, 852; 1831, 453, 191. But these are too low in that they exclude part of the built-up area. 'Manchester' is taken, for instance, to consist only of Manchester Township and Salford. Dr Donald Read has pointed out to me that to contemporaries 'Manchester' also included the townships of Cheetham, Hulme, Chorlton Row and Ardwick. If these are included, the 1801 Manchester figure, rises from 84,020 to 88,886, and the 1831 figure from 182,812 to 222,554.

17. Not all boroughs had started as popular and open constituencies. Some, especially in Cornwall, had been 'already rotten when they were enfranchised': Porritt, i.91.

18. *Parl. Deb.*, N.S., xxv.1253; *Morning Chronicle*, 28 July 1830; E. Montagu to Countess of Harrowby, 29 July: Harrowby MSS, mlvii, f. 22. Writer succeeded as (5th) Lord Rokeby, 1831.

19. John Mortlock (*c.* 1755–1816). See Namier and Brooke, *History of Parliament, 1754–90*, i.219.

20. *Parl. Papers*, 1831–2 (112), xxxvi.538.

21. Newcastle Poll Book. I am grateful to Dr T. J. Nossiter for this information. He has classified by occupation 1639 of the 2856 who voted. His conclusions are supported by *Parl. Papers*, 1835 (116), xxv.235, showing the low proportion of freemen occupying houses valued at £10 and above.

22. *Votes and Proc.*, 1830–1, App. vol., p. 621. The petitioners seem to have stated the facts more or less correctly. 841 voted in 1826. *Parl. Papers*, 1831–2, xxxvi.324,578, and 1835 (116) xxiv.185, give the freemen as just over 1000, of whom in 1833 547 resided in the city, or within seven miles of it. There were 991 houses worth £10 annually and above in the old borough, 1124 in the new.

23. Eight manufacturers were returned in the 1826 election: see G. P. Judd, *Members of Parliament, 1734–1832* (1955), p. 94 (app. 21).

24. Countess of Airlie, *Lady Palmerston and Her Times* (1922), i.131.

25. See D. C. Moore, *Victorian Studies*, xiii (1969), 5–36. For Professor Moore's other articles see Ch. 4, n. 85.

26. *Parl. Deb.*, N.S., xxii.882 (Lushington); *Morning Chronicle*, 12 Oct. 1829 (see also Ch. 4, n. 4), 2 Nov. 1830.

27. There were five single-Member English boroughs before 1832, Banbury being one of them.

28. An accusation of partisanship against the Northampton magistrates after the 1826 election reached the London press and the Court of King's Bench. See *The Times*, 25 Dec. 1827 (letter from 'Constant Reader'), 10, 11 June 1828 (law reports).

29. *Votes and Proc.*, 1830–1, App. vol., pp. 699–700.

30. 26 July.

31. The corporation were up against a rich manufacturer, William Evans, who admitted spending £17,000 'or a little more' on the contest (*Parl. Papers*, 1830, HL (82), xvii.157) and said privately that it had cost him £22,000 (W. Gardiner, *Music and Friends*, Leicester, 1838, iii.13). For the whole episode see R. W. Greaves, *The Corporation of Leicester*, 1689–1836 (2nd ed., 1970), ch. 7; A. Temple Patterson, *Radical Leicester* (1954), ch. 8.

32. *Parl. Deb.*, N.S., xvi.624.

33. ibid., xix.1745–6. See also *Diary and Correspondence of Lord Colchester*, Ed. C. Abbott (1861), iii.516 (13 June 1827).

34. Petition, 16 Nov. 1830: *Votes and Proc.*, 1830–1, App. vol., pp. 153–5.

35. Temple Patterson, *Radical Leicester*, pp. 203–4. A group of merchants decided in Apr. 1830 to bring a case in order to test the legality of the Liverpool freemen's exemption: *Parl. Papers*, 1835, xxvi.625.

36. On the unfairness of the Municipal Corporation Commissioners' Report (*Parl. Papers*, 1835, xxiii.5–49) see S. & B. Webb, *Manor and Borough* (1908), ii.718.

37. There were twelve general elections from 1784 to 1831, inclusive, and forty English counties returning Members. 90 of these 480 elections were contested. The highest number of English county contests in an election was ten. This was reached in 1807, 1818, 1826, 1830 and 1831. I am grateful to Mr. K. Roberts for these figures.

38. N. Gash, *Proc. Leeds Phil. Soc.*, viii, pt. 1 (1956), 20, 34, n. 4. See also *Parl. Deb.*, N.S., xxv.1252. A large sum was subscribed for Wilberforce in 1807, chiefly by opponents of the slave trade. Such subscriptions were rare in county contests.

39. *Morning Chronicle*, 26 July 1830.

40. 20 Geo. III c. 17, which brought an Act of 1712 up to date.

41. *Manchester Guardian*, 5 and 12 Dec. 1829. The influence of 'town freeholders' on the old county system received much attention in 1831–2. See *Parl. Deb.*, 3rd ser., iii.1063, xii.1393, xiii.22 (Brougham on Yorks and Lancs); vi.190–1 (Dalrymple, Holdsworth); vii.1194 (Wellington); ix.993 (W. Peel); xiii.27–8 (Malmesbury); Peel to H. Hobhouse, July 1831: Add. MSS, 40, 402, f. 98; *Blackwood's* xxx (Oct. 1831), 613: this article is identified in D. C. Moore, 'The Other Face of Reform', *Victorian Studies*, v. 29, as being by A. Alison. Some of the towns to which these passages relate were wholly unlike Manchester; and many of the freeholders concerned cannot be classed as urban. In 15 of the 19 cities and towns that were counties of themselves the freeholders had no votes for the county. For the electoral changes created by land tax redemption see

C. W. W. Wynn to Harrowby, 4 Feb. 1832: Harrowby MSS, xix, f. 238; *Parl. Deb.*, iv.1219 (Sugden). For the information provided by Land Tax 'duplicates' see *Parl. Papers*, 1831–2, xxxvi.483–7 (Kesteven, Holland). The debates of Aug. 1831 on the 'town freeholders' are described in Ch. 6.

42. The Scottish system is described in E. Porritt, *The Unreformed House of Commons* (1903, repr. 1963), ii, chs. 38 & 39.

43. To J. Lockhart, 27 Aug. 1828: Sir Walter Scott, *Letters*, Ed. H. J. C. Grierson (1936), x.493.

44. *Croker*, i.369. The phrase was used in connexion with an earlier and less complete version of the list; but it applies equally to the total of 276.

45. See the comparisons between rotten borough Members and other MPs in Judd, *Members of Parliament*, p. 75, n. 2.

46. No. 1074, p. 561, 31 Aug.

47. The word denotes here independence of party. Often it also connoted independence of the government, or the possession of an income which gave an MP no temptation to seek a government place. It could also connote independence of constituents.

48. *Parl. Deb.*, 1st ser., xvii.565.

49. ibid, xxxv.428; *Courier*, 24 Sept. reporting speech at Newcastle, 19 Sept.

50. Sir Robert Heron, *Notes* (2nd ed., Grantham, 1851), p. 225. For connotations of 'the people', as Melbourne used the phrase, see Ch. 4, n. 78. See also *Diary of B. R. Haydon*, Ed. W. B. Pope, iv (1963), 97. For a similar view by another Canningite, J. W. Ward (later Visc. Dudley and Ward, and Earl of Dudley), see *Letters of the Earl of Dudley to the Bishop of Llandaff* (new ed., 1841), p. 277: Ward to Copleston, 16 Feb. 1821.

51. See R. S. Neale, *Victorian Studies*, xii (1968), 4–32.

52. See N. McCord, *Hist. Journal*, x (1967), 376–90.

53. *Tour in Germany, Holland and England* (publ. anon., 1832), iv.9. I am grateful to Sir Isaiah Berlin for telling me of this book.

54. *England and America* (1833), i.80–106.

55. For an introduction to this controversial subject see E. J. Hobsbawm and R. M. Hartwell, 'The Standard of Living during the Industrial Revolution: a Discussion', *Ec. Hist. Rev.*, xvi (1963), 119–46. For the importance of the first five years of peace in the development of class solidarities see Harold Perkin, *The Origins of Modern English Society, 1780–1880* (1969), ch. 6.

56. Thompson, *Making of the English Working Class*, gives a detailed and compelling account of these developments. It is a matter of controversy, however, whether working-class consciousness had gone as far by 1832 as Mr Thompson suggests.

57. *Memorials of His Time (1856)*, ch. 2. The *Memorials* were written between 1821 and 1830 and first published in 1856. They have been republished several times in various versions, the 1971 edition (Edinburgh) being a facsimile of 1856.

58. J. M. Keynes, *Two Memoirs* (1949), p. 99.

59. Dissenters served on some corporations, and controlled that of Nottingham. Their exclusion from most corporate bodies did not result from the retention, until 1828, of the Test and Corporation Acts, since Indemnity Acts were passed annually in their favour. It originated in the fact that nearly all corporations were self-electing. Anglican monopolies thus tended to be perpetuated.

60. The methodist ministers were the chief champions of quietism. Their rule over the laity was not challenged until the Leeds organ affair of 1827. See B. Gregory, *Sidelights on the Conflicts of Methodism, 1827–52* (1898), pp. 51–61.

61. Vol. x, p. 410. Jeffrey wrote the article concerned: see J. Clive, *Scotch Reviewers* (1957), p. 104. Prof. Clive points out (p. 110) that in an article of Oct. 1808 Jeffrey and Brougham took a different tone. See also A. Prentice's account of Manchester opinion at this time: *Personal Recollections of Manchester, 1792–1832* (2nd ed., 1851), pp. 33–4.

62. Neither term was yet a party label. But conservative already had party connotations. See *Quarterly Rev.,* xlii (Jan. 1830), 276: 'what is called the tory and . . . might with more propriety be called the conservative party'. The writer was Fullerton or Miller: see M. F. Brightfield, *J. W. Croker* (Univ. of California, 1940), p. 403, n. 19. For Grey's use of 'conservative' see Ch. 9, n. 27.

63. *Peel's Memoirs,* Ed. Earl Stanhope (formerly Visc. Mahon) and E. Cardwell (1856), i.101–2.

64. The term is used here in the popularly accepted sense. How far the ideas put forward in the *Westminster* were those of Bentham is open to dispute.

65. B. Holland, *Duke of Devonshire* (1911), i.406.

66. G. M. Trevelyan, *Grey* (1920), p. 371.

67. ibid., p. 373.

68. A. Mitchell, *The Whigs in Opposition, 1815–30* (1967), p. 155. See also same author in *Historical Studies, Australia and New Zealand,* xii (1965), 22–42.

69. Russell's plan is outlined in *Parl. Deb.,* N.S., vii.78.

70. Mitchell, *Whigs in Opposition,* pp. 154, 168.

71. For such fears see *Parl. Deb.,* xii.947 (Inglis), *W.N.D.,* viii.18. Melbourne spoke against Russell's 1826 Reform motion: *Parl. Deb.,* N.S., xv.712–14.

72. ibid., vii.87.

73. James Mill attacked Russell's 1826 proposals. See W. E. S. Thomas, 'James Mill's Politics', *Hist. Journal,* xii (1969), 268.

74. See also G. A. Legh-Keck's statement on 8 May 1827 that 'the inhabitants of Leeds' were not anxious to have the seats to be made available by the disfranchisement of Penryn (*Parl. Deb.,* N.S., xvii.684), and Yonge, *Liverpool,* ii.137–8. For distrust of manufacturers among the governing class see N. McCord, 'The Government of Tyneside, 1800–50', *T.R.H.S.,* 5th ser., xx (1970), 5–30.

75. 31 Oct. Quoted A. Briggs, 'Thomas Attwood and the Economic Background of the Birmingham Political Union', *Camb. Hist. Journal,* ix (1948), 193.

76. See Prof. I. R. Christie's introd. to 1964 repr. of G. S. Veitch, *The Genesis of Parliamentary Reform* (1st publ., 1913). John Cannon, *Parliamentary Reform, 1640–1832* (1973), gives an excellent account of the early Reform movement.

77. A. S. Foord, 'The Waning of the Influence of the Crown', *E.H.R.,* lxii (1947), 484–507; B. Kemp, *King and Commons* (1957), pp. 103–9.

78. Lauderdale to Lonsdale, 18 Feb.: Lowther MSS. See also Ellenborough. *Parl. Deb.,* xii.36.

79. See *Morning Chronicle,* 10 July 1829, editorial; *Manchester Times,* 15 Aug. 1829. See also Ch. 8, n. 52.

80. A. G. Stapleton, *George Canning and His Times* (1859), p. 350.

81. Mitchell, *Whigs in Opposition*, p. 185, n. 4.

82. *Table Talk* (2nd ed., 1836), p. 66.

83. *Parl. Deb.*, N.S., xvii.544. See n. 3 above.

84. Seven resigned, but one of them (Bexley) then decided to stay. There were more than forty resignations in all: *Formation of Canning's Ministry*, Ed. A. Aspinall (1937: Camden 3rd ser., lix), pp. xxxix, 127.

85. 11 August 1831. Greville's mother was a Bentinck. Canning had been connected with that family through his wife's sister.

86. J. J. Hope-Vere to J. P. Wood, 26 Apr. 1827: Linlithgow MSS, Hope-Vere vol., f. 18.

87. See n. 38 above and *The Times*, 17 Mar. 1827.

88. See Russell's comments on the 1826 contests: *Parl. Deb.*, iv.337.

89. A. G. Stapleton, *Political Life of George Canning, 1822–7* (1831), iii.297–8.

Chapter 2. Catholics, corn and currency

1. From this point, one of Canning's friends who joined Wellington's government is termed a Huskissonite, and one who did not join it a Canningite.

2. Notes 77–80 below bear on the East Retford case. For the petition against the return brought by Newcastle's supporters, and the Fitzwilliam counter-petition, see *Commons Journals*, lxxxii.71–3,521–2. For private statements of the Fitzwilliam case see John Parker to Fitzwilliam, 10 June 1826; H. S. Foljambe to same, 10, 25, 30 June, 23 July 1826: Fitzwilliam–Northants MSS. For general accounts see *Parl. Papers*, Election Committee Evidence and Report, 1826–7 (288), iv.757–952; Disfranchisement Bill Evidence, 1828 (80), iv.37–132; HL Evidence, 1830 (HL. 82), xvii.1–770; Mun. Corp. R. Comm., pp. 1870–3, 1835 (116), xxv.462–5; *Parl. Deb.*, N.S., xxv.1239–74.

3. *Mrs Arbuthnot*, ii.171,179,187–9. No one thought East Retford very important at this time. See (1) Granville to Huskisson, 30 May, 'the wretched trumpery East Retford Bill': Add. MSS, 38, 756, f. 212; (2) Huskisson to Wellington, 20 May; to Anglesey, 26 May; memo. on resignation: *W.N.D.*, iv.449, Add. MSS, 38, 756, f. 175, 38, 762, f. 186; (3) Broughton, *Recollections*, v.203–4 (Palmerston's statement that Huskisson was undecided how to vote until the last moment). Huskisson's statements just after his resignation should be treated with reserve, since by representing the occasion of his 'dismissal' as trivial he could make the Duke's conduct to him look unreasonable and unfeeling. But it is clear that the issue on which he left the government was thought to be of little intrinsic importance.

4. The Royal Assent had been given to the repeal of the Test and Corporation Acts on 9 May.

5. *Peel's Memoirs*, Ed. Earl Stanhope (formerly Visc. Mahon) and E. Cardwell (1856), i.103.

6. During a Lords debate on 28 Apr. 1828 Wellington re-affirmed his opposition to emancipation (*Parl. Deb.*, N.S., xix.179). Very few of his followers knew that in 1825 he had suggested a concordat with Rome on the basis of allowing emancipation while safeguarding Protestant interests (*W.N.D.* ii.592–607).

7. Ceased to apply to the first nine months after a general election by Act of 1919: repealed altogether in 1926. See Ch. 9.

8. *W.N.D.*, iv.455.

9. W. Cooke-Taylor, *Peel*, i (1846), 347; R. L. Sheil, *Legal and Political Sketches* (1855), ii.106–7.

10. *Dublin Evening Mail*, 18 June.

11. Parker, *Peel*, ii.99.

12. ibid, ii.64.

13. It was doubted in political circles whether, given normal circumstances, the new Irish county electorate would be more amenable than the old to the Protestant landlords: *Lord Ellenborough's Political Diary, 1828–30*, Ed. Lord Colchester (1881), i.350–1; G. J. W. Agar-Ellis to R. Sneyd, 29 Mar. 1829: Sneyd MSS. But a £10 electorate would give some protection against 'demagogues'.

14. E. Pellew, *Sidmouth* (1847), iii.425n. See also Lady Salisbury's notes of conversations with Wellington, 20 Apr., 24 May, 1832: Salisbury MSS; *W.N.D.*, v.489–92.

15. *Croker*, ii.15.

16. G. I. T. Machin, *The Catholic Question in English Politics, 1820–30* (1964), p. 173. Two of the sixty 'converts' were whigs.

17. Contemporary estimates which follow the registers and put the pre-1829 Irish county electorate at 200,000 or above are far too high. The Irish electoral registers contained the names of many people who had died or lost their qualifications. No accurate estimate can be made. See N. P. Leader's comments: *Parl. Deb.*, xiii.581. J. A. Reynolds concludes (*The Catholic Emancipation Crisis in Ireland*, 1954, p. 168, n. 30) that there were 'a little over 100,000' electors, of whom 16,000 kept their votes. The first figure may be accepted as a guide. The second seems too low, in that it neglects those who remained qualified under the £50 and £20 franchises. See Table 5 (p. 313).

18. *Parl. Deb.*, N.S., xx.933–4. See also Cobbett's Letter to Winchilsea in *Weekly Political Register*, 14 Mar. 1829, lxvii.338–51.

19. *Diary*, 22 Feb.: see also entry of 6 Feb. For more direct predictions that Emancipation would be followed by Reform see Lord John Russell, *Recollections and Suggestions* (1875), p. 59, and E. Hodder, *Shaftesbury* (1886) i.109 (Ashley's diary, 25 Feb. 1829).

20. For statements during the Reform debates indicating that the anti-catholic view had been that of the majority see *Parl. Deb.*, N.S. xxiv.1229–30, 3rd ser., ii.1171,1308, iv.885–6, vii.306,450,999,1137,1168, ix.539, x.929. This series is not confined to anti-reformers. It includes Macaulay. For Burdett's dissentient view, ibid., iv.899. Gladstone thought in the 1870s that Reform, if passed first, would have delayed Emancipation: *Nineteenth Century*, ii (1877), 540, repr. *Gleanings* (1898), i.136. See also Ch. 9, n. 66; *Morning Chronicle*, 14 July 1829, editorial.

21. See W. G. Hoskins, *Devonshire Studies* (1952), pp. 412–18.

22. Peel to Aberdeen, 23 Aug. 1829, and reply of 25 Oct.: Add. MSS, 40, 312, ff. 65–8, 73.

23. *Parl. Deb.*, iii.1036.

24. ibid., iv.335.

25. ibid., xii.111. See also Lansdowne to Stanley, 9 Mar. 1829: Derby MSS;

Russell, *Recollections*, p. 59; Hodder, *Shaftesbury*, i.109; *Mirror of Parliament* (1829), i.720 (Huskisson).

26. See J. Golby, 'A Great Electioneer and his Motives', *Hist. Journal*, viii (1965), 201–18.

27. Visc. Sandon to the Earl of Harrowby, 12 Feb. 1829: Harrowby MSS, v, f. 158.

28. 9 May.

29. Cobbett's *Political Register*, 18 July. A similar suggestion was made at Leeds in Sept. 1829: *Morning Chronicle*, 26 Sept. For Association's 'Address to the People' see *Chronicle*, 20 Oct.

30. *Manchester Times*, 15 Aug. Speech reproduced in Cobbett's *Political Register*, lxviii, 212–18. See also *Examiner*, 14 June (Reform dinner, Chichester), 20 Sept. (radical Reform mtg., Oldham).

31. 7. Geo. IV c. 6.

32. 'Distressed State of the Country' (report of 8 May meeting, Birmingham, 1829), p. 17.

33. He had contemplated founding a Political Union in 1819: speech, 18 Jan. 1836, C. M. Wakefield, *Thomas Attwood* (1885), p. 294.

34. *Birmingham Journal*, 12 Nov. 1836: report of speech.

35. A. Briggs, *Cam. Hist. Journal*, ix (1948), 211.

36. See Parkes's speech, 22 Nov. 1831: *The Times*, 25 Nov.

37. MS record of Town Meetings, etc., 1827–32, pp. 48–9: Birmingham City Library.

38. See *Manchester Guardian*, 30 Jan. 1830.

39. *Cam. Hist. Journal*, x (1952), 305.

40. Attwood was also supported initially by Joseph Allday, the powerful, though anonymous, editor of the tory–radical *Birmingham Argus*. Place noted, however, that A.'s currency theories had deterred some potential members: Add. MSS, 27, 789, f. 137.

41. Putting Burdett in the chair at the first annual meeting in July 1830 cost Attwood the support of both Cobbett and Allday. Burdett was too whiggish for the first (see n. 102 below), too radical for the second.

42. *Parl. Deb.*, N.S., xxii.347–8.

43. *London Radicalism, 1830–43*, Ed. D. J. Rowe (London Record Soc., v. 1970), p. 10.

44. 39 Geo. III c. 79 (1799) and 57 Geo. III c. 19 (1817). For effect of these Acts see *London Radicalism*, p. 67, and *Lord Melbourne's Papers*, Ed. Lloyd C. Sanders (1889), p. 151. Prof. C. T. Flick has recently assessed the influence of Thomas Attwood and Francis Place in *Huntington Library Quarterly*, xxxiv (1971), 355–66.

45. The resentment which the Political Union had aroused came to the surface at the Town Meeting held in Birmingham on 11 Aug. 1830 to congratulate the French. A plea for Reform was included in the resolutions after hot controversy: *Birmingham Gazette*, 16 Aug.

46. Palmerston's account is given in Lorne, *Palmerston* (1892), pp. 56–62. See also Sir H. Knatchbull-Hugesson, *Kentish Family* (1960), pp. 177–87 (based on the Vyvyan MSS).

47. *Parl. Deb.*, N.S., xx.315 (Grey); *The Times*, 8 Dec. 1834, report of Totnes

speech: see also Broughton, *Recollections*, iv.121 (Russell). See also *Parl. Deb.*, N.S., xxi.1685 (Hobhouse), 1688 (W. Smith); *Examiner*, 7 June; *Manchester Guardian*, 8 Aug.; *Manchester Times*, 15 Aug. 1829.

48. Sir Walter Scott, *Letters*, Ed. H. J. C. Grierson, xi (1936), 162, n. 3.

49. Lady Salisbury's notes, 5 Mar. 1830: Salisbury MSS.

50. Letter, 28 Sept. 1829, read to a Newark meeting, 5 Oct. M. T. Sadler, Newcastle's candidate in the election, had used the phrase in his *Ireland: Its Evils and Their Remedies* (2nd ed., 1829, pp. 117–18). Wilde, the opposing candidate, pointed out that N. was upholding the view which Sadler had condemned: *Nottingham Review*, 9 Oct. 1829. See J. Golby, 'A Great Electioneer', *Hist. Journal*, viii (1965), 204, stating that the evicted tenants had enjoyed rent concessions as 'loyal' Newcastle voters. The matter was debated in the Commons, 1 Mar. 1830: *Parl. Deb.*, N.S., xxii.1077–122.

51. Moreover loyalty to the King hardly implied support for His Government, since George IV's dislike of the Emancipation Bill had been well known.

52. *Correspondence of Charles Arbuthnot*, Ed. A. Aspinall (1941), p. 115.

53. ibid., p. 130.

54. See *Quarterly Rev.*, cxvii (1865), 551–2, 558. This article was by Visc. Cranborne, lately Lord Robert Cecil, and, from 1868, Marquess of Salisbury.

55. See *The Extraordinary Black Book* (1831 ed.).

56. *Diary*, 12 Dec. 1830. In edition by Lytton Strachey and Roger Fulford (1938), ii.85. Not printed in earlier editions.

57. 11 Oct.: Ellice MSS, E.17, ff. 136–7.

58. A. Mitchell, *The Whigs in Opposition 1815–30* (1967), pp. 220–1. Grey had incurred the king's enmity by his part in 'the Queen's affair' in 1820. Moreover, he had succeeded many years earlier, where George had failed, in becoming the lover of Georgiana, Duchess of Devonshire. The duchess bore a child by Grey and it had been well known in the fashionable world that he was the successful rival. Political gossip attributed the strength of George IV's dislike to this humiliation long ago. Talking to Knighton in 1829 the king referred to Grey as 'my bane through life': *Mrs Arbuthnot*, ii.273. See also *W.N.D.*, iv.75 and *Recollections of Louisa, Countess of Antrim* (privately printed, 1937), p. 9.

59. *Lieven–Grey Correspondence*, Ed. G. Le Strange (1890), i.423–4.

60. For opposing contemporary views about this see *Parl. Deb.*, i.173 (Denman), v.616 (Baring), xi.744 (Peel), and Peel's refusal of Huskisson's Liverpool seat: Parker, *Peel*, ii.162–3.

61. The nickname Brunswicker indicated that the opponents of emancipation were loyal to the protestant principles of the House of Brunswick.

62. Ellice MSS, E. 18, ff. 13–14, 23.

63. 14 Mar.: Grey MSS.

64. W. W. Rostow, *British Economy of the Nineteenth Century* (1948), p. 125.

65. D. Bythell, *The Handloom Weavers* (1969), pp. 129–30.

66. A memorandum by Anglesey in June 1830 records the King-to-be as speaking 'very favourably' of Grey: Marquess of Anglesey, *One Leg* (1961), p. 230. Prof. N. Gash writes of William after the Reform Act: 'if he is to be placed in any political category, he was an "Old Whig":' *Reaction and Reconstruction in English Politics* (1965), p. 5. William's Queen, Adelaide, was a tory, as is well illustrated by the extracts from her diary in P. Ziegler, *King William IV* (1971).

She did not discuss political questions with the king when others were present: Ziegler, p. 175.

67. *W.N.D.*, vii.106–8. The episode is analysed in N. Gash, *Mr Secretary Peel* (1961), pp.633–5.

68. See *Mrs Arbuthnot*, ii.337–8,349; Ellenborough, *Political Diary* (1881), ii.195; Grey to Howick, 21 Mar. 1830: Grey MSS. According to G. R. Gleig *(Personal Reminiscences of the Duke of Wellington*, Ed. M. E. Gleig, 1904, p. 107), Wellington spoke later as if he had wished to avoid a dissolution. But the evidence the other way from the early months of 1830 is convincing.

69. Peel was unavoidably absent on some difficult nights. His father died on 3 May.

70. Visc. Normanby to Devonshire: Devonshire MSS. The writer succeeded in Apr. 1831 as Earl of Mulgrave.

71. *Lieven–Grey Corresp.*, ii.21; *Corresp. of Charles Arbuthnot*, pp. 184–5.

72. Add. MSS, 40, 340, f. 223.

73. *Corresp. of Charles Arbuthnot*, p. 183.

74. Journal of Visc. Howick (later 3rd Earl Grey), 27 June: Grey MSS. Part printed, G. M. Trevelyan, *Grey* (1920), p. 218.

75. 7 July: Spencer MSS.

76. The account which follows is highly selective. No mention is made, for instance, of Blandford's Reform motion of 18 February.

77. There was a higher rate for a 'plumper' when the elector used only one of his votes. But the managers in East Retford discouraged plumpers which were apt to make for bad blood between the two candidates and their respective backers. I am grateful to Mr R. A. Preston for his advice on East Retford.

78. Their existing candidate, Sir Robert Dundas, was Fitzwilliam's nephew.

79. The whigs seem to have made no effort to prevent these proceedings. Possibly they believed East Retford to be Newcastle's borough. He was its Lord High Steward and the largest local landowner; and T. H. B. Oldfield, in his *Representative History of Great Britain and Ireland* (1816), app. to vol. vi, had given Newcastle as its patron. The *Courier*, 7 Apr. 1827, reported the Committee's discovery that Fitzwilliam had paid election expenses as being accidental. The subsequent whig argument that Fitzwilliam's actions 'had no bearing whatever on the case' was a weak one: *Parl. Deb.*, N.S., xviii.1083 (Tennyson).

80. *Parl.Deb.*, N.S.,xxv.1269. See also ibid.,xvii.1215–16 (Forbes),xviii.1269–70 (Howick), xxii.707 (Burdett), 3rd ser. iii.144 (Howick); *Diary of B. R. Haydon*, 20 May 1833, Ed. W. B. Pope, iv (1963), 84: 'I date the whole from East Retford'.

81. 10 Feb.: Grey MSS. Latter part in J. R. M. Butler, *The Passing of the Great Reform Bill* (1914), p. 66, n. 3.

82. Althorp was a strong supporter of ballot and voted on 15 Mar. for O'Connell's amendment to include it in the East Retford Bill.

83. *Parl. Deb.*, N.S., viii.1269, xxiv.1225.

84. J. R. M. Butler, *The Passing of the Great Reform Bill* (1914, new imp. 1964), p. 63, n. 3.

85. *Morning Chronicle*, 9 Mar.

86. First public meeting held 22 May. Founder was Lt. Col. Leslie Grove Jones (1779–1839).

87. *Parl. Deb.*, N.S., xxiii.182.

88. ibid., xxiv.1215,1223.

89. *Parl. Deb.*, iii.87. The essay by Dr Fraser in *Popular Movements, c. 1830–1850*, Ed. J. T. Ward (1970), pp. 31–53, provides an interesting account of the Reform agitation.

90. ibid., ii.1065.

91. For early comments in Parliament on the B.P.U. see *Parl. Deb.*, N.S., xxiii.515 (Radnor) and n. 42 above.

92. *Birmingham Journal*, 21 Aug. In Oct. it was given as '7000 male adults, and ... still rapidly increasing': Political Union Dinner, 11 Oct. 1830, *Summary Report* (Birmingham), p. 3.

93. Littleton, diary, 6 Dec. 1831: Hatherton MSS. L. had the information from Joseph Parkes.

94. M. I. Thomis, *Politics and Society in Nottingham, 1785–1835* (1969), pp. 223–5.

95. A. to his wife, 13 Oct. 1831: Wakefield, *Attwood*, p. 184.

96. *London Radicalism*, pp. 1–7; W. Lovett, *Life and Struggles* (1967), pp. 45–6.

97. For the inaugural meeting of the London Political Reform Society, 16 July 1830, see Cobbett's *Political Register*, 31 July.

98. The Rotunda was used by the Radical Reform Association and others. Carlile thus acted as host to various organizations.

99. *Parl. Papers*, 1830–1, iii.421–32.

100. xxvii.640–58. Author was David Robinson: *Wellesley Index to Victorian Periodicals, 1824–1900*, Ed. W. E. Houghton, i (1966), 34. See also Ch. 3, n. 10. *The Standard*, 28 Jan. 1830, announced that 'any plan of Reform which should proportion ... representation to the property ..., or to the numbers of the represented, or to a scale compounded of both, would return at least three-fourths good tories to Parliament'.

101. *Morning Chronicle*, 9 July. By 'universal' the authors meant manhood suffrage. See Ch. 9, n. 28. At a Radical Reform Association meeting, 2 Feb. 1830, Henry Hetherington (1792–1849) said that Westminster was 'palpably compromised by the character of its representatives': *Morning Chronicle*, 3 Feb.

102. *Political Register*, 17, 31 July, 7 Aug.

103. John Doherty, leader of the Lancashire spinners(see Ch. 3), was conscious of 'the misrepresentation of the people': *Manchester Guardian*, 27 Feb. 1830. But recommending his National Association for the Protection of Labour on 26 Apr. 1830, he asked: 'what chance had the poor man ... with his employer when the latter both made and administered the laws?' The speech was made at Bury which had no MP until 1832. Doherty clearly regarded the employers of Bury as needing no Reform Act to increase their power. *United Trades Cooperative Journal*, 1 May 1830 (see H.O. 40, 27, f. 277).

104. *The Times*, 13 Mar. 1830. For status of County Meetings see B. Keith Lucas, *Law Quarterly Rev.*, Jan. 1954, pp. 109–14.

105. For this failure see *Camb. Hist. of the Brit. Empire*, ii (1940), 316–25. Murray's despatches of 3 and 15 Sept. 1828 are in *Parl. Papers*, 1829 (333), xxv.158,161 (version for Jamaica). It became known in spring 1830 that illegal slavery practices had flourished in Mauritius: *Parl. Deb.*, N.S., xxiv.672,774; C. Buxton, *Memoirs of Sir T. F. Buxton* (1849), p. 191.

106. xxxix.343 (Apr. 1829). See also *British Critic*, v (1829), 454.

107. *Morning Chronicle*, 17 May; Sir G. Stephen, *Anti-Slavery Recollections* (1854), pp. 120–2.

108. When William Knibb, the Jamaica missionary, was told that the Reform Bill had been passed he rejoined: 'Thank God; now I'll have slavery down': J. H. Hinton, *Life of W. Knibb* (1847), p. 138.

109. xxviii.729 (Nov. 1830).

110. xii.232.

111. *Parl. Deb.*, N.S., xxii.879 (Morpeth). See also Address debate, ibid., 73 (Blandford), 76 (Western), 77 (Protheroe).

112. *Parl. Deb.*, iii.316. See also Russell, *Recollections*, p. 60. The reference must be to the 28 May proposals.

113. Broughton, *Recollections*, iv.24.

114. See also Liverpool's statement on the Grampound seats: *Parl. Deb.*, N.S., v.629–32.

115. *Political Diary*, ii.318.

116. New Shoreham, Cricklade, and Aylesbury had been successively convicted of corruption and sluiced during George III's reign. See Ch. 1, n. 15.

117. A smaller interest than was generally supposed. See J. Golby, *Hist. Journal* (1965), viii.205. See also *Parl. Deb.*, N.S., xxii.1394–5.

118. Peel's statement in *Parl. Deb.*, N.S., xxii.897. See Gash, *Mr Secretary Peel*, p. 610.

Chapter 3. The 1830 election

1. No attempt has been made in the passage which follows to give a comprehensive account of the election. Features which had no great bearing on Reform are omitted. This applies especially to Ireland.

2. See *The Result of the General Election* or *What has the Duke . . . Gained by the Dissolution?*, anon, but attributed to Brougham, and the *Reply*, giving the ministerial version, by 'Oxon Graduate'. The fullest private statement of the whips' calculations is in J. Planta to Wellington, 30 Aug.: Wellington MSS. Brougham's private comments are in B. to Devonshire (8 Sept.): Devonshire MSS. See also n. 57 below on the Treasury list.

3. See Abercromby to Lansdowne, 17 Aug. 1830: Lansdowne MSS. Quotation in A. Mitchell, *The Whigs in Opposition, 1815–30* (1967), p. 233. I would like to thank Dr Mitchell for drawing various unpublished letters to my attention.

4. *Edinburgh Evening Courant*, 12 Aug.

5. See Ch. 2, n. 13. It was not supposed, either before or after the 1830 election, that the £10 voters of Ireland would be much more amenable to control by the protestant landlords than the old forty-shilling freeholders had been (see Spring Rice to Stanley, 11 Oct. 1829: Derby MSS). But the effect of the 'legislative package'—the three Acts taken together—had been to keep most of the Irish counties under their usual allegiances.

6. ch. 35.

7. 27 Jan., 26 July. Contemporaries constantly exaggerated the increase in the

number of voters: J. Cannon, *Parliamentary Reform, 1640–1832* (1973), pp. 40–2, 145.

8. 28 July.

9. *The Times*, 29 July.

10. xxvii.658. See Ch. 2, n. 100.

11. *Parl. Deb.*, N.S., xxv.1074. See also ibid., 622 (O'Connell).

12. Bedford to Lord William Russell, 16 Nov. 1830: Bedford MSS.

13. *Aris's Birmingham Gazette*, 9 Aug.

14. See Tavistock to Lord William Russell, (a) 18 Aug., (b) 15 Oct. 1830: (a) Georgiana Blakiston, *Lord William Russell and His Wife, 1815–46* (1972), pp. 220–1; (b) Bedford MSS. Three vols. of letters to *Lord G. William Russell* were privately printed, 1915–20. A derogatory passage about the Methodists in his *Memoirs of the Affairs of Europe*, i (1829) cost Lord John support: John Prest, *Lord John Russell* (1972), p. 37. Lord John's draft reply on the incident, 22 July, is in Russell MSS (Ann Arbor).

15. The anti-catholics in the Carnarvon Boroughs had tried to remove Lord William Paget in 1828: G. I. T. Machin, *The Catholic Question in English Politics 1820–30* (1964), pp. 149–50: see also ibid., p. 121. Anglesey's brother, Rear Admiral the Hon. Sir Charles Paget (1778–1839), who stood in 1830, was reluctant to spend money or indeed to become the family's candidate at all. He did not want either to give up his post in the Royal Household or to support Wellington. If elected he would be obliged to do one or the other: Anglesey MSS (Plas Newydd). Lord William's debts had lately aggravated Anglesey's family troubles: Marquess of Anglesey, *One Leg* (1961), pp. 234–7. I am grateful to Mr Llewellyn Jones for information on this contest.

16. *Spectator*, 26 Feb. 1831.

17. See petitions in *Votes and Proc.*, 1830–1, App. vol., pp. 3–6, 12–13, 615–17. For Calne see also Ch. 4, n. 120.

18. *Parl. Papers*, 1835 (116), xxiii.616–19.

19. *The Times*, 2 Aug.

20. ibid., 9 Aug.

21. *West Briton* (Truro), 6 Aug. Falmouth, being an ultra tory, believed that the government had 'countenanced' this 'vile attempt to radicalize Truro'; F. to Lord Kenyon, 5 Aug.: Kenyon MSS.

22. Professor John Wilson ('Christopher North'), Constitutional meeting, Edinburgh, 28 Nov. 1831: pamphlet giving *Report of the Speeches*. The same point is made in *Blackwood's*, xxix (Mar. 1831), 439 (probably by Wilson).

23. *Globe*, 26 Oct.; *The Times*, 27 Oct. 1830.

24. *Parl. Papers*, 1831–2, xxxvi.499. It is possible that only two of the voters were resident.

25. To Countess of Harrowby, 18 Aug.: Harrowby MSS, lxii, f. 243. Writer's husband was Secretary to the Board of Control in Wellington's government from Jan. 1830.

26. *The Times*, 12 Aug.; *Suffolk Chronicle*, 7, 14 Aug. See also the Revd. W. P. Seagill, *The Peace of the County* (Bury St Edmunds, 1830).

27. D. Le Marchant to F. T. Baring, 14 Aug.: *Journals and Correspondence of F. T. Baring*, Ed. Lord Northbrook (1905), i.66.

28. *Courier*, 6 Aug. (H. Sumner's speech). See Jolliffe's petition, *Votes and*

Proc., 1830–1, App. vol., pp. 93–4. Jolliffe had been challenged in Petersfield, an attempt being made in 1830 to 'open' that borough. In mid-July the Surrey reformers were looking for a candidate who would stand 'on the popular interest' and were ready to pay most, if not all, of his expenses: Howick's journal, 15 July: Grey MSS.

29. C. M. Wakefield, *Thomas Attwood* (1885), p. 143.

30. Quoted D. C. Moore, *Hist. Journal*, ix (1966), 50.

31. *Dyott's Diary*, Ed. R. W. Jeffery (1907), ii.87.

32. *Aris's Birmingham Gazette*, 9 Aug.

33. See Fitzwilliam MSS, Northants.

34. See N. Gash, *Proc. Leeds Phil. Soc.*, viii (1956), 19–35; A. S. Turberville and F. Beckwith, *Thoresby Soc. Miscellany*, xli (1943), 1–33.

35. Mitchell, *Whigs in Opposition*, p. 233, n. 4.

36. Fitzwilliam MSS, Sheffield.

37. ibid., Althorp to Milton, 22 July. Stapylton kept the poll open for two days, during which he received 94 votes. Each of the other four candidates received more than 1000.

38. Baines had originally suggested Brougham for the county in 1812: Gash, n. 34 above, p. 24.

39. Gally Knight to Milton, 12 Aug.: Fitzwilliam MSS, Sheffield.

40. Term coined by the tory *Leeds Intelligencer*, 29 July.

41. On the town freeholders see Ch. 6, n. 81. Yorkshire was also unrepresentative in containing '6 to 10 country gentlemen of equal pretensions among whom it was impossible to make a choice which should rest on any satisfactory ground of preference'; W. Empson to T. Spring Rice, 26 July 1830: Monteagle MSS, Nat. Library of Ireland, MS 13370(4). I am grateful to Mr W. E. S. Thomas for drawing my attention to this letter.

42. *The Result of the General Election* (1830), p. 21.

43. xxviii (Oct. 1830), 691–2.

44. *The Times*, 14 May 1832 (The Revd. W. Shepherd).

45. 16 Oct. Brougham was sensitive to this type of criticism. See report of his Sheffield speech in *Sheffield Independent*, 2 Oct. 1830.

46. *Notes* (2nd ed., Grantham, 1851), p. 186.

47. 3 Dec. 1830, Fitzwilliam MSS, Northants. Fazakerley (c. 1788–1852) had been returned for Peterborough on 24 November in a by-election. See also F. to Lansdowne, 28 Jan. 1831: Lansdowne MSS.

48. Lansdowne MSS. See n. 3 above. Those who predicted that the new House would be unmanageable were not all whigs. See Croker to Lowther, 13 Aug. (heading to this chapter), quoted *Three Diaries*, p. xxiii, and Greville, *Diary*, 14 Aug.

49. *Parl. Deb.*, iii.165. Grant referred also to 'the events of the last session'. His Norwich election address had called for 'practical correction of every abuse, including such as prevail in electing representatives of the people'.

50. Hatherton MSS.

51. For Fazakerley see Littleton's diary, 18 Jan. 1832: Hatherton MSS; Broughton, *Recollections*, iv.345, where F. is called 'the simmering saucepan of Lansdowne House'.

52. *Mirror of Parliament* (1830), iii.2730–1.

53. *Staffordshire Advertiser*, 17 July. *Colchester Gazette*, 10 July, gives a slightly different version. Whittle Harvey said in this speech that since he began contesting the Borough in 1812 he had spent over £25,000 on it.

54. *Colchester Gazette*, 14 Aug.

55. *Nottingham Journal*, 10 July. Quoted in, for instance, *Staffordshire Advertiser*, 17 July.

56. R. S. Carew to Milton, 27 Aug.: Fitzwilliam MSS, Sheffield.

57. The Treasury list for the election, classifying the whole of the new House into 'Friends', 'Foes', 'Doubtfuls', etc., has survived in the Peel MSS: Add. MSS, 40, 401, f. 181.

58. *Manchester Courier*, 8 Dec. 1832. *Manchester Guardian* of same date gives a slightly different version.

59. Political memories are conveniently short, however. In 1834 Croker maintained in the *Quarterly Rev.* (iii.289) that the July revolution had made little impression on British opinion until the incoming whig ministers showed their sympathy with the tricolour. By then the reaction to Wellington's speech of 2 Nov. 1830 (see Ch. 4) had been largely forgotten.

60. *Parl. Deb.*, viii.285. See also xii.161 (Wellington).

61. In the Armagh City election three cheers were given for the French revolution. But there appear to have been few, if any, other Irish contests where events in France made a stir. On this point, as on all others concerning the election in Ireland, I have received most valuable help from Dr A. D. Macintyre.

62. *Essays Presented to Sir Lewis Namier*, Ed. R. Pares and A. J. P. Taylor (1956), pp. 287-8.

63. See *Spectator*, 23 Apr. 1832, p. 351.

64. Cobbett was quick to foresee its effects: *Weekly Political Register*, 14 Aug. 1830.

65. 30 Nov.: *W.N.D.*, viii.110.

66. 12 Aug.

67. *The Times*, 14 Aug.

68. 28 July. See also *Standard*, 15 July.

69. The Beer Act illustrates the difficulties of an alliance between whigs and ultra tories. In his Leeds speech on 27 July Brougham commended the government for having, by the Act, 'taken away from the justices that power which is liable to be abused in crushing an obnoxious individual, who might choose to have his own opinion upon . . . state policy' (*The Times*, 30 July). Vyvyan was playing on his audience's dislike of centralization and government placemen, Brougham on the unpopularity, in places such as Leeds, of JPs who bullied radicals. For the Act, and its effects during the Reform crisis, see Brian Harrison, *Drink and the Victorians* (1971), ch. 3.

70. *Standard*, 9 Aug.

71. Mitchell, *Whigs in Opposition*, p. 233, n. 6.

72. *The Times*, 1 Oct. 1830.

73. 30 Sept.: Grey MSS. On 13 Sept., however, Huskisson had reported the trade and manufactures of Lancashire to be flourishing: *Lord Melbourne's Papers*, Ed. Lloyd C. Sanders (1889), p. 119.

74. J. T. Ward, *Sir James Graham* (1967), p. 92.

75. Earl of Ellesmere, *Personal Reminiscences of the Duke of Wellington*, Ed.

Countess of Strafford (1903), p. 62. See also Shaw (from Manchester) to Sir H. Bouverie, 23 Oct.: 'the political feeling of the working classes is very strong and bad, and getting worse', and Sir H. Bouverie to Lord Fitzroy Somerset, 30 Oct.: H.O. 40, 26, ff. 93, 106.

76. Sel. Cttee. on Combinations, Q. 3395, 3446, 3450, *Parl. Papers*, 1837–8, viii.256,259; H.O. 40, 27, f. 274.

77. H.O. 40, 26, f. 119.

78. 5. Geo. IV c. 95, 6. Geo. IV c. 129.

79. J. F. Foster to Home Office, 26 Oct.: H.O. 40, 27, f. 314. See also Ch. 1, n. 74.

80. J. Richardson to Sir Walter Scott, 21 Oct.: *Sir Walter's Postbag*, Ed. W. Partington (1932), p. 297.

81. To Governor, Bank of Ireland: Bank of England MSS, letter book no. 6, p. 178.

82. See n. 25 above. Harrowby MSS, lxii, f. 271.

83. M. Sadleir, *Bulwer: Edward and Rosina, 1803–36* (1931), p. 156, n. 2.

84. 15 Sept.: Add. MSS, 38, 758, f. 242.

85. The railway helped the reformers, since it ran near the rotten borough of Newton and made the 'rottenness' of the system visible to thousands of travellers: A. Prentice, *Personal Recollections of Manchester, 1792–1832*, 2nd ed., (1851), p. 369; *Parl. Deb.*, xii.696–7 (Radnor).

86. Letters of 19 Sept., 8 Oct.: Grey MSS, letter of 25 Sept.: Mitchell, *Whigs in Opposition*, pp. 239–40.

87. Littleton to R. Wellesley, 20 Dec. 1830: Hatherton MSS. Peel had wanted to neutralize the whig leader as well as secure Huskissonites, and had apparently suggested offering the Paris Embassy to Grey: Wellington to Mrs Arbuthnot, 26 Aug.: Wellington MSS.

88. To Peel, 17 Sept.: Add. MSS, 40, 340, f. 236.

89. Vesey Fitzgerald had just been invited to join the government and had declined on grounds of health, *W.N.D.*, vii.240–1,256.

90. A. Aspinall, *Lord Brougham and the Whig Party* (1927), p. 182.

91. E. Ashley, *Palmerston* (1879), i.213.

92. *Mrs Arbuthnot*, ii.389 (Ld. Clive), 395. For a last foredoomed overture from Croker to Palmerston see Dalling (Bulwer), *Palmerston* (5 vol. ed., completed by E. Ashley, 1870–6), i.364.

93. See n. 49 above.

94. J. T. Ward, *Sir James Graham* (1967), p. 88.

95. Contrast Greville, 31 Aug.: 'the urgency of the danger will unquestionably increase the impatience of those who already think the government incapable of carrying on the public business.'

96. Countess of Longford, *Wellington: Pillar of State* (1972), p. 216.

97. To Mrs Arbuthnot, 31 Aug.: Wellington MSS.

98. Wellington MSS.; part in Longford, op. cit., p. 222.

99. ibid.

100. Lord Cockburn, *Memorials of His Time* (1856), p. 468.

101. To her mother, Lady Harrowby, 2 Oct.: Harrowby MSS, lxii, f. 291. For an earlier controversy involving Newcastle see Ch. 2, n. 50.

102. 6 Oct.: *Lieven–Grey Correspondence*, Ed. G. Le Strange (1890), ii.101–2.

Reformers regarded resistance to political evictions as part of the Reform struggle See *Sun*, 4 Nov.: 'Stamford has led the way—Newark is not far behind— Manchester, Leeds, and Birmingham are bestirring themselves. . . . the conviction is rapidly spreading among all classes that Reform can no longer be delayed with safety'. Exeter's reported evictions were at Stamford, Newcastle's at Newark.

103. To Lord William Russell, 6 Oct.: Bedford MSS.

104. 29 Sept.

105. H. F. Cooke to Raikes, 'September': *Private Correspondence of T. Raikes to Wellington*, Ed. H. Raikes (1861) p. 49.

106. *The Times*, 15 Sept. Wilton disclaimed any wish 'to stem the tide of knowledge', but regretted 'that the higher classes . . . should be overwhelmed by it'. A more hostile view of the educational improvements of the day appeared in *Blackwood's* xxviii (Oct. 1830), 691–2, for which see also n. 43 above.

107. *The Times*, 25 Sept.

108. *Leicester Chronicle*, 11 Sept. (Brewin).

109. *Manchester Guardian*, 28 Aug. The speaker, Mark Philips, was later one of Manchester's first MPs.

110. 1 Nov.

111. *Parl. Deb.*, i.156; 145–6 (Maberly).

112. Cooke to Raikes p. 50: see note 105 above.

113. Wellington MSS. See also the quotation from Wellington's letter to Sir James Shaw, 17 Oct., in Longford, op. cit., p. 224.

114. ibid.

115. The *Morning Chronicle* editorial mentioned in n. 45 above was occasioned by the report of this speech.

116. Peel to Planta, 18 Oct. (enclosing note from Wellington, 17 Oct.): Add. MSS, 40, 401, f. 232; *Courier*, 18 Oct.

117. Among the whigs Grey did not dismiss the rumour: Grey to Holland, 17 Oct.: Grey MSS. See G. M. Trevelyan, *Grey* (1920), p. 234, n. 3. The date on this letter is not clear. Prof. C. T. Flick gives it as 19 Oct. in *Journal of Mod. Hist.*, xxxvii (1965), 69, n. 32.

118. Parker, *Peel*, ii.164.

119. Le Marchant, *Althorp*, pp. 252–3.

120. See n. 117 above for this letter.

121. Prest, *Russell*, p. 38.

122. Fortescue MSS, 1262M/FC–86. I am grateful to Dr I. D. C. Newbould for drawing my attention to this letter.

123. Prest, *Russell*, p. 38.

124. Add. MSS, 51, 751, ff. 46–7.

125. Durham to his wife, 2 Nov.: Durham MSS. For this letter see C. W. New, *Durham* (1929), pp. 101–2, and Flick, n. 117 above, p. 69.

126. Le Marchant, *Althorp*, pp. 254–5.

127. *Parl. Deb.*, i.52–3.

128. Lord John Russell, *Recollections and Suggestions* (1875), p. 62. The colleague is identified as Aberdeen in Russell's draft (now in the W. L. Clements Library, Ann Arbor), but not in the published text. *Edinburgh Rev.*, clviii (Oct. 1883), 577, containing Gladstone's version, gives Aberdeen as the author of a different

reply. Sir T. Martin's view that the Lord Chancellor made the remark (*Lyndhurst*, 1883, p. 272) appears to be unfounded.

Chapter 4. The whigs in office

1. Lady Salisbury's note, 8 Dec. 1836: Salisbury MSS partly published in Countess of Longford, *Wellington: Pillar of State* (1972), p. 224. Another of the notes, 20 Apr. 1832, records a similar statement by the Duke. For a hint of the view which Wellington attributed to Lonsdale see *Observations on Two Pamphlets ... Attributed to Mr Brougham*, pp. 66–7. *Observations* appeared on 23 Oct. 1830.

2. Littleton to Wellesley, 20 Dec. 1830, Hatherton MSS; Tavistock to Ld. G. William Russell, 5 Nov. 1830, Bedford MSS. See also *Globe* editorial, 17 Nov.; *Morning Chronicle*, 6, 13 Nov.; *Westminster Rev.*, xiv.233–4; *Croker*, ii.126; *Parl. Deb.*, i.146 (Maberly), 148 (Wood).

3. 15 Nov.: John Gladstone MSS.

4. See Brougham's speech, 28 Mar. 1831: *Parl. Deb.*, iii.1060–1; *Morning Chronicle*, 12 Oct. 1829 (leader comment on Cheshire Whig Club dinner).

5. Le Marchant, *Althorp*, p. 309.

6. For Peel see *Letters of Princess Lieven*, Ed. L. G. Robinson (1902), pp. 277–8. Lyndhurst, Ellenborough, and Murray, whose views are mentioned in the text, seem to have been the only cabinet ministers of reforming inclinations.

7. *W.N.D.*, vii.353: *Conversations of Wellington with G. W. Chad*, Ed. 7th Duke of Wellington (1956), p. 11. According to Guizot, Peel held a different view: F. P. G. Guizot, *Peel* (1857), p. 51.

8. *Parl. Deb.*, i.37.

9. See Ellenborough, 2 Nov.; 'the tone of the debate was very good and will do good': *Political Diary, 1828–30*, Ed. Lord Colchester (1881), ii.411.

10. G. R. Gleig, *Life of Wellington* (Everyman ed., 1909), pp. 300, 311, 416.

11. Entry of 8 Dec. 1834.

12. *W.N.D.*, i.80. See also *Three Diaries*, p. 93 (Ellenborough), and *W.N.D.*, viii.287.

13. Robert Blake, *The Unknown Prime Minister* (1955), p. 439. The fact that Mrs Arbuthnot did not greatly like Peel lessened Wellington's chances of hearing unpalatable truths from his Leader of the Commons. Peel disapproved of the way in which Mrs Arbuthnot had 'usurped' the Duchess of Wellington's place: *Private Letters of Peel*, ed. G. Peel (1920), pp. 96, 110. Mrs Arbuthnot may well have detected, and resented, Peel's disapproval.

14. *The Times*, 30 Oct., report taken from *Kent Herald*. See also *Maidstone Journal*, 2 Nov.

15. See also *Morning Chronicle*, 15 Nov.

16. J. H. Hawkins, *Parl. Deb.*, iii.1623.

17. C. S. Parker, *Graham* (1907), i.97–8.

18. Greville, *Diary*, 15 Dec. 1830; *Parl. Deb.*, viii.317 (Grey).

19. *Wm. IV–Grey Corresp.* i.186; *Parl. Deb.*, vii.933, xii.442; *Croker*, ii.160.

20. Add. MSS, 40, 401, f. 267. Quoted A. A. W. Ramsay, *Peel* (1928), p. 140. See also Wellington to Mrs Arbuthnot, 26 Dec. 1830: *Wellington and His Friends*,

Ed. 7th Duke of Wellington (1965), p. 91; *Three Diaries*, p. 249 (Littleton, 11 May 1832); Lord John Russell, *Essay on the History of the English Government and Constitution*, introd. 1865 ed., p. xliii.

21. *Gladstone Diaries*, Ed. M. R. D. Foot, i. (1968), 329. *Gladstone*, Ed. T. Wemyss Reid (1899), contains facsimile of the minute recording the result at p. 120.

22. Wellington MSS. He was whiggish and had held office under Canning. He joined Wellington's ministry in 1830. The Duke's reply is printed in *W.N.D.* vii.352–3. See also Londonderry to Buckingham, 28 Aug. 1830: Duke of Buckingham, *Courts and Cabinets of William IV and Victoria* (1861), i.49–50.

23. See Vyvyan's statement on 13 Sept. 1831: *Parl. Deb.*, vi.1406.

24. Peel to Henry Hobhouse, 24 Nov.: Ramsay, *Peel*, p. 140

25. Lady Salisbury's notes, 24 May 1832: Salisbury MSS. For the story that Peel meant to retire from office by Christmas even if the government survived see Lady Salisbury's notes, ibid., and 8 Dec. 1836; Parker, *Peel*, ii.171–2; Lord Stanhope, *Conversations with the Duke of Wellington* (2nd ed., 1888), pp. 185–6.

26. *Three Diaries*, p. 1 (Le Marchant). Greville gives a different version.

27. See *Diary of B. R. Haydon*, Ed. W. B. Pope, iv (1963), 370–1. Wellington soon came to regret his readiness to resign: Countess of Longford, *Wellington*, p. 264.

28. Wellington to Camden, 8 Dec. 1832: Sir Keith Feiling, *Second Tory Party* (1938), p. 403.

29. Hon. Lloyd Kenyon's diary, 15 Nov.: Kenyon MSS. See also Ellenborough, *Political Diary*, ii.434.

30. *Parl. Deb.*, i.548 n.; Broughton, *Recollections*, iv.66–7; F. T. Baring to his wife, 12, 15 Nov.: *Journals and Correspondence of F. T. Baring*, Ed. Lord Northbrook (1905), i.69,71; Grey to Princess Lieven, 12 Nov.: *Lieven–Grey Correspondence*, Ed. G. Le Strange (1890), ii.116.

31. Grey's friendship with Lady Lyndhurst had aroused comment. See Greville, *Diary*, 12 Dec. 1830, 8 July 1831, 6 Mar. 1832 (none of the passages complete in earlier editions). Hardinge also was said to have been sounded about staying in office: Le Marchant, *Althorp*, p. 230.

32. A. Aspinall, *Lord Brougham and the Whig Party* (1927), p. 187.

33. The Rolls would have involved Brougham in the expense of re-election for Yorkshire, unless he had been prepared to retire to a cheaper seat. It is a measure of the degree to which his ambition had become inflamed that he overlooked this drawback in Nov. 1830. Writing to Lansdowne in Sept. 1861 he used the expense of re-election to support his contention that he had not 'very much desired' the Rolls (Aspinall, *Brougham and the Whig Party*, pp. 185–6). In fact, he had desired the post with equal ardour and imprudence.

34. The king may have been prompted by the outgoing ministers to give this advice. The evidence is conflicting. At the time Croker hinted that something had been said to the king. In 1857 he wrote that Wellington and Peel gave no such warning. (*Croker*, ii.80; *Three Diaries*, p. 4, n. 1; C. W. New. *Brougham to 1830*, (1961), p. 416, n. 2.)

35. Le Marchant, *Althorp*, p. 261.

36. A number of leading whigs pleaded with Brougham that morning. Althorp's intervention seems to have been decisive.

37. To Duke of Portland: Portland MSS.

38. *Parl. Deb.*, N.S., xvii.1261.

39. Lord Byron's *Letters and Journals*, Ed. R. E. Prothero (1898–1903), v.176, 15 Jan. 1821. See also *Journal of the Conversations of Lord Byron with Lady Blessington* (1893), pp. 47–8.

40. On Grey's preference see *Lieven*, Ed. Robinson, pp. 278–9.

41. For the earlier position see Sir Lewis Namier, *Structure of Politics at the Accession of George III* (2nd ed., 1957), pp. 10–11.

42. Broughton, *Recollections*, iv.28; Lady Salisbury's notes, 18 Sept. 1830: Salisbury MSS. Attwood's remark suggests that he realized the frailty of the alliance between middle and working classes on which the Birmingham Political Union rested.

43. Earl Gower to Countess of Harrowby, undated: Harrowby MSS, xvii, f. 160.

44. Sir Robert Heron, *Notes* (2nd ed., Grantham, 1851), pp. 189–90; Hon. Marianne Kenyon to Hon. Lloyd Kenyon, 29 Nov. 1830: Kenyon MSS; Croker to Hertford, 19 Jan. 1831: Croker MSS (Ann Arbor), letter book 25, p. 161; Lowther to Lonsdale, 22 Jan. 1831: Lonsdale MSS. Opinion in the provinces, even among propertied people, was more sympathetic to the labourers than in London. See E. J. Hobsbawm & G. Rudé, *Captain Swing* (1969), p. 261, giving examples of petitions chiefly from the disturbed areas.

45. *Three Diaries*, p. 49; Greville, *Diary*, 24 Feb. 1831.

46. ch. 18.

47. *Parl. Deb.*, ii.712.

48. See also F. T. Baring, 27 Feb.: *Journals*, i. 81–2.

49. See on the ultra groups B. T. Bradfield, (1) 'Sir R. Vyvyan and the Country Gentlemen, 1830–34', *E.H.R.*, lxxxiii (1968), 729–43, (2) 'Sir R. Vyvyan and the Fall of Wellington's Government', *Univ. of Birmingham Hist. Journal*, xi (1968), 141–56.

50. Broughton, *Recollections*, iv.178. See also Littleton, diary, 29 June 1831: Hatherton MSS. Russell is said to have drafted the Reform scheme during a stay in Streatham Rectory: F. Arnold, *History of Streatham* (1886), p. 154. I owe this last reference to the kindness of Prof. M. R. D. Foot.

51. Richmond was proposed for the committee; but Russell objected. See R.'s account in Greville, *Diary*, 22 Nov. 1842; Lord John Russell, *Recollections and Suggestions* (1875), pp. 68–9.

52. Broughton, *Recollections*, iv.257; H. P. Brougham, *Life and Times* (1871), iii.380; Le Marchant, *Althorp*, p. 292.

53. In 1834 Durham and Brougham quarrelled publicly over their roles in the preparation of the Bill. Their statements, and the subsequent correspondence, provide a good deal of information on the committee's doings. Durham's speeches on the subject were reported in *The Times* on 28 Oct. 1833, 17 Sept., 10, 31 Oct. 1834: Brougham's on 13 Oct. 1834. See also *Ed. Rev.*, lx (Oct. 1834), 248–51; *The Times*, 31 July 1837 (Russell's Stroud speech).

54. Parker, *Graham*, i.120. The wording is Graham's: he was writing in 1851.

55. *Early Correspondence of Lord John Russell, 1805–40*, Ed. Rollo Russell (1913), ii.52–3.

56. Russell, *Essay*, pp. xxxvii–viii. Original is in P.R.O. 30/22/1A, ff. 275–6.

57. It was argued against ballot both that it increased facilities for casting fraudulent votes and that it would not protect voters, since their politics would be known even if the actual voting process were secret. The effect of ballot was one of the many issues on which both sides cited American experience. See *Parl. Deb.*, i.898–9 (Sir R. Wilson); H. Grote, *Personal Life of G. Grote* (1873), pp. 76–7; *Liverpool Mercury*, 10 Oct. 1834, *Liverpool Courier*, 29 Oct. 1834; Lord Morpeth's American diary, 25 Oct. 1841: Harvard College Library (MS copy). For a view of ballot in France see *West Briton* (Truro), 23 July 1830.

58. *Parl. Papers*, 1830–1, iii.421–32.

59. See W. E. S. Thomas, 'James Mill's *Essay* and Reform', *Hist. Journal*, xii (1969), 249–84; D. C. Moore, 'Political Morality in mid-nineteenth century England', *Victorian Studies*, xiii (1969), 5–36.

60. *Liverpool Chronicle*, 27 Nov. (G. P. Payne). See also (1) *Morning Chronicle*, 16 Dec., 1st leader (2) C. T. Flick, 'The Class Character of the Agitation . . . ', *South Atlantic Quarterly*, lxviii (1969), 39–55.

61. Durham to Russell, 21 Oct. 1834: Grey MSS (copy).

62. *Parl. Deb.*, xxviii.451,457 (Russell, Stanley); S. J. Reid, *Durham* (1906), i.238. Russell seems to have been the only committee member to object to ballot. Duncannon agreed to it at Althorp's request: Russell to Brougham, 15 Nov. 1837; Brougham MSS, U.C.L. 14, 426. See also W. F. Monypenny (and G. E. Buckle), *Disraeli* (2 vol. ed., 1929), i.392.

63. See Russell's later views on ballot: *Parl. Deb.*, xl.1192. After 1832 J. C. Hobhouse thought ballot too democratic: Broughton, *Recollections*, v.120–1.

64. Grey told the Lords, 3 Dec. 1830, that 'he might perhaps have very strong objections to . . . ballot': *Parl. Deb.*, i.756.

65. The king sanctioned the proposal for quinquennial parliaments which was still included when the scheme was submitted to him: *Wm. IV–Grey Corresp.*, i.103.

66. Althorp was careful to dispel any idea that the choice of a minister outside the cabinet indicated lack of cabinet support for the scheme: *Parl. Deb.*, ii.131.

67. On the speed with which the king assented to the proposals see Lady Salisbury's diary, 28 Jan. 1837: C. Oman, *The Gascoyne Heiress* (1968), p. 232.

68. The annual value was to be established through jury service, or assessments to poor rate or inhabited house duty: *Wm. IV–Grey Corresp.*, i.462.

69. See *The Journal of Sir Walter Scott*, Ed. W. E. K. Anderson (1971), p. 641, 25 Mar. 1831, 'the curse of Cromwell on those whose conceit brought us to this pass'; Sydney Smith, *Works* (1850), p. 633, 'Lord John Russell . . . would perform the operation for the stone—build St Peter's—or assume (with or without ten minutes' notice) the command of the Channel Fleet'.

70. *Parl. Papers*, 1830–1, x.10–17. John Wilks (c. 1765-1854, see *D.N.B.*) moved for the return.

71. *Parl. Deb.*, iv.343. Russell guessed at the time that 'the poor rate returns would give a greater number', R. to Durham, 13 Feb. 1831: Grey MSS.

72. *Three Diaries*, p. 12, n. 1.

73. Le Marchant, *Althorp*, pp. 294–5 (Grey, Melbourne). Grey thought the French electorate during the Orleans monarchy too small in proportion to the population.

74. *Politics in the Age of Peel* (1953), ch. 3.

75. Russell to Durham, 13 Feb.; F. T. Baring, *Journals*, i.83n.

76. For deference of lower classes see *Examiner*, 13 Sept. 1829; *Morning Chronicle*, 16 Oct. 1829. For 1780 proposal of equal electoral districts see John Cannon, *Parliamentary Reform, 1640–1832* (1973), p. 82.

77. *Parl. Deb.*, xii.580 (Stanley).

78. Most politicians agreed that the people should not be confused with the populace. The reformers protested that they kept the distinction between the two categories in mind and deferred only to the people; their opponents rebutted these claims. See *Parl. Deb.*, ii.1143 (Althorp), iii.1774 and v.114–15 (Peel), vii.228 (Bunbury), viii.251 (Brougham), viii.323 (Grey), xi.479–80, defective pagination (Croker); *The Times*, 17 Aug. 1830 (Brougham's election dinner speech at York); *Manchester Guardian*, 13 Nov. 1830. Sandon, writing to Stanley on 16 Oct. 1831, referred to the difficulty of agreeing 'as to what shall be called the people': Harrowby MSS, xix, f. 342. For a contemporary analysis see G. C. Lewis, *Political Terms* (1832), p. 150; for a modern analysis C. S. Emden, *The People and the Constitution* (2nd ed., 1956), app. 1. The restrictive use of 'the people' was not universal at the time of the Bill. In the quotation from Thomas Attwood on p. 133 the phrase is used to include the working class.

79. *Lieven–Grey Corresp.*, ii.189. See also Grey, 3 Oct. 1831: *Parl. Deb.*, vii.955.

80. 24 Mar. 1832.

81. *Liverpool Mercury*, 27 May 1831 (John Gladstone).

82. *Parl. Deb.*, ix.420.

83. Smith, *Works*, p. 570. See also *Parl. Deb.*, iv.780–1 (Macaulay), xxiv.569, xxxix.69 (Russell). The problem is discussed in J. Milton-Smith's article, *Hist. Journal*, xv (1972), 72–4.

84. See *Parl. Deb.*, viii.105 (Carnarvon), xi.415–16 (Mahon), 775–6 (Stanley), xiv.875 (Peel). Lord Salisbury is reported by Littleton in Nov. 1831 as having declared that 'the moment the Bill passed he would . . . sell as much of his property as he could, invest it in foreign funds . . . ' (*Three Diaries*, p. 159). In June 1831 Southey reported that Wordsworth had 'invested all the money he could command in the American funds' (*Selections from Letters of R. Southey*, Ed. J. W. Warter (1856), iv.225). Lord Hertford made a large investment in USA at the same time; see Ch. 9, n. 25.

85. D. C. Moore, 'Concession or Cure: the Sociological Premises of the First Reform Act', *Hist. Journal*, ix (1966), 39–59. See also Professor Moore's articles in *Victorian Studies*, v (1961), 7–34; xiii (1969), 5–36; xiv (1971), 328–37—reply to Dr E. P. Hennock; *Ideas and Institutions of Victorian Britain*, Ed. R. Robson (1967), pp. 20–57. These articles are of great interest, though some of the views in them have been controverted.

86. G. Huxley, *Lady Elizabeth and the Grosvenors* (1965), p. 98.

87. J. A. Roebuck, when collecting materials for his *History of the Whig Ministry of 1830* (1852), could not understand the cabinet's boldness. See Parker, *Graham*, i.114–22.

88. Brougham, *Life and Times*, iii.53–4,92: for the errors in this work see A. Aspinall, *E.H.R.*, lix (1944), 87–112; *Parl. Deb.*, iii.991 (Wharncliffe), 1332 (Carnarvon), 1341 (Brougham—better reported in *Mirror of Parliament*, 1831, ii.1402), vii.784–6 (Brougham); Brougham to Graham, 1 Nov. 1830, in New,

Brougham to 1830, p. 413 (also printed, less accurately, in Parker, *Graham*, i.96); H. P. Brougham, *Speeches* (1838), ii.552–4. Contemporary statements about Brougham's plan (Greville, *Diary*, 22 May 1831; Broughton *Recollections* iv.214) need to be used carefully. Brougham announced the plan in his Yorkshire speeches. He put it into outline form at the end of Oct. He then extended it 'in several essential points' in response to Wellington's speech on 2 Nov. Remarks about the plan may be based on its features, actual or supposed, at any of these three stages.

89. See, for instance, Russell, *Parl. Deb.*, iv.341.

90. Howick's journal, 6 Nov. 1830: Grey MSS; *Parl. Deb.*, iii.1082. Althorp told his friends that office had strengthened his Reform convictions: A. to Milton, 28 Dec. 1830: Fitzwilliam MSS (Northants Record Office): Littleton to his wife: Hatherton MSS.

91. John to William Gladstone, 18 Mar. 1831: John Gladstone MSS. I would like to thank Sir William Gladstone, Bt., for helping me over this letter. On the background to it see S. G. Checkland, *The Gladstones* (1971), pp. 233–4. *Croker*, ii.80, gives the story of the pilots. The *Poll Book* for the election (Liverpool, J. Gore, 1830, p. lviii) puts the expenditure at £112,000–£115,000. Borough polling was limited to eight days under 9 Geo. IV c. 59.

92. *Parl. Deb.*, xii.696–7 (Radnor); A. Prentice, *Personal Recollections of Manchester, 1792–1832* (2nd ed., 1851), p. 369.

93. Petition given in *Votes and Proc.*, 1830–1, App. vol., pp. 340–1.

94. 1 Jan, 1831. The franchise at Preston was even wider than the potwalloper classification suggests: all inhabitants could vote.

95. See Russell's MS memo. endorsed 'Paper read with Lord Grey, Panshanger, Jan. 1831': P.R.O. 30/22/1B, ff. 257–8. For Althorp's part see Littleton's diary, 29 June 1831: Hatherton MSS.

96. Durham MSS. This letter is printed with omissions in J. R. M. Butler, *The Passing of the Great Reform Bill* (1914), p. 179.

97. Spencer Walpole, *Life of Lord John Russell* (1889), i.285. See also Brougham to Ld. Granton (Feb. 1845): Brougham–Granton MSS.

98. G. M. Trevelyan, *Grey*, (1920) p. 237n.

99. For this viewpoint see Holland to his son, Henry, 5 Nov. 1830: Add. MSS, 51, 751, ff. 46–7.

100. G. Pellew, *Sidmouth* (1847) iii.439n.

101. See, for instance, Robert Lowery, anon. articles in *Weekly Record*, no. 8, p. 69, 24 May 1856; no. 43, p. 34, 24 Jan. 1857.

102. *Wm. IV–Grey Corresp.* i.52,92,118.

103. Howick to his brother Charles Grey, 31 Jan.: Grey MSS.

104. *Creevey Papers*, Ed. Sir H. Maxwell (3rd ed. 1905), p. 558.

105. 1 Mar.: Anglesey MSS (Belfast), T1068/30.

106. *Croker*, ii.108.

107. Grey told colleagues the same; Holland's diary, 6 Mar. 1832: Add. MSS, 51, 868, f. 389. Grey had not been quite so truthful as a young politician: see Trevelyan, *Grey*, pp. 18–23.

108. As a *Quarterly* reviewer remarked in Jan. 1832: xlvi.553.

109. For Grey's ignorance of the Commons see Broughton, *Recollections*, iv.287.

110. A. Aspinall, 'The Cabinet Council, 1783–1835,' *Proc. Brit. Acad.*, xxxviii (1952), 187.

111. Lord David Cecil, *Lord M.* (1954), p. 192.

112. Littleton's note on letter of 1 Jan. 1831 to him from Althorp: Hatherton MSS.

113. See Sir J. MacDonald to Lansdowne, 17 Jan. (1831): Lansdowne MSS.

114. 500,000 was Russell's estimate on 1 Mar. As there was no registration system (outside Ireland) before 1832, pre-Reform electoral figures are liable to error. John Cannon, *Parliamentary Reform, 1640–1832* (1973), p. 259 and app. 4, argues convincingly that the long-accepted figure of 300,000 for the total increase over the three countries is too low.

115. Grey admitted in the Lords that Schedule B was 'the weakest part of the measure': *Parl. Deb.*, viii.326.

116. The committee recommended extending the vote to all £20 householders 'within the town or borough and parish': *Wm. IV–Grey Corresp.*, i.462. See also Lansdowne to Grey, 18 Jan.: Grey MSS.

117. *Parl. Papers*, 1831–2, xxxvii.2.

118. Bowood Liberty, which had a population of 63 in 1821, caused the discrepancy between the 'borough and parish' figure and that for the entire parish: *Parl. Papers*, 1822, xv.356.

119. ibid., 1830–1, x.63.

120. The Calne corporators showed some independence but Lansdowne defeated challenges to his authority in 1826 and 1830. For the attempt in 1830 to open the borough, and the petition, see *Votes and Proc.*, 1830–1, App. vol., pp. 4–5; *Parl. Papers*, 1831–2, xxxvi.507.

121. *Parl. Deb.*, xiii.514-7 (Croker).

122. Lonsdale MSS.

123. See Croker to Hertford, 8 Mar.: Croker MSS, letter book 25, pp. 241–2; Greville, *Diary*, 13 Dec. 1831.

124. Stanhope, *Conversations with the Duke of Wellington*, p. 30; Buckingham, *Courts and Cabinets of Wm. IV and Victoria*, i.240; *W.N.D.*, vii.409: see also *W.N.D.*, viii.293. In G. R. Gleig, *Personal Reminiscences of the Duke of Wellington*, Ed. M. E. Gleig (1904), p. 53, the duke is said to have wanted to refuse leave to introduce the Bill. The date of Wellington's remark to this effect to Gleig is uncertain, however, whereas the statement and letters cited above originated soon after the event. They must be preferred to Gleig's evidence. According to the *Courier*, 28 Feb. 1831, Wellington proposed to the meeting 'that the Bill should be met by a direct negative', but deferred to Peel and others who planned to reserve opposition 'for the details of the Bill'.

125. *Parl. Deb.*, ii.1344.

126. William George Adam, K.C., and Henry Stephenson. Both had been briefed to appear before the Lords by the petitioners against the East Retford disfranchisement. Le Marchant's opinion of them is in *Three Diaries*, p. 14.

127. Lowther to Lonsdale, 28 Feb. (Lonsdale MSS) bears signs of inside knowledge. But when he wrote it Lowther had no idea how extensive disfranchisement would be. He predicted 'the abolition of 10 or 12 boroughs', and that 'one Member will be taken from about 40 more'. He was near the mark on Schedule B, but not on Schedule A.

128. Brougham, *Life and Times*, iii.102–3; Broughton, *Recollections*, iv.93.

129. As on emancipation in 1829, the less popular side impugned the validity of some of the signatures collected by their opponents: *Parl. Deb.*, ii.997 (Dundas).

130. Le Marchant, *Althorp*, p. 297.

Chapter 5. *The Bill in the Commons (I): A dreadful race*

1. Le Marchant, *Althorp*, p. 299 (f.n. by Ld. Lyttelton).

2. See Greville, *Diary*, 13 Dec. 1831, 22 Nov. 1842; *Parl. Deb.*, viii.460, ix.177–9. Russell was moving for leave to bring in the Bill. The debate ended on 9 Mar. when leave was given without a division.

3. On this point see Goulburn to his wife, 2 Mar.: Goulburn MSS, iii.9.

4. J. A. Roebuck, *History of the Whig Ministry of 1830* (1852), ii.87–8n. H. P. Brougham, *Life and Times* (1871), iii.105–6, gives a rather different version. Roebuck had his information from Brougham.

5. Grey had expected a majority of 70 (see p. 154) even if the Bill had been opposed on 1 Mar.: G. to Anglesey, 1 Mar.: Anglesey MSS (Belfast), T1068/30.

6. Compare Broughton, *Recollections*, iv.87, with Le Marchant, *Althorp*, p. 298.

7. Broughton, *Recollections*, iv.88: *Lieven–Grey Correspondence*, ii.178n.

8. Grey MSS. For the discussions with Palmerston just before 1 Mar. see J. Milton-Smith, 'Grey's Cabinet and the Objects of Parliamentary Reform', *Hist. Journal*, xv (1972), 67, citing Palmerston MSS (Broadlands).

9. Le Marchant, *Althorp*, p. 301.

10. See Graham Wallas, *Place* (1898). Place was an assiduous archivist: the abundance of material on his doings makes it easy for the historian to exaggerate his importance. For a recent regional study on the political importance of the shopkeepers see T. J. Nossiter, 'Shopkeeper Radicalism in the Nineteenth Century', in *Imagination and Precision in the Social Sciences*, Ed. T. J. Nossiter, A. H. Hanson and Stein Rokkan (1972).

11. *London Radicalism, 1830–43*, Ed. D. J. Rowe (London Record Soc., v, 1970), pp. 13–14.

12. Brougham, *Life and Times*, iii.92.

13. For a radical who objected to omission of ballot see the account of the Leeds meeting, 10 Mar., in A. S. Turberville, *Thoresby Soc. Miscellany*, xli (1943), 35.

14. See C. T. Flick, 'Class character of the Agitation for . . . Reform', *South Atlantic Quarterly*, lxviii (1969), 48.

15. *Parl. Deb.*, iii.181.

16. For petitions in favour of the Bill from outvoters who would lose their votes by it see *Votes and Proc.*, 1830–1, App. vol., pp. 827–8, 910, 1163–4. For views in Steyning (Schedule A) see *Parl. Deb.* v.373.

17. The usual estimate for the borough electorate of England and Wales in 1831 is 188,391: C. Seymour, *Electoral Reform in England and Wales, 1832–1885* (1915), p. 533. J. Cannon (see Ch. 4, n. 114) reduces this to 164,000. The ancient

right voters were put at 108,219 in 1833. This latter figure is not accurate, however. In some boroughs no figure is available for ancient right voters until 1836.
See *Parl. Papers*, 1833, xxvii.21–249,1837–8, xliv. 553–858, 1866,lvii. 235n, 242.

18. *Works* (1850), p. 559. Quoted in *The Times*, 7 Apr. 1831. For Wellington's
defence of the system in this aspect see *W.N.D.*, viii.18.

19. See, for instance, the clash between Smithson and Mann in the Leeds
meeting of 10 Mar.: A. S. Turberville, 'Leeds and Parliamentary Reform,
1820–32', *Thoresby Soc. Miscellany*, xli (1943), 35–6. For a later appraisal see
Parl. Papers, Handloom Weavers' Petitions: Sel. Cttee. Rep., p. 181, Q. 2569–71;
1835 (341), xiii.203.

20. *An address to the Working Classes* . . . (Oct. 1831), pp. 10–11. For Carpenter
see *D.N.B.*, P. Hollis, *The Pauper Press* (1970), pp. 308–9, and E. P. Thompson,
The Making of the English Working Class (1963), p. 812. The pamphlet was much
praised in the 'respectable' Reform press. See *Morning Chronicle*, 2 Dec. 1831.
Doherty took the same line: see *Voice of the People*, 18 June 1831 (reporting D.'s
speech, 13 June). For retrospective comments on this view see *Weekly True Sun*,
11 June 1837 (I am indebted to Mr John Lello for drawing my attention to this
passage) and *Parl. Deb.*, clii.1015 (W. J. Fox, 28 Feb. 1859).

21. Althorp to Graham, n.d. [early 1833]: Graham MSS.

22. For rules of N.U.W.C. see *London Radicalism*, pp. 29–33.

23. Thompson, *Making of the English Working Class*, p. 778.

24. Even the *Poor Man's Guardian* spoke favourably of the Bill on 26 May
1832. A report to the Home Office, 27 Oct. 1831, put its circulation at 2200 per
week: H.O. 64, 11.

25. 18 Mar.

26. *The Times*, 8 Apr.

27. *Journals and Correspondence of F. T. Baring*, Ed. Lord Northbrook (1905),
i.83–4.

28. Croker MSS (Ann Arbor), letter book 25, p. 258.

29. Hickleton MSS, A.2.34. It was hard to persuade magnates to move quickly
enough. See, for instance, Cockburn to Sir T. Dick-Lauder, 7 Mar.: 'a good
meeting today is better than a better one tomorrow': *Some Letters of Lord Cockburn*, Ed. H. A. Cockburn (1932), p. 31.

30. Lonsdale MSS.

31. When the king agreed to dissolve, Lyndhurst is said to have commented:
'All is now lost', W. McC. Torrens, *Melbourne* (1878), i.369. But see Croker's
remark in n. 71 below.

32. *Three Diaries*, p. 14 (Le Marchant).

33. See Stanley to Anglesey, 12 Mar.: Derby MSS (letter books).

34. *Parl. Deb.*, iii.367–72,455–68,540.

35. See Goulburn to his wife, 19 Mar.: Goulburn MSS, iii.9.

36. The Canadian timber trade was particularly important to the Atlantic
shipping interest in that the older ships were used in it. For the budget proposals
see Lucy Brown, *The Board of Trade and the Free-Trade Movement 1830–42* (1958),
pp. 46–50.

37. Royal Archives, Windsor Castle. The name is left blank in *Wm. IV–Grey
Corresp.*, i.169. Brudenell succeeded as Earl of Cardigan in 1837 and is best known
as the commander of the Light Brigade during the charge at Balaclava.

38. Christopher North, in *Noctes Ambrosianae*, says, 'I now almost begin to blame myself for the hand I had in turning out their (the cabinet's) predecessors': *Blackwood's*, xxx (Aug. 1831), 416.

39. Knatchbull was taken ill a few hours before the debate began. He missed the division, being paired against an absent reformer. Strictly, Vyvyan moved that the Bill be read 'this day six months'.

40. See F. T. Baring, *Journals*, i.84.

41. Sir G. O. Trevelyan, *Life and Letters of Lord Macaulay*: Macaulay to Ellis 30 Mar. (1908 ed., p. 147).

42. C. W. New, *Durham* (1929), p. 139.

43. See Goulburn to his wife [23 Mar.]: Goulburn MSS iii.8.2.

44. See T. M'Crie, *Agnew* (1850), pp. 103–12.

45. *Coventry Herald and Observer*, 29 Apr.

46. G. Woodbridge, *Reform Bill of 1832* (New York, 1970), p. 84.

47. Croker to Hertford, 24 Mar.: Croker MSS (Ann Arbor), letter book 25, p. 297.

48. See also Abercromby to Lansdowne [10 Mar.]: Lansdowne MSS.

49. *Parl. Deb.*, vii.959–61 (Grey). Russell gave a slightly different figure: iii.1511–12. For Peel's speech, *Parl. Deb.*, N.S., xx.739–40.

50. To Henry Wynn, 25 Mar.: Wynn MSS.

51. Diary, 26 Dec. 1909: Marquess of Lincolnshire's MSS.

52. Devonshire's diary: Devonshire MSS. Text in *Derby and Chesterfield Reporter*, 24 Mar., is nearly the same. See also *Parl. Deb.*, v.113 (Althorp).

53. See Grey to Lansdowne, 24 Mar.: Lansdowne MSS.

54. *Creevey Papers*, Ed. Sir H. Maxwell (3rd ed., 1905), p. 567.

55. For Wharncliffe's first reactions to the Bill see *The First Lady Wharncliffe and Her Family*, Ed. C. Grosvenor and Lord Stuart of Wortley (1927), ii.61–4.

56. *Parl. Deb.*, iii.993, 1008.

57. *Parl. Deb.*, iii.1173.

58. See Lansdowne to Russell, n.d.: Add. MSS, 38, 380, ff. 50–2.

59. *Parl. Deb.*, iii.1274–5,1517.

60. See memorial in *Parl. Papers*, 1830–1, x.135–6. Census of 1821 gave 'Truro, St Mary's, borough and parish' as having a population of 2,712. According to the f.n., 'the town of Truro . . . is said to be nearly three times as populous as the borough': ibid., 1822, xv.39.

61. *Parl. Deb.*, v.481.

62. See Palmerston's undated letter to Lansdowne in P. Guedalla, *Palmerston* (1926), p. 159; H. C. Bell, *Journal of Mod. Hist.*, iv (1932), 188–9; W. Whewell to Palmerston, 20 Mar.: Palmerston MSS.

63. Palmerston to Grey, 8 Apr.: see also Durham to Grey, 'Saturday night' [9 Apr.]: both Grey MSS.

64. Russell's memo, 4 Apr.: Russell MSS, P.R.O. 30/22/1b, ff. 27–37.

65. Broughton, *Recollections*, iv.99.

66. For planning of the amendment, ibid., iv.101.

67. For a whig's comment see *Life of Lord Campbell*, Ed. Mrs M. S. Hardcastle (1881), i.511.

68. Sir Robert Wilson, one of the Members for Southwark, was in this position. When he learned that the cabinet would not accept defeat he abstained: *Parl.*

Deb., iii.1637–41. He had apparently been told by Ellice that the question would not be made one of confidence; Wilson to Durham, 28 July 1831: Durham MSS.

69. *Manchester Guardian*, 9 Apr. Compare reports of Hunt's remarks in Commons on 11 Mar. and on 12 Apr.: *Parl. Deb.*, iii.373,1245–6.

70. *Croker*, ii.114–15.

71. The beliefs (which Peel seems to have held) that, if Gascoyne won, the cabinet would try to dissolve, and that an election would produce a majority for the Bill, were not universal among the opposition leaders. Croker wrote on 19 Apr. that the ministers would accept defeat from Gascoyne, and reported on 22 Apr. that, according to rumour, they would not gain in an election: *Croker*, ii.115; Croker MSS, letter book 25, p. 384.

72. Holmes predicted an opposition majority of eight during the debate: Lord John Russell, *Recollections and Suggestions* (1875), p. 74.

73. Croker to Hertford, 20 Apr.: Croker MSS (Ann Arbor), letter book 25, p. 377.

74. For Stanley's denial of a compromise with O'Connell see *Parl. Deb.*, iii.690.

75. Grey MSS. O'Connell had been allowed to alter his plea on condition that he did not move for an arrest of judgment if convicted.

76. To Anglesey: Derby MSS (letter books).

77. J. R. M. Butler says (*The Passing of Great Reform Bill*, 1914, p. 212) on the authority of C. S. Parker, *Graham* (1907), i.109–10, that the decision was taken 'apparently against the advice of Brougham and Russell'. The Russell letter cited by Parker was written in Mar., however, and establishes merely that Russell was willing, in the last resort, to maintain the numbers of the House. The Brougham letter cited is undated. Neither letter provides convincing evidence that Brougham and Russell were willing to accept an amendment which entailed either increasing the total numbers or abandoning the increases for Scotland and Ireland. Melbourne appears to have spoken last, and decisively, in favour of dissolution: see A. Aspinall, *Proc. Brit. Acad.*, xxxviii (1952), 193, n. 2.

78. Devonshire's diary, 21 Apr.: Devonshire MSS.

79. The king's account of his reasons, in a memo. dated 14 Jan. 1835, is in Baron von Stockmar, *Memoirs* (1872, Ed. F. Max Müller), i.317–19.

80. *Letters of Harriet Countess Granville*, Ed. F. Leveson Gower (1894), ii.97.

81. Brougham, *Life and Times*, iii.114–15. See also Holland, diary, 31 Aug. 1831, Add. MSS 51, 867, f. 115.

82. Roebuck, *History of the Whig Ministry*, ii.151. Roebuck had his information from Brougham. The version in Brougham, *Life and Times*, iii.116, is slightly different. See also (Emma Sophia) Countess Brownlow, *Eve of Victorianism* (1940), p. 148.

83. Broughton, *Recollections*, iv.108.

84. H. Martineau, *History of England, 1816–46* (1850), ii.35. Harriet Martineau achieved success as an author early in 1832 and came to know several leading whig and radical politicians.

85. Hon. Mrs (Louisa Honoria) Cadogan to Scott, 25 Apr.: *Private Letter-Books of Sir Walter Scott*, Ed. W. Partington (1930), p. 46; *Creevey Papers*, pp. 570–1; R. H. Gronow, *Reminiscences and Recollections* (1889), i.288. See also Littleton, diary, 1 Dec. 1831: Hatherton MSS; Lord Albemarle, *Fifty Years of*

My Life (1876), ii.292–3. The author's father had been Master of the Horse in 1831.

86. *Mirror of Parliament* (1831), ii.1639.

Chapter 6. The Bill in the Commons (II): The reformers' high tide

1. *Private Letter-Books of Sir Walter Scott,* Ed. W. Partington (1930), p. 46.

2. 23 Apr.

3. Kenyon MSS.

4. To Ewart, 27 Apr.: Derby MSS (letter books).

5. To Cartwright, 25 Apr. Cartwright read out part of the letter in an election speech: *Northampton Mercury,* 14 May.

6. W. McC. Torrens, *Graham* (1863), i.375–6.

7. Robert Palmer (Berks) and John Wilson-Patten (Lancs) were rejected for supporting Gascoyne, though they had voted for the second reading.

8. For later reports showing this see (Cumberland election) *Carlisle Journal,* 7 May, speeches of Visc. Lowther and E. Stanley; (Westmorland election) *Westmorland Advertiser,* 14 May, speeches of John Hill and Col. H. C. Lowther.

9. *The Times,* 30 Apr. The reports had appeared in the local press several days earlier: *Kentish Chronicle,* 27 Apr., *Kent Herald,* 28 Apr.

10. Bristol was the only city to produce a notable anti-Reform petition before the Bill was introduced: *Parl. Deb.,* ii.996–7.

11. One Member for Bucks, Huntingdonshire, Monmouthshire, and Westmorland: both for Shropshire. For Bucks see R. W. Davis, *Political Change and Continuity, 1760–1885* (1972), pp. 92–8.

12. Cleveland to Ellice, 'Sunday night' (24 Apr.), offering £10,000 and stating C.'s '*extreme anxiety* to secure a place' for Hope-Vere: Ellice MSS, E. 56, f. 47.

13. Some rioting affected results, however. After a riot at Rye the patron was prevailed on to compromise and allow the return of one reformer: *The Times,* 2 May.

14. He seems to have exposed himself to danger imprudently: Lord Cockburn, *Journal* (1874), i.14.

15. Stamford, where the Exeter interest were accused of strong-arm methods, may have been an exception to this.

16. For this shortage see *The Times,* 30 Apr.; Devonshire to Lady Granville, 1 May: Devonshire MSS.

17. Advert. in *The Times,* 27 Apr. Maria Edgeworth thought ill of the play: *Letters from England, 1813–44,* Ed. C. Colvin (1971), p. 540.

18. For Grey's rejoinder see *Parl. Deb.,* xii.14.

19. To Harrowby, 13 May: Harrowby MSS, lxiii, f. 119.

20. Ellenborough told the Lords in Apr. 1832 that none of the new Reform Members 'selected by the people' in the election had shown 'even ordinary ability': *Parl. Deb.,* xii.34. For Long-Wellesley, see Countess of Longford, *Wellington: Pillar of State* (1972), pp. 250–7.

21. Deputies' letter book, 1826–34, pp. 229–38; minute book, viii.33–7,46–7: Corporation of London, Guildhall Library, MSS 3085, 3083/8. See also B. L.

Manning, *The Protestant Dissenting Deputies*, Ed. O. Greenwood (1952), p. 474.
I am grateful to Dr K. R. M. Short for drawing my attention to this episode.

22. See N. Gash, *Politics in the Age of Peel* (1953), 302-4.

23. Wilberforce had been supported in the 1807 Yorkshire election by a nation-wide subscription. But this related to a single contest, and was for a cause regarded as humanitarian rather than strictly political.

24. At Bristol the Reform committee, 'unable to effect a coalition between the Reform candidates, . . . appealed to the electors to sign a declaration that they would not vote for any candidate who would not pledge himself to support the Bill': *The Times*, 2 May. This committee, which consisted largely of Bristol's leading middle-class reformers, operated throughout 1831 and 1832. It was less suspect than a political union among people of property. But relations between the committee and the Bristol Political Union (formed in June 1831) were gener-ally good. I am grateful to Mr A. P. Hart for information on Bristol politics.

25. *The Times*, 31 May. This was additional to £15,000 subscribed through Brooks's Club soon after the dissolution. The committee for the fund helped Reform candidates in twenty contests. See also Broughton, *Recollections,* iv.109; *Sun*, 28 Apr. The fund may have been less important than the reformers' ability to switch money collected for one contest, and not needed there, to another. On this see Lowther to Croker, 12 May: Croker MSS (Ann Arbor).

26. *The Times*, 3 May (Shaftesbury); Ellice to Stanley, 11 May: Derby MSS (Dorset).

27. 6 May.

28. 'The Patriot King to His People': copy in Bedford MSS. Richard Ryder (for whose fears see n. 19 above) conceded in the same letter that some of the new Reform MPs were 'men of character and respectability, and, with the exception of pledging themselves to the Bill, not inclined to promote revolutionary measures'.

29. D. C. Moore in *Ideas and Institutions of Victorian Britain*, Ed. R. Robson (1967), p. 26. Professor Moore's chapter is important for any study of the use of influence in this election. For a criticism of it see John Cannon, *Parliamentary Reform, 1640-1832* (1973), pp. 246-50.

30. John Gladstone MSS (Hawarden).

31. G. M. Trevelyan, *Grey* (1920), p. 301.

32. J. R. M. Butler, *The Passing of the Great Reform Bill* (1914), p. 229. See also J. Hume to Graham, 7 June: Graham MSS; Abercromby to Lansdowne, post-mark 8 June: Lansdowne MSS.

33. See on this point Melbourne, 4 Oct. 1831: *Parl. Deb.*, vii.1179-80.

34. ibid., iv.890.

35. ibid., ii.1344.

36. For some of the wilder predictions, ibid., vii.1197-1204 (Wellington); *W.N.D.*, viii.110.

37. *Parl. Deb.*, ii. 1353.

38. ibid., xiv.875. Butler comments that the anti-reformers, could they have surveyed the modern scene, would have hailed some 'changes as a dire fulfilment of their forebodings'; but 'they must surely have been also surprised at the essential sameness of English politics and the acquiescence of the people in the alternate rule of the old aristocratic parties. They had not foreseen the development of the

Caucus, the inevitable parasite which feeds on democracy and saps its strength'
(*Great Reform Bill*, p. 258). These remarks appeared in 1914, when M. Ostro-
gorski's *Democracy and the Organization of Political Parties* (1902) was the leading
authority, and soon after the publication of *The Party System* (1911) by Hilaire
Belloc and Cecil Chesterton.

39. Lowther wrote in Dec. 1831 that mechanics' institutes and newsrooms produced 'the greatest mass of *floating* discontent that pervades this country and
France': quoted in A. Aspinall, *Politics and the Press* (1949), p. 12.

40. See Lord John Russell, *Memoirs of the Affairs of Europe from the Peace of
Utrecht*, i (1824), 70–1. I am very grateful to Mr John Prest for allowing me to see
his biography of Russell while it was in typescript.

41. It was not perhaps a coincidence that the only member of the cabinet to
develop doubts in the crisis of May 1832 was Richmond, its one ultra tory. He
dissented from the peer-making recommendation of 8 May.

42. *Lord Melbourne's Papers*, Ed. Lloyd C. Sanders (1889), pp. 95, 101. See also
Melbourne to Anglesey, 8 Apr. 1833, 'change is of itself a great danger and a
great evil': Anglesey MSS (Belfast). Hartington expressed similar views in the
1880s: B. Holland, *Duke of Devonshire* (1911), ii.72.

43. *Girlhood of Queen Victoria* (diaries, Ed. Lord Esher, 1912), ii.178. See also
journal of Visc. Howick, 30 Jan. 1836: Grey MSS.

44. *The Times*, 21 May. Peel told Goulburn (24 May) that the reporter 'was
either sent from the political union of Birmingham or is connected with that
society'.

45. See Goulburn to Peel, undated and 2 June: Add. MSS, 40, 333, ff. 115–16;
Peel to Goulburn 24 May, 5 June: Goulburn MSS, ii,18. 5 June letter printed in
part in Parker, *Peel*, ii.187–8 and 170–1. The 'letter' on pp. 170–1 is, in fact, the
second half of the one on pp. 187–8. For press comment see, as an instance,
Liverpool Mercury, 27 May, 'Peel will not only let it (the Bill) pass, but will
commend its passing'.

46. See Harrowby, 4 Oct.: 'the ministers have done what no ministers ever
ought to do: they have brought forward a measure which it may be almost
equally dangerous to adopt or to reject': *Parl. Deb.*, vii.1168.

47. Ellenborough diary, unpublished, 22 Mar.: P.R.O. 30/12/28/2.

48. *Parl. Deb.*, iv.892.

49. xxx.894. The remark about 'leading ministerial journals' and the violence
offered to anti-Reform candidates refers particularly to *The Times*, 30 Apr. 1831
(3rd leader)

50. *Parl. Deb.*, iv.221,223–5,368–71. The question was raised by Lord Stormont
on the Address (21 June). Despite Stanley's reply Lord Chandos asked for publication of the correspondence (27 June). Wetherell, supporting Chandos, said that
expiry of the statute was 'no excuse' for dropping the prosecution.

51. G. D. Ryder to Harrowby, 17 May 1831: Harrowby MSS, lxiii, f. 121;
Mrs Arbuthnot, ii.421. See also Lord Malmesbury, *Memoirs of an Ex-Minister*
(2nd ed., 1884); i.38; *Parl. Deb.*, iii.1320–1 (Buccleugh). The stories were not
confined to opposition circles: see 2nd Earl of Lytton, *Life of Edward Bulwer,
First Lord Lytton* (1913) i.409–10.

52. *Trans. Hon. Soc. of Cymmrodorion*, session 1965, pt. 2, p. 226. I am grateful
to Dr T. M. O. Charles-Edwards for drawing my attention to this.

53. *Three Diaries*, p. 109 (Ellenborough).

54. *Parl. Deb.*, iv.749 (Vernon).

55. Le Marchant, *Althorp*, p. 342.

56. ibid., p. 326. See A. D. Kriegel, 'Irish Policy of Lord Grey's Government', *E.H.R.*, lxxxvi (1971), 28, n. 6.

57. *The Times*, 9 May 1832. For earlier varieties of the same remark see Baines, as reported *Leeds Mercury*, 1 Oct. 1831; Macaulay, *Parl. Deb.*, ix.381–2.

58. Littleton, diary, 4 Aug.: Hatherton MSS.

59. Grey told Attwood on 30 June that the restriction would be abandoned. Attwood announced this to the Birmingham Political Union on 4 July. At the same time the qualifying period of occupation of 'the £10 house' was lengthened from six to twelve months.

60. *Parl. Deb.*, v.354.

61. *Recollections and Suggestions* (1875), p. 92. For accusations of gerrymandering see *Parl. Deb.*, vii.323–8 (Croker on counties selected for division), 338–48 (on Boundary Commissioners); ix.822–5 and Broughton, *Recollections*, iv.161 (division of Lincolnshire); xii.1378–90 and *Three Diaries*, p. 272 (Gateshead and Co. Durham); xiii.114–16 ('seven mile provision', cl. 27). Only one instance of a gerrymandering decision by the ministry is known to the author. It occurred in the Boundary Bill discussions. Littleton, chairman of the Boundary Commissioners, wanted to include Eton in Windsor Borough. Grey objected. 'The real cause of the objection', Littleton noted in his diary (29 Dec. 1831, Hatherton MSS), 'is with Mr Stanley, who very wisely suspects that the Eton parsons are not with the Government'. S. was one of the members for Windsor. For discussion of this in the Commons see *Parl. Deb.*, xiii.972,977.

62. E. Herries, *Memoir of J. C. Herries* (1880), ii.120–1. See also nn. 45 and 63. Peel's coldness to the ultra tories has been attributed by Prof. N. Gash partly to the fear that 'he and Wellington [might] be asked to form a ministry and pass a modified Reform act as the only way of unseating the whigs': *Sir Robert Peel, Life of Peel after 1830* (1972), p. 19. Peel's letters do not seem to provide conclusive support for this interpretation. Wellington reported a suggestion that a modified Reform should be sponsored from the opposition benches. Peel gave his reasons for rejecting this idea to the duke on 24 May, and to Goulburn on 5 June. He told them that the new House of Commons would not accept a small Reform. To Goulburn he added simply that he saw 'great embarrassment' in admitting the principle of a large Reform (Parker, *Peel*, ii.185–6,188). In a later passage of the same letter to Goulburn he wrote of his 'growing aversion' to office 'under any circumstances' (ibid., p. 170). It is hard to judge from these passages whether Peel's fears were as specific in May–June 1831 as Prof. Gash suggests.

63. See Peel to Goulburn cited in n. 45 above, and to Herries 2, 7 June (extracts in *Three Diaries*, p. xl). Peel did not attend the Pitt Dinner, 28 May.

64. J. J. Hope-Vere to J. P. Wood, 21 Apr. 1831 (Linlithgow MSS, Hope-Vere vol., ff. 258–9) gives a picture of Peel in the Gascoyne debate: 'the sight of him hushed the uproar in a moment and while he spoke the deepest silence prevailed, only interrupted by vehement cheering.'

65. Sir H. Maxwell, *Wellington* (1900), ii.257.

66. Le Marchant, *Althorp*, p. 400. Althorp is the subject of one of W. Bagehot's

Historical Essays. It was first published in the *Fortnightly Review*, Nov. 1876, and is in B.'s *Collected Works*, Ed. N. St John Stevas, iii (1968), pp. 200–31.

67. Althorp to Spencer, 17 Mar. 1832: Spencer MSS.

68. *Diary*, 5 Apr. 1843 (not precisely dated in Strachey & Fulford ed., 1938). Greville had the story from Arbuthnot who had been told by Althorp.

69. *Life of Lord Campbell*, Ed. Mrs M. S. Hardcastle (1881), i.483.

70. Wearing black was then unusual, except for a clergyman or during mourning. Althorp's wife had died in childbirth in 1818. Thereafter he wore black.

71. Greville, *Diary*, 21 Mar. 1829. In Ellenborough, *Political Diary*, i.406 the remark is attributed to Horace Twiss.

72. H. P. Brougham, *Life and Times*, iii.253–4. For Althorp's methods of preparation see Littleton, diary, 1 Dec. 1831. Hansard records Althorp as speaking 238 times in the Reform Bill debates. I am grateful to Mr K. Roberts for this figure.

73. Le Marchant, *Althorp*, p. 400. There are several versions of this story. See Lord John Russell, *Essay on the History of the English Government and Constitution*, introd., 1865 ed., p. xliv; Greville, *Diary*, 5 Apr. 1843; R. Whately, annotation to *Bacon's Essay on Praise* (6th ed., 1864), p. 562, where it is related in connexion with the Poor Law Amendment Bill.

74. *Parl. Papers*, 1830–1, x.53,100.

75. *Parl. Papers*, 1831–2, xxxvi.134; xxxvii.257–8.

76. Entry of 26 July: Hatherton MSS.

77. Greville, *Diary*, 14 Feb. 1841. See Graham to Grey, 17 June: Graham MSS. I am grateful to Prof. C. T. Flick for knowledge of this letter.

78. *Parl. Deb.*, v.1227.

79. See Peel to Goulburn, 17 Aug.: Goulburn MSS, ii,18.

80. Littleton, diary, 11 Aug. 1831; see also entries of 11, 24, 25 July 1831, 28 Jan. 1832: Hatherton MSS.

81. Prof. G. Woodbridge (*Reform Bill of 1832*, New York, 1970, p. 86) gives a table of ten English counties showing the approximate percentages of pre-1832 county voters who resided in what were to become new boroughs. The percentage is 45 for Yorkshire: elsewhere it does not rise above 15. This table is valuable in that it highlights the aspect of the borough freeholder question which engaged the most attention in 1830. But it leaves unresolved the still more complex problem of how Reform affected freeholders within existing boroughs (or within the area eventually included in these boroughs after their enlargement). Anything approaching a full tabulation of the change brought by the Act would be very difficult; and it would not reveal much about the hopes of the tory reformers.

82. Russell's speeches, 27 Jan., 1 Feb. 1832, contain the clearest ministerial statements to this effect: *Parl. Deb.*, ix.983–5,1134–6. Professor D. C. Moore has argued (*Hist. Journal*, ix.53) that the ministerial amendment to the town freeholder arrangements represented an effort to counteract the anticipated effects of the Chandos clause, and that Russell's arguments cited above reflect the ministers' reaction to Chandos rather than their original intent. In view of Holland's diary, 14 Aug., and of other evidence mentioned in the text, this theory is very hard to accept. It is, however, not a coincidence that Russell's point was put most clearly

late in the debates. In Aug. 1831 the ministers not only made an apparently 'anti-landlord' change on the town freeholder: they also acquired in the Chandos clause a powerful argument for having done so. After their defeat on the clause they were less inhibited about arguing that the landed interest must not be set up in isolation from, and opposition to, other interests. Littleton and Ebrington were active in deprecating any idea of confining freeholders to the boroughs; see Littleton's diary, 7 and 8 Dec. 1831, 29 Feb. 1832: Hatherton MSS.

83. 29 Dec.

84. 19 May.

85. D. C. Moore, *Victorian Studies*, v. 29, n. 53. See also *Blackwood's*, xxx.613.

86. *Parl. Deb.*, ix.1136. See n. 82 above. Althorp feared from an early stage that too much influence was being given to the landed interest; A. to Littleton, 1 Jan. 1831 (Hatherton MSS); to Milton, 6 Mar. 1831 (Fitzwilliam MSS, Northants); to Brougham, 17 Jan. 1841 (Spencer MSS).

87. To Henry Hobhouse, 15 July 1831: Add. MSS 40, 402, f. 98.

88. *Parl. Deb.*, iii.779, v. 580. Baring's view was later echoed by Wellington: ibid., vii.1194.

89. *Parl. Papers*, 1866, lvii.16–21 (giving total of 101,158), 207 (giving 91,974). The first total is to be preferred, being based on fuller returns. It may still be an underestimate, in that no returns were made for a few county divisions which had failed to differentiate borough freeholders from the rest. On the other hand, some freeholders with qualifying property in the part of the parish outside the borough concerned were included. This would do something to counteract the factor mentioned above. Copyholders and leaseholders in boroughs who did not qualify as borough voters were given county votes in the Act. In Aug. 1831 this privilege was confined to freeholders.

90. For this problem in general see E. P. Hennock and D. C. Moore, *Victorian Studies*, xiv.321–37. The discussion on the 1859 proposals is recorded in *Parl. Deb.*, clii.990–2 (Disraeli), cliii.390–3 (Russell).

91. See Praed's statement, 26 July, that ministers had transferred St Germans to Schedule A because they 'found it no longer necessary to conciliate the landed interest': *Parl. Deb.*, v.349.

92. *Mirror of Parliament* (1831) ii.1332 (13 Aug., Hughes Hughes). The *Mirror* reports are fuller than Hansard for an episode such as this.

93. *Parl. Deb.*, v.1316–19.

94. *Mirror* (1831), ii.1270 (Col. Davies).

95. Holland, diary, 14 Aug.: Add. MSS, 51, 867, ff. 79–80. 'Lansdowne, Palmerston and Richmond . . . had strong objections' to the change, Holland noted, 'founded on the apprehension of town votes overwhelming the land'. See also Lansdowne to Grey, 18 Jan. 1831: Grey MSS.

96. *Mirror* (1831), ii.1422.

97. ibid., 1488. Sibthorp said that he had given notice of the amendment 'so long back as the last Parliament' and had renewed the notice on 24 June.

98. Holland, diary, 14 Aug.: Add MSS, 51, 867, ff. 30–1.

99. C. A. W. Pelham, later 2nd Earl of Yarborough, publicly repented in 1838 of having voted for the amendment: *Parl. Deb.*, xliii.682.

100. See Graham to Abercromby, 6 Sept.: Graham MSS. On 19 Aug. Althorp had the clause extended to others than farmers: *Parl. Deb.*, vi.297–9.

101. *Three Diaries*, p. 122.

102. *Parl. Papers*, 1866, lvii.207.

103. For Russell's later views, see R. to Melbourne, 13 Aug. 1837: 'I reckoned that we gave seats enough to the landed interest in the counties to compensate for the close boroughs.... But we overdid it, owing chiefly to the Chandos clause': P.R.O. 30/22/2F, f. 9. I owe this reference to Dr I. D. C. Newbould. See also *Parl. Deb.*, xxxix.107 (Russell, 21 Nov. 1837); R's *Essay*, pp. liii–liv.

104. *Mirror* (1831), ii.1626.

105. ibid., 1694. Before the Bill became law the landed interest received one small concession. In the five English cities and towns which were counties of themselves where the freeholders already qualified for borough votes they were to continue to do so.

106. Peel's absence gave rise to the usual rumours; Hardinge to Peel, 12 Sept., and reply, 13 Sept.: Add. MSS, 40, 313, f. 159, and Hardinge MSS.

107. The opposition speaker, Scarlett, missed his cue on 19 Sept. As a result the debate and division were held, not on third reading, but on the motion that 'this Bill do pass'. For Bulwer's description of the final scene see *Lytton*, i.417–21.

108. 23 Sept.: Spencer MSS.

Chapter 7. The Bill in the Lords (I): The whisper of a faction

1. See Holland to Grey, 21 Apr., recommending 'one or two callings up forth-with' or even 'a batch of peers at once': Grey MSS.

2. To Stanley: Derby MSS.

3. On 27 May Rosslyn wrote to Wellington doubting the staunchness of the anti-reform peers in the face of government pressure: *W.N.D.*, vii.448–9.

4. Baronies of the United Kingdom went to seven holders of Scottish and Irish peerages and to nine commoners. One of the sixteen (Belhaven) was already a Scottish representative peer.

5. Marquess of Anglesey, *One Leg* (1961), p. 254; Grey to Anglesey, 3 Sept.: Anglesey MSS (Belfast) T1068/30; reply, 5 Sept.: Grey MSS.

6. Grey MSS. See also Grey to Stanley, 18 Sept.: Derby MSS.

7. O'Neill was an ultra tory and Grand Master of Orangemen who had been dismissed from the post of Irish Postmaster General by Wellington for various anti-Catholic indiscretions.

8. Littleton, diary, 15 July 1831: Hatherton MSS.

9. 6 Sept.: Devonshire MSS.

10. On 5 Feb. 1832 Holland noted the view, expressed in the cabinet, that the king's insistence on eldest sons might lose the ministry 'some votes' in the Lords: Add. MSS, 51, 868, f. 327.

11. They had enough by-election trouble already. In the week 17 to 24 Oct. the anti-Reform candidates won in Dorset and Pembrokeshire, and Harrowby's eldest son, Visc. Sandon, defeated a thorough-going reformer at Liverpool. Sandon was a reformer; but 'he always', according to Althorp, 'tried to steer a middle course and was full of crotchets': Littleton, diary, 12 Dec. 1831: Hatherton MSS.

12. Holland, diary, 5 Sept., Add. MSS, 51, 867, ff. 121–6, gives a full account.

13. Sir G. O. Trevelyan, *Life and Letters of Lord Macaulay* (1908 ed.), p. 178.

14. A tactical resignation was mentioned privately by Althorp on 7 Oct. He told Baring that the government's best course would have been to 'resign, show the tories that they cannot form a government, come in and carry the Bill'. Althorp knew by 7 Oct. that the government would be 'beat to hell' in the Lords, and that the opposition's majority would be 'about 40'. His remark was thus made in the light of a last-minute realization that this majority would be too large to be erased by peermaking. Significantly, even when Althorp stated the stark facts, Baring was doubtful about the tactic of resignation. 'Are you . . . sure that you will come back?' he asked: *Journals and Correspondence of F. T. Baring*, Ed. Lord Northbrook (1905) i.99. Brougham's view resembled Baring's. He thought that the opposition might be able to form a ministry 'at the close of the session': Holland, diary, 8 Oct., Add. MSS, 51, 867, ff. 174–5. For the feeling against tactical resignation see *Parl. Deb.*, xii.934 (Sugden).

15. Grey MSS.

16. H. Grote, *Personal Life of G. Grote* (1873), p. 68.

17. *W.N.D.*, vii.493. Radnor is named as an objector, Tavistock and Titchfield as the eldest sons who have refused (latter misprinted as Lichfield in Duke of Buckingham, *Courts and Cabinets of William IV and Victoria* (1861), i.341–2); *Blackwood's* xxx (Sept. 1831), 555.

18. *W.N.D.*, vii.531.

19. ibid., 563.

20. *Works* (1850), p. 564.

21. *Lord Melbourne's Papers*, Ed. Lloyd C. Sanders (1889), p. 130.

22. *Three Diaries*, p. 132 (Ellenborough); Broughton, *Recollections*, iv.131; *Correspondence of Charles Arbuthnot*, Ed. A. Aspinall (1941), p. 147; *Parl. Deb.*, vii.980–1,1320–1.

23. xxx.413. The writer expected Grey to resign after defeat on second reading in the Lords.

24. *Parl. Deb.*, vii.1157 (4 Oct.).

25. *Three Diaries*, p. 132 (Ellenborough).

26. See C. Greville to R. Sneyd, 11 Oct.: Sneyd MSS.

27. *Corresp. of Charles Arbuthnot*, p. 146. For the bishops' general attitude to the Bill see E. Hughes, *E.H.R.*, lvi (1941), 459–90; W. G. Simon, *Hist. Magazine of the Protestant Episcopal Church*, xxxii (1963), 361–70.

28. *Diary*, 20 Jan. 1832.

29. To R. Sneyd, 'Saturday' [8 October]: Sneyd MSS.

30. Wellington MSS.

31. *Lieven–Grey Correspondence*, Ed. G. Le Strange (1890), ii.284.

32. *W.N.D.*, vii.559.

33. *Parl. Deb.*, vii.1309–10.

34. M. Van Buren, *Autobiography*, Ed. J. C. Fitzpatrick (Washington, 1920), p. 483; Countess Bathurst to R. Sneyd, 'Saturday' [8 Oct.[: Sneyd MSS; Sir H. Maxwell, *Clarendon* (1913), i.65. Van Buren had arrived in London as American Minister designate in Sept. 1831. He was President of the United States, 1837–41.

35. 1st Earl of Dudley's *Letters to 'Ivy'*, Ed. S. H. Romilly (1905), p. 375; *Three Diaries*, p. 144 (Ellenborough).

36. W. E. Gladstone, then at Oxford, attended each night. See *Gladstone Diaries*, Ed. M. R. D. Foot, i (1968), 385–7. The reformers claimed, with much exaggeration, a large majority for the Bill among the peers of older creation. For the facts see Gerda C. Richards, *Am. Hist. Rev.*, xxxiv (1928), 53. The 'not contents' were strongest among the bishops and the Scottish and Irish representative peers. Those sitting solely as representative peers cast 26 votes against the Bill and 7 for it.

37. *Parl. Deb.*, viii.461.

38. 8 Oct., Grote to Parkes: *Posthumous Papers of George Grote*, Ed. H. Grote (privately printed, 1874), p. 40.

39. Le Marchant, *Althorp*, p. 354.

40. The motion had been accepted by a meeting of nearly 200 reformers on 8 Oct.: Holland, diary, 8 Oct., Add. MSS, 51, 867, f. 176.

41. *Parl. Deb.*, viii.460. For Palmerston's objections see P. to Grey, 9, 10 Oct.: Grey MSS; Grey to P. (1) 10 Oct.: *Wm. IV–Grey Corresp.*, i.375–8, P.'s name witheld by editor (2) 14 Oct.: Grey MSS (copy); Durham to Grey, 'Tuesday' [11 Oct.]: Grey MSS, quotations in S. J. Reid, *Durham* (1906), i.269, C. W. New, *Durham* (1929), p. 153. For cabinet approval of statements, Holland, diary, 8 Oct., Add. MSS, 51, 867, ff. 179, 186–7.

42. Littleton's diary, 13 Feb. 1832: Hatherton MSS; the wording is different in Parker, *Peel*, ii.199. See also *W.N.D.*, viii.258 (Newcastle to Harrowby, 22 Feb. 1832); on Wharncliffe, Holland, diary, 8 Oct., Add. MSS, 51, 867, f. 181.

43. *Croker*, ii.115. See Ch. 5, n. 70.

44. Derby MSS. This correspondence survives in both Derby and Harrowby MSS.

45. Peel to Aberdeen, 14 Oct.: Add. MSS, 43, 061, ff. 138–40. An opposition role was not thought suitable for a bishop; see Holland, diary, Add. MSS, 51, 868, f. 450 (William IV on Bishop of Exeter). Nor was it congenial for a bishop who hoped for translation to a better see.

46. See M. I. Thomis, *Politics and Society in Nottingham, 1785–1835* (1969), pp. 225–31. The news arrived when Nottingham was crowded for Goose Fair.

47. Littleton, diary, 12 Oct. 1831: Hatherton MSS; *Keene's Bath Journal*, 14 Nov.; O. Chadwick, *Victorian Church*, i (1966), 27; *Courier*, 1 Nov. 1831.

48. Spencer Walpole, *Life of Lord John Russell* (1889), i.172.

49. Broughton, *Recollections*, iv.148.

50. J. R. M. Butler, *The Passing of the Great Reform Bill* (1914), p. 294. For ministerial complaints that Place misrepresented what Grey told the deputation see *Parl. Deb.*, viii.850; Place's letter in *Morning Chronicle*, 19 Oct.; Althorp to Grey 'Sunday' [13 Nov. 1831]: Spencer MSS (part in Butler, *Great Reform Bill*, p. 320). The member of the deputation who appears in Butler as Carpell, and in Broughton, *Recollections*, iv.149n., as Carpire was J. C. Carpue (1764–1846): see *D.N.B.* According to Althorp, 9 Jan. was the date originally chosen for the reassembly of Parliament.

51. *The Times*, 18 Oct.

52. *Leicester Chronicle*, 15, 22 Oct.

53. *Manchester Guardian*, 15 Oct. See also *Parl. Deb.*, viii.636 (Hunt).

54. W. Brimelow, *Political and Parliamentary History of Bolton* (1882), i.111–14.

55. A. S. Turberville, *Thoresby Soc. Miscellany*, xli (1943), 46–7.

56. The Birmingham Union was very short of money for a long campaign. See Grote to Parkes, 29 Oct.: *Posthumous Papers of G. Grote*, pp. 41–2; Broughton, *Recollections*, iv.164.

57. The proposal was not new. See *Three Diaries*, p. 19 (Stanhope's remark to Ellenborough, 18 Nov. 1830), and Joseph Hume, *Parl. Deb.*, iv.396 (27 June 1831).

58. See also *Globe*, 29 Oct., *Ballot*, 30 Oct., *Scotsman*, 9 Nov.

59. S. & B. Webb, *Manor and Borough* (1908), ii.468–74; *Parl. Papers*, Mun. Corp. R. Comm., pp. 1222–3, 1835 (116), xxiv.562–3; *Bristol Gazette*, 16 Sept. 1830.

60. Mayor of Bristol (Charles Pinney) to Melbourne, 4 Nov. 1831: *Bristol Gazette*, 17 Nov.

61. Read to a meeting of the Bristol Pol. Union, 25 Oct., and published *Morning Chronicle*, 7 Nov. 1831. Wetherell's statement in the Commons on 27 Aug. (*Parl. Deb.*, vi.698,699) that support for the Bill had 'abated' in Bristol helps to explain Protheroe's attitude.

62. Ld. Fitzroy Somerset to Melbourne, 6 Dec. 1831: H.O. 48, 28, f. 135: anon. [the Revd. John Eagles], *The Bristol Riots, their Causes, Progress and Consequences* (Bristol, 1832), app., p. 300. Eagles's account was coloured by his strong anti-reforming views.

63. Text in Eagles, pp. 52–3. See also W. Herapath to Alderman Daniel, 26 Oct.: *Morning Chronicle*, 7 Nov.

64. Lt. C. Claxton to Melbourne, recd. 17 Oct.: H.O. 40, 28, ff. 9–10.

65. *Bristol Gazette*, 27 Oct., *Bristol Mirror*, 29 Oct. According to T. J. Manchee, *The Origin of the Riots of Bristol* [1831], p. 12, the cavalry paraded the Bristol streets. This does not agree with Eagles's account.

66. Mackworth to Ld. Fitzroy Somerset, 31 Oct. 1831: H.O. 40, 28, f. 16.

67. Brereton to Ld. Fitzroy Somerset, 3 Nov. 1831: ibid., f. 71.

68. 'Mackworth's Personal Narrative': published in Bristol and London papers Nov. 1831 (*Morning Chronicle*, 22 Nov.). See also Mackworth to Ld. Fitzroy Somerset, 3 Nov.: H.O. 40, 28, ff. 81–2; Herapath's letter, *Bristol Mercury*, 22 Nov.

69. C. Kingsley, 'Great Cities and their Influence for Good and Evil', in *Sanitary and Social Lectures and Essays* (1880), p. 190.

70. See Place in Add. MSS, 27, 791, f. 101.

71. 10 Nov. On 18 Nov. the *Chronicle* explained that this passage had been based on a 'partial misreport' of the Union's proceedings.

72. H.O. 40, 29, f. 352, see also unsigned copy to Melbourne, 14 Nov., H.O. 48, 28, no. 34; Magistrates of Blackburn to Melbourne, 9 Nov.: H.O. 52, 13.

73. See Ch. 8, n. 127.

74. See also *Quarterly Rev.*, xlvi (Jan. 1832), 548.

75. *Examiner*, 30 Oct., p. 690. See also issue of 13 Nov., p. 722. The *Examiner* was not uniformly hostile to the scheme. The *Spectator*, 29 Oct., would 'not pronounce decidedly on the necessity' for a National Guard.

76. See editorial, 29 Oct.

77. To C. Buller, 6 Nov. 1831: W. N. Bruce, *Napier* (1864), i.363–5.

78. Melbourne MSS.

79. *The Times*, 18 Nov.

80. Report, endorsed 7 Oct.: H.O. 64, 11; *Poor Man's Guardian*, 8 Oct. Date

given wrongly as Aug. in D. J. Rowe, *Hist. Journal*, xiii (1970), 36–7, and as 2 Oct. in Add. MSS, 27, 791, f. 301.

81. ibid., f. 303. Place dates wrongly to 5 Oct. in another ref. to the meeting, Add. MSS, 27, 790, f. 11; *Poor Man's Guardian*, 15 Oct., i.128.

82. *London Radicalism, 1830–43*, Ed. D. J. Rowe (London Record Soc., v., 1970), p. 45.

83. ibid., p. 48.

84. Broughton, *Recollections*, iv.147.

85. See also H.O. 64, 11, report endorsed 26 Oct.

86. J. Hamburger, *James Mill and the Art of Revolution* (1963), p. 247.

87. For statement on these laws by N.P.U. see *The Times*, 19 Nov. During the crisis of May 1832 Place was prepared to defy them; see Add. MSS, 27, 793, f.26.

88. For Holland's admiration of Melbourne's efforts see diary, 7 Nov., Add. MSS, 51, 868, f. 197, and Holland to Grey, 8 Nov.: Grey MSS.

89. *London Radicalism*, p. 64.

90. Holland, diary, 7 Nov., Add. MSS, 51, 868, f. 201 (sheet marked '12 Nov.' by H. in error).

91. See also *Standard*, 4 Nov.

92. The king to Melbourne, 1, 5 Nov.: Melbourne MSS; Holland, diary, 7 Nov., Add. MSS, 51, 868, ff. 203–4.

93. *W.N.D.*, viii.143.

94. Holland, diary, 19 Nov., Add. MSS, 51, 868, ff. 218–19. As early as 26 Oct. Holland had used the possible need to act against 'armed associations' as an argument for early reassembly of Parliament (his letter of that date to Grey: Grey MSS).

95. On 2 Jan. 1832 Grey told the cabinet that he had been wrong to oppose the December date: Holland, diary, Add. MSS, 51, 868, f. 287. Parliament had been prorogued until 22 Nov. The decision on reassembly between Dec. and Jan. was therefore needed by 19 Nov. at latest.

96. To Melbourne, 19 Nov.: H.O. 48, 28, no. 34. See also *Brighton Guardian*, 16 Nov.

97. *Melbourne's Papers*, p. 135.

98. H.O. 64, 11, endorsed 22 Nov. See also *Poor Man's Guardian*, 26 Nov., i.182, and P. Hollis, *The Pauper Press* (1970), p. 42. E. G. Wakefield published a pamphlet just before 22 Nov., 'Householders in Danger from the Populace'. Drawing on his own convict experiences, he produced in it a plea that London householders should be armed against Huntite 'desperadoes'; mentioned in *The Times*, 22 Nov.

99. See Althorp to Parkes, 18 Nov.: Parkes MSS, U.C.L.; Althorp to Grey, undated and 20 Nov., Grey to Althorp, 20 Nov.: J. K. Buckley, *Joseph Parkes* (1926), pp. 85–7; Parkes to Grote, 28 Nov.: Add. MSS 35, 149, f. 128. News of Althorp's initiative soon reached the press: *Courier*, 19 Nov. See also Grey to Lansdowne, 18 Nov.: Lansdowne MSS; to Melbourne, 18 Nov.: Melbourne MSS. Melbourne proposed to use Sir Francis Lawley, Bt., one of the Members for Warwickshire, as a channel of communication with Attwood.

100. *Melbourne's Papers*, pp. 140–2.

101. See, for instance, Holland, diary, 19 Nov., Add. MSS, 51, 868, f. 215.

102. *Wm. IV–Grey Corresp.*, i.470.

103. Lansdowne to Stanley, 21 Nov.: Derby MSS; Stanley to Grey, 22 Nov.: Derby MSS, letter book 168, pp. 148–50. For Durham see H. P. Brougham, *Life and Times* (1871), iii.133. Within a few days of this meeting Graham suggested obtaining the king's consent to create 'the requisite number of peers': C. S. Parker, *Graham* (1907), i.129.

104. Wharncliffe to Harrowby, 22 Nov.: Harrowby MSS, xix, f. 184; *W.N.D.*, viii.90; *Wm. IV–Grey Corresp.*, i.446–7, where names left blank are Henry Drummond and Pascoe Grenfell (Royal Archives).

105. Letter to *The Times*, 29 Nov. See also *The Times*, 23, 24, 25, 26 Nov.

106. *Three Diaries*, p. 163 (Ellenborough). See also Holland, diary, 11 Dec., Add. MSS, 51, 868, ff. 244–5.

107. Spencer MSS. Compare Ellice to his son, 4 Nov.: Ellice MSS, E.61, f. 20. Ellice then thought a meeting about 6 Dec. 'absolutely inevitable'.

108. See Holland, diary, Add. MSS, 51, 868, ff. 210–11, for an account of 15 Nov. cabinet meeting (which Holland missed). By 18 Nov. Grey himself was wavering; 'the recommencement of the fires, and the general state of the country' he told Lansdowne (see n. 99 above), might point to a Dec. date.

109. See, for instance, Althorp to Grey, 26 Nov.: Spencer MSS.

110. 'Saturday evening' [19 November]: Harrowby MSS, xix, f. 211.

111. See Wharncliffe's memo., with Grey's annotations, *Wm. IV–Grey Corresp.*, i.471–8; the copy in Harrowby MSS, xix, ff. 187–90, carries Visc. Sandon's marginal notes; Althorp to Parkes, 6 Nov.: Parkes MSS, U.C.L., and reply, 13 Nov.: Spencer MSS, partly in Buckley, *Parkes*, pp. 78–80.

112. Holland, diary, Add. MSS, 51, 868, f. 223.

113. xxx.910.

114. See County Fire Office to Home Secretary, 15 Dec. 1831, asserting that the burnings were more frequent than they had been in the previous winter: H.O. 40, 29, f. 533. This seems to have been an exaggeration; but burnings were frequent in 1831–2: E. J. Hobsbawm & G. Rudé, *Captain Swing* (1969), pp. 284–5 and app. iii.

115. See Russell's plan with Althorp's comments: P.R.O. 30/22/1b, ff. 64–6; Russell's memo., 1 Dec.: Grey MSS; Althorp to Grey, 20 Oct. and later undated letter: Spencer MSS; Littleton, diary, 15 Nov., 2 Dec.: Hatherton MSS.

116. See Ch. 6, n. 82. For Wharncliffe's views see also *Parl. Deb.*, iii.999.

117. *Wm. IV–Grey Corresp.*, i.468,474.

118. Littleton, diary, 12 Dec.: Hatherton MSS.

119. For the first concession on freemen see *Parl. Deb.*, iii.1521–2. The extent of the Dec. concession may be judged by comparing clause 22 in the Bill, as re-introduced in June 1831 (*Parl. Deb.*, iv.6), with clause 32 of the Act. Greville, *Diary*, 22 Nov. 1842, records Russell's later defence of the change. For an example of political creation of freemen see *The Times*, 8 Nov., on Liskeard. Holland, diary, Add. MSS, 51, 868, ff. 250–1, gives the cabinet's reasons for not extending the concession to Ireland, where it would have helped to perpetuate protestant ascendancy.

120. Compare cl. 21 of the Bill as published in June 1831 (see n. 119 above) with cl. 27 and 30 of the Act).

121. Annotations to Wharncliffe's memo. of 23 Nov. 1831 by Visc. Sandon, headed 'Lord Grey, 29 Nov.': Harrowby MSS, xix, f. 188. This note is against the

passage printed in *Wm. IV–Grey Corresp.*, i.473 (see n. 111 above). Stanley told Sandon, 24 Oct., 'out of 26,000 rate-payers in Liverpool the number who have actually paid in any one year is not above 7,000': Harrowby MSS, xix, f. 324. See also Althorp to Parkes, 6 Nov. (n. 111 above); *Three Diaries*, pp. 157, 162–3; *Parl. Deb.*, vi.602,617, ix.1256–7.

122. The formula was devised by Thomas Drummond (1797–1840), then an R.E. Lieutenant, afterwards Althorp's private secretary, finally under-secretary at Dublin Castle. See Lord John Russell, *Recollections and Suggestions* (1875), pp. 88–9; Le Marchant, *Althorp*, p. 544n. The formula put Calne in Schedule B at last. Russell had wanted, in Feb. 1831, to include the 'number of houses assessed to the house tax' as one of the criteria for disfranchisement: P.R.O. 30/22/1b, f. 385.

123. For O'Connellite complaints see Holland, Add. MSS, 51, 868, ff. 226, 247–8. There are excellent short accounts of the Irish Reform Bill in N. Gash, *Politics in the Age of Peel* (1953), pp. 50–64, and A. Macintyre, *The Liberator* (1965), pp. 29–37.

124. Unpublished entry: Hatherton MSS. Lansdowne was a strong advocate of the ruralized borough. Holland judged L.'s 'real object' to be 'infusing landed interest in town elections' (diary, 20 Dec.): Add. MS, 51, 868, f. 262. For Littleton's appointment as a Boundary Commissioner see *Parl. Deb.*, vi.1397–1412, vii.338–40. *Parl. Papers*, 1831–2, xxxvi.11,20, give the instructions to the Boundary Commissioners, dated 8 Aug., 24 Nov. 1831.

125. Calculation based on *Parl. Papers*, 1859, xxiii.121–4. Sudbury (see p. 221), having escaped from Schedule B, was eventually enlarged so that Ballingdon came within the borough boundary. See *Parl. Deb.*, xiii.977, and S. Lewis, *Topographical Dictionary of England* (1835), iv. Sudbury was disfranchised for corruption in 1844.

126. 12 Dec., unpublished part of entry: Hatherton MSS.

127. Add. MSS, 27, 791, ff. 119–20.

128. Le Marchant, *Althorp*, p. 375, where letter wrongly dated 20 Dec.; date should be 1 Dec. See Holland, Add. MSS, 51, 868, ff. 234–6.

129. Add. MSS, 27, 791, f. 119. Place's ideas were not so well known in the cabinet now that Durham's influence had declined. Thus there may have been a personal element in his criticisms. They were borne out by events, however. In 1832 Althorp apparently gave a hint to overseers in London to allow householders on to the register despite payment of rates being late. By an Act of 1843 three months were allowed for payment. In 1849 this was lengthened to six months: C. Seymour, *Electoral Reform in England and Wales, 1832–1885* (1915), pp. 144–8. For an example of how the clause was said to have worked in 1832 see W. F. Monypenny (and G. E. Buckle), *Disraeli* (1929), i.224.

Chapter 8. The Bill in the Lords (II): 'To Stop the Duke'

1. *The Times*, 9 Jan.
2. The cabinet were more demanding in May 1832: see p. 304. So was Asquith in the Parliament Bill crisis: see R. Jenkins, *Mr Balfour's Poodle* (1954), p. 134.

3. Holland, diary, 16 Feb. 1832: Add. MSS, 51, 868, f. 349. See *Wm. IV–Grey Corresp.*, ii.224–5.

4. ibid., ii.415. See also ii.205–6. A creation of fifty or sixty was mentioned to the king as a possibility shortly before the second reading debate. William IV 'seemed to shudder at the number': Holland, diary, 2 Apr. 1832: Add. MSS, 51, 869, f. 442.

5. See Grey's statement to the cabinet on 18 Dec., for instance; ibid., f. 258.

6. By 5 Feb. Durham was telling the cabinet that a creation 'of 50 or even 60' was needed: ibid., f. 325.

7. *John Bull*, 15, 22 Jan.; *Morning Chronicle*, 6 Feb.; Littleton's diary, 26 Feb.: Hatherton MSS (part printed in *Three Diaries*, p. 202); Althorp to Spencer, 17 Jan.: Spencer MSS; *The First Lady Wharncliffe and Her Family*, Ed. C. Grosvenor and Lord Stuart of Wortley (1927), ii.121–2; *Three Diaries*, p. 183 (Littleton); *The Times*, 24 Jan. For Radnor, see Ch. 7, n. 17.

8. Holland, diary, 27 Feb. 1832, Add. MSS, 51, 868, f. 372.

9. *Wm. IV–Grey Corresp.*, ii.91,92. It was agreed between the waverers and the government that there were elements in the Bill on which the latter could accept no defeat, and that if these were altered Grey would apply for a creation. No agreement was ever achieved, however, about what was included under this heading. Each side wanted to tie down the other while remaining free themselves. *Wm. IV–Grey Corresp.* and Holland's diary refer constantly to this question. For the change in Wharncliffe's views about it contrast *Three Diaries*, p. 183, with Wharncliffe to Greville, 12 Feb.: Harrowby MSS, xix.367–70.

10. 12 Feb.: Melbourne MSS.

11. Taylor wrote in Jan. 1832 that he had 'never been a party man nor a politician' (*W.N.D.*, viii.202). Though not a whig he had connexions with two moderates in the cabinet. Stanley's wife was his niece. His wife and Goderich's were first cousins.

12. *W.N.D.*, viii.177. Lord Stanhope, *Miscellanies*, 1st ser. (2nd ed., 1863), pp. 73–4, has a slightly different version, dated 25 Jan. Harrowby to Jersey, 27 Jan., is a different letter, though much the same points are made: T. H. Duncombe, *Life and Correspondence of T. S. Duncombe* (1868), i.118. There are complete copies of the first circular in Harrowby MSS, xix, ff. 253–60, 267–74.

13. Second circular letter, 14 Feb.: Harrowby MSS, xix, ff. 252, 266.

14. Parker, *Peel*, ii.199–202.

15. *Correspondence of Charles Arbuthnot*, Ed. A. Aspinall (1941), p. 154.

16. *W.N.D.*, viii.271.

17. See Londonderry to Wellington, 14 Oct., 23 Nov. 1831: Wellington MSS; L. to Mrs Arbuthnot, 21 Jan. 1832: *Corresp. of Charles Arbuthnot*, p. 155. Croker reported on 14 Feb. 1832 that Wharncliffe was 'intriguing for power': *Croker*, ii.149.

18. C. Greville to Harrowby, 24 Feb.: Harrowby MSS, xix, f. 62. Grantham eventually voted against the second reading. See Lowther to Croker (Croker MSS), Goulburn to his wife (Goulburn MSS), both 11 Apr. 1832.

19. See *Annual Register* (1832), History, p. 146. The change from an opposition majority of 41 to a government majority of 9 was produced as follows:

| | Gain or loss to | |
	Government	Opposition
1. Changed votes: waverers proper	+17	−17
2. Did not vote having previously voted against		−10
3. Did not vote having previously voted for	−3	
4. Voted for: did not vote previously	+12	
5. Voted against: did not vote previously		+3
	+26	−24

A few of those in classes 2 and 4 above were not waverers. Thus Dudley is in 2: he did not vote in April 1832, because he had lately become insane. Accident, as well as activity by the diehard opposition, contributed to classes 3 and 5. Thus class 5 includes the Marquess of Abercorn who came of age only in Jan. 1832.

20. The third leader was the Earl of Haddington (1780–1858). He had been a Canningite. Styled Lord Binning before succeeding to the Earldom in 1828.
21. Harrowby MSS, xix, f. 95.
22. Kenyon MSS.
23. Broughton, *Recollections*, iv.191; J. Scholefield to Durham, 10 Mar. 1832: Durham MSS.
24. See Lansdowne to Holland in Holland, diary, Add. MSS, 51, 868, f. 384.
25. Broughton, *Recollections*, iv.174.
26. ibid., iv.190.
27. Althorp's letter and Grey's reply are in Le Marchant, *Althorp*, pp. 403–14.
28. Holland, diary, 14 Mar.: Add. MSS, 51, 868, ff. 406–7.
29. Greville's *Diary* provides much information on the waverers, not all of it reliable. In reading his account it is necessary to keep in mind that his views sometimes differed from those of the waverer leaders. See Wharncliffe to Greville 12 Feb. (n. 9 above).
30. For last-minute estimates of the probable government majority see *Journals and Correspondence of F. T. Baring*, Ed. Lord Northbrook (1905), i.93–5.
31. *Wm. IV–Grey Corresp.*, ii.296. For the king's earlier remarks to the same effect see Holland, diary, Add. MSS, 51, 867, ff. 128, 159–60.
32. Grey MSS. By the second reading the government had arranged parliamentary business so that there could be a prorogation 'without public inconvenience': Holland, diary, Add. MSS, 51, 868, f. 524.
33. 3 Apr. (1st leader).
34. *Three Diaries*, p. 224 (Le Marchant).
35. *Parl. Deb.*, xii.447. Grey told Lord Somers, 23 Apr., that the same applied to the new metropolitan members; Grey MSS.
36. *Parl. Deb.*, xii.452.

37. Lord Cockburn, *Jeffrey* (1852), i.330.

38. Speech at Rochdale, 25 Sept. 1877: John Bright, *Public Addresses*, Ed. J. E. Thorold Rogers (1879), p. 415.

39. Spencer MSS.

40. For a picture of the cabinet's peers facing the horrors of the committee stage without the help of either Althorp or a majority see Holland, diary, Add. MSS, 51, 869, f. 433.

41. Ellenborough's 'Protocol No. 2': Ellenborough MSS, P.R.O. 30/12/20/6: see *Three Diaries*, p.234.

42. 'Protocol No. 3': Ellenborough MSS, P.R.O. 30/12/20/6.

43. Ellice to Parkes, undated: Ellice MSS, E.41, f. 5; *Tyne Mercury*, 24 Apr.; *Morning Chronicle*, 27 Apr. (giving Parkes's defence against Cobbett); J. K. Buckley, *Joseph Parkes* (1926), pp. 91–4. Charles, chairman of the Northern P.U., Newcastle-upon-Tyne, and Thomas Attwood were brothers. According to G. J. Holyoake (*Sixty Years of an Agitator's Life*, 1892, i.26) Thomas Attwood would have been willing to see the £10 qualification raised had not the Northern Political Union made this stand. Baines made a similar stand at the Leeds meeting, 19 Apr. (*Leeds Mercury*, 21 Apr.). In *Birmingham Journal*, 5 May, Parkes pointed out that the £10 clause would produce only about 5000 voters in Birmingham. On 7 May he told the Birmingham Political Union that £10 was 'a qualification too high, not too low' (*The Times*, 9 May).

44. To Harrowby, 21 April: Harrowby MSS, xix.207.

45. Greville, *Diary*, 12 May; *Three Diaries*, p. 242.

46. Holland, diary, Add. MSS, 51, 869, f. 472. There are several accounts of how the ministers learned the truth before the debate. In using them, it is necessary to keep in mind the distinction between learning that Lyndhurst would move postponement and learning that the waverers would vote for it. See J. R. M. Butler, *The Passing of the Great Reform Bill* (1914), p. 370, n. 1; Greville, *Diary*, 12 May; Lord John Russell's introd. to his *Speeches* (1870), i.73; H. P. Brougham, *Life and Times* (1871), iii.190–1. The *Morning Chronicle's* story (10, 11 May) that Mulgrave discovered 'the intrigue' through dining with Lyndhurst on 6 May seems to have been unfounded.

47. For Grey's statement that 'a collision between the two Houses' would justify a creation see *Parl. Deb.*, xii.452–3. Harrowby's contention that the government's resignation was at variance with this is given in same, xiii.353–5. Burdett wrote to Grey, 4 May, 'with or without the metropolitans and £10 clauses you will not resign I anxiously hope': Grey MSS. Greville, 12 May, thought the cabinet's immediate resignation after their defeat on 7 May 'remarkable'. According to Creevey, Grey referred a few weeks later to the opposition's blunder in not believing 'that he would resign . . . on an apparent question of form': *Creevey Papers*, Ed. Sir H. Maxwell (3rd ed., 1905), p. 589.

48. *Blackwood's*, xxxi (May 1832), 855, gives an indication of these attitudes.

49. *Three Diaries*, p. 238.

50. xxix (Mar. 1831), 437, 441.

51. *W.N.D.*, viii.287.

52. For discussion of the radical dilemma on manhood suffrage see *Examiner*, 13 Sept., 25 Oct. 1829; *Morning Chronicle*, 16 Oct. 1829. See also Ch. 1, n. 79.

53. Buller, 23 June 1835: *Mirror of Parliament* (1835), ii.1509.

54. *W.N.D.*, viii.293. See also Wellington to Mrs Arbuthnot, 10 May 1831, 'there is no safety or success but in profound secrecy': Wellington MSS.

55. W. F. Monypenny (and G. E. Buckle), *Disraeli* (2 vol. ed., 1929), i.391–2.

56. These resolutions were reproduced in full in *Morning Chronicle*, 30 Apr. See also speeches of Parkes and McDonnell at the Birmingham Political Union meeting, 7 May 1832 (*The Times*, 9 May). For the belief at this stage that it was useless to petition the Lords see *London Radicalism, 1830–43*, Ed. D. J. Rowe (London Record Soc., v, 1970), pp. 78–80.

57. See Ellenborough, diary, 8 Oct. 1831: *Three Diaries*, p. 144; Holland, diary, 12 Oct. 1831, Add. MSS, 51, 867, f. 182.

58. Lady Lyndhurst had been intimate with Lord Dudley who had lately gone mad. She was said to have tried to accept a cheque for £5000 from him when he was already deranged: *Morning Chronicle*, 17 Apr.; *Three Diaries*, pp. 225–6 (Le Marchant); Benbow to Littleton, 20 Apr., Littleton diary, 8 May, 26 June 1832, 9, 22, 30 Mar. 1933: Hatherton MSS.

59. *Three Diaries*, p. 232 (Ellenborough).

60. Holland, diary, Add. MSS, 51, 869, ff. 459–60.

61. See Althorp, 17 May: *Parl. Deb.*, xii.1042. Holland thought Lyndhurst 'as nervous as his nature, destitute of shame, well could be': diary, Add. MSS, 51, 869, f. 474.

62. Le Marchant, *Althorp*, p. 419.

63. Winchilsea said in his speech that, when he entered the House, he did not know the amendment was to be moved: *Parl. Deb.* xii.712.

64. ibid., 694 (Bexley).

65. Richmond's opposition to a creation had been known to his colleagues for some weeks: Holland, diary, 3 Apr. 1832, Add. MSS, 51, 869, ff. 444–7.

66. Broughton, *Recollections*, iv.219. See also F. T. Baring, *Journals*, i.96. Holland seems to have expected the king to agree: P. Ziegler, *King William IV* (1971), p. 217. Althorp to Spencer, 7 May (Spencer MSS), gives Grey's view before the debate.

67. For the cartoon by 'H.B.' (John Doyle) depicting this dinner see *British Museum Catalogue of Personal and Political Satires*, xi (Ed. M. D. George, 1954), 618.

68. *Croker*, ii.155; *Parl. Deb.*, xii.966.

69. Althorp to Spencer, 'Thursday' [10 May]: Spencer MSS.

70. *Three Diaries*, p. 246 (Le Marchant).

71. *W.N.D.*, viii.340.

72. *Despatches, 1799–1818*, Ed. J. Gurwood, ii (1835), 616n.

73. *Parl. Deb.*, xii.1075.

74. *Croker*, ii.181.

75. For comments on the division list see *The Times*, 14 May.

76. See Add. MSS, 27, 794, ff. 344–7. John Cannon, *Parliamentary Reform, 1640–1832* (1973), p. 238, points out that most of the petitions arrived too late to affect the event.

77. *Parl. Deb.*, xii.877.

78. *Birmingham Journal*, 12 May.

79. *The Times, Morning Chronicle*, 11 May. Just over 5000 members had joined Place's National Political Union in Nov. 1831, on its formation. About 5600

joined between 1 and 15 May 1832: J. Hamburger, *James Mill and the Art of Revolution* (1963), p. 130.

80. 19 May.

81. A. S. Turberville, 'Leeds and Parliamentary Reform, 1820-32', *Thoresby Soc. Miscellany*, xli (1943), 51-3.

82. *London Radicalism*, pp. 87-8.

83. *The First Lady Wharncliffe and Her Family*, Ed. C. Grosvenor and Lord Stuart of Wortley (1927), ii.145.

84. Add. MSS, 27, 794, f. 58. Final petition was presented 21 May: H. of C. *Journals*, lxxxvii.326.

85. C. M. Wakefield, *Thomas Attwood* (1885), p. 195. Mr G. de B. Attwood's narrative.

86. Graham Wallas, *Place* (1898), pp. 300-1.

87. See *Parl. Deb.*, v. 1379. *The Radical Reformer*, an unstamped paper, suggested on 15 Oct. 1831 that auctioneers would not deal in goods distrained from radical working men.

88. *Morning Post*, 12 May.

89. For Place's attitude to a run after the defeat of Oct. 1831 see P. to Hobhouse, 11 Oct.: Add. MSS, 35, 149, f. 84. The O'Connellites had used this tactic with some success in 1828: see p. 54 and J. A. Reynolds, *The Catholic Emancipation Crisis in Ireland* (1954), pp. 151-2. O'Connell had also tried to employ it in June 1830 and Jan. 1831.

90. Grote, who was a banker, wrote to the press dissociating himself from the placard. See Add. MSS, 27, 794, ff. 4-9; *London Radicalism*, p. 91. See also *Report* (Birmingham, 1832), p. 5, Birmingham meeting, 16 May (G. F. Muntz's speech).

91. *London Radicalism*, p. 90. See *Morning Chronicle*, 14 May, on the placards and Holyoake, *Sixty Years of an Agitator's Life* (1892), i.219-20.

92. *Parl. Papers*, 1831-2 (722), vi.24 (Q.291—Horsley Palmer), 79 (Q.1060, 1062—Stuckey), 103-4 (Q.1482, 1492—Forster), 455 (Q.5611, 5613—Attwood).

93. Add. MSS, 27, 793, f. 143.

94. *Parl. Papers*, 1831-2 (722), vi.398 (Q.4984); J. J. Hope-Vere to J. P. Wood, (endorsed 15 May): Linlithgow MSS, Hope-Vere vol., f. 372.

95. ibid., 80 (Q.1064—Stuckey), 398 (Q.4981—Richards). cf. vi.371 (Q.4712—Grote).

96. ibid., 399 (Q.4999).

97. Wakefield's speech: *The Times*, 14 May.

98. *Life of Lord Campbell*, Ed. Mrs M. S. Hardcastle (1881), ii.10.

99. See, for instance, Baring to his wife, 11 May: F. T. Baring, *Journals*, i.98.

100. *W.N.D.*, viii.316. See also Lyndhurst to Wellington, 14 May: P. Fitzgerald, *William IV* (1884), ii.111.

101. W.O. 3.84, p. 226. See also W.O. 3.436, p. 231.

102. *Weekly Dispatch*, 14 May, had the same story. See also Grey to Lord Hill, 14 May, quoted in G. M. Trevelyan, *Grey* (1920), p. 340; *Standard*, 18 May.

103. *Parl. Deb.*, xii.908,916,923,930,947,975,952-3,957.

104. Greville, *Diary*, 17 May.

105. *W.N.D.*, viii.308. Arbuthnot's account, 12 May, of an interview with Rothschild. See also *Lady Holland to Her Son*, Ed. Earl of Ilchester (1946), p. 137; Holland, diary, Add. MSS, 51, 869, f. 487; *Three Diaries*, p. 264.

106. Broughton, *Recollections*, iv.229.

107. To Spencer: Spencer MSS. See also Holland, diary, 17 May, Add. MSS, 51, 869, ff. 498–9.

108. To Spencer, 17 May: Spencer MSS.

109. George Augustus Frederick Fitzclarence (1794–1842), eldest child of the King, then Duke of Clarence, by Mrs Jordan; cr. Earl of Munster, June 1831: see *D.N.B.*

110. Broughton, *Recollections*, iv.231.

111. *Lady Holland to Her Son*, p. 137.

112. Lord John Russell, *Recollections and Suggestions* (1875), p. 103.

113. For the fate of this paper see A. Aspinall, *E.H.R.*, lix (1944), 95–6.

114. *Parl. Deb.*, xii.1050.

115. *Wm. IV–Grey Corresp.*, ii.444.

116. Brougham wrote more than once in later life that, if the peers had not seceded, he and Grey might still have been unwilling, at the moment of decision, to put a creation in hand. All the evidence from May 1832 runs counter to these statements and they must be rejected. See Butler, *Great Reform Bill*, pp. 413–14; and *Edinburgh Rev.*, cxxxiv (1871), 291–4 (3rd Earl Grey's letter on Broughton, *Recollections*).

117. *London Radicalism*, pp. 92–3 (Place to Hobhouse, 18 May); Parkes to Grote, 14 May: Add. MSS, 27, 794, f. 10.

118. *Parl. Papers*, 1831–2 (722), vi.192 (Q.2678—Norman). For press estimates of Bank's reserve see Hamburger, *James Mill and the Art of Revolution*, pp. 105–6. It was known that the reserve had fallen, but not how far the fall had gone. See, for instance, *Quarterly Rev.*, xlvi (Jan. 1832), 563.

119. Add. MSS, 27, 794, f. 286–8.

120. Lord Cockburn, *Journal* (1874), i.30; Sir Robert Heron, *Notes* (2nd ed. Grantham, 1851), p. 196.

121. Wakefield, *Attwood*, p. 195.

122. *Parl. Deb.*, xii.1037–8.

123. There was some foundation for the rumour. Alexander Somerville, *Public and Personal Affairs* (1839), p. 25; Parkes to Grote, 14 May: see n. 117 above; Wakefield, *Attwood*, pp. 196–7. For the placard, 'Will the Soldiers Fight?', displayed in London, 16 May, see *Cosmopolite*, 19 May.

124. See H.O. 40, 30, ff. 99–102, 106–8 (Sir H. Bouverie's reports, Jan. 1832); *Sheffield Independent*, 19 May. General Sir George Cockburn had advised, in a letter published in the *Morning Chronicle*, 6 Dec. 1831, that, if no national guard were formed, 'the citizens, who by law may keep arms for their defence, should immediately procure them'.

125. H.O. 64, 12, 12 Mar. 1832; *Poor Man's Guardian*, 31 Mar.; *Parl. Papers*, 1833 (718), xiii.610,795 (Q. 214–222; 5161–3); Hamburger, *James Mill and the Art of Revolution*, p. 236; P. Hollis, *The Pauper Press* (1970), pp. 41–2.

126. G. W. E. Russell, *Collections and Recollections* (1904), p. 108.

127. Most of the *Poor Man's Guardian*, 11 Apr. 1832, was taken up with Macerone's 'Instructions'. See also R. Carlile's *Cosmopolite*, 14, 28 Apr. F. Macerone's account is in his *Memoirs* (1838), ii.458–9,468. Among stamped papers, *The Times* and *Morning Chronicle* had devoted space to Macerone's views in Oct./Nov. 1831.

128. Add. MSS, 27, 794, f. 282. In this passage Place mentions a plan to seize 'the families of the tory lords' and take them as hostages to the towns held by the reformers. For this see also W. Lovett, *Life and Struggles* (1967), p. 179, f.n.

129. J. M. Ludlow and Lloyd Jones, *Progress of the Working Classes* (1867), p. 22. See also Croker's encounter with two Manchester workmen at Molesey: *Croker*, ii.169–70.

130. Private estimates of the crisis by Place and Parkes, written as it ended, are in *London Radicalism*, pp. 94–6, and H. Grote, *Personal Life of G. Grote* (1873), pp. 78–80. Parkes's retrospective view should be read with some scepticism. He probably was not either as important or as revolutionary during the crisis as his account suggests. I would like to thank Mr W. E. S. Thomas for showing me the draft of an important paper on Parkes.

131. Add. MSS, 27, 794, f. 87.

132. *Personal Life of G. Grote*, pp. 79–80; Add. MSS, 27, 790, f. 243.

133. *The Times*, 10 Oct. 1848. For the circumstances in which the story became public see H. A. Bruce, *Sir William Napier* (1864), i.542–5, ii.59–60,270–6.

134. He was said to have been a 'captain in the national army of Poland' during the revolution in that country (*Morning Chronicle*, 25 Feb. 1832). See also *Parl. Deb.*, x.965–6.

135. *Morning Chronicle*, 17 May (Potter's speech).

136. Wellington does not seem to have repented of this secession. See C. Oman, *The Gascoyne Heiress* (1968), p. 135 (Lady Salisbury's diary, 10 Sept. 1834).

137. See Add. MSS, 27, 795, ff. 116–7. Place apparently supplied the figures for the speech.

138. *Creevey Papers*, p. 589.

139. *Three Diaries*, p. 273 (Le Marchant). The king told Melbourne that government offices were not to be illuminated and that there were to be no fireworks in the royal parks: Ziegler, *King William IV*, p. 220.

Chapter 9. It may work

1. C. M. Wakefield, *Thomas Attwood* (1885), p. 215.

2. Grey to Ellice, 1 Dec. 1832: Ellice MSS, E.18, f. 124; B. R. Haydon, *Autobiography and Memoirs*, Ed. A. P. D. Penrose (1927), p. 419.

3. *Parl. Deb.*, xv.143.

4. T. Raikes, *Journal* (2nd ed., 1856), i.34–5. Persons are identified as 'Duke of R.' and 'Lord W.'.

5. *Early Correspondence of Lord John Russell, 1805–40*, Ed. Rollo Russell (1913), ii.38.

6. *Earlier Letters*, Ed. F. E. Mineka (1963, xii, University of Toronto ed. of Mill's Works), p. 78.

7. G. M. Trevelyan, *Grey* (1920), p. 358. See also Le Marchant, *Althorp*, pp. 448–9; Grey to Russell, 25 Oct. 1832: Add. MSS, 38, 080, ff. 58–9.

8. Broughton, *Recollections*, iv.261–2.

9. Morpeth told Althorp on 26 Dec., after canvassing the West Riding of Yorkshire, 'the general feeling is very keen in favour of a full measure of Church

Reform': Le Marchant, *Althorp*, p. 448. Some idea of the support which pro-government candidates derived from the dissenting interest may be gained from the records in pollbooks of dissenting ministers' votes. In Dec. 1832 at Bolton, Dover, Durham City, Hereford, Ipswich, Leicester, and Maidstone, dissenting ministers cast 30 votes for, and none against, pro-government candidates: J. Vincent, *Pollbooks* (1968), p. 67.

10. At its first beginnings the Oxford Movement gained the support of those who wished to uphold a specifically *protestant* Church. Newman and his friends received a promise of support from the Duke of Newcastle, for instance: *Newman, Letters,* Ed. A. Mozley (1891), i.482.

11. Graham Wallas, *Place* (1898), p. 327.

12. To Henry Wynn, 28 Nov.: Williams Wynn MSS, National Library of Wales, N.L.W. 4817, f. 400. See also A. de Tocqueville, *Journeys to England and Ireland,* Ed. J. P. Mayer (1958), p. 56.

13. No two observers agreed whether to label certain Members 'whig' or 'radical'; see Sir H. Taylor to Ellice, 15 Dec. 1832: Ellice MSS, E.52, ff. 34–5.

14. It is now generally accepted that Melbourne did not actually resign, though his remarks gave the king every chance to end the government. See *Lord Melbourne's Papers,* Ed. Lloyd C. Sanders (1889), pp. 219–27.

15. ibid., pp. 269–76.

16. *Creevey Papers,* Ed. Sir H. Maxwell (3rd ed. 1905), p. 650.

17. See Lucy Brown, *The Board of Trade and the Free-Trade Movement, 1830–42* (1958), pp. 220–1.

18. Wakefield, *Attwood,* pp. 355–65.

19. C. B. R. Kent, *The English Radicals* (1899), p. 347.

20. Raikes, *Journal,* i.171. Raikes is quoting from a letter written by Wellington in Mar. 1833. The duke was quick to recognize his mistake. See Greville, *Diary,* 21 Feb. 1835.

21. See Ch. 6, n. 103, and C. Seymour, *Electoral Reform in England and Wales, 1832–1885* (1915), pp. 79–81. Seymour probably exaggerated the differences between Chandos clause voters and the rest of the county electorate.

22. According to Londonderry (to Buckingham, 3 Sept. 1834), even Durham admitted this: Duke of Buckingham, *Courts and Cabinets of William IV and Victoria* (1861), ii.126.

23. 1795–1871. Mayor of Newcastle, 1838–9. Knighted, 1840. W. Hutt (then MP for Hull) claimed to have obtained the knighthood for Fife (Hutt to Brockett, 19 June 1840: Brockett MSS, Gateshead Public Library, viii.910). I am grateful to Dr T. J. Nossiter for supplying these details.

24. *England and The English* (Univ. of Chicago Press, 1970), p. 52. Bulwer assumed surname of Lytton in 1843, and was created Lord Lytton, 1866. See also Haydon, 21 Feb. 1835, 'the capitalists . . . prefer the steadiness of existing abuse to the unsettled nature of reforming it': *Diary of B. R. Haydon,* Ed. W. B. Pope, iv (1963), 268. G. Kitson Clark, *The Making of Victorian England* (1962), ch. 5, contains a stimulating analysis of the radicals' difficulties.

25. Raikes, *Journal,* iv.136.

26. See Ch. 6, n. 103.

27. On the conservatives in the 1830s see G. Kitson Clark, *Peel and the Conservative Party* (2nd ed., 1964); D. Close, 'The Rise of the Conservatives in the

N

Age of Reform', *Bull. Inst. Hist. Res.*, xlv (1972), 89–103. Grey stressed his own conservatism. See G. to Anglesey, 11 June 1832: Anglesey MSS (Belfast), T.1068/30, f. 239; *Lieven–Grey Correspondence*, Ed. G. Le Strange (1890), iii.18. He told the Lords that the Reform Bill was a 'conservative . . . measure': *Parl. Deb.*, viii.335.

28. The phrase then in use. More strictly, the Charter embodied manhood suffrage. Votes for women were included in the petition drawn up for the London Working Men's Association, Feb. 1837; but the Chartists did not sustain this demand.

29. See *Blackwood's*, xlvi (Sept. 1839), 289.

30. The middle-class element during the first phase of Chartism may have been underestimated by some historians; see D. J. Rowe, *Past and Present*, xxxvi (Apr. 1967), 73–86.

31. *Memoirs of Chateaubriand*, Trans. A. Teixeira de Mattos (1902), iv.92.

32. *Private Letters of Peel*, Ed. G. Peel (1920), pp. 285–6. Peel was speaking to the Comte de Jarnac (1821–75). Translated from Jarnac's article in *Revue des Deux Mondes*, July 1874.

33. Tennyson's reference to 'the red fool-fury of the Seine' was published in June 1850 (*In Memoriam*, cxxvii). In *Our Mutual Friend* (published in 1864–5) Dickens satirized the complacency of the British about their governmental arrangements: Mr Podsnap remarks that the British constitution 'was bestowed on us by providence' and that 'no other country is so favoured as this country'. See also Kingsley's 1862 preface to *Alton Locke*: 'young lads thirty or forty years ago believe(d) . . . that they might have to fight . . . any day for the safety of their property and the honour of their sisters': quoted in W. E. Houghton, *The Victorian Frame of Mind, 1830–70* (1957), p. 57. Compare De Tocqueville's views in the 1830s on England, *Journeys to England and Ireland*, pp. 73–4, with those that he held by 1857: *Oeuvres Complètes*, vi (1867) 394, vii (1866) 461. In 1861 *The Times* referred to 'a degree of general contentment to which neither we, nor any other nation we know of, ever attained before': quoted in G. M. Young, *Victorian Essays* (1962), p. 135.

34. *Amberley Papers*, Ed. B. & P. Russell (1937), ii.267.

35. *Essays on Parliamentary Reform* (1883), p. 169.

36. See, among recent studies, D. E. D. Beales, 'Parliamentary Parties and the "Independent" Member, 1810–60' in *Ideas and Institutions of Victorian Britain*, Ed. R. Robson (1967); D. Close, *E.H.R.*, lxxxiv (1969), 257–77.

37. *Parl. Deb.*, iv.1243, v.714 (Russell), vii.1184 (Melbourne). Brougham was doubtful whether a change should be made: ibid., viii.250. There were ministerial denials of rumours about an impending change in the law on vacating seats: ibid., v.616–17, xi.528, xiii.384. Russell announced in 1854 that his Reform Bill would repeal the requirement to vacate: ibid., cxxx.508–10.

38. Littleton's diary, 28 June 1832 (misdated 27 June by L.): Hatherton MSS. By 'his minister' Littleton means 'his Prime Minister'.

39. *Diary*, 16 May 1833.

40. Diary, 9 Apr. 1835: Hatherton MSS.

41. See D. E. Butler, *The Electoral System in Britain since 1918* (2nd ed., 1963), pp. 52–4. *The Times*, 17 Feb. 1919, calculated that, in the 284 by-elections caused by ministerial appointments since 1868, there had been only eight government

defeats. But the re-election requirement ruined the career of one twentieth-century politician of great ability—C. F. G. Masterman (1874–1927).

42. 59 Geo. III c. 12, cl. 19.

43. *Parl. Deb.*, vi.670–2,677–83.

44. Seymour, *Electoral Reform in England and Wales*, p. 150.

45. *Parl. Papers*, 1867 (136, 305), lvi.461,466. M. Cowling, *Disraeli, Gladstone and Revolution* (1967), and F. B. Smith, *The Making of the Second Reform Bill* (1966) explain how the problem of the compounder was resolved in 1867. For the aftermath of the 1867 Act see H. J. Hanham, *Elections and Party Management* (1959), pp. 400–2.

46. *Parl. Papers*, Sel. Cttee. Votes of Electors, pp. 183–90, 1846 (451), viii.371–8; *Parl. Deb.*, xcii.399 (Bright).

47. W. Whateley to Althorp, 31 Jan. 1834: printed copy in Derby MSS.

48. Increased to £5 in 1865: Seymour, *Electoral Reform in England and Wales*, pp. 160–1.

49. *Parl. Papers*, 1846 (451), viii.175–615. In 1845 the League's Manchester office handed in 23,000 objections during the last few days before the deadline: ibid., 267. See N. McCord, *The Anti-Corn Law League* (1958), pp. 148–54.

50. After the 1835 election reduced to one day in boroughs: 5 and 6 Wm. IV, c. 36.

51. W. McC. Torrens, *Melbourne* (1878), i.406.

52. *Parl. Deb.*, cxxv.207. Cited in G. Kitson Clark, 'The Electorate and the Repeal of the Corn Laws', *T.R.H.S.*, 5th ser., i.124. *Parl. Papers*, 1835, viii, records the evidence given to the Sel. Cttee. on Bribery at Elections.

53. See C. O'Leary, *The Elimination of Corrupt Practices* (1962), chs. 3, 4 and 5. The Ballot Act of 1872 did not end bribery.

54. See *Parl. Papers*, 1842, viii.607. A Southampton coachmaker told the committee that, with one exception, the electors he had met 'would be glad if the town was disfranchised'.

55. Russell told the Commons on 24 June 1831 that he hoped 'in the present session' to introduce a Bill to tighten up the laws against electoral corruption: *Parl. Deb.*, iv.339–40. N. Gash, *Politics in the Age of Peel* (1953), ch. 5, gives an excellent account of the post-1832 system in this aspect.

56. For the defects of the Scottish Reform Act see W. Ferguson, *Scot. Hist. Rev.*, xlv (1966), 105–14; J. T. Ward, *Scot. Hist. Rev.*, xlvi (1966), 89–94.

57. Littleton's diary, 14 June 1932: Hatherton MSS.

58. See Ch. 4, n. 82.

59. See S. F. Woolley, 'The Personnel of the Parliament of 1833', *E.H.R.*, lii (1938), 240–62. Professor W. O. Aydelotte has done notable work recently in this field on the 1841–7 House of Commons. See especially *History*, xxxix (1954), 249–62, and Kitson Clark, *The Making of Victorian England*, app., pp. 290–305.

60. Hedworth Lambton told Durham, 1 Jan. 1833, that the family would lose its supporters in newly-enfranchised Sunderland 'if you sent anyone down at any time who was not in every way most eligible, as regards talents, political attainment and high character': Durham MSS. According to T. H. S. Escott the Reform Act had a marked effect on aristocratic manners: 'the man of pleasure ceased to be the type to which it was expected . . . that all those born in the

purple should conform': *England; Its People, Polity and Pursuits* (rev. ed., 1885), p. 331.

61. It is also arguable that the increasingly widespread acceptance of free trade doctrines lessened the anxiety of business men for political influence.

62. Anon. broadsheet by 'Fair Play': Liverpool City Library. See also Ch. 4, n. 81.

63. *Politics in the Age of Peel*, pp. 193–201, 439. The list gives 59 Members as returned by patrons, with a further 14 'queried'.

64. See Althorp to Milton, 6 Mar. 1831: Fitzwilliam (Northants) MSS; to Brougham, 1 Aug. 1837: Spencer MSS. For Baring's view see Ch. 6, n. 88.

65. 17 Jan. 1841: Spencer MSS. See also Spencer Walpole, *Life of Lord John Russell* (1889), i.372–3; undated note by Spencer Cowper in Palmerston MSS; and Ch. 6, n. 103.

66. *Nineteenth Century*, ii (1877), 540, repr. *Gleanings* (1898), i.136. C. P. Villiers held the same view; V. to Bright, 25 Dec. 1859: Add. MSS, 43, 386, f. 288. For the whole problem see D. C. Moore, 'The Corn Laws and High Farming', *Ec. Hist. Rev.*, 2nd ser., xviii (1965), 544–61.

67. I am grateful to Mr Michael Maclagan for showing me this list. Some statesmen naturally appear in it more than once.

68. A. P. Stanley, *Thomas Arnold* (12th ed., 1881), ii.86–7.

69. John Prest, *Lord John Russell* (1972), p. 303.

70. *The English Constitution*, introd., 1872 ed.

71. 3 Sept.: Ellice MSS, E.19, f. 90. For an earlier suggestion of Grey's disillusionment see Haydon, *Diary*, iv.195. Rienzi (*c.* 1313–54), tribune of the Roman people, was the subject of a play by Mary Russell Mitford, produced in 1828, and a novel by E. L. Bulwer (from 1843 Bulwer-Lytton), published in 1835. Wagner's opera, based on the novel, was first produced in 1842.

72. Diary, 11 Dec.: Harvard College Library (MS copy).

73. *Melbourne's Papers*, p. 389; Lord David Cecil, *Lord M.* (1954), p. 129. See also M. to Russell, 24 Oct. 1837, quoted in Prest, *Russell*, p. 157.

74. *Edinburgh Rev.*, lxxxiii (Jan. 1846), 255. For authorship of this article see Walpole, *Russell*, i.404.

75. Prest, *Russell*, p. 331.

76. *Parl. Deb.*, cxxx.498.

77. See passage cited in n. 66 above; *Church Quarterly Rev.*, iii.474–5,477, repr. *Gleanings*, i.77,81; 'C.R.L.F.' (Fletcher), *Mr Gladstone at Oxford, 1890* (1908), pp. 42–3. Gladstone was apt to add qualifications to this view as to others. In 1877 he conceded that the 1832 Act had 'proved . . . a safe and strengthening measure': *Nineteenth Century*, ii.548. In 1891 he hinted at a similar judgment in saying that 'the golden age of administrative reform was from 1832 to the Crimean War': John Morley, *Gladstone* (2 vol. ed., 1906), ii.705. In 1892 he thought 'the opposition to the first Reform Bill . . . less unreasonable than the opposition offered . . . to subsequent measures': Gladstone's *Autobiographica*, Ed. J. Brooke & M. Sorensen (1971), p. 37. Shaftesbury's later views on the Act were, if anything, more severe than Gladstone's; see S.'s letter to *The Times*, 6 June 1882: quoted E. Hodder, *Shaftesbury* (1886), i.125.

78. *L'Ancien Régime et la Révolution*, bk. i, ch. 1.

79. See, for instance, Melbourne to Russell, 5 Jan. 1843 (on the corn law

question): 'there is but one party in the country that can create a real feeling and agitation and that is the government' (*Melbourne's Papers*, p. 517). Melbourne had evidently forgotten what he had thought of the Reform agitation during the last months of Wellington's government.

80. Speech at Birmingham, 29 Jan. 1864: *Public Addresses*, Ed. J. E. Thorold Rogers (1879), p. 29.

81. 6 Dec.: Durham MSS.

82. The number of working-class people eligible to vote was underestimated in the 1860s. This was probably true of the 1830s also. See C. P. Villiers to Russell 23 Dec. 1865: P.R.O. 30/22/15H, ff. 149a–50 (cited Prest, *Russell*, p. 405), and *Parl. Papers*, 1866, lvii (170), 47–51. By official calculations working men comprised some 26 per cent of the electorate in England and Wales in 1865–6. It seems likely that the percentage thirty years earlier would have been much the same, or a little less. On this presumption the decline in the importance of the ancient right voters was balanced by the rise of the 'labour aristocracy', the working men just over the £10 line increasing a little faster than the electorate as a whole. During these years the composition of the working-class vote probably altered more than the proportion of the electorate which this vote represented. The influence of non-voters is analysed in J. Vincent, *The Formation of the Liberal Party, 1857–68* (1966), pp. 100–4.

83. *Parl. Deb.*, i.613. See also Lord John Russell, *Recollections and Suggestions* (1875), p. 70.

84. See A. V. Dicey, *Law and Public Opinion in England* (1905), p. 7, quoted in G. Watson, *The English Ideology* (1973), p. 45.

THE REFORM CRISIS: DATES OF EVENTS

1830

26 June	Death of George IV
24 July	Parliament dissolved
	General election:
29 July	first returns
1 Sept.	last return
28 Aug.	Agricultural unrest: first destruction of a threshing machine
15 Sept.	William Huskisson killed in an accident
31 Oct.	Meeting of whig MPs in Althorp's rooms, Albany: Brougham announces his intended Reform motion
2 Nov.	Address debate: Wellington declares against Reform
13 Nov.	Meeting of whig MPs: terms of Reform motion decided
15 Nov.	Government defeated on Civil List: 233 to 204 (Parnell's amendment)
16 Nov.	Wellington resigns: Grey summoned to form a government

1831

14 Jan.	Reform proposals: committee of four sign their report
30 Jan.	Reform proposals: Grey presents cabinet's scheme to king
1 Mar.	Russell outlines Reform Bill to Commons
18 Mar.	Government defeated in Commons, 236 to 190, on timber duties
23 Mar.	Reform Bill, second reading: passed by 302 to 301 *(early morning)*
18 Apr.	Russell outlines amendments to Bill to be made by government: General Gascoyne moves that number of MPs for England and Wales be not reduced
20 Apr.	Government defeated on Gascoyne's motion by 299 to 291 *(early morning)*
23 Apr.	Parliament dissolved
	General election:
28 Apr.	first returns
1 June	last return
24 June	Reform Bill reintroduced in Commons
7 July	Second-reading division: Bill passed by 367 to 231 *(early morning)*
12 July	Government motion for Bill to go to committee (usually regarded as first day of committee stage, though House resolved itself into committee only at very end of sitting)

7 Sept.	Fortieth and last committee sitting
21 Sept.	Back-bench reforming MPs meet and protest against suggestion that government might resign if defeated in Lords
22 Sept.	Bill passes Commons by 345 votes to 236 on final division and is brought up to Lords
8 Oct.	Second-reading division in Lords: government defeated by 199 to 158 (*early morning*)
8–10 Oct.	Riots at Derby and Nottingham
18 Oct.	Open letter by Grey, promising 'not less efficient' Bill, published in *The Times*
29–31 Oct.	Bristol riots
22 Nov.	Proclamation against organization of political unions on military lines
6 Dec.	Reassembly of Parliament
12 Dec.	New Reform Bill introduced in Commons
18 Dec.	Second-reading division: Bill passed by 324 to 162 (*early morning*)

1832

13 Jan.	Cabinet minute sent to the king, asking for promise that peers will be created if this is needed to prevent defeat of the Bill
15 Jan.	William IV agrees to a creation of this kind
20 Jan.	First committee sitting on the Bill
10 Mar.	Twenty-second and last committee sitting
22 Mar.	Third reading, Commons: Bill passed by 355 to 239
26 Mar.	Bill brought up to Lords: declarations by waverer leaders
14 Apr.	Second reading, Lords: passed by 184 to 175 (*early morning*)
7 May	Government defeated by 151 to 116 on Lyndhurst's motion to postpone disfranchising clauses
9 May	The king refuses the cabinet's demand for the creation of 50 to 60 peers and accepts their resignations
10 May	Ebrington's motion in Commons of support for outgoing ministers passed by 288 to 208
15 May	Wellington advises the king to recall Grey
18 May	William IV gives Grey full authority for a creation of peers
4 June	Third reading, Lords: passed by 106 to 22
7 June	Royal Assent given to Bill by commission

(Reform Act for Scotland received Royal Assent on 17 July, Act for Ireland on 7 August.)

INDEX

Places which appear in the text principally as parliamentary constituencies are asterisked. All pre-1832 English boroughs are listed in Table 2, pp. 20–1. No index entries have been made for that list.

The index shows the names and titles under which people appear in the text, and those changes of name and title which seem relevant in a book on this subject. Christian names which were not commonly used are sometimes omitted. Some index entries do not correspond to names in the text. Thus the first entry for Viscount Howick refers to a passage in which he appears simply as Grey's son.

Notes and references are not indexed.

Abbreviations   cr. = created   succ. = succeeded

N*